The Public Policy Process

The Public Policy Process is essential reading for anyone trying to understand the process by which public policy is made. Explaining clearly the importance of the relationship between theoretical and practical aspects of policy making, the book gives a thorough overview of the people and organisations involved in the process.

Fully revised and updated for a seventh edition, *The Public Policy Process* provides:

- Clear exploration, using many illustrations, of how policy is made and implemented.
- A new chapter on comparative theory and methods.
- New material on studying advocacy coalitions, policy changes, governance and evaluation.
- More European and international examples.

Michael Hill is Emeritus Professor of Social Policy at the University of Newcastle, UK. Since leaving Newcastle he has held visiting appointments at London University, Goldsmiths College, Queen Mary College, the London School of Economics and Brighton University.

Frédéric Varone is Professor of Political Science at the University of Geneva, Switzerland. He also taught policy analysis at the universities of Louvain, Belgium, and Lille, France, and was a visiting scholar at the University of California, Berkeley.

"A fresh edition of a classic textbook. It provides an even-handed, concise and considerate overview of a range of theories and approaches in the study of the policy process."

Mark Bovens, *Utrecht University, the Netherlands*

"The seventh edition consolidates *The Public Policy Process* is one of the leading textbooks in the field of public policy-making. It provides a rich and accessible overview of relevant theory and essential concepts along with illustrative examples from a diverse set of cases. The book is a great source of knowledge and inspiration that is certain to be of interest to academics and practitioners and all those interested in understanding the policy process."

Daniel Nohrstedt, *Uppsala University, Sweden*

"This book presents an excellent contribution to the study of the policy process. Michael Hill and Frédéric Varone performed an invaluable service by authoring this new edition of the very successful textbook. It is a 'must read' for students and researchers interested in policy theories ant their application to various aspects of the policy process."

Sabine Kuhlmann, *University of Potsdam, Germany*

"In the seventh edition of *The Public Policy Process*, Hill and Varone have transformed what has been one of the best introductory books on policy process research into one that is an even better. In doing so, they recognize and describe the complexities inherent in policy processes without reverting to overly simplified and distorted depictions. Based on crisp conceptualizations and comprehensive theoretical foundations, this book offers a firm foundation for new students and experienced scholars for understanding, studying, and influencing policy processes."

Chris Weible, *School of Public Affairs, University of Colorado Denver, USA*

The Public Policy Process

MICHAEL HILL and FRÉDÉRIC VARONE

Seventh Edition

WITHDRAWN

Routledge
Taylor & Francis Group

LONDON AND NEW YORK

Seventh edition published 2017
by Routledge
2 Park Square, Milton Park, Abingdon, Oxon OX14 4RN

and by Routledge
711 Third Avenue, New York, NY 10017

Routledge is an imprint of the Taylor & Francis Group, an informa business

© 2017 Michael Hill and Frédéric Varone

First edition published by Pearson Education Limited 1997
Sixth edition published by Pearson Education Limited 2013

British Library Cataloguing-in-Publication Data
A catalogue record for this book is available from the British Library

Library of Congress Cataloging in Publication Data
A catalog record for this book has been requested

ISBN: 978-1-138-90949-6 (hbk)
ISBN: 978-1-138-90950-2 (pbk)
ISBN: 978-1-315-69396-5 (ebk)

Typeset in Stone Serif
by RefineCatch Limited, Bungay, Suffolk
Printed and bound by CPI Group (UK) Ltd, Croydon, CR0 4YY

Contents

| Part 2 | Analysis of the policy process |

Illustrations

Figures

Tables

Boxes

Preface

This is a book about the process by which public policy is made. Efforts to influence the policy process, the concern of much policy analysis writing, need to be grounded in an understanding of it. Making policy embraces the emergence of policies on the agenda, policy formulation and policy implementation. It is a continuous process, with many feedback loops, carried out by diverse actors.

Part 1 of the book starts with an introductory chapter which sets the study of the policy process in the context of the wider policy studies literature and examines some of the key underlying concepts and methodological issues. It is then followed by six chapters which explore the various theoretical approaches to policy process analysis. As the study of the policy process essentially investigates the exercise of power, these chapters discuss how power is distributed in society and embedded in political institutions. Part 2 comprises eight chapters which explore application of those approaches. These start with a chapter examining the implications of policy diversity for analysis and emphasising the importance of seeing the policy process as a political process. This is followed by separate explorations of agenda setting, policy formulation and policy implementation. Two particular aspects of the implementation process are explored in the next two chapters: the significance of formal organisations and the importance of the roles of 'street-level' workers for that process. Then follows a chapter on governance, looking at how inter-organisational complexity within the nation state and changing relationships between states impact upon the policy processes. Finally, the conclusion to the book explores the impact of concerns about evaluation and accountability for the operation of the policy process.

During the history of this book substantial changes have been made over time. There have been two occasions when these have been particularly substantial. One of these was when the original partnership between Michael Hill and Chris Ham ended in 1997. The other is with the publication of this edition in which Frédéric Varone has joined with Michael in a partnership that extends the scope of the book and makes it more international in character. Changes have been made throughout the text, updating the range of ideas discussed and drawing diverse illustrations.

Throughout the history of the book there have been changes of publishers as well as changes of authors. The original commissioner of the book was

Edward Elgar, long before he formed his own company, and the book followed him from St. Martin's Press to Harvester Wheatsheaf. Further changes in the publishing world moved it on, first to Prentice Hall and then to Pearson Education. Now, fortunately, continuity is secured by the fact that Andrew Taylor moved to Taylor and Francis when they took over the Pearson list. Andrew has been a great help in encouraging Michael Hill in his aspiration to seek a collaborator for this new edition, and in negotiating the new arrangements for the book.

Despite all the changes, the book still owes a great deal to the original collaboration with Chris Ham, and Michael is very grateful to him for his original contribution and for then letting the book evolve. *The Policy Process in the Modern Capitalist State* was developed when Michael and Chris worked together on a teaching programme on the policy process for the master's course in public policy studies at the School for Advanced Urban Studies at Bristol University.

Over the years that Michael has been engaged on writing about the policy processes debts to colleagues and students, both in the institutions in which he has worked and in many other places at home and abroad, have cumulated to the extent that he cannot acknowledge them all. He does however want to highlight his collaboration with Peter Hupe of Erasmus University, Rotterdam. In 2002 they wrote *Implementing Public Policy,* now in its third edition.

Acknowledgements

The following excerpts have been granted permission for their use from the publishers in which they first appeared:

Kisby, B. (2007) 'Analysing policy networks: Towards an ideational approach', *Policy Studies*, 28(1). Taylor & Francis Ltd, www.tandfonline.com, reprinted by permission of the publisher.

Hall, P.A. (1993) 'Policy paradigms, social learning and the state: The case of economic policy making in Britain', *Journal of Comparative Politics*, 25. This article first appeared in the *Journal of Comparative Politics* and has been reprinted with the publishers' permission at CUNY.

Taylor, I. (2003) 'Policy on the hoof: The handling of the foot and mouth disease outbreak in the UK, 2001', *Policy and Politics*, 31(4), pp. 535–46. Reprinted with the permission of Policy Press: University of Bristol.

Exworthy, M., Berney, L. and Powell, M. (2002) ' "How great expectations in Westminster may be dashed locally": The implementation of national policy on health inequalities', *Policy and Politics*, 30(1), pp. 79–96. Reprinted with the permission of Policy Press: University of Bristol.

Part

1

Policy theories

1 Studying the policy process

SYNOPSIS

This book is divided into two parts. Part 1 (Chapters 1–7) explores, after this introductory chapter, a range of theories that have been developed to explain all of, or key aspects of, the policy process. Then Part 2 (Chapters 8–15) looks at various aspects of the policy process, essentially developing and applying some of the main ideas from the first part. Connections between the theories in the first part and the discussions of the issues in the second part will be made in various ways, including summarising observations at the ends of chapters.

This introductory chapter looks at some important overall considerations about the study of the policy process. It explores the implications of the three key words in the title in reverse order. Thus it starts with an exploration of what is implied in examining the policy process. That examines the relationship between the 'descriptive' aim of this book and the 'prescriptive' objectives that motivate much policy analysis. A particular aspect of this that requires some introductory exploration here is the fact that many prescriptive approaches involve very explicit views about the 'staged' shape that the policy process should take, whilst a descriptive approach involves a much more agnostic perspective on that. This leads on to a general exploration of the relationship between the study of the policy process and political science, and other social science disciplines. Two policy examples are used at the end of this discussion to illustrate these points. They are then also used to illustrate the examination of what may be meant by policy. Here it will be shown again that a distinction may be drawn between approaches to this concept that endeavour to use a very precise, and perhaps prescriptive, meaning and the stance taken in this book that political and ideological contests make that activity difficult and/or contentious. Finally there is consideration of what is distinctive about the study of public policy. The examination of this topic involves a recognition of the extent to which there are problems with identifying a distinctive public sector, something which is emphasised in modern stresses upon the extent to which 'government' needs to be seen to have been replaced by 'governance'.

Introduction

We are all critical of public policies from time to time. Most of us have ideas about how they could be better. When we engage in ordinary conversations about the defects of policies, we put forward, or hear advanced, various propositions about why they are defective. Those propositions tend to involve views about policy makers as ignorant or misled or perhaps malign. They often embody views that policies would be better if only different people had more influence on policy, including, of course, perhaps ourselves.

This book is based on the belief that before you can really start to suggest alternative policies to the ones we have, or to suggest alternative ways of making policy, it is essential to try to understand how policy is made. Many of the popular prescriptions for improving policy rest upon essential misunderstandings of the nature of the policy process. For example:

- views about the need for policy makers to be more aware of the 'facts' often disregard the way the facts are actually matters of dispute between different 'interests', 'beliefs' and 'values';
- suggestions for taking 'politics' out of policy making disregard the fact that politics is much more than simply the interplay of politicians;
- statements about the role of politicians (including many they themselves make) suggest that they have much more influence over the policy process than in fact they do. It may be said that there is both extravagant 'claiming' and 'blaming'.

The view taken in this book is that the policy process is essentially a complex and multi-layered one. It is essentially a political process, but in the widest sense of that term. The policy process is a complex political process in which there are many actors: politicians, pressure groups, civil servants, publicly employed professionals, academic experts, journalists and even sometimes those who see themselves as the passive recipients of policy.

To explore further what studying the policy process implies, it is appropriate to start with an examination of the place of this approach in the context of the many different approaches adopted to what can be generically called 'policy analysis'. That then leads on to some more specific considerations about adopting a process perspective. From there we can go to what that implies for the way public policy is examined in this book.

Description and prescription in policy analysis

Some policy analysts are interested in furthering understanding of policy (analysis *of* policy); some are interested in improving the quality of policy (analysis *for* policy); and some are interested in both activities (see Parsons, 1995, for an overview of the many approaches). Further, cutting across the distinction between 'analysis of' and 'analysis for' policy are concerns with *ends* and concerns with *means*.

The typology set out in Box 1.1 identifies a range of different kinds of policy analysis.

| Box 1.1 | Different kinds of policy analysis |

Analysis *of* policy

- Studies of policy *content*, in which analysts seek to describe and explain the genesis and development of particular policies. The analyst interested in policy content usually investigates one or more cases in order to trace how a policy emerged, how it was implemented and what the results were. A great deal of academic work concentrates on single policies or single policy areas (social policy, environment policy, foreign policy, etc.).
- Studies of policy *outputs*, with much in common with studies of policy content but which typically seek to explain why levels of expenditure or service provision vary (over time or between countries or local governments).
- Studies of the policy *process*, in which attention is focused upon how policy decisions are made and how policies are shaped in action.

Analysis *for* policy

- *Evaluation* marks the borderline between analysis of policy and analysis for policy. Evaluation studies are also sometimes referred to as impact studies as they are concerned with analysing the impact policies have on the population. Evaluation studies may answer descriptive questions (which intended impacts are observed?), causal questions (which factors explain the missing impacts?) and/or normative questions (which policy modification would improve the intended impacts?).
- *Information* for policy making, in which data are marshalled in order to assist policy makers to reach decisions. An important vein of contemporary studies of this kind manifests a pragmatic concern with 'what works', trying to ensure that policy and practice are 'evidence based' (Davies et al., 2000).
- *Process advocacy*, in which analysts seek to improve the nature of the policy-making systems through the reallocation of functions and tasks, and through efforts to enhance the basis for policy choice through the development of planning systems and new approaches to option appraisal. Much of the academic work in the sub-fields of 'public administration' and 'public management' has this concern.
- *Policy advocacy*, which involves the analyst in pressing specific options and ideas in the policy process, either individually or in association with others, perhaps through a pressure group.

Typology based upon ones offered by Gordon et al. (1977) and by Hogwood and Gunn (1981; 1984).

This book's concern is with the policy process, the third of the varieties of policy analysis identified in Box 1.1. However, many studies of policy outputs contribute to our understanding of the policy process. Similarly, evaluation studies give much attention not merely to what the policy outputs or outcomes were but also to questions about how the policy process shaped them. Much the same can be said of studies that seek to offer information for policy making, since 'what works' may be determined by the way the policy process works. Overall it is often not easy to draw a clear line between 'analysis of' and 'analysis for' policy.

The desire to examine how the policy process works was in many respects a minor concern in the period between 1950 and 1980, when policy studies in their own right mushroomed dramatically. If the right policies could be found, and their design difficulties solved, then progress would be made towards the solution of society's problems. Only a minority – radical analysts on the 'Left' who doubted that modern governments really had the will to solve problems, and radical analysts on the 'Right' who were sceptical about their capacity to do so – raised doubts and suggested that more attention should be paid to the determinants of policy decisions. While many of the leading figures in the development of policy analysis certainly moved between prescription and description – endeavouring to ground solutions in political and organisational realism – prescription was dominant in policy studies.

This book's original predecessor (Ham and Hill, 1984) was comparatively unusual at that time in asserting that it was appropriate to concentrate on description, to explore the nature of the policy process. Our justification was the need to help to ensure that proposals about policy content, or about how to change policy, should be grounded in the understanding of the real world in which policy is made. Nowadays that is a much less exceptional stance to take towards the study of policy. Rather, the problem may instead be that scepticism is so widespread that it is hard to make a case for the development of more sophisticated approaches to the policy process. That contributes to a widening gulf between the practical people – politicians, civil servants, pressure group leaders, etc. – whose business is achieving policy change and the academic analysts of the policy process – who aim to describe and interpret causal mechanisms at work in policy processes.

This book's stance, then, is to assert that we must continue to try to understand the policy process – however irrational or uncontrollable it may seem to be – as a crucial first step towards trying to secure effective policy making. The stance taken here can be compared to one in which effective engineering needs to be grounded in a good understanding of physics. While – at least in the past – many successful engineers have operated pragmatically, using trial and error methods and accumulating experience with only an intuitive understanding of physics, the modern view is that the physics should inform their practice. When things go wrong, moreover, for example when a bridge collapses, questions will be asked about the extent to which the practice was based upon the relevant body of scientific knowledge.

However, as will be indicated below, there is a need to be cautious about use of the word scientific in relation to the study of political and social life.

In reality, much of the so-called knowledge of the policy process derives from the observations of practical people who are much more interested in prescribing than in describing. The aim here is merely to try to stand back critically from their eagerness to prescribe, leading often to either complicity with the goals of the powerful or, as Rothstein has put it, to 'misery research' (1998, pp. 62–3) reflecting how often what is prescribed fails to be realised.

Does a process perspective need to start with any assumptions about the shape it takes?

If you are engaged in one of the prescriptive forms of policy analysis, you are likely to be relating your activity to one of the stages of the policy process: helping agenda setting or policy formulation through the provision of information, advising how actors might seek to steer or control the implementation process or evaluating policy outcomes. But if you are engaged in description you may even need to be sceptical about notions that policy development follows a staged process. There seem to be common-sense reasons why we should expect there to be stages in a policy process. Many human activities are staged in this way. Take for example going on a journey; you may typically:

- determine where you want to go;
- work out the best way to go there;
- go on the journey; and
- (perhaps) reflect on that process for future reference.

However, this activity does not always take that shape. You may go for a walk in which choices of the route and even the ultimate destination emerge as you engage in the process, depending on how you feel and what you see as you go along. Similarly, it is important not to assume that policy processes will necessarily take the shape embodied in the journey model set out systematically above. The problem, then, is that much of the activity observed by the student of the policy process is presumed by key actors to take that form, and that (as suggested above) much analysis of it takes that for granted.

The issues about the extent to which the 'stages model' of the policy process is, can or should be used will be explored further (in Chapter 8). However, there is one point about it that must be mentioned here. Readers of the last paragraph may have said to themselves that, while that statement about the book apparently presents an open-minded view of whether the policy process involves stages, several of the chapter headings of this book seem to take some of those stages for granted. The defence against a charge of inconsistency here is that any textbook, or teaching activity, needs a structure. The topic examined needs to be divided up in some way. The justification for the divisions adopted – as John, one of the stages model's severest critics, has recognised – is that there is a pragmatic case for the model as it 'imposes some order on the research process' (1998, p. 36). What had to be recognised in shaping this book was that if every process is continuously seen as interacting with every other process, there is no way to divide up discussion into separate chapters or sections. Hence, limited use is made of the stages model by recognising that there are somewhat different things to say about agenda setting, policy formulation and implementation respectively. At the same time, interactions are regularly stressed. Moreover the view taken here is not quite as radical as John's: very many policy processes do take shape along staged lines (albeit often with feedback loops).

Studying the policy process

As an issue for academic study, the exploration of the policy process is most evidently a part of political studies or political science. We are concerned here with the explanation of the outputs of politics – the 'how' aspect of Lasswell's terse definition of the study of politics as being about 'who gets what, when, and how' (1936). At the same time, much of the study of politics is about how power is acquired and used, without reference to policy outputs, inasmuch as it is concerned with elections, legislative processes and so on.

Any discussion of the public policy process needs to be grounded in an extensive consideration of the nature of power in the state. Any consideration of how the process works will tend to involve propositions about who dominates. Omission of this, in statements about the policy process, will tend to have the implication that there are no dominant elements in the state. That is in itself a stance on this much-debated subject, congruent with the pluralist perspective that power is evenly spread and openly contested. This has been widely opposed by views which draw upon Marxist theory or elite theory, which see power as very distinctively structured or which suggest that dominance is very much embedded in the nature of the machinery of the state itself.

An important element in the controversy about control over the state concerns the nature of power itself. This will be explored further in the next chapter. Controversy about the state and about power is closely related to the debate about democracy. Broadly, there is a conflict about the extent to which it is possible to identify, in the society that is under scrutiny, a system of power over the state which can be regarded as reasonably according with some of the criteria for a democracy. While modern political scientists recognise problems about the realisation of any ideal model of democracy, there are differing views about the scope any specific system offers for public participation. Sometimes these differences seem like little more than debates about whether the bottle is half full or half empty. However, there has been a strong division between a pluralist camp taking an optimistic view of democracy, particularly American democracy, and a neo-Marxist or elitist camp emphasising, for example, the dominance of the 'military–industrial complex' (Mills, 1956) or the structural power of business (Przeworski and Wallerstein, 1988; Swank, 1992).

Having identified the study of the policy process as so closely related to the study of politics, it is pertinent to note, without going too deeply into the argument, the problems about adopting too restrictive a view of the 'political'. Hay, in exploring what is meant by 'political analysis', makes the following point:

> The political should be defined in such a way as to encompass the entire sphere of the social. The implication of this is that events, processes and practices should not be labelled 'non-political' or 'extra-political' simply by virtue of the specific setting or context in which they occur. All events, processes and practices which occur within the social sphere have the potential to be political and, hence, to be amenable to political analysis. The realm of government is no more innately political, by this definition, than that of culture, law or the domestic sphere.
>
> (2002, p. 3)

Hay goes on from there to argue for the need for political analysis to include 'extra-political variables', to be concerned with economic and cultural processes, for example. He thus argues: 'Political analysts cannot simply afford to leave the analysis of economics to the economists, history to historians and so forth' (ibid., p. 4). But there is also a need to turn that argument the other way about and acknowledge that economists, historians, etc. can make a contribution to the understanding of the policy process.

In some parts of this book attention will be paid to arguments about the nature of the policy process that derive from economics. These particularly rest upon a view that it can help us to understand the policy process if we identify some or all of those engaged in it as 'rational actors'. This notion, with much in common with the way economists analyse human behaviour in the 'marketplace', assumes people will follow their interests, and engage in forms of gaming. We will also have to examine a very different kind of economics which sees decision making as determined by powerful economic forces.

Another discipline which contributes to the understanding of the policy process is sociology. It may be argued that analysis of political behaviour is political sociology. But quite apart from that, the sociology of organisations makes an important contribution to the study of the policy process, inasmuch as most policy making occurs within institutions. The sociology of organisations is particularly important for the interpretation of the translation of policy into action, exploring issues about the behaviour of workers within complex organisations (amongst which state bureaucracies loom large).

It is important to stress that there is no reason to suggest that the study of policy processes is any different from any other social science research enterprise. However, a little more needs to be said about the way in which the characteristics of the policy process pose certain challenges for research.

The object of study is normally a unique sequence of events. This means that there will be little scope for testing earlier research by looking for a situation in which a process is replicated. Policy experiments are rare, and when they occur they are not necessarily set up in ways which make research evaluation easy (Booth, 1998; Bulmer, 1987). The political environments in which they are conducted mean that they are very unlikely to run their course without ongoing adjustments. When they do occur, the very fact that they are atypical limits the lessons that can be drawn from them.

Policy process studies are very often case studies, using qualitative methods such as documentary analysis, discourse analysis, interviews with key actors or direct observation. Where quantitative methods are used, they are likely to deal with impact, from which deductions can be made back to process. Perhaps the ideal here is some combination of qualitative observation of process with quantitative work on the inputs and outputs of this process (e.g. written surveys of interest groups, secondary analysis of official statistics, quantitative coding of the votes in legislatures, the consultations procedures organised by the administration, etc.). For example, many empirical studies establish a causal link between the increasing saliency of an issue and the subsequent policy change (see John et al., 2013, for British examples). Concretely, a major policy change is expected only when a particular issue attracts the attention of the media, interest groups and elected officials. Quantitative and longitudinal studies are required to capture the media coverage of an issue (e.g. a dramatic nuclear accident, such as in Fukushima in 2011), the mobilisation of pressure groups (e.g. street-demonstrations and protest activities by environmentalist organisations) and the reactions of elected politicians (e.g. bills proposed by green parties), and how the increase of issue saliency might eventually translate into a major policy change (e.g. the phasing out from nuclear power).

However, there are many relevant activities that are very hard to observe, to measure and to quantify. This brings us back to the issue of power. The fact that many power processes are not readily accessible to analysis but are kept covert – indeed, their very success may depend upon them being so – is acknowledged in many colloquial expressions (the 'power behind the throne', the 'kitchen cabinet', the '*éminence grise*'). Official secrecy is openly used as a justification for restricting access to situations or data necessary to evaluate policy processes. Very much more is just kept secret without any attempt to offer a justification for doing so.

Analysts of policy processes are thus thrown back on methods which must involve inference from the data they can secure. They also find themselves in situations in which – like journalists or private detectives – they cannot validate their findings by revealing their sources. All social scientists are open to accusations that their theories and ideologies predispose them to particular interpretations of their qualitative and/or quantitative data. Those who study the policy process are particularly vulnerable to this charge.

One interesting way of trying to deal with this problem is to acknowledge openly the validity of competing theoretical frameworks of reference and then to explore a case study using each as an alternative lens (likely to amplify some parts of the subject and obscure others). Allison's (1971) use of this approach is described in Box 8.2. A number of other writers have followed Allison's lead, using different models. A particular concern has been to try to evaluate the evidence for the interpretations of policy processes to be discussed in the next chapter, as fairly open and competitive ones or as ones that are strongly structured or biased in favour of particular actors or interests (Blowers, 1984; Ham, 1992; Hill et al., 1989).

A second complementary way is to investigate and then to compare several policy processes. The comparison of similar or different cases is very often a promising research strategy to move beyond the singularities of a specific policy process, and to identify common patterns across policy domains, across countries or over time. In Chapter 6 we will address both ways by illustrating how a compound research design can combine various theoretical frameworks and types of comparisons.

Nevertheless, in the social and political sciences we recognise how complexity, change and the consciousness of the actors we are studying limit our scope for the establishment of generalisations (that is, propositions going beyond the investigated cases). We also recognise how, particularly in a field like the study of policy process, the use of experimental methods remains rather exceptional (see Smith et al., 2011, for such applications), and we must often use qualitative techniques in single or comparative case studies to grasp social and political phenomena. Hence, whilst the study of the policy process is claimed to be an academic discipline (Lasswell, 1951; 1968; 1970) upon which the more active contributions to policy analysis need to be based, there is a need not to overwork the distinction between academic and practical approaches. People describe and try to understand because they want to prescribe. Conversely, people who dedicate themselves directly to prescription will always want to root what they have to say in a realistic appreciation of what 'is', whether derived from academic studies or from their own practical experience.

There is a need to recognise the extent to which this activity may be considered as a form of historical study. Obviously the events observed have taken place in the past, though of course often the immediate past. Two issues emerge from that comparison. One is that what is involved are efforts to generalise from observations of past events in order to predict future ones or identify patterns. Historians differ on the feasibility of this (see MacMillan, 2009, for a cautious statement on this, or Hobsbaum, 1997, for a strong one). The other concerns the veracity of the observations of the past and the objectivity of the observer (see Evans, 2000, for a discussion of this).

A number of books have taken these observations further to pose a challenge to efforts to generalise about the policy process. This is not a book on methodology, let alone one which will extend into some of the difficult questions about the philosophy of the social sciences. But the fact that even the cautious empiricism set out above is challenged by some writers, including some who have discussed policy processes, cannot be left entirely without comment. Some theorists (who are here labelled 'postmodernist') argue that it is impossible to draw a distinction between 'analysis of' and 'analysis for' policy. The starting point for their argument is a view that few realistic social scientists will contest, namely that when we attempt to study a topic on which we have strong views on what 'ought' to happen, that may distort our interpretation of what does happen. That distortion is then even more likely if we have difficulties in developing a methodology for our work which enables the establishment of undisputable facts. What we face here, of course, are the issues about the extent to which social or political studies can be called 'scientific'.

In recurrent debates about the claim that social sciences are scientific, the core of the argument is about the extent to which 'positivist' methods can be used, involving the formulation and testing of causal hypotheses. The difficulties about doing this are partly practical problems about the extent to which it is possible to set up experimental situations or to design comparative research projects to control some of the variables so that the (net) impact of others may be isolated. These problems are tackled by those who subscribe to positivist approaches by seeking situations in which there are variations between research sites in the extent of the presence of key variables. Sophisticated statistical methods are used to sort out the impact of a complex mix of variables (Haynes, 2003). But there are other problems. When we try to develop explanations of what people do, we need to be aware that they have their own explanations of their behaviour, and their behaviour is influenced by the way they think and speak about what they are doing. Then we must also not forget that researchers themselves are people developing hypotheses about other people. Hence, not only do they bring biases to their studies, but they are also likely to be in situations in which their views and what they are doing will be communicated to those whose activities they are researching, and thus will be influencing future behaviour. While even in the physical sciences there are some problems about the relationship between researchers and the 'matter' they study, in the social sciences these problems are more fundamental. The objects of studies can understand what is being hypothesised and can react to that.

Postmodernist theorists go further to argue that when reporting 'facts', the observer is an active shaper both of the message sent and of the message received. For postmodernists, the language with which evidence is reported is important. The social construction of reality involves discourses and the presentation of 'texts' in which issues about language usage are at the core of the postmodern argument (Farmer, 1995). At its strongest, the postmodernist perspective challenges all attempts to generalise about the policy process. It is often not clear in this 'postmodernist' writing whether it is only being argued that more attention needs to be paid to discourse, and the need to deconstruct dominant discourses, or whether an entirely relativist stance is being taken. In much postmodernist writing there is an emphasis on the need for the 'democratisation of discourse' (Dryzek, 1990; Fischer, 2003; Fox and Miller, 1995). This is particularly important for the issues about evidence in political analysis.

The position taken in this book is to support the positivist 'project' inasmuch as it involves the systematic search for truth, in a context in which there are great difficulties about either accumulating good evidence or avoiding biases. But there must be a concern to recognise the significance of discourse and to allow for the possibility of alternative interpretations of evidence. This position has been described as 'critical modernist', explained by Pollitt and Bouckaert as still holding to 'the importance of the empirical testing of theories and hypotheses, although accepting that this is only one kind of test, and that arguments concerning whether the appropriate conditions for falsification will be met will never cease' (2000, p. 23). They go on to emphasise that 'reality is socially constructed, but not all constructions have equal claim to our credulity', and that there is a need to 'discriminate between more – and less – adequate descriptions and explanations' (ibid.).

Focusing on the policy process: exploration through examples

This section will use two examples from the UK to clarify some of the issues that have been discussed so far and to introduce the issues about the definition of policy that are the concerns of the rest of this chapter. The examples have been chosen to offer a clear contrast between example 1 (Box 1.2), a case where a comparatively straightforward process analysis is possible, and example 2 (Box 1.3), a case that is difficult and may be controversial.

Box 1.2	The right to roam

The roots of the quest for wider rights of access to the countryside than embodied in the long-standing English and Welsh 'rights of way' goes back to efforts by ramblers to gain access to privately owned moorland in the 1930s. In its 1997 manifesto the Labour Party promised, 'Our policies include greater freedom for people to explore our open countryside. We will not, however, permit any abuse of a right to greater access'.

That promise was kept and a right of access to specifically designated land was included in the Countryside and Rights of Way Act 2000. That Act contains very specific provisions on the land involved. This is designed to exclude cultivated land, parks and gardens, golf courses, military land, etc.; in other words, it confines the right to roam to open, comparatively wild country. The land remains in private ownership, and owners have rights to make use of it in various ways (including putting animals to graze on it); conversely there are also limitations on the things the public can do on it (horse riding, camping, driving a vehicle on it). The land in question has to be designated on official maps, and 'access authorities' (local governments or National Parks Authorities) have explicit powers to manage it (setting up entrance points, fences, notices, etc.).

Box 1.3	The reduction of child poverty

The attack on child poverty is of course a topic that is a widespread subject of policy advocacy. Pressure groups exist that address themselves wholly or partly to this; note for example the Child Poverty Action Group in the UK. Unlike the legislation discussed in Box 1.2, the 1997 Labour manifesto contained no specific commitment to an attack on child poverty but did include a variety of measures that might be expected to make a contribution to that goal either quite directly (the reduction of unemployment, the introduction of a minimum wage, reduction of taxes that imposed heavy burdens on lower income families) or indirectly (measures to improve health, education and housing, for example). However, in 1999 the then Prime Minister, Tony Blair, proclaimed that the government had a '20 year mission' 'to end child poverty for ever' (see Stewart in Seldon, 2007, p. 411; also Hills and Stewart, 2005, for wider discussion of this policy issue). That pledge was followed by the specification of interim targets, and various official indications about how the pledge might be interpreted. Crucial here is the use by the government of a definition of poverty in terms of below 60 percent of 'equivalised' (meaning a technique for taking into account household composition) median income after meeting housing costs.

This policy was put into an Act of Parliament (the Child Poverty Act 2010), setting goals not for the eradication of child poverty, but for specific improvements in respect of indicators by 2020–21. The measure had cross-party support and was not repealed when the Conservative-led Coalition Government assumed power in 2010, despite the fact that expenditure cuts have made the goals of the Act harder to achieve. The debate about the precise definition of the issue, however, rumbled on, and at the time of writing the measure seems likely to be replaced by an even more ambiguous Life Chances Act.

There has been extensive academic activity to track progress towards the specified goals (Stewart, 2011), and of course pressure groups have paid careful attention to evidence on that subject. More specific policy changes (in particular the development of tax credits) have been evaluated in terms of the contributions they make to the proclaimed goal.

Both of the policy examples in the boxes are set out in terms which can be seen as descriptive rather than prescriptive. But both developments can be seen in terms of wider goals, which can be (and in the case of the poverty issue very much are) the concerns of policy analysts. The chain of events following Blair's poverty pledge involved the translation of that into something to which actual government activity might be related; prescriptive analysts have much to say about how that has been done. But from a descriptive point of view there is also much to be said. In the case of the right to roam the original manifesto commitment may be seen, from its cautious terms, to be a product of an agenda-setting process in which the influence of interests contrary to those eager to open up the countryside can be detected. The actual elaborate designation process set up testifies to the further importance of this. What is then interesting is the extent to which the freedom of access acquired in practice has depended upon a quite complex, and indeed expensive, implementation process concerned with the designation, mapping and setting out of the access land. The anti-poverty pledge offers a much more extreme example of how complex a policy process may be. It was itself quite meaningless until accompanied by an official definition and until a very long-run goal was accompanied by interim goal statements. But even then, where the countryside access pledge implied a quite specific measure, the poverty pledge required realisation in terms of the development of a sequence of activities (in fact, further policies; we will come back to that in the next section).

In terms of what was said earlier about the notion of policy as 'staged', it may also be noted that it is quite easy to separate out agenda setting, more detailed policy formulation and implementation in respect of the 'right to roam'. The logical sequence predicted by the stages models was followed. But then it was a comparatively low-profile measure (it is not even mentioned in Seldon's two edited volumes on the Blair governments: Seldon, 2001; 2007) with fairly low implications either for those opposed to it or for other public policies. On the other hand, actually following through the events since Blair's anti-poverty pledge takes us down a tortuous path of interacting policies, some of which advance the nation towards that goal whilst others lead away from it.

At this point some readers may protest that comparing 'right to roam' with 'anti-poverty' policy is not comparing like with like. Some may even want to say that the first is a policy, the second just an aspiration. It does indeed seem probable that Blair's famous pledge may have been meant as a vague rhetorical aspiration (Dean, 2011, chapter 6). However, it was then set out in an Act of Parliament and passed with all-party support, containing targets which were not specifically repudiated by later governments formed from the parties in opposition at the time. The important point is that the word 'policy' is regularly used about both the policies discussed. This obviously leads us to the issues about the definition of policy.

The meaning of 'policy'

The *Chambers Dictionary* defines policy as 'a course of action, especially one based on some declared and respected principle'. That definition clearly sees policy as something more than simply a decision: it embodies the idea of action – indeed, rational action – inasmuch as some 'principle' is involved. In everyday speech we sometimes say things like 'my policy is always to . . .'.

This book is, of course, about *public* policy. Interestingly, the *Oxford English Dictionary* describes the following as 'the chief living sense' of the word 'policy': 'a course of action adopted and pursued by a government, party, ruler, statesman . . .'. In the next section we come back to the implications of the word 'public'.

These definitions do not get us very far towards identifying a policy. Perhaps we can do no more than adopt the very British pragmatism of Cunningham, a former top British civil servant, who argued that 'policy is rather like the elephant – you recognise it when you see it but cannot easily define it' (1963, p. 229). A rather similarly vague approach is adopted by Friend and his colleagues, who say 'policy is essentially a *stance* which, once articulated, contributes to the context within which a succession of future decisions will be made' (Friend et al., 1974, p. 40). However, others have sought to do better than that. Box 1.4 sets out some examples.

The definitional problems posed by the concept of policy suggest that it is difficult to treat it as a very specific and concrete phenomenon. Policy may sometimes be identifiable in terms of a decision, but very often it involves either groups of decisions or what may be seen as little more than an orientation. The attempts at definition also imply that it is hard to identify particular occasions when policy is made. There is a temptation here to adopt a more specific definition of policy for the purposes of this textbook, since there are grounds for seeing some usages as too vague for systematic analysis. This is perhaps the case with the poverty policy example discussed above. But it is unhelpful for social scientists to give terms in wide general use specific meanings for the purposes of their own analyses. In analysing the policy process it is important to recognise that different actors will be using the word policy in different ways, often with the specific objective of influencing how others view their actions.

Box 1.4	Definitions of policy

- Heclo's definition of policy, like the *Chambers Dictionary* one set out in the text, emphasises action: 'a policy may usefully be considered as a course of action or inaction rather than specific decisions or actions' (1972, p. 85).

- Easton offers a variant of this, noting that 'a policy . . . consists of a web of decisions and actions that allocate . . . values' (1953, p. 130).

- W.I. Jenkins sees policy as 'a set of interrelated decisions . . . concerning the selection of goals and the means of achieving them within a specified situation . . .' (1978, p. 15).

- B.C. Smith suggests that 'the concept of policy denotes . . . deliberate choice of action or inaction, rather than the effects of interrelating forces': he emphasises 'inaction' as well as action and reminds us that 'attention should not focus exclusively on decisions which produce change, but must also be sensitive to those which resist change and are difficult to observe because they are not represented in the policy-making process by legislative enactment' (1976, p. 13).

Let us look a little more at the implications of the fact (emphasised in Easton's and Jenkins' definitions in Box 1.4) that policy involves a course of action or a web of decisions rather than just one decision. There are several aspects to this. Perhaps the most important of these is that the term 'policy' is being applied to many very different substantive topics. When we move away from talking about policy in general terms we discover very different usages. We return to this issue in a later section. Meanwhile, we list the general issues to be considered.

First, a decision network, often of considerable complexity, may be involved in producing action. A web of decisions, taking place over a long period of time and extending far beyond the initial policy-making process, may form part of the network. Both of the examples above (Boxes 1.2 and 1.3) involve this; it is very clear in respect of the issue of anti-poverty policy but even the right to roam policy was shown to imply a quite elaborate pattern of implementation actions.

A second point is that policy is not usually expressed in a single decision. It tends to be defined in terms of a series of decisions which, taken together, comprise a more or less common understanding of what policy is. That is, of course, crucial for the anti-poverty policy example, where from the very start a pragmatic response to the core issue of how to define poverty was of fundamental importance.

Third, policies invariably change over time. Yesterday's statements of intent may not be the same as today's, either because of incremental adjustments to earlier decisions, or because of major changes of direction. Also, the experience of implementing a decision may feed back into the decision-making process. This is not to say that policies are always changing, but simply that the policy process is dynamic rather than static and that we need to be aware of shifting definitions of issues. Again the way in which a decision that something should be done about poverty led on to a sequence of other decisions is quite evident. But the much more concrete policy making around the right to roam also had implications for related actions. There remain issues about the extent to which the originally designated access land can be extended, and it may be noted that later legislation (the Marine and Coastal Access Act 2009) goes on to set up related new approaches to access to the coast.

Fourth, it is therefore important not to fall into the trap of seeing the policy process as if it exists on a desert island. Most of the policies that are likely to be studied in the modern world are changes to existing policies. Even when they seem to address a new issue or problem they will nevertheless be entering a crowded policy space, impacting upon and being influenced by other policies. Hence, as Wildavsky puts it, 'any major move sets off a series of changes, many of which . . . inevitably transform any problem they were originally supposed to solve' (1979, p. 71). If we take a broad policy issue like the reduction of poverty it may be noted that this extends more widely to redistributional issues in society as a whole. Someone has to pay for any gains made by the poor. Furthermore, the concentration on raising incomes close to the poverty threshold has implications for the situations of those further up the income 'ladder'. Perhaps most significantly of all, the fact that the incomes of many who secure state benefits are below the officially defined poverty level generates a dilemma for the government, which they find easier to respond to in terms of efforts (often controversial) to get people off benefits than to change the rates of benefit.

Fifth, a development of this fourth point is that much policy decision-making is concerned, as Hogwood and Gunn (1984) have stressed, with attempting the difficult task of 'policy termination' or determining 'policy succession' (see also Hogwood and Peters, 1983). In this sense the anti-poverty pledge may be seen as crucial for partial shifts in the benefit system from basic social assistance guarantees to tax credits only available to those in work. This implication has been very evident of the way in which more recent governments have approached this issue.

Sixth, the corollary of the last three points is the need to recognise that the study of policy has as one of its main concerns the examination of non-decisions. This is what Heclo and Smith are pointing to (see Box 1.4) in their references to inaction. It has been argued that much political activity is concerned with maintaining the status quo and resisting challenges to the existing allocation of values. Analysis of this activity is a necessary part of the examination of the dynamics of the policy process.

Seventh, the definitions cited raise the question of whether policy can be seen as action without decisions. It can be said that a pattern of actions over a period of time constitutes a policy, even if these actions have not been formally sanctioned by a decision. Dery takes this point even further to argue that often we can write of 'policy by the way . . . the by-product of policies that are made and implemented to pursue objectives other than those of the policy in question' (1999, pp. 165–6). In this sense policy may be seen as an outcome which actors may or may not want to claim as a consequence of purposive activity. Having proclaimed that they have an anti-poverty policy, a government may be able to claim credit for reductions of the numbers of those below the poverty line whether or not this is a result of their interventions.

Writers on policy have increasingly turned their attention to the action of lower-level actors, sometimes called 'street-level bureaucrats' (Lipsky, 1980), in order to gain a better understanding of the policy process. It has been suggested that in some circumstances it is at this level in the system that policy is actually made. It would seem to be important to balance a decisional, top-down perspective on policy with an action-oriented, bottom-up perspective. Actions as well as decisions may therefore be said to be the proper focus of policy analysis. Later we will explore some of the issues surrounding the evolution of policy, noting writers who see the policy process as involving distinctive stages or a cycle and a literature which draws a stronger distinction between policy making and implementation. Such an approach rests very much upon a taken-for-granted version of the *Chambers* definition set out above. It may be contrasted with a view that in many respects policy needs to be seen as what happens, rather than as what politicians say will happen.

The view that policies may simply be outcomes of political and bureaucratic processes as opposed to courses 'of action adopted and pursued' leads to two important themes for the study of the policy process: (1) the relationship between policy and politics, and (2) the dominance in much that is said and written about policy of the view that political action is (or should be) purposive.

A deeper exploration of the *Oxford English Dictionary* reveals that the word 'policy' has an interesting history in English. Amongst usages of the word that are now obsolete are the notions of policy as a 'prudent, expedient or advantageous procedure' and as a 'device, expedient, contrivance ... stratagem, trick'. Parsons points out that Shakespeare used 'policy' in various ways:

> Policy encompassed the arts of political illusion and duplicity. Show, outward appearance and illusions were the stuff of which power was made. Shakespeare employed the terms of Machiavellian philosophy ... Power cannot be sustained purely with force. It needs, in a Machiavellian sense, *policy*: and 'policy sits above conscience', as the bard tells us in *Timon of Athens*.
>
> (Parsons, 1995, p. 14)

Furthermore some languages do not draw a clear distinction between 'policy' (i.e. *'les politiques'* in French), 'politics' (i.e. *'la politique'* in French) and 'polity' (i.e. *'le politique'* in French). Therefore, French handbooks on policy analysis explicitly refer to the English language to distinguish between 'polity' as the institutional frame of the game, 'politics' as the political power game, and 'public policies' as the outcome of the game. At the same time, they insist on the strong interrelationships between these three dimensions (Meny and Thoenig, 1989, p.129; Muller, 2003, pp. 5 and 122; Knoepfel et al., 2006, p. 27; Lascoumes and Le Galès, 2007, p. 40).

Richard Jenkins argues that the 'apparently objective distinction between politics and policy is actually likely to be deeply political in its own right; in this sense, the other European languages have definitely got it right' (2007, p. 27). Thus he attacks the 'technocratic illusion of "rational" policy' (ibid.). We have here another aspect of the distinction between descriptive and prescriptive approaches to the policy process. Much prescriptive writing depends upon taking an explicit stance on what policy *should* be, but in the study of the policy process it is important to be aware of the complexity and ambiguity of the concept of policy. Hence, the purpose of this very brief excursion into linguistic history is to emphasise not merely that policy has been seen as a simple and expedient, even duplicitous, ingredient in political strategy but also that this may still be an appropriate way to think of it. We need to ask: what is being said when someone stresses that they have a policy? May they not simply be trying to convince us that they are acting effectively and purposefully? Edelman (1971; 1977; 1988) has devoted considerable attention to the 'symbolic' uses of the concept of policy. Further, even if people can convince us, we still need to ask: what are the implications of their policy? Phenomena like the proclaimed 'anti-poverty policy' particularly need unpacking in this way. The notion here that policies are 'claims' takes us back to the simplest of the dictionary definitions, that is, that when we (and by the same token politicians) say we have a 'policy' we are in a sense making a claim to have a 'property'. And, of course, then – as has been shown in respect of anti-poverty policy – such claims may provoke challenges.

It is a particular feature of the modern discourse about policy that it is seen as desirable that politicians should have policies – so that electorates may make choices – and that governments should enact those policies in a systematic way. It was suggested above that the very rise of the study of policy was dominated by that perspective, and that many contributions to policy analysis are motivated by a desire to assist a rational policy-making process. Yet politicians do not necessarily see their roles in this way – power may be more important to them than policy, and power may be used for personal ends rather than to try to solve problems in the way presumed in discussions of policy analysis.

What, then, needs to be understood as we examine the policy process is that, although the concept of policy is vague and elusive, it is nevertheless widely used to suggest a rational process. Readers need to be sceptical about writing which takes it for granted that a policy-making process is organised and has specific goals. It may be desirable that it should be like this, but whether it actually is or not must be an issue for research.

Public policy

The *Oxford English Dictionary* definition of policy quoted above refers to action 'by a government, party, ruler, statesman, etc.' But it goes on to note the more private usage of 'any course of action adopted as advantageous or expedient'. It was noted that individuals sometimes talk of adopting 'policies'. Organisations of all kinds regularly do so. This book is about 'public policy'. Is there anything intrinsically different about the definition arising from the fact that it is the state or state organisations that are seen as the makers of the policy? The answer to that is surely 'no' as far as the simple characteristics of policy are concerned, but 'yes' inasmuch as special claims are made about the legitimacy of state policy and its primacy over other policies. This takes us into two difficulties – one about the nature of the state, the other about the special justifications used for the role of the state as a provider of policies.

A basic definition of the state is enshrined in Max Weber's definition of it as (1) 'an administrative and legal order subject to change by legislation' and (2) claiming 'binding authority . . . over all action taking place in the area of its jurisdiction' (Weber, 1947, p. 156). It can be identified in terms of both the institutions that make it up and the functions these institutions perform. State institutions comprise legislative bodies, including parliamentary assemblies and subordinate law-making institutions; executive bodies, including governmental bureaux and departments of state; and judicial bodies – principally courts of law – with responsibility for enforcing and, through their decisions, developing the law. State institutions are located at various levels – national, regional and local.

But there are also inter- and supra-state institutions which act, to some degree, as superordinate states. These include both international organisations – the United Nations, the World Trade Organization, the World Health Organization, the World Bank, etc., which may seek to impose policies on nation states – and supra-national institutions like the European Union, which operate quite specifically as superordinate law makers. The very fact that this supra-national power is controversial and is to some degree challenged by nation states offers a reminder of the fact that many states have gone through a process of struggling to achieve a legitimate superordinate role.

The identification of a complex of institutions as making up the state introduces another complication. This is that the state may operate through institutions which have many features that are regarded as private rather than public. In the past, particularly in the early years of state formation, states hired mercenary armies, subcontracted tax collection and delegated law enforcement to local, quasi-autonomous barons. In many of the early nation states the whole apparatus of government was initially no more than an extension of the royal household. In other societies the establishment of a centralised governmental system was very much a partnership between the sovereign and a religious body.

The modern manifestation of the phenomena discussed in the last paragraph has been a deliberate shift to the delegation of what had become accepted as governmental functions. What this implies is a contract between government and a 'private' body to operate all or part of a public service. This is often presented as simply a mechanism for policy 'implementation' with policy making remaining in government hands, but it will be shown later that this policy-making/implementation distinction is not easily drawn. The delegation of a major activity, particularly a monopoly activity, tends to involve some shift of control over policy. A related phenomenon is a public/private partnership where resources are drawn from both publicly collected revenues and private sources; policy control is obviously particularly likely to be shared in these circumstances. Finally, in introducing this subject the word 'private' was deliberately put in inverted commas. Like the concept 'public', this is hard to define when there is a complex partnership between different elements, including state ones. Furthermore, 'private' does not necessarily imply a private profit-making organisation – in this respect institutions bringing voluntary organisations into association with the state may be seen as ways of further integrating state and society and increasing democratic participation.

These complications, arising both from the increasing importance of supra-state bodies and from changes within the nation state (sometimes described as the 'hollowing out' of the state – see Milward et al., 1993 – have led many contemporary writers to speak of a movement from 'government' to 'governance'. Richards and Smith thus say:

> 'Governance' is a descriptive label that is used to highlight the changing nature of the policy process in recent decades. In particular, it sensitises us to the ever-increasing variety of terrains and actors involved in the making of public policy. Thus, it demands that we consider all the actors and locations beyond the 'core executive' involved in the policy making process.
>
> (Richards and Smith, 2002, p. 2)

That definition perhaps gives insufficient emphasis to the supra-state issues, that is, that the key actors may be outside as well as inside the nation state. There is a debate (see section on globalism in Chapter 2) about the extent to which globalisation and the development of international governing institutions are important for contemporary governance (see Pierre, 2000).

Pierre and Peters' exploration of the use of the term 'governance' suggests that it is confusing since it is used both to describe empirical phenomena and to explore how those phenomena operate (2000, p. 12). Some writers emphasise a need for a shift from government to governance because of new realities, while others use this terminology to analyse how processes are actually changing.

To sum up then, there is an obvious objection to seeing the public policy process as only about policies delivered and/or enforced by governments. Private actors may do this for governments. But that still leaves a problem about identifying governments in situations of overlapping supra-national and sub-national governments, even perhaps competing governments. To return to the example of anti-poverty policy: the European Union, the United Kingdom government, the devolved governments in Scotland, Wales and Northern Ireland, and many local authorities all claim to have anti-poverty policies (the actual terms may vary – for example, in the European Union case the issue is often embraced within the notion of 'social exclusion'). Moreover since, as has already been stressed, effective action in this area depends upon many different activities it is implicit that this may involve different governments, whose actions may or may not be consistent with each other.

CONCLUSIONS

This chapter has stressed that this book deals with the description of the policy process. However, it has been noted that it is impossible to maintain a rigid distinction between description and prescription because so many of those who have written about the policy process have combined the two.

(continued)

Descriptions have been offered in order to justify or criticise the way policies are made and implemented. Some of the most important controversies in policy analysis have been between analysts who differ on what they observe and what they want to observe.

One widely quoted proposition from Karl Marx is 'the philosophers have only *interpreted* the world in various ways; the point, however, is to *change* it' (1845, in Marx, 1958, vol. 2, p. 405). Marx was clear that he needed to offer a realistic description of the world in order to establish his political programme. The study of policy processes has been dominated by people concerned to show how power is concentrated or how politicians may be called to account or how administrators distort the intentions of their political chiefs and so on. Whilst this account attempts to achieve a measure of neutrality in that respect, it would be foolish of the writers to pretend that their prescriptive biases will not show through from time to time. And in the last resort Marx is right – the justification for trying to understand is a desire to do things better.

2 Theories of power and the policy process

SYNOPSIS

This chapter, the first of six exploring theoretical and methodological approaches to the analysis of the policy process, deals with the general issues about power in society that are of importance for explaining the policy process.

The chapter shows how a pluralist perspective on representative government was developed. This perspective saw power as fragmented yet relatively widely distributed. A dialogue developed between that perspective and alternative views that stressed ways in which power is concentrated. Amongst the latter is Marxist theory, which has a very explicit approach to explaining power inequalities in terms of economic inequalities.

The chapter then shows that much Marxist theory involves a perspective on the state embodying a form of structural determinism: seeing state action as determined by the economic order (capitalism, in the modern world). That leads on to a general consideration of forms of structural determinism, the most important of which – amongst theories in current vogue – is globalist theory. The exploration of globalist theory suggests that some of its forms are closely related to Marxist theory and that most aspects of it raise important questions about the complex nature of the relationship between social structure and political action. Reasons are then suggested for recognising structural constraints, moving beyond narrow economic determinism to embrace considerations about inequalities introduced by analysts of gender and ethnic inequalities, but avoiding a narrowly determinist approach to them.

Introduction

The study of the policy process is essentially the study of the exercise of power in the making of policy and cannot therefore disregard underlying questions about the sources and nature of that power. These questions have been the subject of widespread controversy. In the last chapter the close connections between analysis of the policy process and concerns to suggest ways to change or influence that process were noted. Similarly in the study of the power within the state, 'explanatory and normative theories are intertwined' (Dryzek and Dunleavy, 2009, p. xii). The discussion here highlights explanatory issues, but we are inevitably influenced by the ways theories may help us to justify or challenge forms of power. In that controversy there are two particularly important themes: about the extent to which systems have power distributed in a relatively egalitarian way and about the extent to which power is concentrated or fragmented.

Table 2.1 expresses these as two dimensions. All four positions represent generalised versions of different theoretical positions which will be discussed further here and in the following chapters. The two top positions (1 and 2) show what are often presented as alternative models of democracy, but the concern here is the extent to which power is structured, not with the arguments about what constitutes a democratic system of government. The diagram has been deliberately drawn to involve four quadrants rather than axes, but of course in reality, different theories take different positions about the extent of the structuring (or conversely the fragmentation) of power or about the extent to which its distribution is egalitarian. In the process of arguments between theorists, new modified positions are adopted. This means that contemporary exponents of any of these perspectives are likely to take positions closer to the axes than their predecessors. For example, a classical Marxist position would be way out on the margins of quadrant 3 if a continuum was used, and a classical pluralist one would be at an alternative extreme position in quadrant 2, but many modern theorists will be much closer to the axis. A great deal of the literature on power and theories of the state does indeed focus upon the arguments between theorists who are broadly in quadrants 2 and 3. The perspective represented by quadrant 1 has come under considerable attack from all sides, while in quadrant 4 will be found some recent writers who see the political process as exceptionally incoherent (see section on policy networks in Chapter 4).

Table 2.1   A simplified representation of the main approaches to describing the policy process

	Power structured	Power fragmented
Power distributed relatively equally	1. Representative government in which a unified executive is responsive to popular will	2. Pluralist government in which popular will prevails through competition between groups
Power distributed unequally	3. Government by an unrepresentative elite, or in the grip of external influences	4. Unpredictable and chaotic government, buffeted by multiple pressures

Origins of pluralist theory: rescuing the theory of representative democracy

The issue mentioned about the way explanatory and normative perspectives often interlock lies right at the centre of the debate about pluralism. Defenders of democratic ideals have had to come to terms with the large and complex institutional structures of states. An Athenian ideal of democracy – that is, one involving direct participation – has been seen to offer an unworkable model. In several political systems, popular votes are organised to adopt an amendment to the Constitution or a legislative act. In some circumstances, citizens may even formulate the policy proposition to be voted upon and launch a so-called 'popular initiative'. This direct-democracy instrument is very frequently used in Switzerland, in California and in other American States. In the UK referenda are used from time to time; there was one on continuing membership of the European Union in 1975 (2016), one on devolution in 1997 and one on Scottish independence in 2014.

However, even in democratic regimes where direct legislation is a key institutional feature, the legislative and executive institutions are based on the indirect representation of citizens and on the delegation of policy-making powers to elected officials. In a representative system, a limited number of people participate in the day-to-day business of government but they may be the representatives of the people as a whole. The early model for this representation was still seen to involve a relatively personal relationship between the elected politician and the comparatively small electorate that elected him (it was almost always 'him' at that stage of the development of political institutions).

With the enlargement of the electorate and the increasing need to organise within the legislature, another institution developed to make the connection between elector and elected more indirect – the political party. Schumpeter (1947) defines democracy as 'that institutional arrangement for arriving at political decisions in which individuals acquire the power to decide by means of a competitive struggle for the people's vote' (p. 269). While there are important examples around the world of efforts to facilitate more continuous democratic participation, it is very often the case that general representation has been limited (merely the chance to make choices every few years between a limited number of options). However alongside political parties, processes of government involve other groups or organisations of public interests who will try to influence voting decisions at elections or the legislative programmes of political parties. Once established, moreover, these 'pressure groups' will try to influence the policy process at any stage – negotiating the details of legislation, establishing links to influence the implementation process, monitoring policy outcomes and so on. Thus, it is argued that the pressure groups that have grown up alongside the formal institutions of government have come to play an important direct part in representing the views of specific interests.

Talking about the United Kingdom, Beer (1965) notes the development of a collectivist theory of representation legitimising a much greater role for groups than earlier conceptions of representative government. Beer argues that as governments sought to manage the economy, they were led to bargain with organised groups of producers, in particular with worker and employer associations. Governments of both political parties sought the consent and cooperation of these associations, and needed their advice, acquiescence and approval. Such 'neo-corporatist arrangements' – prevalent in many countries – between state actors, private business organisations and workers' unions are discussed further in Chapter 4.

Similarly, the evolution of the welfare state stimulated action by organised groups of consumers, such as tenants, parents and patients. The desire by governments to retain office led them to consult and bargain with these consumer groups in attempts to win support and votes. Beer's thesis has been developed in the work of Richardson and Jordan (1979; see also Jordan and Richardson, 1987), who have argued that the United Kingdom is a 'post-parliamentary democracy' in which policies are developed in negotiation between government agencies and pressure groups organised into policy communities. According to Richardson and Jordan, pressure groups influence public policy from the point at which issues emerge onto the agenda to the stage of implementation.

What has been described here, then, is a replacement of the view of government portrayed in quadrant 1 of Table 2.1, 'representative democracy', in which an executive responsible to a legislature was seen as making policy on behalf of the people, by a more complex pluralist model (as in quadrant 2). As far as some countries are concerned, particularly the United Kingdom, this perspective on the system is still contested – if not by political scientists then at least by some politicians – inasmuch as claims are made that the government 'in parliament' is still paramount, with a mandate to legislate. The empirical question to which we will need to return, therefore (particularly in the section on the impact of electoral mandates in Chapter 9), is the extent to which policies emerge directly and untainted by the influence of pressure groups from political manifestos and promises in some societies.

The pluralist school of thought in political science described and charted the developments described above, exploring how political parties really worked and the roles played by pressure groups. But many in this school also argued that this was how a modern democracy should work. Theorists like Truman (1958) and Bentley (1967) gloried in the institutional complexity of their society, contrasting it favourably with less open societies where they perceived much group activity to be limited or even suppressed. Hence pluralism should be seen, in Schwarzmantel's words, 'both as a normative theory and as a way of explaining and analysing the power structure of the liberal-democratic system' (1994, p. 48). Schwarzmantel amplifies this as follows:

> Because pluralism takes its starting point to be a modern society in which there are different interests, popular power is realised through group activity, the working of political parties and pressure groups or interest

groups, each of which represents one of the many interests into which a developed society is split. Pluralist perspectives salute and emphasise this diversity of interest, and like liberal theorists they see this variety as a necessary and positive dimension of social life.

(1994, p. 50)

Clearly, then, opposition to the pluralist perspective can take two forms. One of these is to argue that this is not a satisfactory model for democracy (it is too indirect or it is impossible to realise the 'general will' through such diversity). This is not the concern of this discussion. The other is to argue that pluralism provides a misleadingly optimistic picture of the way power is organised in those societies described as pluralist. This may, of course, then lead back to a critique of the ideal, or, as in the case of the work of the socialist pluralist Herbert Laski (1925), to a set of proposals for strengthening pluralism by countering the biases in the system (see also Cohen and Rogers, 1995, for a modern version of this approach).

Dahl and his followers

Perhaps the most influential exposition of pluralist theory, and certainly a very important one for the study of policy processes, was in the early work of Robert Dahl. While he shifted his position later in his career, Dahl (1958) originally argued that power in many Western industrialised societies is widely distributed among different groups. No group is without power to influence decision making, and equally, no group is dominant. Any group can ensure that its political preferences and wishes are adopted if it is sufficiently determined.

Dahl and colleagues such as Nelson Polsby (1963) argue that their position is not that power is equally distributed. Rather, pluralist theory argues that the sources of power are unequally but widely distributed among individuals and groups within society. Although all groups and interests do not have the same degree of influence, even the least powerful are able to make their voices heard at some stage in the decision-making process. No individual or group is completely powerless, and the pluralist explanation of this is that the sources of power – like money, information, expertise and so on – are distributed non-cumulatively and no one source is dominant. Essentially, then, in a pluralist political system power is fragmented and diffused, and the basic picture presented by the pluralists is of a political marketplace where what a group achieves depends on its resources and its 'decibel rating'.

There is an issue here, to which we will return in the next four chapters, about the way that pluralist theory deals with the role of government agencies. In much pluralist work, the state, as such, is little investigated. While some writers argue that government is neutral and acts essentially as a referee in the struggle between groups (Latham, 1952), the dominant theme in the work of Dahl is that government agencies are one set of pressure groups among many others. According to the latter interpretation, government both pursues its own preferences and responds to demands coming from outside interests.

The critique of pluralism

Much of the theoretical work expounding the pluralist perspective, and particularly Dahl's contribution, was an attack on earlier work which stressed power concentrations. Dahl argued that 'the evidence for a ruling elite, either in the United States or in any specific community, has not yet been properly examined so far as I know' (p. 469). In Dahl's view, there is a need for researchers interested in the power structure to examine neither the 'reputation' for power of local leaders (Hunter, 1953) nor their key positions in large-scale organisations (Mills, 1956), but rather to focus on actual decisions and to explore whether the preferences of the hypothetical ruling elite are adopted over those of other groups. Only in this way is it possible to test the assertion that a ruling elite exists.

Underpinning Dahl's approach is a straightforward definition of power which states: 'A has power over B to the extent that he can get B to do something that B would not otherwise do' (Dahl, 1957, p. 203). This draws attention to the fact that power involves a relationship between political actors. These actors may be individuals, groups or other human aggregates, and Dahl emphasises that power must be studied in cases where there are differences of preferences between actors. Actors whose preferences prevail in conflicts over key political issues are those who exercise power in a political system. It follows that the student of power needs to analyse concrete decisions involving actors pursuing different preferences. Careful study of these decisions is required before the distribution of power can be described adequately.

The problem with this is that it treats the exercise of power as something that is likely to be very visible. Critics have pointed out that much power is exercised more covertly and through the subtle cultural processes which influence how people determine their activities and interests. Attempts have been made to deal with this issue by using other words – 'authority', 'influence' and 'domination', for example. Changing the words does not really solve the problem, but it does draw attention to the variety of ways in which power is exercised. Knoke offers a useful approach, using 'influence' to describe what 'occurs when one actor intentionally transmits information to another that alters the latter's actions' (Knoke, 1990, p. 3) and 'domination' where 'one actor controls the behaviour of another actor by offering or withholding some benefit or harm' (ibid., p. 4). This helps to get away from a simple model of the way power is exercised, but it does not deal with the problem of deeply structured power.

Dahl came under attack from Bachrach and Baratz, who, in an article published in 1962, argue that power does not simply involve examining key decisions and actual behaviour. Bachrach and Baratz assert that 'power is also exercised when A devotes his energies to creating or reinforcing social and political values and institutional practices that limit the scope of the political process to public consideration of only those issues which are comparatively innocuous to A' (1963, p. 948). Borrowing a term from Schattschneider, Bachrach and Baratz describe this as 'the mobilisation of bias' (Schattschneider, 1960, p. 71), a process which confines decision making to safe issues. What this suggests is the existence of two faces of power: one operating, as Dahl indicates, at the level of overt conflicts over key issues; the other operating, through a process which Bachrach and Baratz term 'nondecision-making', to suppress conflicts and to prevent them from entering the political process. The implication of Bachrach and Baratz's analysis is that the methodology adopted by researchers such as Dahl is inadequate, or at least partial. A more complete analysis needs to examine what does not happen, as well as what does happen, and to unravel the means by which the mobilisation of bias operates to limit the scope of debate.

But what does nondecision-making actually involve? Bachrach and Baratz define nondecision-making as 'the practice of limiting the scope of actual decision-making to "safe" issues by manipulating the dominant community values, myths, and political institutions and procedures' (1962, p. 642). Bachrach and Baratz argue that a nondecision-making situation can be said to exist 'when the dominant values, the accepted rules of the game, the existing power relations among groups, and the instruments of force, singly or in combination, effectively prevent certain grievances from developing into full-fledged issues which call for decisions' (ibid.). In this respect Bachrach and Baratz distinguish nondecision-making from negative aspects of decision making such as deciding not to act and deciding not to decide. In their view, nondecision-making differs from these other phenomena in that when nondecision-making occurs, issues do not even become matters for decision. That is, issues remain latent and fail to enter the decision-making process because of the impact of the mobilisation of bias.

Bachrach and Baratz emphasise the means by which vested interests are protected by nondecision-making. In their model of the political process, Bachrach and Baratz argue that demand regulation is not a neutral activity, but rather operates to the disadvantage of persons and groups seeking a real-location of values. These may be expected to be those who are disadvantaged by the status quo.

The pluralists responded to Bachrach and Baratz's critique by claiming that nondecision-making was un-researchable (Merelman, 1968; Wolfinger, 1971). How, they asked, could nondecisions be studied? On what basis could social scientists investigate issues that did not arise and conflicts that did not emerge? Bachrach and Baratz replied by amplifying and to some extent modifying their position. In their book, *Power and Poverty,* published in 1970, they maintain that the second face of power operates to keep grievances covert. A nondecision – defined as 'a decision that results in suppression or thwarting of a latent or manifest challenge to the values or interests of the decision-maker' (p. 44) – can be investigated through the identification of covert grievances and the existence of conflicts that do not enter the political arena. If no grievances or conflicts can be discovered, then a consensus exists and nondecision-making has not occurred (see Box 2.1).

Box 2.1	Bachrach and Baratz's examples of the different forms that nondecision-making can take

- The use of force to prevent demands from entering the political process. For example, the terrorisation of civil rights workers in the southern United States.
- The use of power to deter the emergence of issues. The co-optation of groups into decision-making procedures is an illustration.
- Rules or procedures used to deflect unwelcome challenges. Referring issues to committees or commissions for detailed study is one example; labelling demands as unpatriotic or immoral is another.
- Reshaping rules and procedures to block challenges.

Bachrach and Baratz also argue that power may be exercised by anticipated reactions. That is, an actor, A, may be deterred from pursuing his or her preferences because he or she anticipates an unfavourable reaction by another actor, B. Anticipated reactions may operate when a community group fails to mobilise because it anticipates an unfavourable response by decision makers, or when decision makers themselves do not act because they expect opposition from key political actors. Although these examples involve an exercise of power, Bachrach and Baratz note that this 'is not nondecision-making in the strict sense' (1970, p. 46).

The debate about power was taken a stage further by Lukes (1974), who argues that power must be studied in three dimensions. First, there is the exercise of power that occurs in observable, *overt* conflicts between actors over key issues: the pluralists' approach. Second, there is the exercise of power that occurs in *covert* conflicts between actors over issues or potential issues: Bachrach and Baratz's method. Third, there is the dimension of power that Lukes adds, which involves the exercise of power to shape people's preferences so that neither overt nor covert conflicts exist. In other words, when the third dimension of power operates, there is *latent* conflict. He draws here on Crenson's (1971) arguments about 'anticipated reactions', where it is recognised the situation is so loaded in favour of existing power (e.g. the economic power of the steel industry), that efforts to achieve change (e.g. air pollution policy) are pointless.

Lukes states that latent conflict exists when there would be a conflict of wants or preferences between those exercising power and those subject to it

were the latter to become aware of their interests. In this context, the definition of power employed by Lukes is that 'A exercises power over B when A
affects B in a manner contrary to B's interests' (1974, p. 27). In Lukes' view
the existence of a consensus does not indicate that power is not being exercised, he argues:

> is it not the supreme and most insidious exercise of power to prevent
> people, to whatever degree, from having grievances by shaping their
> perceptions, cognitions and preferences in such a way that they accept
> their role in the existing order of things, either because they can see or
> imagine no alternative to it, or because they see it as natural and unchange-
> able, or because they value it as divinely ordained and beneficial? To
> assume that the absence of grievance equals genuine consensus is simply
> to rule out the possibility of false or manipulated consensus by defini-
> tional fiat.
>
> (Lukes, 1974, p. 24)

The difficulty with Lukes' formulation is that it suggests that 'true interests'
can be identified, and that in this sense the researcher can identify something that the objects of his or her study cannot. While there is something
to be said for this when what is at stake are policies (like pollution) that may
actually poison us and shorten our lives, there is otherwise a problem about
this approach. Hay suggests that one way out of this problem is not to follow
Lukes in identifying a third dimension of power but to suggest that there are
two uses of power, which he describes as 'conduct shaping' and 'context
shaping'. He argues about the latter that '[t]o define power as context-shaping
is to emphasise power relations in which structures, institutions and organisations are shaped by human action in such a way as to alter the parameters
of subsequent action' (Hay, 2002, pp. 185–6).

Hay's formulation fits with the way in which Lukes' third dimension of
power suggests for Gaventa (1980) and others a 'deep structure' conditioning
policy options. It also draws attention to identifiable actors in the policy
process whose indirect influence is difficult to chart, in particular the mass
media.

The shaping of power can be studied, for example through the examination of 'social myths, language, and symbols and how they are manipulated
in power processes' (Gaventa, 1980, p. 15). In his elaboration of Lukes' work,
Gaventa explores the way in which power is exercised in all three dimensions and stresses the need to see how successful operation on one 'dimension' affects another, as 'the total impact of a power relationship is more
than the sum of its parts. Power serves to create power. Powerlessness serves
to reinforce powerlessness. Power relationships, once established, are self
sustaining' (Gaventa, 1980, p. 256).

Identifying a 'shaping' activity in respect of power can, however, also
suggest scope for activities that do not take existing power structures for
granted. From the point of view of Marilyn Taylor, exploring the possibilities
for the empowerment of disadvantaged communities, it carries a 'more

positive message that power is not fixed and immutable and that it is possible to seize opportunities to redefine assumptions and divert the flow of power into new directions' (2003b, p. 102).

In an edition of the original book published in 2005, Lukes has reproduced the first edition in its entirety but added chapters that (a) offer some qualifications of his original argument and (b) respond to his critics. He defends his approach but criticises his original position in the following way:

> Following others in the 'power debate' it focuses on the *exercise* of power, thereby committing the exercise fallacy': power is a dispositional concept, identifying an ability or capacity, which may or may not be exercised. Secondly, it focuses entirely on the exercise of 'power over – the power of some A over some B and B's condition of dependence on A. Thirdly, it equates such dependence-inducing power with *domination*, assuming that A affects B in a manner contrary to B's interests, thereby neglecting . . . the manifold ways in which power over others can be productive, transformative, authoritative and compatible with dignity. Fourthly . . . it offers no more than the most perfunctory and questionable account of what such interests are and, moreover treats an actor's interests as unitary . . . And, finally, it operates (like most of the literature on power) with a reductive and simplistic picture of binary power relations . . .
>
> What is clear is that the underlying concept here defined is not 'power' but rather the securing of compliance to domination.
>
> (ibid., pp. 109–10)

The issues about the faces of power have been given considerable attention by theorists who have explored issues about the role of discourses in the power structure. Habermas (1987) has emphasised the importance of communication in securing the acceptance of the unequal distribution of power, and of the policy consequences that flow from it. Foucault (1980) goes further, to see power relations as flowing from taken-for-granted discourses. This approach has something to offer in respect of the debate about how power is exercised but contributes little to the issues about the bases of power and power inequalities.

What seems to have been given relatively little attention before the development of discourse analysis is the role of the media (newspapers, radio, television). It is surprising that there are not indexed references to the media in either Bachrach and Baratz's book or Lukes' book (including the recent edition). The balance is redressed, to some extent at least, by writers like Fischer, who says that discourse analysis requires attention to be given to 'the distribution of discourse capabilities across society' (2003, p. 80). He then goes on to point out:

> A key aspect of modern society is the role of the media, particularly how it is controlled. As is well documented the media in the United States and Europe is increasingly controlled by smaller numbers of people and the content is more and more influenced by the advertisers who pay for

the programmes. This strongly supports the ideological complex with a distinctive consumer-oriented business bias. Moreover much of the news is limited in the perspectives it offers.

(Ibid.)

It is undisputable that mass media take a pivotal role in information exchanges between the various stakeholders of a policy process. In particular, mass media function as mediators between the political elite, organised interests and citizens. Through the media elected officials communicate policy priorities, proposals and decisions to their electoral constituencies and policy clienteles and, vice versa, interest groups voice their grievances to influence the governmental agenda and decision-making process. However, the mass media should not be conceived as neutral conveyors of policy relevant information. Media owner and journalists obviously exercise a strong power by selecting – and, as corollary, by neglecting – specific issues, by framing policy problems or solutions in a particular way, and by covering in a differentiated manner the activities of various actors.

A relatively new strand of literature insists on the 'mediatisation' of policy and politics as 'a long-term process through which the importance of the media and their spill-over effects on political processes, institutions, organizations and actors have increased' (Strömbäck and Esser, 2014, p. 6; see also Mazzoleni and Schulz, 1999; Meyer, 2002). The media logic dominates the political communication and the policy process. Furthermore, as contemporary mass media are mainly motivated by a commercial logic, they use specific frames and storytelling techniques such as simplification, personalisation, stereotyping, polarisation and 'spectacularisation' (Strömbäck and Esser 2009, pp. 212–13). If mass media are leading the 'tango', then policy actors adapt their strategies to capture a large audience and try to 'self-mediatise' their own policy positions and actions. Empirical studies focusing on the mediatisation of policy processes demonstrated that populist parties (e.g. radical-right parties in many European countries) are more frequently covered by mass media than other policy actors participating in a concrete policy process (e.g. Landerer 2014). In sum, mass media are not the neutral providers of pluralist information and (some) policy actors proactively adapt their communication strategies to increase their 'newsworthiness': this colonisation of the media logic into the political sphere has probably major impacts on the balance of power between policy actors and, eventually, is challenging for a pluralist democracy.

The pluralists rethink?

It is important to note again that all of the more sophisticated exponents of the pluralist position, and in particular Dahl, do not claim that power is likely to be equally distributed. Their theory has two crucial components:

one is that the political stage is accessible to all; the other is that the elites who mount that stage do so largely as the representatives of larger groups of people.

Such statements need to be located in times and places: they cannot be taken to be generalisations about everywhere. They might only be applicable to the places that were studied. However, much of the debate was carried in relation to local studies in the United States and then applied to the whole country. Much of the work (Bachrach and Baratz's studies are an exception) was comparatively 'race blind'. New historical work such as Katznelson's study of Roosevelt's new deal (2013) shows how strongly concerns to sustain white dominance (particularly in the South) constrained progressive discourse. That is not to belittle the important methodological and conceptual issues discussed above, but it is to stress that the degree of concentration of power and the extent of suppression of interests ought to be regarded as empirical questions not simply resolvable by taking sides in the debate. The contributions from Bachrach and Baratz and from Lukes raised issues about how power should be studied that cannot be disregarded.

It is interesting to note, therefore, a significant shift in position adopted by some of the key protagonists in the debate on the pluralist side. Dahl and Lindblom's 1953 collaboration *Politics, Economics and Welfare* was revised in 1976 and prefaced with a strong statement on political inequality. Parsons describes it as reflecting on

> many of the failures of policy-making which were becoming evident in the 1970s . . . After Vietnam, Watergate, the 'imperial presidency', the growth of urban decay, and social and economic inequality, Dahl and Lindblom confessed to changing their minds on the question of who governs.
>
> (Parsons, 1995, p. 253)

Lindblom's *Politics and Markets* (1977) also offers powerful evidence on the limitations imposed upon pluralist democracy by the working of business and markets. Since that time writers who may be loosely seen as belonging within the pluralist tradition have observed a changing relationship between politics and markets, with a strong power shift towards business.

In terms of the quadrants in Table 2.1, these qualifications to pluralist theory can be seen as bringing it closer to the perspective embodied in quadrant 3, emphasising inequalities and recognising, as Schattschneider so memorably put it, that 'The flaw in the pluralist heaven is that the heavenly choir sings with a strong upper-class accent' (1960, pp. 34–5).

However, there are two rather different ways of conceptualising a revised pluralist position, both of which represent compromises between the pluralist perspective and other perspectives, though they are rather different in character. One is to reconceptualise pluralism as 'democratic elitism' (Bachrach, 1969), which involves a sort of reconciliation between Dahl and the writers, like Hunter (1953) and Mills (1956), whom he originally set out to attack. The other is to take the arguments about the limitations upon pluralism in a much more structuralist direction. The next section addresses the first of these options, leading discussion on towards the stronger statements about power concentration that are associated with Marxism. That then leads on to the discussion of structuralist perspectives.

The elitist perspective

The classical elitist position was set out at the end of the nineteenth century by an Italian, Gaetano Mosca:

> Among the constant facts and tendencies that are to be found in all political organisms, one is so obvious that it is apparent to the most casual eye. In all societies – from societies that are very meagrely developed and have barely attained the dawnings of civilisation, down to the most advanced and powerful societies – two classes of people appear – a class that rules and a class that is ruled. The first class, always the less numerous, performs all political functions, monopolises power and enjoys the advantages that power brings, whereas the second, the more numerous class, is directed and controlled by the first, in a manner that is now more or less legal, now more or less arbitrary and violent.
>
> (1939, p. 50; original publication in Italian, 1896)

The classical elitist thesis maintains that political elites achieve their position in a number of ways: through revolutionary overthrow, military power, or the command of natural resources. It is a perspective that most obviously applies to pre-democratic states. However, it may be argued that in the modern state, the position of elites is related to the development of large-scale organisations in many areas of life, with the result that there are different kinds of elites, not just those holding formal political power. Bottomore makes a distinction between the political *elite*, which is made up of 'those individuals who actually exercise power in a society at any given time' and which 'will include members of the government and of the high administration, military leaders, and, in some cases, politically influential families of an aristocracy or royal house and leaders of powerful economic enterprises', and the political *class*, comprising the political elite but also leaders of political parties in opposition, trade union leaders, businessmen and politically active intellectuals (1966, pp. 14–15, for the use of a similar distinction in the analysis of power in the United States see Domhoff, 1978). Defined in this way, the political elite is composed of bureaucratic, military, aristocratic and business elites, while the political class is composed of the political elite together with elites from other areas of social life. What this suggests is that elite power may be based on a variety of sources: the occupation of formal office, wealth, technical expertise, knowledge and so on. To a certain extent, these resources may be cumulative, but power is not solely dependent on any one resource.

In the twentieth century, the growth of large firms, the establishment of trade unions, and the development of political parties – all institutions in which effective power is likely to rest with an oligarchic leadership – underline the significance of organisational control and institutional position as key political resources. Of particular importance in this context was the creation of bureaucratic systems of administration to carry out the increasing responsibilities taken on by the state from the nineteenth century onwards. As Weber (1947) notes, bureaucracies have both positive and negative aspects: positive, in that they offer an efficient way of organising administration; negative, because they open up the possibility of power being vested in officials who are accountable neither to the public nor to politicians. The growth of bureaucracies may, in Weber's view, lead to control of the economy by bureaucrats. In this line of argument, elite theory draws attention to the need to look at the state itself. This theme has been echoed by various writers who have seen the modern state as a technocracy (Ellul, 1964; Meynaud, 1965). We will also see other variants on this theme in some aspects of the rational choice theory explored in Chapter 3, theories stressing the importance of policy communities in Chapter 4, and the examination of the impact of institutions in Chapter 5.

C. Wright Mills (1956) draws attention to institutional position as a source of power, and suggests that the American political system is dominated by a power elite occupying key positions in government, business corporations and the military. The overlap and connection between the leaders of these institutions helps to create a relatively coherent power elite. But can a realistic distinction be drawn between the sort of modified pluralist perspective set out in the last section and the elitist one? The elitist case is not helped by the fact that many alternative sources of elite power have been suggested. That tends to reinforce the pluralist case, and may be seen as the basis of the theory of 'democratic elitism'. That theory argues that regular elections based on competition between the leaders of political parties, together with participation by pressure group elites in between elections, and interaction between these elites and the bureaucratic elites, are the ways in which democracy operates in the modern state. The fact that different elites operate in different issue areas is a protection against domination by one group.

There is a problem with sustaining a simple elite theory position inasmuch as there are difficulties in specifying the mechanisms by which power is seized and the techniques used to hold on to it. Similar problems may be noted with critiques of power popular in the UK which use the concept of 'the establishment', exacerbated by a tendency to adopt a conspiratorial tone without being able to show how different parts of that entity reinforce each other (see Jones, 2014, for a recent example). One now very unfashionable elite theorist, Pareto, who worked in Italy around the same time as Mosca, offered an answer to these problems inasmuch as he saw elite domination as based upon the special qualities possessed by the elite (Pareto, 1966). In this respect it is relevant to bear in mind that Pareto belonged to a generation that attached more importance to immutable genetic characteristics than do most modern theorists. But even he posited a kind of pluralist process by which the 'circulation of elites' occurs as old elites weaken and new ones arise.

There are, however, two ways in which the debate about how power is exercised needs to be taken further. One, as indicated above, is to bypass the question about how power is acquired but to argue that once that has happened then the institutions of the state offer the means for an elite to perpetuate its power. The detailed examination of this will have to await Chapter 5. The other approach to this question is to emphasise the importance of economic power. Where it does this, elite theory begins to merge with another very important approach to the study of power, Marxist theory, to the extent that some of the key exponents of the position set out above (for example, Mills) are only distinguishable from Marxists by their comparative reluctance to quote Marx in their support. The next section therefore picks up on those aspects of Marxist theory that concentrate on the role of individual actors in the pursuit of power.

Elite theory, in both classical and modern guises, represents an important alternative to pluralism. Yet, while some writers have attempted to reconcile elitism and pluralist democracy, others have used the findings of elitist studies to argue that the power elite is but a ruling class by another name. That is, it is suggested that institutions may well be run by minority groups, but that these groups come from similar social backgrounds and are therefore exercising power in the interests of a dominant group.

It must be noted that the bridging concept between elitism and Marxism is the idea of a 'ruling class'. However, until recently this class analysis has led to a disregard of the extent to which other forms of social stratification, particularly stratification in terms of gender and ethnicity, may be significant for the distribution of power. Now, both within feminist literature and in the analysis of racism, a lively debate has developed about the extent to which these other forms of stratification may operate independently of, or in association with, class divisions, to structure and bias the policy process. We will return to this later.

Marxism

When the original book from which this version has developed was published (Ham and Hill, 1984) Marxist theory was much more influential amongst social science academics than it is today; Karl Marx's own propositions had been developed by a wide variety of theorists. One of those with things to say that are particularly pertinent for the examination of the policy process was Ralph Miliband. In his book *The State in Capitalist Society* (1969), Miliband takes as his starting point not the political process itself but the form of economic organisation (the mode of production). In advanced Western industrialised societies, the capitalist mode of production dominates, giving rise to two major social classes – the bourgeoisie and the proletariat. Miliband's analysis of the distribution of income and wealth, and changes in this distribution over time, demonstrates the continued concentration of wealth in a small section of the population. The question Miliband then asks is whether this economically dominant class exercises decisive political power. In other words, he explores the relationship between economic power and political power.

Taking their cue from Karl Marx, writers like Miliband argue that the state is not a neutral agent, but rather is an instrument for class domination. Marx expressed this view in the *Communist Manifesto*, where he wrote that 'The executive of the modern state is but a committee for managing the common affairs of the whole bourgeoisie' (quoted in McLellan, 1971, p. 192). Miliband suggests three reasons why the state is an instrument of bourgeois domination in capitalist society. First, there is the similarity in social background between the bourgeoisie and members of the state elite – that is, those who occupy senior positions in government, the civil service, the military, the judiciary and other state institutions. Second, there is the power that the bourgeoisie is able to exercise as a pressure group through personal contacts and networks and through the associations representing business and industry. Third, there is the constraint placed on the state by the objective power of capital. In these ways, Miliband contends, the state acts as an instrument which serves the long-term interests of the whole bourgeoisie.

Marxism is today seen, above all, as the ideology that sustained the Soviet empire until its collapse and is – increasingly unconvincingly – argued to continue to hold sway in China. But it must be remembered that Marx's original purpose was to analyse the system of economic power dominant within capitalist societies and to show how that system contained within it the seeds of its own downfall. The fact that it has not fallen in the way Marx predicted does not necessarily invalidate the whole of his analysis, particularly those parts relating to the significance of ownership or control of the means of production for power within the state. It should be added that continuing to give attention to that argument does not necessarily imply an acceptance of the model of ownership and control over economic enterprise, involving primarily individual entrepreneurship, that prevailed in Marx's time. In the modern world key controllers may well not be, formally speaking, the owners of economic enterprises, and ownership is in any case very complex.

The original theory set out by Karl Marx, though complicated and stated in rather different ways at different times in his life, postulated a theory of history in which the means of production is a dominant and determining force. The 'executive of the modern state' was a committee to manage the 'affairs of the whole bourgeoisie' not because the latter was able to control it, but because it could be nothing else so long as society remained capitalist. In other words, mainstream Marxist theory takes the issues about the determination of policy in a very different direction to the concerns of this chapter so far, to suggest that a power *structure* determined by the means of production is of dominant importance. Box 2.2 explores the theory discussed here using the example of the bank bailout in 2008.

| Box 2.2 | The Instrumental and structural power of business: the banks bailout in the United States of America and the United Kingdom (2008) |

Culpepper and Reinke (2014) revisit the seminal work of Ralph Miliband (1969) and Hacker and Pierson (2002) by distinguishing between the instrumental and structural power of business, and by applying these concepts to explain the bailouts of big banks in 2008:

- *'Instrumental* power comprises the various means, unrelated to the core functions of the firm, through which business influences politics: donations for campaigns, privileged access to policymakers, and lobbyists and organizations that defend business interest.'

- *'Structural* power, by contrast, inheres in fact that firms are agents of economic activity in capitalist democracies. Because the state relies on firm investment to generate growth, the abilities of companies not to invest can cause damage to the economy and thereby to the politicians governing it. Because a negative policy, or even the anticipation of one, may lead firms to lower their rate of investment, scholars have characterized the democratic state as structurally dependent on capital. Governments are predisposed to adopt policies that promote firm investment, even without business leaders necessarily having to do anything' (Culpepper and Reinke, 2014, p. 429).

Furthermore, Culpepper and Reinke argue that both forms of business power have *automatic* aspects, when policymakers anticipate the potential behaviour of private firms (e.g. disinvestment), even if firms take no actions. In addition, business can also use instrumental and structural power more proactively and *strategically*, when firms exercise their power (e.g. the threat of delocalisation) during bargaining and policy-making processes.

The comparative study of the 2008 bailouts of big banks, that were perceived as 'too big to fail' in the United Kingdom and the United States of America, illustrates how business power influences policy making. Despite the fact that both countries are liberal market economies, and that Wall Street and London are two leading financial centres, the American and British banks' bailout policies were quite different. The American policy required the participation of all banks, even the healthy ones (Wells Fargo or JP Morgan), to the state bailout plan. On the contrary, the British plan was based on the voluntary participation of major banks, with the self-selection of only the sickest ones (RBS and Lloyds/HBOS). In addition, the United Kingdom spent about 21 percent of the Gross Domestic Product for the bailouts, far more than in the United States (6 percent). Last but not least, the United States plan eventually made money for the taxpayers (estimated at $8–10bn), whilst the United Kingdom bailout policy generated large losses for the state (estimated at $14bn). How can these significant differences be explained? Culpepper and Reinke claim that the American banks were much more vulnerable to government policy, because their business activities and income depend on the internal market (i.e. no credible exit option for the banks). By contrast, the income from the British

(continued)

banks came mostly from outside the United Kingdom (i.e. credible threat to delocalise banking activities) and they could strategically exercise their structural power. The American government could thus get a better policy deal from their banks than it was possible for the British government.

Structuralist aspects of the Marxist perspective

This section will deal fairly briefly with Marxist structuralism since direct use of this form of analysis has declined significantly in recent years. Yet it is worth a little attention as an alternative approach to the explanation of unequal power in the policy process, seeing what may be called 'economic imperatives' as a crucial influence, a view that we will then see echoed by some theorists who would not see themselves as Marxists.

According to classical Marxist theory, the social structure of a capitalist society is essentially a 'class structure'. The two classes that confront each other in a capitalist society (at least in the last resort) are the bourgeoisie (the owners of the means of production) and the proletariat (who work for the bourgeoisie). Some of Marx's work deals with other classes, but his logic indicates that they will eventually be sucked into the fundamental class struggle. That struggle will then intensify, as the nature of competitive production forces the bourgeoisie to systematically reduce the rewards going to the proletariat. This process of 'immiseration' will eventually lead the increasingly unified proletariat to rise up to overthrow the bourgeoisie. That revolution will lead to the replacement of capitalism by socialism, just as earlier the logic of industrial change led capitalism to replace feudalism. In other words, at the core of classical Marxist theory there is an essentially determinist argument. Our position in relation to the means of production determines our long-run political interests. Our fate is set by the working out of that dialectic. Notwithstanding that position, Marx urged the proletariat to organise politically, to work towards the ultimate revolution. In that sense there is a contradiction at the core of classical Marxism, which has left it open for some to reinterpret the theory in a very much less deterministic way.

The concern here is with the role of the state in the determinist model. The idea, set out above, of the state as 'the executive committee of the bourgeoisie' is, in this interpretation, the only thing it can be. Its role is a supportive and subsidiary one in relation to capitalism. In his determinist 'mood' Marx was not very interested in the role of the state. The problem is that in his more activist 'mood' he urged the organisations of the proletariat to mobilise to try to take over the state. This engendered an argument within Marxism about the purpose of such activity. Was it just to prepare for, or practice for, or advance, the revolution, since the state could neither be transformed nor transform capitalism? Or was there a peaceful road to revolution by way of securing control over the state? It was this alternative that engendered a social democratic form of Marxism which the revolutionary followers of Marx repudiated.

Hence, whilst generating an elaborate controversy about the state within Marxist ranks (which became increasingly complicated as the role of the state changed in the twentieth century in ways that did not seem to accord with Marxist predictions), the classical Marxist position is to suggest that the capitalist state's main function is to assist the process of capital accumulation. This means creating conditions in which capitalists are able to promote the production of profit. The state is seen as acting to maintain order and control within society.

Twentieth-century Marxist theory has elaborated this in a variety of ways, partly to explain phenomena that Marx had not expected to occur. In specific terms, assisting accumulation means providing physical resources such as roads and industrial sites, while maintaining order is carried out both through repressive mechanisms like the police and through agencies such as schools, which perform an important legitimation function. The accumulation process is further assisted through state intervention in the provision of services such as housing and health care to groups in the working population. One of the functions of these services is to reduce the cost of labour power to capital and to keep the workforce healthy.

O'Connor (1973) classifies these different forms of state expenditure as social investment, social consumption and social expenses. Social investment increases labour productivity through the provision, for example, of infrastructure and aid to industry; social consumption lowers the cost of reproducing labour power as, for example, in the provision of social insurance; and social expenses serve to maintain social harmony. In practice, nearly all interventions by the state perform more than one of these functions.

O'Connor's analysis suggests that state expenditure serves the interest of monopoly capital, and that the state is run by a class-conscious political directorate acting on behalf of monopoly capitalist class interests. In a similar vein, Gough (1979) makes use of O'Connor's typology to show how the modern welfare state serves the long-term interests of the capitalist class.

The key point overall is that Marxist theory tends to take a stance which treats state action as to a considerable extent constrained and *determined* by economic institutions. It will be suggested below that this proposition is restated today by many who would certainly not wish to be portrayed as (neo)Marxists.

Other structuralist perspectives

Thompson puts the underlying theoretical issue about the relationship between explanations of social action that emphasise actions and those that emphasise structure as follows:

> The problem of the relation between the individual and society, or between action and social structure, lies at the heart of social theory and the philosophy of social science. In the writings of most major theorists . . . this problem is raised and allegedly resolved in one way or another. Such resolutions generally amount to the accentuation of one term at the expense of the other . . . the problem is not so much resolved as dissolved.
>
> (1989, p. 56)

Structuralist theories that see political action as determined by powerful forces outside human control have a long history in the social sciences. Writers have postulated distinct patterns of human evolution or a determinist approach to history which challenge the view that individuals have the capacity to determine their own social and political institutions. Theories of this kind have taken forms that suggest a need to accept the status quo, and/or to regard political choices as predetermined by demographic, social and economic factors. They have also come in 'critical' forms – concerned to analyse what are seen as powerful constraints upon human action which have to be attacked in order to achieve fundamental change. That contrast draws attention to the problem within much of this theory: that in dealing with the factors that determine social stability in changing societies it has to try to specify conditions under which change can occur.

Structuralist theory has, in short, to take a stance on the relationship between structure and action. The former determines the latter yet the latter feeds back to alter the former. All but the most simplistic forms of structural theory – with which we need not bother ourselves because they are so unrealistic – acknowledge some measure of scope for action to secure change. Further distinctions can be made between different kinds of structural theory about the extent to which they are totally determinist. These differences particularly concern the extent to which there are strong evolutionary forces in societies.

Related to this issue of variations in the extent to which theories are determinist is the issue of what is seen as the source of that determinism – demography, technological evolution and economic forces being perhaps the most widely identified sources. A sort of determinism, which lies at the very weakest end of structural theory, simply sees the institutional and ideological configurations that have been established as imposing strong constraints upon future actions (Chapter 5 returns to this theme).

Hence, structuralist Marxism sits alongside other structuralist perspectives. In sociology 'structure functionalist theory' has been influential but is now seen as fairly dated. Yet it is worth a brief mention (a) because of the way in which it poses questions about structural influences that – at least when postulated in a very weak form – still need attention, and (b) because as a theoretical perspective it occupies an important place in relation to Marxism as a set of propositions which partly support and partly offer a contradiction of that perspective.

Structural functionalism involves a fusion in sociological theory between propositions from early anthropological studies – which suggested that social institutions reinforce each other in ways which support the status quo in allegedly 'static' societies – and propositions from social Darwinism, which traced processes of social evolution. Sociologists in this tradition in the United States or Western Europe saw their own societies as 'progressing', with their institutions adapting in response to evolving social needs. Where Marxists saw an evolutionary process leading towards social crisis, these theorists saw a progressive adaptation occurring.

What this perspective implied for political choices – and thus for the policy process – was a series of imperatives to which the political system would respond. The evolutionary element in this perspective led some scholars to proclaim that their own societies had reached 'the end of ideology' (Bell, 1960) – in which political battles would be muted by a common acceptance of the benefits of the status quo – and less 'developed' societies would follow to evolve along the same progressive path. Economic development is seen as the generator of a wide range of social changes (Kerr, 1973). In addition to its contribution to the growth of the standard of living it is a source of urban development. These changes are then held to have influenced patterns of social behaviour, including choices about marriage and family size.

Comparative studies have thus aimed to explain the emergence of public policies – particularly social policy – by correlating their incidence with the phenomena of economic growth, industrialisation, urbanisation and demographic change linked together in a package of ingredients of 'modernisation' (Hofferbert, 1974; Wilensky, 1975).

Some versions of the modernisation thesis go beyond these issues to try to identify a postmodernist or a post-industrial order with its own distinctive policies. We will find some traces of this approach later in the book when we examine organisational arrangements and find that there are suggestions that we are now in a postmodernist, or more specifically post-Fordist, era in which old bureaucratic and hierarchical models for the organisation of industrial and administrative life are giving way to new forms. Clearly, technological changes – the development of computers and other electronic control devices – facilitate the development of these new forms of organisation. But readers should be suspicious of arguments about these phenomena which come in deterministic forms, however. It is one thing to say that people are trying new approaches to the organisation of complex activities, aided by new technology, but quite another to dress this up in a technologically determinist form which seems to deny any role for human choice.

The question is: have we here a set of determinist theories suggesting that public policy developments can be read off from these economic and social developments? Or are these theories merely making the point that there is

a) a general association between economic growth and state growth across the broad band of prosperous nations in the past, together with (perhaps)

b) a certain critical threshold that nations have to pass before significant levels of public services, imposing high costs on the nation, become feasible in developing societies, and

c) further – picking up on the last part of this section – that there is a later generation of technological developments which are further transforming some of the record keeping and surveillance options open to governments?

To go further would be to pay too little attention to the choices made by actors or to variations in response from place to place (Ashford, 1986).

Economic determinism without Marxism

Perspectives can be identified on economic determinism which either diverge so far from classical Marxism that it is inappropriate to call them Marxist, or which involve propositions about the dominance of economic considerations in the policy process of a kind that have no foundations in Marxist theory. The most important of these propositions are those that stress the significance of 'global' economic forces. These will be discussed separately following this comparatively brief look at other theories that embody forms of economic determinism.

There is a perspective which suggests that there is built into the politics of any but the poorest societies a set of concerns about the need for advances in the standard of living that any politicians will disregard at their peril. Note how issues about the requirement to secure growth are so salient in political discourse. Related to this – particularly since the collapse of communism – is the view that only capitalist economic institutions can provide those advances. This perspective is obviously advanced in philosophical works which celebrate capitalist economic institutions (Hayek, 1944; 1960), and is more generally taken for granted in much contemporary political analysis. The pronouncement by the Chinese leader Deng Xiaoping – to justify his flirtations with capitalism – that it does not matter what colour the cat is so long as it can catch mice (Shambaugh, 1995, p. 88), perhaps sums up this post-Marxist consensus.

It is interesting to note how implicit economic determinism crops up in the ranks of thinkers from all parts of the ideological spectrum. There is a thread of thinking from the 'Right' which is very like Marxist structuralism, but without any theory of change or revolution. This is the view that there has been a process of evolution to the ideal economic order (capitalism) and the ideal political order (representative democracy) and that the kind of 'directional history' embodied in the theories of Hegel and Marx has come to an end (Fukuyama, 1992). Such a perspective suggests that:

All countries undergoing economic modernisation must increasingly resemble one another: they must unify nationally on the basis of a centralized state, urbanize, replace traditional forms of social organisation like tribe, sect and family with economically rational ones based on function and efficiency, and provide for the universal education of their citizens . . .

the logic of modern natural science would seem to dictate a universal evolution in the direction of capitalism.

(Fukuyama, 1992, pp. xiv–xv)

Fukuyama explores this theme with a caution not evident in the quotation, but he does in many respects advance there a 1990s version of Bell's earlier 'end of ideology' thesis. Since he wrote that book he has adopted a much more nuanced perspective on development, still in a sense seeing an ideal goal – which he describes as 'getting to Denmark' (2011, p. 14; idealising that country instead of the United States) – dependent on the coming together of 'the state, the rule of law, and democratic accountability' (Fukuyama, 2011; 2014). At the same time he does not give this an evolutionary aspect, and even expresses doubt about contemporary developments in the United States inasmuch as the role of the state is being undermined.

This recent work from Fukuyama argues that 'It is the balance between a strong state and a strong society that makes democracy work' (2011, p. 482), leaving on one side whether a capitalist economy is a necessary feature of a strong society. Other perspectives on modernisation involve assumptions about the need to secure economic growth or to limit public expenditure and taxation – with the implicit consequences of this for other policies – in the interests of the maintenance of the capitalist economy. Clearly there may be here a kind of structuralist perspective, specifying a distinct limit to the extent to which politicians can disregard economic forces.

Globalism

A closely related kind of determinist theory, deserving of a section of its own because of the wide attention it is given, is globalism. This sees a sequence of worldwide economic developments as of determining importance for contemporary policy making. Globalist theory has developed on a massive scale, and in the process branched in many directions. It embodies various themes – the development of global financial markets, the cross-national diffusion of technology, the emergence of transnational or global corporations (and the increasing economic pressure upon large corporations to 'think globally'), the development of international organisations and the emergence of global cultural flows. It is given particular relevance for the policy process by policy problems – pollution, conflicts over scarce resources, poorly regulated international trading, movements of people as economic migrants and refugees – that have global implications. All these trends offer challenges to state autonomy and stimulate new political formations beyond the nation state. More cautious statements on this topic stress the extent to which this is in some respects a gradual change, acknowledge that complex supra-national economic developments have a long history and recognise that the speed of modern communications heightens awareness of the phenomenon.

There are variants of globalism that are close to classical Marxism, in that they see the processes described by Marx as now taking place on a world scale (Wallerstein, 1979; Cox, 1987). This is a view that George and Wilding describe as 'Marxissant', with 'the fundamental premise that the driving logic of capitalism for constantly increased profitability has been the major force behind globalisation' (2002, p. 7). This is a view that is not particularly new: it was set out originally by Lenin in 1917. It suggests that there is a complicated working through of the postulated conflict between capitalists and proletariat across the world, postponing the eventual crisis and raising difficult tactical problems for international Marxists who have to face difficulties in getting the proletariat to think globally rather than to accept national interpretations of exploitation.

Within globalist thinking there are distinctions to be found between those who see capitalism as an increasingly international phenomenon and those who argue that companies are rather more supra-national than global (that is, they spread out from a national base) and that their power is not necessarily an external imposition upon nation states but something established within them (see Panitch, 1994). As Panitch puts it in a rhetorical question, 'Is it really to international finance that governments in London or Ottawa are accountable when they prepare their budgets? Or are they accountable to the City of London or to Bay Street?' (1994, p. 74).

Globalist theory may accept that capitalist economic relationships are increasingly organised on a world scale but not set out that view in Marxist terms. The question that emerges for this discussion is then to what extent a globalist position is really a determinist one. Is globalist theory saying that here is a series of structural developments about which politicians can do little? Or is it merely saying that the issues about the power of economic interests need to be analysed in supra-national terms? In other words, this is not so much a determinist point of view as one which emphasises *either* that national policy makers must increasingly be able to deal with interests organised outside their country *or* that if they are to be effective policy processes need to be supra-national too (Hirst and Thompson, 1992). Streeck (2014) adds a specifically European twist to this argument by exploring the increasing difficulties of controlling the Eurozone in the interests of the nation state members (either collectively or individually). But his analysis may be generalised to take in the international agreements about free trade.

The latter position may lead to a pessimistic stance on the feasibility of achieving solutions to political problems in the face of institutional complexity, but it is not ultimately a determinist stance. It is obviously important for contemporary arguments about 'governance' inasmuch as the policy process is complicated both by the way it goes beyond the single nation state and involves private business actors that are able to operate alongside or in partnership with governments. Indeed it has become a commonplace to observe the existence of companies that are larger than many nation states. While companies will have their headquarters in one country and face limitations upon complete mobility, they can influence national policies inasmuch as they may be able to make choices about the location of many of their activities.

A related 'global' phenomenon that has been observed is the capacity of such companies to affect taxation policies inasmuch as they can use accounting devices to ensure that activities are taxed wherever tax rates are lowest (Shaxson, 2011).

Hay offers a useful alternative slant on the determinist element in the globalist perspective arguing that 'whether the globalist thesis is "true" or not may matter far less than whether it is *deemed* to be true – or, quite possibly, just useful – by those employing it' (2002, p. 258). Hence, Hay argues that decision makers may believe either that there is no alternative but to respond to perceived global economic forces, or that globalisation 'may provide a most convenient alibi, allowing politicians to escape the responsibility they would otherwise bear for reforms which might otherwise be rather difficult to legitimate' (ibid., p. 259). That puts a very interesting slant on the structure/action relationship, seeing decision makers as active 'agents' within structures. But those structures are not all determining, and how those structures are perceived or 'used' may be crucial.

That observation on globalism leads to two others. First, it is obviously not a determinist approach in itself to pay attention to the extent to which pressures upon policy decisions come from sources outside the nation state. In that sense it is quite feasible to adopt a pluralist analysis (whether modified or not by concerns about power concentrations), taking into account the extent to which interest groups organised outside the nation state or across several nation states have an impact upon policy in any specific state.

Second, if governments are more aware of international developments then this may affect how they respond to economic interests within their own country. Hence, as Pierre and Peters put it, 'the need to develop closer links . . . with private industry is driven by a strategy to maintain or increase the international competitiveness of the domestic industry' (2000, p. 60).

Dryzek and Dunleavy argue:

> The more a state becomes integrated into the global economy, the more it has to worry about the reactions of international markets to its policies. And markets worry only about what is good for business, not for social justice, human rights or environmental protection. Friedmann (1999) calls this a 'golden straightjacket', golden because this integration allegedly fosters the generation of wealth.
>
> (2009, p. 315)

Other variants of structuralism

Some of the structuralist arguments originating from feminism link very closely with Marxist theory. For some writers, gender divisions in society are seen as further ways in which the proletariat are divided and controlled. The growth of a female workforce which is poorly paid and insecure is seen as a particularly insidious development in the 'reserve army of labour' that keeps the proletariat cheap and weak (Barrett, 1980).

Other feminist theory focuses rather more upon male domination of economic and political institutions *per se*, not seeing it in the Marxist context of class divisions (Millet, 1970; Delphy, 1984). Inasmuch as this perspective is structuralist in nature, it opens up a very important issue with ramifications beyond the relations between the genders. What is involved is an argument that there is a range of institutions – the family, the church, the economy, the state – that are linked together in a structure that has a powerfully determining impact upon what gets on the agenda. We are back here with Lukes's third face of power. This structure influences culture, discourse and behaviour, defining the political agenda. As such it *defines out* many female concerns. Schwarzmantel makes a direct parallel with Marxism using the concept of 'deep structure':

> Both feminism and Marxism take a common stance, in that both are concerned to reveal . . . a 'deep structure' or power dimension which exists in the liberal-democratic state and the society that surrounds it, and in other forms of state and society as well. The power dimension is in both cases seen as a 'fault line' or basic division which is to some extent hidden from view.
>
> (1994, p. 115)

Rhetorics of equality are seen as masking real inequalities of power. An ideology of male domination is seen as embodied in a division between the 'public' sphere and the 'private' sphere. The public sphere for long excluded women, whilst in the private sphere, behaviour within the household was regarded as outside the realm of political interference. This had the effect of keeping issues about domineering behaviour by men within the household off the policy agenda.

Schwarzmantel perhaps takes the parallels between feminist theory and Marxist theory too far. What the general feminist position brings into the discussion is a good example of how policy processes have been structured with the effect that they support the status quo and suppress certain issues in the way described by Lukes. Some feminist scholars go one step further and argue that mainstream policy studies also contribute to reinforcing the status quo. For instance, the 'Feminist Comparative Policy' approach (Mazur and Hoard, 2014) insists on the need to 'gender' the study of policy processes and outputs. Feminist approaches claim that policy studies should investigate these issues and assess how the state promotes or hinders gender equality. They take us into a more general approach to the way in which policy processes are structured.

Before we look at that it is important to recognise that the arguments deployed here also apply to ethnic divisions. The equivalent of radical feminism's development of Marxist theory is a body of work that stresses the way ethnic divisions function to keep the proletariat divided (Solomos et al.,

1982). The term 'ethnicity' needs to be interpreted widely here – going far beyond recognised biological differences (which are in any case ambiguous and contestable) to comprise national, linguistic, cultural and religious divisions which create or are used to create divisions of an 'ethnic' kind. In this case there is a connection back, too, to the issues about globalism. There are economic differences associated with divisions between countries, where the 'national interest' is invoked to both attack and defend inequalities. The world 'division of labour' has ethnic dimensions. Migration has then further complicated this by contributing to the reproduction of these divisions within countries (Cohen, 1987).

Just as there is a conflict within feminist theory between those who link gender and class issues and those who focus primarily on gender, so too in the analysis of ethnic divisions there are those whose analyses are embedded in Marxist theory and those who see that perspective as too limiting for a satisfactory analysis of the exploitation of ethnic groups (Rex, 1986). In the analysis of ethnic divisions, as in the exploration of gender divisions, there is a need to analyse structural constraints upon political action in historical terms, examining both the establishment of institutions which privileged some and disadvantaged others, and the development of ideologies which set out to justify inequalities. In the case of ethnicity, the establishment and maintenance of cohesive nation states involves the deployment of rules to define who do and who do not belong, and ideologies to justify those rules. At the time of writing this issue is becoming highlighted by questions about the cultures and values of Islamic minorities and the integration of migrants.

In this section it is open to question whether the phenomena being explored should be described as 'structural'. What is being described is divisions within societies, which are maintained and reinforced in various ways. It is implicit in feminist theory and in attacks upon ethnic divisions that there is a politics of challenge to these divisions. Where the structuralism comes in is in regarding challenging such divisions as a difficult political task. It is a task, moreover, where policy processes have to involve not just changing distributive or regulatory rules but also challenging the ideologies that have underpinned those rules. Here we are back to the point made by Hay in relation to Lukes' analysis of power, that we have here ideas about society and its culture – discourses, if you like – that sustain patterns of power.

It is very important to recognise how the perspective set out in the last paragraph embodies cultural concepts and ideologies within 'structural' influences. With this in mind we can go back to the objection to Lukes' suggestion that the third face of power is in evidence when people are seen to act in ways that conflict with their true interest, that this involves an 'Olympian' condescension on the part of the scholar who claims to know better than the actors what their interests are. If a policy change with implications for the reduction of some disadvantage is rejected by many who would gain from it, we cannot necessarily know whether this is because of 'false consciousness' or of a consciousness which for some reason has not been articulated because the disadvantaged know, or assume, that efforts to secure it would in the end be frustrated (or worse). There is then a need to look more widely at the things that seem to help us explain events if we look (as has been characteristic of work inspired by Foucault) into the cultural context of the arguments, the forms that arguments take, the uses made of ways (education, media presentations, etc.) that structure it and so on. In such circumstances we do not need to impute particular forms of false consciousness.

Faced with a policy issue on which a disadvantaged group has something specific to gain the counter-argument may come from elite groups who deploy a wide and general argument as to why they should *instead* be supported. This may be seen as the use of a general 'conservative' ideology. There are three obvious forms of this:

- Traditional conservatism – we are the best guardians of society.

- Neo-conservatism and forms of nationalism that do not challenge the status quo – we can protect you from big dangers out there.

- Neo-liberalism – the maintenance of market arrangements are the least worst ways of dealing with social problems.

Opposed to these are ideas for change advocated by 'radical' groups that so-called 'false conscious' people may recognise good reasons to distrust. After all the history of the twentieth century is littered with false dawns, false prophets and false expectations offered by socialist, radical, populist, etc., movements. As Tilly notes, in one item in a checklist of answers to the question 'why do people not rebel' this may be 'as a result of mystification, repression, or the sheer unavailability of alternative ideological frames' (1991, p. 594). He might have added words like 'convincing' or 'acceptable' before 'alternative' there.

This discussion of structural determinants of policy processes has moved from theories which seem to be strongly determinist – structural functionalism and classical Marxism – to perspectives that many would not call structuralist at all since they merely spell out factors which are likely to have a strong influence on political choices. Parsons (1995, pp. 608–9) argues that some of these may simply be incorporated into accepted constraints as '[t]he distinction between politics and economy and society . . . needs to be revised to take account of the argument that the world of "facts" and social and economic forces is not simply "out there"'. He goes on to explain that 'it may well be that external environments are better understood as mirrors or projections of the values, beliefs and assumptions which frame the internal policy-making process'. That is, however, perhaps to make too little of some powerful forces at work. The case for a discussion of structuralist theory lies not primarily in a need to outline what are in many respects rather over-deterministic theories, but in a need to stress that there is running through any policy process a series of strong biases or influences on action. This may be described as an influential 'deep structure' (Schwarzmantel, 1994) or in terms of Lukes's 'third face of power' or Hay's 'context-shaping power' (see p. 34). Social change – in which the policy process plays an important part – involves a dynamic in which structure influences action and is at the same time altered by that action.

It has been shown that structural perspectives do not necessarily put 'class interests' and 'economic forces' as the only kinds of determining agents. Implicit in the concept of structure is a system which gives dominance to a range of powerful groups (see Degeling and Colebatch, 1984). Such groups will include professional and bureaucratic elites, males, specific ethnic, religious, linguistic groups, and so on. This dominance is given structural form by customary practices and modes of organisation. It may well be built into language, and manifested symbolically in a variety of ways.

Structures are not fixed and immutable. In giving attention here to formalised political institutions, it must not be forgotten that they vary considerably in strength and in the extent to which they are formalised. A distinction may perhaps be drawn between structures and institutions, where the latter are seen as 'regularized practices *structured* by rules and resources deeply layered in time and space' (Thompson, 1989, p. 61). They are changed by action, and some actions may be specifically directed at trying to change structures. The prevailing order is continually being renegotiated. This is clearly not an easy process, but in addressing the determinants of decision making, it is one which must not be entirely disregarded (this sort of approach to the relationship between structure and action is explored in the sociological writings of Giddens, 1976; 1984). In this context the word that has become widely used in relation to action is 'agency', expressing the extent to which people are able to operate autonomously.

CONCLUSIONS

This long chapter started by outlining a simple way to classify discussions of power in terms of four quadrants illustrating arguments about the extent to which it is structured and the extent to which it is distributed equally. It rather quickly dismissed the 'representative government' model (Table 2.1, quadrant 1) which sees power as, broadly speaking, structured but not unequally distributed.

The discussion showed that the main arguments seem to have been between pluralists who see power as fragmented but relatively evenly distributed, and a variety of theorists who identify ways in which it is concentrated in the hands of small groups, often described as elites. Identifying Marxism as, at least historically, the most important version of the latter theory, it went on to explore the way in which Marxists have been split between those who identify capitalists as actors in their own interests and those who adopt a more structuralist explanation of the (for them temporary) dominance of capitalism.

(continued)

Since it may be argued that there is little difference between a neo-pluralist position that sees no real balance between interests, inasmuch as economic interests (loosely business) dominate, and a simple Marxist position that similarly stresses the power of capital it is, then, the structuralist version of Marxism that tends to continue to exert influence. This is particularly true, if it is detached from its origins in evolutionary theory, of the variety of ways in which economics is seen as exerting a deterministic influence upon the policy process. The most important modern form of this determinism is globalist theory.

The chapter went on to look at challenges to determinism, seeing the extent to which it involves discourses used to support the existing distribution of power or to enhance the power of specific interests. In the end it needs to be conceded that actions occur within structures, and are influenced by those structures, but that what this implies in practice is very complex. The next four chapters pick up this theme in different ways, since much of the theoretical work considered is concerned, if not explicitly then implicitly, with the relationship between structure and action.

3 Rational choice theory

SYNOPSIS

Rational choice theory involves the application of notions from economics (and to some extent from mathematics) to the analysis of the way in which self-interested behaviour by individuals may influence the policy process. It suggests that predictive propositions can be derived from generalisations which equate self-interest and rational behaviour and assume that they will be dominant. It assists the analysis of the policy process by reminding us of the importance of self-interest and of the extent to which public policy problems emerge from the incapacity of market mechanisms to solve many collective action problems.

In order to understand the key underlying issues about rational choice methodology, involving deductions from assumptions about self-interest, an examination of the issues about use of deductive, inductive and iterative in policy research is interposed early in the chapter. Then the basic notion of the political marketplace is introduced. This is followed by a discussion of the way in which collective action problems have been analysed from an economic perspective, principally to assist with the development of prescriptive approaches, but in ways which also help with the analysis of the development of public policies. Game theory, with its roots in mathematics rather than economics, is then briefly examined as a further extension of that approach.

Finally, the economic theory of bureaucracy and principal-agent theory are examined. These are seen as theoretical approaches which contribute to insights about the behaviour of public sector bureaucrats, particularly when modified in ways which retain the concern to stress self-interested behaviour but show that they may lead to varied predictions of the way in which actual behavioural choices will be structured. A final note warns against the underlying determinism of theory that puts self-interest into so strong a predictive role.

Introduction

This chapter looks at a number of approaches to the analysis of the policy process which draw upon economic theory. These are given various names, but essentially they are variants of what is called rational choice theory or public choice theory. Assumptions about choices made in competitive market situations are applied to political processes. A key characteristic of this sort of theory is the way its assumptions are derived from the notion that individuals act in their own best interests. It is in this sense that the word 'rational' is used. Many rational choice scholars consider that individuals have a 'thin' rationality (Elster, 1983): their preferences are both complete and transitive. When an individual has to make a political choice, he or she can rank all potential outcomes that result from a course of action (completeness). In addition, if this individual prefers A to B, and B to C, then he or she will also prefer A to C (transitivity). While there are good grounds for arguing that economists have appropriated the word 'rational' for a rather particular restricted use, it will be used here since it seems now to be the term most commonly used to describe this kind of theory.

We will look here at a linked group of theories about choices in political processes, about the relationship between individual interests and collective interests and about how actors inside the policy system (particularly bureaucrats) may also have predictable interests. This kind of theoretical work offers a corrective to an idealistic view of the policy process as involving impartial problem solving, but it will be shown that it, too, suffers from problematic simplifying assumptions.

These theories are seen by some writers as providing a coherent framework for the analysis of politics, giving to political science a similar grounding to that which is claimed to exist for classical economics. This claim is contested (see for example Green and Shapiro, 1994), hence rational choice theory tends either to be rejected in totality by those who see no place for it in political science or to be accepted as a dominant perspective, rendering other ones irrelevant. The position taken here will be neither of these, but rather one which sees rational choice theory as making a contribution to our understanding of the policy process. In this respect the perspective is a 'pick and mix' one, prepared to acknowledge ways in which rational choice theory may enhance analysis whilst not accepting the invitation to accept the basic premises of the approach as an overriding framework.

Hindmoor (2006, pp. 1–5) suggests that the key assumptions of rational choice theory are:

- methodological individualism, accounting for outcomes in terms of individual choice;
- deductive methods using models to predict actions;
- behavioural rationality;

- self-interest;
- subjectivism (political individualism).

Hindmoor suggests that the fifth assumption is relatively uncontroversial, but

> The same cannot be said for the other four assumptions. Many (if not most) political scientists would argue that induction is more productive than deduction, that individuals operate with, at most, a 'bounded' rationality . . . and that structure is either more important than agency or that structure and agency are codetermined. Finally most political scientists would join with casual observers in arguing that people are not simple, self-interested, automata.
>
> (2006, p. 4)

To explain the view taken of this work here, it is appropriate to give particular consideration at this stage in the chapter to the second of those 'assumptions': the use of deductive as opposed to inductive methods. Box 3.1 explains these two alternatives briefly and presents an 'inductive iteration' approach as a midway between the inductive and deductive templates, since in practice a large majority of policy researchers move back and forth between theory and empirical data.

Box 3.1	From deductive and inductive approaches to inductive iteration

- *Inductive* approaches start from empirical observations, try to generalise from them and thus develop theory which may then generate further testable hypotheses.
- *Deductive* approaches start from theory and generate hypotheses, which may then be tested and fed back to improve the theory.
- The *'inductive iteration'* approach differs from both the inductive and the deductive templates. The policy researcher does not start directly from the data or from strong theoretical hypotheses. This involves first developing 'theoretical hunches' as provisional causal explanations. After gathering facts and collecting data, the fit is then assessed between these theoretical hunches and the investigated cases. If the researcher cannot produce a rigorous explanation that accounts for most observed cases, then there is a return to theorising. The investigator repeats this dialogue between data and theory to refine and improve the causal arguments. The aim of an inductive iteration is not to produce a final and decisive hypothesis test, but 'to craft causal explanations under real-world conditions' (Yom, 2015, p. 627). The figure below summarises this eclectic research process.

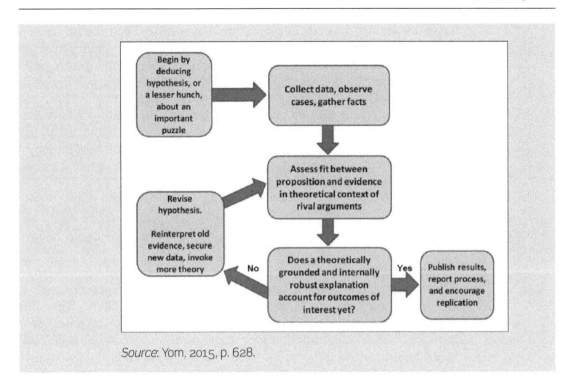

Source: Yom, 2015, p. 628.

This book explores a range of theories which, to a greater or lesser extent, provide potential deductive approaches to the study of the policy process (providing, albeit very tentatively, possible hypotheses on the influence of interests, groups or institutions). However, no one approach alone provides a satisfactory approach to our subject. There is a need instead to combine theories and evidence-based observation to arrive at appropriate analysis of the policy process. Hence there is much to be said in favour of inductive iteration, and it may be pointed out that even those who approach their work purely deductively tend to end up considering to what extent there are theoretical approaches that actually help to explain what they have observed. However, a theory that seeks to offer a comprehensive approach to the explanation of everything is widely regarded – in the social sciences – to claim too much. Rather there is a need to work to and fro between theory and evidence, asking which theories help to explain what happens.

Hence, the trouble about rational choice theory is the extent to which it purports to offer an explanatory approach intrinsically superior to others, using deductively a set of basic assumptions about human behaviour, treating the notion of the rational self-interested actor as the basic building block (a kind of social scientist's notion of gravity) for explanation rather than as something that may or may not be a characteristic of the actors being observed.

The problem is compounded by the fact that, whilst some rational choice theorists defend their perspective as a deductive starting point for the development of hypotheses that may or may not be sustained, others expound their explanatory model of behaviour much more dogmatically. Of course, given the difficulties in doing empirical research, there are many taken-for-granted theoretical propositions in use for which the evidence is limited in amount. However, rational choice theory attracts particular suspicion inasmuch as it has had a substantial impact upon contemporary political behaviour. In that respect it manifests as an ideology rather than a modest theoretical starting point for social science research.

This chapter will explore propositions from rational choice theory that are considered to offer useful sources for generalisations about the policy process, returning to some observations on the other controversial aspects of the theory (centring around the assumptions about self-interest) in a section just before the conclusions.

The development of the idea of the political marketplace

The idea of politics as a marketplace in which leaders compete for votes is developed in the work of Downs (1957). This perspective builds on pluralist theory by adding an element of economistic reasoning which sees self-interest as the dominant motive force in political behaviour. In the political marketplace, parties compete to win power by anticipating the preferences of the median voter and by responding to the demands of pressure groups (see Auster and Silver, 1979; Brittan, 1977; Tullock, 1976). There is a very strong pressure upon governments to yield to those demands, and thus to enhance the role of the state as a giver of benefits (using that word in its general sense, to embrace jobs, contracts, services and tax concessions as well as direct cash benefits). This is not very effectively restrained by the fact that these benefits have to be paid for, because of the extent to which these costs can be hidden in the short run (by deficit financing) or spread in ways which lead benefits to be more readily perceived than the mechanisms to pay for them. For example, in 1991 in Britain, a dramatic cut in an unpopular direct local tax (the 'poll tax') was funded by a percentage increase in an indirect sales tax rate (which had a slight and gradual impact upon prices paid by consumers). Interest groups seek specific benefits for themselves (business subsidies, welfare services, etc.) whose costs are diffused amongst taxpayers as a whole (Moe, 1980). The whole process involves what is often described as 'rent-seeking behaviour' in which interests secure larger gains for themselves than they would if they were competing in a free and open market (Buchanan and Tullock, 1962).

Public choice theorists argue (Brittan, 1977; Tullock, 1976) that as a result of political responses to plural demands, the state grows in power and importance in ways which may be damaging to the working of the capitalist economy. They also suggest that these pluralist (or demand-side) pressures for government growth may be reinforced by monopolistic interests on the part of state suppliers, bureaucrats and professions in enhancing their 'empires'. At this point rational choice theory diverges from classical pluralist theory in giving a significant role to the state as an autonomous actor. This is a theme to which we will return below.

Another theme emerging from this school of thought has been the notion that there is a 'government business cycle' in which government expenditure, to satisfy demands and curb unemployment, is pushed up before general elections (MacRae, 1977; Nordhaus, 1975). The consequences of this are problems of inflation and adverse trade balances that will need to be dealt with in the post-election period. Hence, it is argued that political behaviour may contribute to the cyclical problems of the modern capitalist state. While it is comparatively easy to find specific examples of behaviour to support this thesis, it is less plausible as a general hypothesis. The empirical data is not conclusive (see Mosley, 1984), the feasibility of this kind of behaviour depends upon electoral systems, fitting political activities to economic trends is a difficult activity, and there have been alternative attempts to make economic rectitude a political asset (see Dearlove and Saunders, 1991, pp. 66–7). This is an example of how the widespread propagation of an alleged 'explanation' of behaviour can lead to other behaviour which contradicts it. We will also come later to the opposite kind of human response, behaviour that seems to explicitly reinforce a theoretical prediction.

Rational choice and collective action

Dryzek and Dunleavy's *Theories of the Democratic State* includes a chapter on 'market liberalism' in which they discuss rational choice theory, noting that 'it is possible to deploy microeconomic assumptions without ending up as a market liberal' but that 'most public choice analysts who took a political stand did so on behalf of market liberalism' (2009, p. 105). Hence the particularly ideological tone to much of this theory. Rational choice theory has particularly been developed by those who think it preferable to use market mechanisms to settle collective choice problems. It aims to show that public policy choices are made in ways that are no different from market choices, and that in some respects, therefore, commercial marketplaces deal with choice problems better than political marketplaces. It is argued that policy initiatives ostensibly developed to deal with the deficiencies of markets (market failure) need to take into account corresponding deficiencies of the state (state failure). In this respect, rational choice theory is more concerned with advocacy about the way public policy *should* be made than with analysis of *how* it is made. Hence, there is a close connection between rational choice theory and an economics literature which attempts to define the circumstances in which state (or at least collective) intervention may be justified, for those who believe that market systems are the right ones to settle most social distribution questions.

This literature merits some attention here too, inasmuch as it can be seen as offering explanations about why public policy solutions to problems are adopted, even in the face of strong pro-market ideologies. There are many decision-making situations in which actors will be likely to conclude that following self-interest is problematical, and thus seek other ways of solving collective action problems.

Three key concepts are used in the discussion of this topic:

- Externalities
- Market inefficiencies
- Monopoly.

Externalities arise when market activities have consequences, either *positive* or *negative*, for people who are not party to those activities. Failure to deal with *negative* externalities means that some parties or even all suffer in the long run. One of the most obvious examples of this arises in relation to pollution. In the course of producing something, a manufacturer expels waste products up a chimney or into a watercourse. Direct neighbours but also proximate residents, fish populations, natural habitats, etc. suffer the consequences of this action. And, of course, in the case of activities causing climate change negative externalities are worldwide. Here, then, is a case for collective action that may imply a need for state intervention: to prevent a nuisance which its producer has no incentive to prevent, given that any individual sufferer from it is likely to lack the resources to take action alone. The negative consequences of self-interested individual decisions can even lead, if no regulation exists, to what has been called 'the tragedy of the commons'. This term was originally used by Garret Hardin (Hardin, 1968; see Box 3.2) to describe how rational actors exploiting an unregulated common resource (such as grazing land, but also fish stocks, atmosphere, etc.), for their own gain and with no regards for others, will automatically contribute to the depletion of this common resource.

Box 3.2	The tragedy of the commons

Where there is common land on which peasants are grazing livestock, if there is no regulation of access and numbers, each individual will see it as not in their interest to restrict use. They will reason that a few more animals will not make any difference. Yet when all behave in this way, the consequence is the destruction of the common pasture. This is a specific case of social dilemma in which people's short-term selfish interests are at odds with long-term group interests.

Positive externalities by contrast to negative ones may not seem to be, in themselves, a source of problems. However, there are two difficulties in this case. One is that a positive externality may give some actors substantial advantages over others. The other is that the creator of a positive externality is likely to resent the 'free riders' who will benefit from something they do not pay for. If someone bears the entire costs of building a sea wall to protect their property from flooding, their neighbours are likely to share that benefit for free. There may, of course, in this case also be negative consequences somewhere else down the coast, in which case the combination of positive and negative effects further reinforces the case for collective action.

Faced with a high-cost item, and the likelihood of free riders, an individual is likely to try to secure agreement to collective action (the sharing of the cost amongst the potential beneficiaries). As far at least as the community surrounding the builder of the hypothetical sea wall is concerned, the wall constitutes what is sometimes called a 'public good'. No one can be prevented from benefiting from it. There are other examples where the benefiting community may be very much larger. Perhaps the largest example is a national – or even international – defence system. If it is true that a nuclear deterrent preserves peace, then everyone benefits. The case for state, or even supra-state, monopoly of defence is overwhelming. There are similar issues here with regard to policing within a country.

Furthermore, whilst there have been efforts by states to delegate these tasks, governments often then have to deal with severe control problems. Power has been given – in a very strong sense because weapons are involved – to a body of people who owe no ultimate allegiance to the state. Mercenaries merely have a contract to receive payment and/or spoils in return for their 'work'. It is not surprising that mercenary armies have sometimes switched allegiance, particularly when the capacity of the state to deliver on its part of the bargain has been in doubt (as it may be if the very action for which the mercenaries have been hired seems to be failing). Some rather more modern issues also arise around the nature of the 'contract' between the state and the implementing actors, in the situations in which the latter seem to have no wider basis for 'allegiance'.

Returning, however, to the notion of externalities: how wide are the implications of positive and negative effects? Do they extend well beyond the examples given so far of environmental protection, law and order, and defence? There are some other cases where the free rider problem can be brought under control: roads, bridges and parks may be provided privately, their use paid for through tolls. Then the argument for public provision lies in questions about the inefficient or inequitable use of resources.

But then the externalities argument can be widened further. For example, to what extent does everyone benefit if their fellow citizens are kept healthy? The 'external' impact of infectious diseases is clear enough, but there are other wider senses in which everyone benefits from living in a healthy community. What about education? Do not benefits similarly arise from living in an educated nation? Finally, what about 'externalities' relating to income distribution? If the elimination of extreme inequalities makes people with resources safer – from burglary, assault, revolution even – there are surely externalities which derive from income maintenance policies.

Most economic theorists would probably answer 'no' to some or all of the questions posed in the last paragraph and say that this is stretching the concept too far. If they accepted the case, they would probably want to discuss 'trade offs' with other indirect consequences of state interventions.

However, as stressed above, the concern here is not with the philosophical argument but rather with the fact that there has been a recognition within capitalist economies of a range of justifications for state intervention, often stretching far beyond the obvious examples of 'public goods'. Some economists have added another related concept to the list of special cases – 'merit goods' (Musgrave, 1959), where the collectivity (state) regards it as desirable that people should have something whether they want it or not. Education and health services are sometimes put into this category.

However, there may be reinforcing reasons for state action. One such reason, which lies very close to economic analysis, involves the extent to which state systems make it easier for employers to socialise costs. Public education and training systems reduce costs for employers, and reduce the disadvantage they encounter when other employers poach those upon whom they have spent training money. Help for the old and sick makes it easier for employers to discard inefficient workers. Unemployment benefits similarly may make the laying off of labour at a time of work shortage a less controversial matter and may help those out of work to deal with their relocation problems in a more economically efficient way.

Pure economic theory is based upon assumptions of full awareness by all parties of all their options as buyers and sellers. Real-world economics concedes that there are many imperfections in the market arising from *incomplete knowledge*. That suggests that there may be a role for the state in helping to reduce knowledge imperfections. The case for labour market interventions, introducing buyers of labour to sellers of labour, certainly seems to have been based primarily upon this concern. That example is, however, one designed to deal with an essentially short-run problem. There are also long-term problems inasmuch as citizens may find it very difficult to act in the way the economic model presupposes (this is particularly the case when individuals are unwell or disabled). There was some recognition, even by the tough-minded theorists who designed poor law systems, that there might be individuals who could not be expected to behave like 'economic men'.

Another issue is that of *monopoly*, concerning principally the difficulties that competing suppliers might have in entering a market. Ironically, extreme market liberals accept a role for the state in preventing the abuse of monopoly power – the 'night-watchman state' has a duty to restrain those who try to act in restraint of the market. But another issue concerns the variety of situations in which the nature of the activity is such that it is in practice very hard to sustain competition. The crucial situation here is one in which there is a monopoly or near monopoly supplier and a competing supplier would find the costs of market entry prohibitively high. Examples of this may be found in the supply of telecommunication or postal services, water, electricity, gas, railways and other so-called network industries. To a lesser extent they may also exist in large institutions like hospitals and schools. There may be then an argument for state ownership (i.e. public utilities instead of private operators) or regulation to prevent any existing institution from exploiting its position, or perhaps (more controversially) for state intervention or subsidy to help create a second supplier. However, since the mid-1980s, the European Union and various countries have implemented ambitious liberalisation policies to introduce competition in previously monopolistic sectors. This trend takes the form of simultaneous 'unbundling' (of the incumbent public utilities) and introduction of new competition rules. The unbundling, which is a prerequisite to market opening and fair competition, means that the vertically integrated utility is broken down in two entities: one owning and managing the physical network (e.g. electric grid, railways infrastructure, pipelines, fibre lines, etc.) and one delivering goods and services to final customers (e.g. distribution of household electricity, freight and personal transport, drinking water, internet access, etc.). Whilst the physical network remains a natural monopoly – as it does not make sense to build a second and parallel railways network, for instance – many new (private) operators may enter the market and compete with the previous public incumbent to deliver specific goods and services. This new competition is then regulated by an independent regulatory agency which aims to ensure that all competing operators have a fair access to the physical network.

Economic theory about externalities, incomplete knowledge and monopoly thus provides a series of justifications for public policies, both regulatory and redistributive, of a kind likely to be taken seriously by states in capitalist societies. But there are logical problems about how far to take these arguments. If it is believed that externalities are all-pervasive, incomplete knowledge is the norm and not the exception and monopoly tendencies are endemic, then the logical position reached is a state socialist one. But then, as pragmatic socialists have had to come to recognise, there are arguments to weigh on each side – setting the evidence on 'market failure' against what is sometimes called 'state failure', the incapacity of public institutions to function efficiently or equitably (see Self, 1993, for a good discussion of this issue). Crouch (2011) provides a very thorough analysis of the arguments about these issues, and goes on to suggest that the growth of large firms able to extract monopolistic or oligopolistic advantages needs to be taken into account in making a case for state intervention. However (as noted in Chapter 2; see structural power), he also indicates that these firms may be able to control the state.

It will be evident that much of the analysis in this section relates to arguments about what the state *should* do rather than about what it actually *does*. The implications of this for analysis of the policy process are (1) that justifications for intervention and for non-intervention are embodied in this literature, and (2) that, in the hands of those analysts who are convinced of the general superiority of markets, it offers rather deterministic explanations of policy problems (state failure) which arise when insufficient attention has been paid to the underlying logic.

Finally, it may be suggested that, while the evidence on the extent to which there are collective action problems that are hard to solve provides justifications for state action, it also suggests that such action may be ineffective. If we accept that there is a 'political marketplace' in which politicians compete to win support from voters and organised interests, are there then not reasons why solutions to problems that disadvantage powerful interests will be rejected? Moreover, if on top of this we recognise that there are two levels to the 'marketplace' – one where politicians compete within nations and then another where there is self-interested competition between nations – is the difficulty not further compounded? This pessimistic view may most obviously be set out in respect of the global collective action problems arising out of pollution. The next section explores a theoretical approach that may offer an optimistic response to that.

Game theory

Game theory, while not having its roots in economic theory like the rational choice theory explored so far, has features in common with it, and contributes to the exploration of the issue of why public policy solutions to collective action problems are adopted. This theory arises from a branch of mathematics which has explored the logic of various situations in which there are conflicts of individual interests. Game theory develops a variety of models in which issues are explored about the extent to which individuals do best if they cooperate and those in which they do best if they, in the jargon of the theory, 'defect' – that is, refuse to act cooperatively. It is possible to construct scenarios in which there can only be one winner (zero sum) and games in which collaboration logically brings the best result (positive sum), but much of the relevant work of game theory focuses on games where it is not so easy to point to an obvious choice for the individual players. These games are described as 'mixed-motive games' by Scharpf, who goes on to say that in them:

> The preferences of players are partly harmonious and partly in conflict. Of these, four 'archetypal' constellations have achieved the most notoriety, even among social scientists who otherwise profess to game-theoretic illiteracy. They are known by the nicknames of 'Assurance', 'Battle of the Sexes', 'Prisoners' Dilemma' and 'Chicken'.
>   In discussing the implications of these mixed-motive constellations, the strategies available to both players are conventionally labelled 'cooperate' (C) and 'defect' (D) depending on whether the strategy is intended to realize the common interest of ego and alter or to maximize the advantage of ego at the expense of alter.
>
> (1997, p. 73)

The best known of these games, 'The Prisoners' Dilemma', is set out in Box 3.3. While it uses what may seem a very artificial situation, it can be argued that its equivalent arises in the policy process in many situations in which conflicting actors (particularly actors that may not communicate particularly well with each other, such as nation states) are clear about what they have to do in their own interest and do not trust each other.

Box 3.3	The prisoners' dilemma

Two prisoners who conspired to commit a crime are caught. They are put in separate cells and each told that if they confess they will receive a mild punishment. The dilemma for each is the fear that if the other confesses and they do not, this will result in a severe punishment for themselves. There are therefore four potential outcomes, as shown in the table. The optimum for both is strategy 4, but can they trust each other to stay silent in the face of the temptation to avoid a severe punishment?

It should be noted that some accounts of game theory differ from this one in according slightly different weightings which affect the likelihood of choice of the options. This does not matter, since it is a crucial feature of the way in which game theory is extended that it explores a range of situations where the benefits of self-interest may differ but ignorance of the choices of others remains a constant feature.

	Prisoner A confesses	Prisoner A does not confess
Prisoner B confesses	1. Mild punishments for both	2. Severe punishment for A, light one for B
Prisoner B does not confess	3. Severe punishment for B, light one for A	4. Possible avoidance of punishment for both

The game theory approach is thus used to explore to what extent in the real world situations emerge in which actors will be likely to move from conflicting to collaborative strategies. Particularly pertinent here will be the fact that games are rarely 'one shot' events. There are likely to be repeated interactions between actors so that experience from one game influences the next, and so on. What this leads to is the importance of the fact that games occur within structures. Hence Scharpf argues:

> Actors . . . depend on socially constructed rules to orient their actions in otherwise chaotic social environments and because, if they in fact perform this function, these rules must be "common knowledge" among the actors . . . Institutions have explanatory value because sanctioned rules will reduce the range of potential behaviour by specifying required, prohibited, or permitted actions.
>
> (1997, p. 39)

This comment from Scharpf does not explore the issues about where those rules come from. Later chapters will explore theories that stress the relatively stable structure within which much policy decision making occurs, whilst also acknowledging that there are problems about explaining the processes under which networks (see Chapter 4) and/or institutions (see Chapter 5) are created and change. The democratic model for the creation of a system for solving collective action problems suggests, on the basis of the experience of the consequences of 'blindly' following self-interest, people will come together to create institutions. The mathematical propositions of game theory have been tested in computer tournaments (see the seminal study by Axelrod, 1981) and psychological laboratories, exploring how people actually behave in these games and particularly how experience of repeated games (going beyond 'one shot' games) may change behaviour. Some theorists who share the theory development aspirations of public choice theory recognise from these experiments that individuals may often be motivated to cooperate with each other. It is argued that 'the currently accepted, non-cooperative game theoretical explanation relying on a particular model does not adequately predict behaviour in one shot and finitely repeated social dilemmas' (Ostrom, 1998, p. 9). Experiments suggest that behaviour is very varied, but for some the search goes on to an overarching theory: 'We need a second-generation theory of boundedly rational, innovative, and normative theory' (ibid.).

But perhaps the artificial environment of the psychology laboratory is not the only place to look for theory generation. Scharpf's (1997) treatment of this subject directs us towards deepening our understanding of the institutions which contextualise choice dilemmas.

The economic theory of bureaucracy (and beyond)

The economic theory of bureaucracy applies assumptions about self-interest to the behaviour of public officials. The rational choice theory discussed above sees competition to win political support as an activity that can be analysed like economic 'market' behaviour. This is a 'demand-side' theory about state behaviour. The economic theory of bureaucracy reinforces it by a 'supply-side' argument which is concerned with the consequences of the fact that public bureaucracies tend to be monopoly providers of goods and services. This perspective then draws upon economic theory on monopoly, which stresses the absence of constraints upon costs when these can be passed on to consumers and the extent to which, in the absence of market limitations, a monopolist will tend to oversupply commodities. It is thus particularly central for the notion of 'state failure'. It is argued that bureaucrats will tend, like monopolists, to enlarge their enterprises and to use resources extravagantly (Buchanan and Tullock, 1962; Niskanen, 1971; Tullock, 1967). Thus Tullock argues that '[a]s a general rule, a bureaucrat will find that his possibilities for promotion increase, his power, influence and public respect improve, and even the physical conditions of his office improve, if the bureaucracy in which he works expands' (Tullock, 1976, p. 29). This theory has an intuitive plausibility, but comparatively little empirical evidence has been produced to support it. Peter Self argues that 'these descriptions of the political process can be seen to be . . . overdrawn and exaggerated' (1993, p. 58). Earlier in the same book he describes the work of the key theorist on this topic, Niskanen, as 'logically and mathematically elegant . . . [but] empirically wrong in almost all its facts' (ibid., pp. 33–4). Self goes on to make the following five critical points:

1. The salary of a bureau chief is not closely related to the size of his bureau . . .
2. Bureaus are not necessarily monopolistic . . .
3. Political controllers are not as starved of information as Niskanen claims . . .
4. In any case bureau chiefs are . . . subject to the control of super bureaucrats . . .
5. It is impossible to say that bureaus produce an excessive output if there is no objective way of valuing the output. (Self, 1993, p. 34)

It is not necessarily the case that bureaucratic success is measured by bureau enlargement. Brian Smith (1988, p. 167) points out how some of the most powerful and highly paid roles in civil services – in central finance departments, for example – are in small organisations. Self has observed that 'bureaucratic self-interest takes many different forms, depending on the different career patterns and normative constraints found in different public services' (Smith, 1988, paraphrasing Self, 1985). Indeed, the political attack on big government has led to situations in which civil servants have been rewarded for their skills at cutting budgets, privatising public services and so on.

To be fair, whilst the original argument by Niskanen is put in a form that makes it a very readable polemic, even he modified it a little in a later paper (1991). Others have put the argument in various much more cautious forms. Indeed one of Niskanen's precursors, Downs (1967), offered a typology of 'bureaucrats' with five alternatives, only the first of which closely accords with Niskanen's characterisation:

- 'climbers' who maximise their power, income and prestige;
- 'conservers' who maximise their security;
- 'zealots' who promote specific policies to which they are committed;
- 'advocates' who defend the interests of their department or the wider network of 'interests' within which it belongs;
- 'statesmen' who have a broad commitment to the public interest.

Of course all of these may benefit from working in monopoly situations, but one cannot read off from this any assumptions about how they will operate.

There is a more modern and more limited formulation of the same point in Le Grand's distinction between 'knaves', motivated by self-interest, and the more public-spirited altruists, whom he calls 'knights' (1997; 2003). But then Le Grand's approach also connects this issue up with the influence of structures, providing variations in the extent to which 'knavish' or 'knightly' behaviour is rewarded. In that sense he follows a position taken by institutionalist theorists (to be discussed in Chapter 5). For example, Thelen and Steinmo argue:

> People don't stop at every choice they make in their lives and think to themselves, 'Now what will maximise my self-interest?' Instead, most of us, most of the time, follow societally defined rules, even when so doing may not be directly in our self-interest.
>
> (1992, p. 8)

Last but not least, Perry and Wise (1990) have also suggested that public servants have a strong sense of public interest and are particularly committed to the concerns of others. They develop the concept of 'Public Service Motivation' (PSM) to capture the particular sense of commitment to 'public service values' that can be endorsed by public employees. PSM was originally defined as an 'individual's predisposition to respond to motives grounded primarily or uniquely in public institutions or organisations' (Perry and Wise, 1990, p. 368). However, for most contemporary authors, PSM is better construed as 'the beliefs, values and attitudes that go beyond self-interest and organizational interest, that concern the interest of a larger political entity and that motivate individuals to act accordingly whenever appropriate' (Vandenabeele, 2007, p. 546).

Empirically, Perry (1996) made the first attempt at creating a measurement scale. From then on, PSM was comprised of four sub-dimensions. 'Attraction to politics and policymaking' characterises public employees who prefer to serve public interest by influencing political processes. 'Commitment to the public interest' describes civil servants' aspirations for pursuing the common good (i.e. achieving policy goals). 'Compassion' is a unique feeling of sympathy for the suffering of others that involves emotions and empathy towards others (i.e. target-groups of a given public policy), a sense of understanding and the will to protect. 'Self-sacrifice' is characterised by a devotional desire to help others and a sense of abnegation. Many empirical studies conducted in very different countries demonstrate the presence of PSM among civil servants, as well as its impact on motivation at work, job satisfaction and performance. In addition, the policy environment is a significant antecedent of the PSM level. For instance, civil servants in charge of welfare state policies are inclined to have higher levels of 'compassion', whereas those performing core state functions report lower levels (Anderfuhren-Biget et al., 2014).

The motives encompassed by PSM and highlighted by public management and policy scholars are close to other constructs studied in different academic fields: 'altruism' in sociology (Piliavin and Grube, 2002); 'prosocial behaviours' in organisations studies (Grant, 2008); and 'disinterested motivations' in experimental economics (Fehr and Gintis, 2007; François and Vlassopoulos, 2008). All those theoretical perspectives support the basic idea that civil servants do not strictly behave according to the maximisation of self-interest inasmuch as they have sought jobs that benefit a larger entity than themselves.

Principal-agent theory

The use of an economic model to theorise about public bureaucracy is closely related to what is described as principal-agent theory (Jensen and Meckling, 1976), which focuses on situations in which the 'agent' – that is, the person or persons delegated authority – has motives for disregarding the instruction of 'principals' (Horn, 1995; Wood and Waterman, 1994). This goes beyond the simple proposition about bureau enlargement to explore, from a rational choice perspective, the top-down concern about control over implementation. It has led to a diligent search for situations in which 'perverse incentives' may be built into the day-to-day work of public organisations (see, for example, an influential examination of this issue in relation to the British National Health Service in Enthoven, 1985).

Box 3.4	Basic assumptions of the principal-agent theory

- Principal and agent are interest-maximising and opportunistic.
- The self-interests of principal (i.e. elected official, who delegates a task) and agent (i.e. bureaucrat, who fulfils the delegated task) are divergent.
- The information about the skills and efforts needed to fulfil the task is *asymmetrically* distributed; the agent knows more than the principal.
- The principal may thus select the wrong agent (i.e. *'adverse selection'* problem) and/or may not be able to punish the agent in office if this agent acts detrimentally to the interests of the principal (i.e. *'moral hazard'* problem).
- To solve these two agency problems, the principal has to develop specific tools and mechanisms such as ex ante screening of agents (e.g. competitive selection procedure to make agents reveal their qualities) or ex post control of agents (e.g. define clear performance indicator and financial incentives).

The model has also produced an interesting development which has rather more complex implications. Where market considerations apply, organisations are likely to try to externalise costs. Without the constraints imposed by markets, bureaucracies may also, Dunleavy has suggested (1985; 1986; 1991), internalise costs. Where theorists like Niskanen stress the negative aspects of this – it creates opportunities for the exploitation of public office – there may also be positive ones. Examples of this include exemplary employment practices (in relation to wages, equal opportunities, employee welfare, etc.), responsiveness to clients' needs and interests (appeals procedures, opportunities for participation on policy issues, etc.), and, indeed, general openness to political intervention. Demands that bureaucracies operate as if they are private firms therefore directly challenge a variety of 'benefits' (that is, the costs that have been internalised) that have often been taken for granted as characteristics of the public service. Privatisation of such organisations, Dunleavy (1986) argues, may both undermine the provision of these benefits and create situations in which there are incentives to externalise costs (pollution, income maintenance needs arising out of low wage policies, health consequences of employment practices, etc.).

Dunleavy accepts that bureaucrats will tend to engage in self-interested activities that are directed towards maximising their own welfare; but he shows that whether or not this will involve maximising the size of their organisations will depend upon the task of the organisation, the external (including political) pressures upon it and their own roles within the organisation. He describes their strategies as 'bureau shaping'. He sums up his position as follows:

> Rational bureaucrats therefore concentrate on developing bureau-shaping strategies designed to bring their agency into line with an ideal configuration conferring high status and agreeable work tasks, within a budgetary constraint contingent on the existing and potential shape of the agency's activities.
>
> (Dunleavy, 1991, p. 209)

Hence rational choice theory has both provided a set of arguments to support an attack on public bureaucracy *and* stimulated thinking about how we analyse organisational outputs. The attack on the public sector has taken the form of both outright privatisation and efforts to create competition between or within bureaucracies (see Olson, 1965, 1982, for the development of a rationale for this). Nevertheless, in both this theory and Dunleavy's alternative to it, it must be noted that the emphasis, as in classical economic theory, is upon what can be expected from an individual acting from 'rational' self-interest. There remains a need to test whether actual behaviour is determined in this way.

The limitations of rational choice approaches

To a considerable extent rational choice theories build upon pluralist theories. The discussion of pluralist theories (in Chapter 2) ended not only by challenging the failure of many of the early variations of pluralism for their disregard of inequalities of power but also by setting the individualistic assumptions of pluralism against arguments that identify the importance of structures. Both of these considerations also apply to rational choice theories. While rational choice theories direct us perhaps even more strongly than classical pluralist theory to attach overwhelming importance to self-interest in the explanation of public policy decision making, they do not really deal with the issues about power inequalities within the interest structures they analyse. Clearly they could do this rather more, and in this chapter a number of modifications have been noted (seeing 'games' as actually played in institutional contexts, recognising the way structures influence bureaucratic behaviour). But in general the use of an individual interest model pays little attention to the issues about the manipulation of interests that so concerns theorists like Lukes.

On the other hand, a curious feature of rational choice theory is the way in which, while it can be counterpoised to theories that emphasise the determination of interests, it contains a form of determinism of its own. This has been highlighted by Hay, who argues that the 'rationalism' of rational choice theory

> deals with the problem of the contingency otherwise injected into social systems by agency . . . by denying that agents exercise any meaningful choice at the moment of strategic deliberation. They have, if you like, a nominal choice between rationality and irrationality but, as rational actors, always opt for the former. . . . It relies . . . on a convenient assumption that we know to be false: that individuals in a given context will always choose the same (rational) option. In so doing it translates what would otherwise be a moment of contingency and indeterminism (at least from the political analyst's point of view) into one of complete and absolute determinism.
>
> (Hay, 2002, p. 53)

That formulation is only seeking to deal with the logic of the economic rationality assumption. Behind that, as Hay is of course fully aware, are problems about the notion that self-interested behaviour and rational behaviour can be equated.

Other theorists, although starting out from an economistic mode of reasoning, recognise that other behavioural modes may determine action. We saw that, above, for example in Le Grand's (1997; 2003) distinction between 'knaves' and 'knights'. Ostrom's work was also quoted above, setting simple explanations which emphasise self-interest against 'the growing evidence that reciprocity is a core norm used by many individuals in social dilemma situations' (Ostrom, 1998, p. 4). The work of Jones and Cullis (2003) similarly seeks to apply evidence from psychology to economic analyses of motivation. Yet even with these modifications, surely Hay's strictures about determinism apply. What is merely being pointed out is that what is determined may vary (see also Hay, 2004).

The irony is that inasmuch as rational choice theory has been taken seriously, it has had a certain self-fulfilling effect. Strategies to control bureaucrats and professionals which assume that self-interest is the crucial motivating force in their lives tend to reinforce that phenomenon (through incentive structures) and to undermine altruistic behaviour by controls which send the message that the official is not regarded as trustworthy. Self puts a related point, with particular reference to the use of insecurity as a device to control bureaucrats:

> The problem of moral hazard, according to the theory, is that the bureaucrat will always tend to substitute his own personal wishes . . . However a short-term contractual relationship may well increase this danger . . . An official on limited contract will have less commitment to the public service and may be more disposed to use his position to establish useful contacts and opportunities in the public sector.
>
> (Self, 1993, p. 166)

Yet, earlier in the chapter we have noted, in respect of ideas about the political marketplace, how public choice theory has contributed to alternative behaviour designed to protect against the alleged 'problem' of inflation. So what we are being pointed to here is the significance of belief-systems or ideologies in influencing behaviour.

In this sense the problem about rational choice theory is that, whilst it can be politically neutral, it has been widely propagated as a worldview that defends market capitalism and warns us to distrust the state. But if this means we should distrust its efforts to offer a general theory of policy-making behaviour, it should be pointed out that later in this book, when we look at issues about policy implementation, we will need to come back to examine propositions that suggest circumstances in which markets, or practices that mimic markets, are used for policy delivery to offer ways to enhance efficiency and/or choice. Here, again, care needs to be exercised to distinguish between the advancement of these approaches out of dogma, or the simplistic application of evidence from experimental laboratories, and evidence of negative or positive effects.

CONCLUSIONS

Rational choice theory cannot – despite the claims made by some of its advocates – be seen as an overarching theory of power. Rather, it can be seen, if developed by means of a cautious interplay between deduced hypotheses and empirical evidence, as a source of supplementary ideas for the study of the way power is exercised. Its most close links are with pluralist theory, inasmuch as that makes assumptions about actor self-interest. But some of its more interesting developments contribute to the advancement of propositions about the behaviour of groups and institutions (to be further explored in the next

(continued)

three chapters), where the exploration of issues about choices made within structures is important. If we are unhappy about the way much of the work under this rubric has been motivated by a desire to attack the state and to elevate capitalism, it has performed an important function in reminding us of the role self-interest (on the part of actors inside as well as outside the apparatus of government) plays in the policy process.

4 From pluralism to networks

SYNOPSIS

It was shown earlier (Chapter 2) how classical pluralist theory came under attack both from those who emphasised power inequalities and from those who saw the system of power as in various respects structured. In this chapter, particular attention will be given to approaches to the modification of pluralism which accepted the force of these criticisms without at the same time accepting either the very unitary vision of much Marxist work or going very deeply into the sources of structuration. The chapter will start with a consideration of a body of theory which can be seen as in many respects a precursor of network theory, the theory of corporatism. While it will be argued that much of this theory has been discredited, neo-corporatist tendencies can still be identified in the policy-making systems of many countries. It is also helpful to look at it because of the place it occupies in the evolution of theory. But what is then given primary attention is a variety of approaches to the examination of the policy process which stress the extent to which interest groups are aggregated into networks or policy communities to provide more coordinated systems of power. The chapter ends with consideration of problems about this approach. It has been seen as merely descriptive, and there is a contradiction between a view that networks are essential for policy problem solving and, at the same time, a recognition that they offer mechanisms for the protection of special interests.

Corporatist theory, or corporatism

Schmitter describes corporatism as a system of interest representation. He goes on to put this more specifically as a system

> in which the constituent units are organised into a limited number of singular, compulsory, non-competitive, hierarchically ordered and func-tionally differentiated categories, recognised or licensed (if not created) by

the state and granted a deliberate representational monopoly within their respective categories in exchange for observing certain controls on their selection of leaders and articulation of demands and supports.

(1974, pp. 93–4)

In Schmitter's analysis there are two forms of corporatism: state and societal. State corporatism is authoritarian and anti-liberal. The label is applied to the political systems of Fascist Italy and Nazi Germany. In contrast, societal corporatism originated in the decay of pluralism in Western European and North American political systems. Schmitter hypothesises that in the latter systems, changes in the institutions of capitalism, including concentration of ownership and competition between national economies, triggered the development of corporatism. The need to secure the conditions for capital accumulation forced the state to intervene more directly and to bargain with political associations. We see here a kind of fusion of pluralism with views that stress power aggregations.

Much of the English-language literature on corporatism has explored that concept's applicability to the United States and Britain. Its use to encapsulate the policy process in some of the continental European countries – particularly Scandinavia (see Christiansen et al., 2010; Öberg et al., 2011), Austria, Switzerland and the Netherlands – has been rather more taken for granted. For example, writing about the last-named country, Kickert and van Vucht say:

The threat of labour revolt and rising socialism was countered at the end of the 19th century by the creation of 'corporatism': the institutionalisation of socio-economic cooperation between . . . organised capital, organised labour and government. Based on this . . . the Netherlands developed into an extreme example of the modern non-statist concept of *neo-corporatism*. This concept emphasises the interest representation by a number of internally coherent and well-organised interest groups which are recognised by the state and have privileged or even monopolised access to it.

(1995, p. 13)

But there is no unique model of neo-corporatism. Katzenstein (1985; 2003) distinguishes between liberal and social neo-corporatism. Both are characterised by the inclusion of major 'interest groups' in the policy-making and policy-implementing process, but they differ in other respects. The social corporatist model grows out of a somewhat symmetric relation between business and labour, i.e. a strong labour movement and a strong social democratic party that historically could match business and the centre-right parties. Denmark is an emblematic example of social neo-corporatism (Johansen and Kristensen, 1982). By contrast, in the liberal model unions are weaker and more fragmented, and they are facing strong business associations, representing internationalised companies. Switzerland comes close to this second ideal-type (Mach, 2007; Armingeon, 2011).

This emphasis upon an organised and legally recognised system certainly highlights a difference between the 'coordinated market economies' of corporatist Europe and the 'liberal market economies' echoed in a rather different literature on 'varieties of capitalism' (Hall and Soskice, 2001). In the 1960s and 1970s various writers suggested that the evolution of the liberal market economies towards a more corporatist model was occurring (Winkler, 1976). Middlemas (1979; 1986) went further, arguing that a process of corporate bias originated in British politics in the period 1916–26, when trade unions and employer associations were brought into a close relationship with the state for the first time. As a consequence, these groups came to share the state's power, and changed from mere interest groups to become part of the extended state. Effectively, argues Middlemas, unions and employers' groups became 'governing institutions' (1979, p. 372), so closely were they incorporated into the governmental system.

The impact of Margaret Thatcher's policies led some British writers to dismiss British applications of corporatist theory as merely a description of a passing phase (see, for example, Gamble, 1994). During the 1980s the trade unions were dismissed from the 'triangular' relationship, and at times even the role of business seemed to be downgraded. But this evidence surely only discredits those who proclaimed, borrowing Marxist historicism, that we entered, in the 1970s, the 'age of corporatism'. Corporatism remained in other countries, and could return in Britain, as a way in which the state may 'manage' its relations with key economic actors.

In the United States the relevance of the corporatist thesis has been questioned by observers such as Salisbury (1979), who have argued that Schmitter's model of societal corporatism does not fit the American experience. A different stance is taken by Milward and Francisco (1983), who note important trends towards corporatism in the United States (see Box 4.1).

Box 4.1	Milward and Francisco's (1983) theory of 'corporatist interest intermediation'

This perspective, applied to the United States, stresses the development of corporatist institutions in some policy sectors and particularly those based on government programmes. In these sectors, state agencies support and rely on pressure groups in the process of policy formulation. The result is not a fully developed corporate state but rather 'corporatism in a disaggregated form'. In Milward and Francisco's view, neither federalism nor the separation of powers has precluded the development of corporatist policies because corporatism is based on policy sectors which cut across both territorial boundaries and different parts of government.

Reviewing different approaches to the use of the concept of corporatism, Panitch (1980) argues for a limited definition. In his view, corporatism is not a total economic system, but rather a specific and partial political phenomenon. More concretely, corporatism is a political structure within advanced capitalism which 'integrates organised socio-economic producer groups through a system of representation and cooperative mutual interaction at the leadership level and mobilisation and social control at the mass level' (ibid., p. 173).

This rather cautious approach to the formulation of corporatist theory contributed to generating other ways of conceptualising relationships between interest groups and the state. Grant has summed up the fate of corporatist theory in Britain under the impact of political change and academic elaboration:

> By the time they had developed a conceptual apparatus to analyze the phenomenon, and had managed to organize large-scale research projects, the object of study was already dwindling in importance. The corporatist debate did, however, help to stimulate a new wave of theoretical and empirical work on pressure groups promoting a re-examination of pluralist theory, and thereby encouraging the development of new forms of pluralist analysis such as the idea of policy communities.
>
> (Grant, 1989, p. 36)

It seems on balance as if 'corporatism' is more a descriptive label than a theory. Whilst some corporatist theorists have adopted the Marxist-like argument that there are inevitable tendencies operating in this direction, few have accepted that view, and events in places like the United Kingdom have suggested that corporatist tendencies may come and go as matters of political choice rather than be inevitable developments. Corporatist theory highlights the way in which interests may be aggregated and the extent to which the state may play a role in bringing capital and labour together in ways which may (and this is very much a hypothesis) limit the power of the former. But it pays little attention to interests outside the key productive processes. It belonged to a world in which political conflict could still be seen as involving interaction between the state and the two big organised groups highlighted by Marxist theory: capital and labour. It may be seen as dated, if not by a realisation that the world is more complicated than that, then at least by a recognition that the structure of interests in the modern 'post-industrial' world is rather different. However, this theoretical work thus draws our attention to the possibility that collaboration within networks may be a feature of the policy process.

Policy networks and policy communities

Corporatist theory indicates that there is a need to pay attention to the ways in which powerful interest or pressure groups outside the state and groups within the state relate to each other. But it tends, in a rather generalised way, to develop a single model which gathers the 'parties' to this relationship into three overarching groups: capital, labour and the state. Much other pluralist theory, however, sees neither capital nor labour as single interests which are easily brought together in all-embracing institutions. The same point may be made about the state. Analysts of government have recognised that it is very difficult to get departments to act corporately. Many policy issues are fiercely contested between departments, even within relatively unitary systems of government, between central and local governments and between the many different elements in complex systems like that of the United States.

It has been suggested, therefore, that there may be, rather than corporatist systems, a variety of separate linking systems between interests within government and those outside. One such formulation postulates the existence of a variety of 'iron triangles' embracing the state and both sides of industry and operating in specific industrial sectors and not necessarily across the economy as a whole (Jordan, 1986; Salisbury, 1979; Thurber, 1991).

A related alternative formulation, using the concept of corporatism, comes from Dunleavy (1981), who argues that it is possible to identify systems of 'ideological corporatism' (p. 7) in operation in policy communities. These systems derive from 'the acceptance or dominance of an effectively unified view of the world across different sectors and institutions' (ibid.). In many cases the unified view of the world emanates from a profession – the medical model is a good example – and provides 'ideological cohesion' (ibid.). Dunleavy goes further, suggesting that

> underlying apparent instances of policy shaped by professional influences it is possible on occasion to show that structural parameters and dynamics shaped by production relations and movements of private capital play a key role in shifts of welfare state policy. But I doubt if fairly specific policy changes can ever be reduced to explanation in such terms alone.
>
> (1981, p. 15)

These formulations suggest relatively strong links between actors: *iron* triangles or policy *communities*. Others have borrowed from transaction theory and from the sociological study of inter-organisational relationships to suggest that where powerful institutions need to relate to each other over a period they develop a variety of ways of doing business which assume a measure of stability (see Knoke, 1990). Furthermore, it should not be assumed that these relationships are simply one-way. Pluralist theory can be seen as stressing the amount of competition between groups to try to influence the state. Marxist theory goes to the other extreme of regarding the state as the 'creature' of capitalism. An alternative view is that both sides need each other – the pressure groups need to influence policy, the institutions of the state need support from powerful groups outside it. The exchanges may even be more explicit than that – when the two sides need to trade knowledge, expertise and influence over other actors. Hence, another contribution to the understanding of these relationships comes from the application of exchange theory (see Rhodes, 1981). State institutions and non-state institutions can be seen as linked by both reciprocal connections and more complex network relationships. Smith thus argues that

> The notion of policy networks is a way of coming to terms with the traditionally stark state/civil society dichotomy . . . State actors are also actors in civil society, they live in society and have constant contact with groups which represent societal interests. Therefore the interests of state actors develop along with the interests of the group actors and the degree of autonomy that exists depends on the nature of policy networks.
>
> (1993, p. 67)

Smith explores the relationship between the two concepts outlined above: 'policy networks' (the expression 'issue networks' is also used in this literature) and 'policy communities'. These are closely related ideas, between which there is *no need* to make a choice whilst formulating a policy theory drawing upon them. Communities are stronger versions of networks. Clearly, therefore, networks may cohere into communities and communities may disintegrate into networks. There may be some issues where communities are more likely than networks and vice versa. There may also be some institutional situations, and even societies, where one pattern is more likely than the other and so on.

Smith's analysis was developed from the work of Jordan and Richardson (1987), which tends to use the expression 'policy communities' for a range of relationships of varying stability, and that of Rhodes (1988) and Marsh and Rhodes (1992), which identifies networks of varying cohesiveness. Wilks and Wright (1987) suggest the idea of a continuum from closed and cohesive communities to open and fragmented networks, with the former term reserved for situations in which there is a common policy focus. The main features of *policy communities* and *issue networks,* which represent the two extremes on the policy network continuum, are set out in Table 4.1.

Table 4.1   Comparing policy communities and issue networks

	Policy Community	Issue Network
Membership	Limited with a narrow range of interests	Extensive with a wide range of interests
Integration	Frequent interaction, institutionalised bargaining	Irregular interaction, often consultation rather than bargaining
Consensus or conflict?	Consensus on policy and a relative balance of power between members	Conflict over policy and unequal power

(See also Daugbjerg, 1998, for a similar comparison)

What is particularly important about this work – distinguishing networks and communities from simple pluralist clusters of organisations – is the emphasis upon the state interest in fostering them. Smith (1993), drawing on Jordan and Richardson (1987), identifies, for the British case, four reasons for this:

- networks and communities facilitate a consultative style of government;
- they reduce policy conflict and make it possible to depoliticise issues;
- they make policy making predictable;
- they relate well to the departmental organisation of government. An example of this is the grouping associated with the development of British agricultural policy after the Second World War, which is set out in Box 4.2.

Both concepts – particularly that of policy communities – postulate a stable pattern of interest organisation, so there are some important issues that need to be addressed about how such systems change over time. Smith suggests (1993, pp. 91–8) that change may be engendered by external relationships, general economic and social change, new technology, internal divisions within networks, and challenges between networks and within communities. In the case of agriculture (outlined in Box 4.2) that change has come about partly because of Britain's membership of the European Community, partly because of the growth of a rural population with no commitment to agriculture (people working in or retired from the towns) and partly because of other events that have put consumerist and environmental issues on the political agenda.

Box 4.2	The British agricultural policy 'network' or 'community'

It has been argued that this has involved close consultation between the government department responsible, the associations representing farmers' and landowners' interests and the major suppliers of fertilisers and pesticides. This grouping has been seen as working in a concerted way, resisting influences from consumer interests and anti-pollution lobbies, presenting itself as the manager of the countryside in opposition to other government departments as well as to outside pressure groups (Lowe, 1986). Between the 1940s and the 1970s this could be described as a typical policy community; more recently it has weakened and has had to consult more widely and is perhaps now more appropriately described as a policy network.

In later work with Marsh, Smith has come back to the issues about change (Marsh and Smith, 2000). An important feature of this work has been a concern to take on board issues about networks as 'structures' and actors as 'agents' (see the discussion of the structure/agency issue in Chapter 2). This involves recognising the way in which actors change networks. Marsh and Smith then develop an examination of the impact of exogenous factors, as outlined in the last paragraph, to stress the dialectic relationship between a network, agents and the wider environment.

Other refinements of this theory have sought to be more specific about the way in which networks and communities may relate to each other. Chadwick (2000) and Dudley and Richardson (1999) have argued that more specific communities will often be 'nested' within larger networks.

It is difficult to identify situations in which it is possible to test the extent to which (a) communities really are unified, as there is general agreement that communities vary in this respect, and (b) unified communities get their own way. Box 4.3 offers an exploration of this through an empirical study.

Box 4.3	Toke and Marsh's (2003) study of policy networks and the genetically modified (GM) crops issue

Toke and Marsh describe their study as deploying 'a dialectical model of policy networks' designed to analyse 'the interaction between agents and structure, network and context and network and outcomes to understand and explain how policy change has occurred' (p. 229).

This study explores how a policy on which there appeared to be a cohesive 'policy community' in favour of GM came under challenge. In the process of that challenge the policy community was transformed into a more open network in which some environmentalist groups were incorporated and were able to change policy towards a much more cautious approach to GM crops. It was significant that key actors emerged from relatively 'establishment' pressure groups, notably the widely supported Royal Society for the Protection of Birds and from a government-supported agency English Nature. Also important was wider public recognition of a potential 'problem' with GM crops.

Marsh and Toke's study provides an example of agenda change emerging out of interest group politics. It also indicates the way in which a government minister, sympathetic to the environment protection lobby, may have played a key role. What is interesting about this, however, is that he was in a comparatively junior position, with a viewpoint not supported by the Prime Minister. Here, then, we have an example of low-key policy change coming about not through a direct political initiative but through policy network transformation, yet involving a politician, and a not insignificant movement in public opinion.

There is also a danger here of getting into self-fulfilling statements, like explaining why ideas are on (or off) the policy agenda by arguing that this is because communities want them on or off. The fact that educationalists dominated the United Kingdom education system between 1945 and 1979 can just as plausibly be attributed to the fact that other powerful actors were quite content to let this happen as to the fact that the education policy community had the power to keep it that way. This leads Kisby to argue:

In addition to the interactive relationships that exist between the socioeconomic context, the structure of the network, the agents within the network and the policy outcome, the influence of ideas upon the network may also be seen as constituting something of an interactive relationship with the agents within the network, who do not simply passively accept given ideas but who can use and develop these ideas as well as introducing new ideas themselves.

(2007, p. 83)

Kisby suggests that Toke and Marsh's study, cited in Box 4.3, offers stronger evidence for this viewpoint than they are prepared to acknowledge. Kisby's emphasis upon the role of ideas receives further support in the next chapter where institutional theory that extends the concept of institutions to embrace cultures and dominant ideologies will be explored.

Notwithstanding this, we can at least suggest a simpler proposition: that the policy agenda will be more organised and more predictable when unified policy communities are allowed to dominate (see also the Punctuated Equilibrium model in Chapter 9). There may then be some interesting comparative questions about differences between societies in this respect (corporatist theory propositions are relevant here). But explaining this may be very difficult, particularly when (as seems to have happened in the United Kingdom in the last quarter of the twentieth century) quite dramatic shifts have occurred in the toleration of some forms of policy community domin-ance (particularly in respect of education policy). But the question remains why that ideology should have become so influential, and found echoes (for example in the pro-participation Left) way outside the ranks of the leaders of the attack from the political Right. We are back here to some interesting issues about political choice, undermining social scientists' generalisations about the policy process.

Rhodes, one of the theorists most involved in the development of network theory, has, in his work with Dunleavy, added another element to the analysis of the involvement of networks in government. Rhodes uses the term 'core executive' as referring 'to all those organisations and procedures which coordinate central government policies, and act as final arbiters of conflict between different parts of the government machine' (1995, p. 12). Efforts to define the core executive in Britain may be seen as a contribution to institutional theory (John, 1998) (see the discussion of this approach in the next chapter). However, according to Rhodes, '(the) core executive is the set of networks which police the functional policy networks' (1997, p. 14). As such it needs to be seen as a refinement of network theory.

It is important to recognise how these different emphases upon networks range across a variety of policy issues and concern themselves with different aspects of the policy process. Inasmuch as network theory is an advance upon the pluralist theory of power, it concerns itself with domination (or its absence) across the policy process as a whole. But network ideas can also be found very much in evidence in relation to questions about policy implementation: in concerns about the sharing and modification of policy goals and about the determination of effective action in complex inter-organisational contexts. They have been very important for critiques of the top-down approach to the examination of implementation (see Chapter 11). Clearly, therefore, it is possible that network or community explanations for policy outcomes may be used for parts of policy processes where other explanations (stressing concentrations of power, or even determinist theories, or the institutional theories examined in the next chapter) are offered as prior structuring influences.

The advocacy coalition approach

Sabatier has developed an approach to the analysis of the policy process that has much in common with the work of scholars who emphasise the importance of networks and policy communities. His particular contribution seems to have started from his efforts to try to refine the way the implementation process is analysed (Sabatier, 1986). In work with Jenkins-Smith he has developed what he calls an 'advocacy coalition' approach (see particularly Sabatier and Jenkins-Smith, 1993). This complex theory sees the policy process – from policy inception through to implementation – as involving an 'advocacy coalition' comprising actors from all parts of the policy system. Advocacy coalitions consist of 'actors from a variety of institutions who share a set of policy beliefs' (Sabatier, 1999, p. 9). Sabatier and Jenkins-Smith's approach involves the acceptance of ultimately coordinated action between actors both in favour of and against specific policy goals, and of change over time in response to events inside and outside each 'policy subsystem'. This approach can be seen to be sharing with the other approaches here the notion of a network and of the existence of a degree of consensus (coalition), but going beyond it to embody concerns about the wider political and institutional context. The key features of the advocacy coalition approach are set out in Box 4.4. The approach has been applied to the analysis of a wide range of policy processes, mainly in the United States.

An important feature of more recent elaborations (Sabatier and Weible, 2007; 2014) is more emphasis on a phenomenon that the name given to the theory rather masks: the likely presence of 'minority coalitions' as well as a 'dominant one' (see also the particular importance of this for an issue like nuclear power, as in the use made of the theory in Nohrstedt, 2011). Seeing it as a source of hypotheses Sabatier, Weible and their colleagues advance a view that advocacy coalition theory may be used in comparative analysis. This is explored further in Chapter 6.

| Box 4.4 | The advocacy coalition framework's key features |

Sabatier and Jenkins-Smith summarise their approach as follows:

- reliance upon the policy subsystem as the principal aggregate unit of analysis;
- a model of the individual based upon (a) the possibility of complex goal structures and (b) information-processing capabilities that are limited and, most important, involve perceptual filters;

(continued)

- concern with policy-oriented learning as an important source of policy change;
- the concept of advocacy coalitions as a means of aggregating large numbers of actors from different institutions at multiple levels of government into a manageable number of units;
- conceptualising both belief systems and public policies as sets of goals, perceptions of problems and their causes, and policy preferences that are organised in multiple tiers;
- coalitions that seek to manipulate governmental and other institutions to alter people's behavior and problem conditions in an effort to realise the coalitions' belief systems.

Source: Sabatier and Jenkins-Smith (1999), p. 154.

The network paradox

It has been noted that network theory offers a way to analyse the clustering of interests in the policy process, which has advantages over both simple pluralism and corporatist theory. Rhodes sees policy networks as 'a long-standing feature of British government' (Rhodes in Hayward and Menon, 2003, p. 65). Yet there has been tendency for writers on the contemporary importance of networks to take a stance on the evolution of the policy process very like that taken by earlier theorists who saw the emergence of the 'age of corporatism'. A very different stance will be taken in this book. Issues about networks as one amongst several 'modes of governance' will feature in many places in the book. But the authors very much agree with Lowndes and Skelcher that '[a] crude periodisation of modes of governance can also carry with it the myth of progress – bureaucracy as all-bad, markets as a necessary evil and networks as the "new Jerusalem"' (1998, p. 331).

The account of network theory in this book differs from that of those who have seen networks as fundamental for modern 'governance' in a way which suggests that the role of the state has diminished. Rather, as Hudson and Lowe (2004, chapter 8) argue, Smith's approach to the analysis of networks (on which the account in this chapter has heavily depended) offers the most satisfactory approach to the issue. This involves, for prescriptive approaches to policy analysis, particular concerns about the 'management' of networks; for this discussion the crucial point is that there are important empirical questions about the balance of power within networks and about the extent to which the state (or parts of it) is able to occupy a superordinate role. In a later work Hudson and his colleagues argue 'that some actors are better placed to manage *elements* of the network as a whole' (Hudson et al., 2007,

p. 59) and that in this respect government actors are particularly well placed, hence '[i]t is likely that such a role may provide government actors with the opportunity – contra Rhodes' claim about the autonomy of networks – to attempt to alter a network's design in order to aid the achievement of their own objectives' (ibid.).

'Metagovernance' is then the term used to describe the state's capacity to steer a policy network and, eventually, to ensure its long-term legitimacy (Bevir, 2013). Furthermore, a double perspective is required to assess to what extent a network is legitimate. On the one hand, what may be called 'input legitimacy' focuses on the openness, inclusiveness and transparency of the network. Its democratic quality will be dependent upon the diversity of actors and their level of participation. On the other hand, the expression 'output legitimacy' may be used to refer to the network's ability to deliver expected policy outcomes and, ultimately, its effectiveness in solving collective problems. The key issue is probably to know if there is a basic trade-off between both types of legitimacy or, on the contrary if input and output legitimacy may mutually reinforce each other in some situations (Klijn and Skelcher, 2007; Klijn et al., 2010; Daugbjerg and Fawcett, 2015).

An important body of work, which has been particularly concerned with this issue, has been developed in the Netherlands (see particularly Kickert et al., 1997; Koppenjan and Klijn, 2004). It is pertinent to note two features of Dutch society. One is that – in a place where much land has been reclaimed from the sea and is near or below sea level – cooperation between social actors is important. The other is that a model for such cooperation in a democratic society has been developed in the Netherlands, which entails respect for difference and delegation of powers to quasi-autonomous groups. The latter was a particular product of the need to develop modes of coexistence in a nation within which there were substantial religious divisions, established in an era when these were a fundamental source of political conflict. While this is not so much the case today (at least in respect of conflict between Protestants and Catholics), the so-called 'pillar system' (with separate Protestant, Catholic and social-democratic pillars) remains a model for the organisation of many educational and social services.

Hence there is a paradox here: networks are important in Dutch society but so too is collaboration or coordination between them. Note in Box 4.5 how Koppenjan and Klijn identify both positive and negative features of networks. Thus it is argued that networks are important for the solution of so-called 'wicked problems' where coordination is important (see also Chapter 14). But Koppenjan and Klijn are also very concerned about the difficulties entailed in network management. As Robinson says about their book, 'The reader is left . . . with a sense of how problematic network management really is' (2006, p. 593). Moreover, solving these management problems may come into conflict with representative democracy: from this point of view 'horizontal' coordination needs to be fused with 'vertical' coordination (see Koppenjan et al., 2009). The authors highlight thus the potential conflict between (input-related) democratic legitimacy and (output-related) policy effectiveness.

Box 4.5	Characteristics of networks according to Koppenjan and Klijn

- dependencies between actors, leading to durable interaction patterns;
- those patterns involving shared perceptions: language, rules, trust;
- these may be seen as institutional factors constituting behaviour and influencing cooperation;
- these institutional characteristics contribute to closure in respect of the outside world;
- when problems then cut across these networks cooperation may be inhibited;
- interactions shape and sustain the institutional characteristics.

Source: Summary of part of table 6.1, p. 116, Koppenjan and Klijn (2004).

But the emphasis above on Dutch dilemmas should not be taken to imply the concerns of this Dutch school of academics are not shared by others. Much contemporary writing about ways to solve 'wicked problems', to secure joined up government, or to enhance democracy at the local level alongside national representative democracy, seeks to address these issues (see Chapter 14).

The point here, in a book that is concerned (as noted in Chapter 1) to be primarily descriptive rather than prescriptive, is that much of the literature on networks stresses their all-pervasive nature and identifies therefore that policy-making processes have to involve efforts to work with them.

There is, however, then a problem with policy community and policy network theory rather similar to that with the weaker versions of corporatist theory, that it offers a description of how policy decision processes are organised but not any explanation of why they are organised in that way. This body of theory perhaps only refers to a tendency: one of the ways relationships between the state and interest groups may be regulated. Drawing upon empirical studies it is particularly suggestive of the way in which relationships between the state and interest groups are likely to be regulated in a comparatively stable political system. Smith's (1993) book explores parallels between Britain and the United States, suggesting characteristics of the system of government in the latter that make networks more likely than communities, but he argues that a great deal still depends upon the policy sector. Studies in other societies suggest the existence of similar phenomena (notably the Dutch studies examined above).

John argues that the crucial problem with network theory is that

the all-encompassing nature of networks creates a problem. They are both everything and nothing, and they occur in all aspects of policy-making. But the concept is hard to use as the foundation for an explanation unless the investigator incorporates other factors, such as the interests, ideas, institutions and culture which determine how networks function. The result is an endless circle of argument whereby the network idea is extended to breaking-point to try to explain something it only describes.

(1998, pp. 85–6)

It can perhaps be said that network theory in particular describes rather little except that most activities involve networks. This is the sense in which Dowding (1995) attacks network theory as offering no more than a 'metaphor' for the policy process. A slightly less negative way in which this point may be put is to suggest that it provides a 'framework' rather than a theory. Network theory is not alone in this respect: indeed, a problem running through the study of the policy process is that much theory describes rather than explains. This is an issue to which we will return.

Last but not least, it should not be forgotten that the 'formal network analysis' is a methodological approach, and not a theory *per se*, that offers sophisticated statistical tools to policy scholars applying various theories of policy process (Laumann and Knoke, 1987; Pappi and Henning, 1998; Hanneman and Riddle, 2005; Ward et al., 2011). These quantitative techniques are frequently applied in policy process studies to measure the positions of actors within a network (centrality, prestige, etc.), the coalitions of actors (cliques and dense sub-networks, clustering, etc.) and the relationships between actors (bridge, brokerage, structural hole, etc.). These methodological tools aim at capturing key patterns of relationships and structural features of policy networks. They are thus helpful for describing accurately policy networks and, more concretely, for identifying to what extent state actors or private interest groups are central in a policy network (see the special issue of the *Policy Studies Journal* in August 2012). The formal network analysis can thus travel across various policy process theories and help the conceptualisation and empirical measurement of key concepts such as advocacy coalitions or actors acting as gatekeepers between others and playing thus a broker role (see Ingold and Varone, 2012).

CONCLUSIONS

The emphasis upon networks and communities offers an important corrective to accounts of the political system and the operation of the state which treat them as homogenous and unified entities. It is important to recognise how much policy making depends upon interactions within or between networks.

But network theory lacks explanatory power. Drawing our attention to the importance of issue networks and policy communities tells us little about how they actually influence the policy process. Moreover, it tends to provide too stable a picture of the world of policy makers. While their protagonists recognise the fluidity of networks (indeed, the work analysing the relationships

(*continued*)

between issue networks and policy communities is very concerned with this issue) and that there may be overlapping networks and networks within networks, there is a difficulty in giving any sense of dynamism to the resultant processes. Recognition of the need to explore issues about networks in terms of interactions between actors, and to site them in a wider environment, helps to deal with this. But it does not entirely resolve the problem about its explanatory power, one that is shared with the institutional theory that will be discussed in the next chapter.

5 Institutional theory

SYNOPSIS

This chapter explores the contribution made by institutional theory to under-standing the public policy process. While some writers have argued that it is a relatively recently discovered approach, the first part of the chapter will suggest that it has deep roots in the sociological analysis of policy processes, and that it has also been influenced by institutional economics. Then will follow an exposition of the theory today, showing how the concept of 'institution' has been used very widely to embrace cultural and ideological phenomena. The next part of the chapter explores the way in which theorists have sought to address the problem that an emphasis on institutions tends to imply a stress on stability and either the absence of policy change or the tracking of such change as occurs down an institutionally determined 'pathway'. The two main solutions to this are either to try to develop a way of analysing critical points at which opportunities emerge for system change or simply to stress, as March and Olsen (1984) have, that actually the theory does little more than assert that the organisation of political life makes a difference. This leads to a view that institutional theory faces some of the same problems as network theory, inasmuch as its explanatory uses are limited, but indicates that this in many ways simply emphasises the extent to which the analysis of the policy process is an intuitive art.

One way to solve the problems about using institutional theory may lie in comparative work in which institutional differences between countries suggest reasons for differences in policy processes. Chapter 6 will address this theme.

Introduction

It has been suggested that during the time in the 1950s and 1970s when academic political science developed rapidly in the United States and Britain, there was a tendency to neglect the study of state institutions (March and Olsen, 1984; Nordlinger, 1981). The claim that there was a need for work 'bringing the state back in' (Evans et al., 1985) rather exaggerated the earlier neglect. State functionaries, including the military, figured as key concerns in elite theory, yet it was true that classical Marxist theory tended to see the state simply as a supporting player for the capitalist system and that early pluralist theory largely treated it as a neutral institution which groups in society would compete to control.

Various alternative conceptions of the state are set out in Box 5.1. While it rather exaggerates their positions, it can be said that both early pluralist theory and classical Marxist theory largely embody the first of the models set out in the box. Some elite theory, corporatist theory and some of the public choice models (as discussed in Chapter 3) tend to give the state an active but unitary character (Model 2). Network theory comes close to Model 3 inasmuch as it sees the state as containing members of more than one network or community. The theories discussed in this chapter particularly emphasise Model 4, but in doing so they contain elements of Models 2 and 3.

Box 5.1	Ways the state may be conceptualised

Model 1 As a passive entity to be influenced/captured.

Model 2 As an active entity with interests of its own.

Model 3 As containing actors with potentially conflicting interests.

Model 4 As a structured system influencing and perhaps constraining action.

March and Olsen contrast institutional theory with pluralist and rational choice theory as follows:

> There are two conventional stories of democratic politics. The first story sees politics as a market for trades in which individual and group interests are pursued by rational actors. It emphasises the negotiation of coalition and 'voluntary' exchanges. The second story is an institutional one. It characterizes politics in a more integrative fashion, emphasizing the creation of identities and institutions as well as their structuring effects on political life.
>
> (1996, p. 248)

Their model, at least as expounded in their 1996 essay, sees the need for a fusing of the two approaches: the latter framing the former but being open to change under various circumstances.

The roots of institutional analysis of the policy process

Some writers draw distinctions between different kinds of institutional theory. Hence, John portrays institutional analysis as having a 'central place in political science, particularly during the origins of the discipline', since 'the founding scholars of political science treated institutions, such as legislatures and courts, as a key part of public life and worthy of study in their own right' (1998, p. 38). He then goes on to chart the various ways in which scholars dealt with institutions until about the 1980s, and at the same time notes how behaviourist studies paid little attention to issues about the impact of institutions. After a critique of older institutional studies, John then charts the rise of 'new institutionalism' in the 1980s, which placed the 'state at the centre of analysis' with institutions as 'manifestations of the state' crucial for the explanation of outcomes (ibid., p. 57).

This 'new institutionalism' has its roots in various academic disciplines as well as political science. Three main 'neo-institutionalist schools' are generally distinguished in the literature in terms of these roots (Koelble, 1995; Goodin, 1996; Hall and Taylor, 1996; Lowndes, 1996; Norgaard, 1996). Box 5.2 summarises these, and then in a series of sub-sections we go on to explore further these influences.

Box 5.2 Synopsis of new institutionalism approaches

- The *sociological (or cultural) approach* defines institutions as cultural values, social norms, symbols and rites that limit the cognitive capacities of actors, define the roles and attitudes of the members of an organisation and provide the social legitimacy of this organisation.

- The *historical (or structuralist) approach* defines institutions as the constitutional provisions, legal norms and formal procedures and rules embedded in the structures of the political system that reflect the power relationships between actors and that pre-define access to policy-making arenas.

- The *economic (or calculating) approach* defines institutions as voluntary contracts or arrangements that are the results of repeated interactions between the actors and that ensure a certain degree of predictability to individual behaviour and to the outcomes of collective actions.

The sociological approach

While the revival of interest in institutions is important for the study of public policy, there is no clear distinction between earlier and later work (see Hill, 1972, for an account of relevant earlier sociological work). Certainly, one sociologist whose work will be discussed below, Selznick, has been a seminal figure, saying things still pertinent for modern analyses of institutions. Selznick has, reasonably, been critical of the clear line modern institutionalists have tried to draw between their work and his (1996), but then academics have to try to claim originality!

In some respects institutional analysis is fundamental for the discipline of sociology, raising questions about the extent to which human actions are structurally determined. It is then given an emphasis that is particularly important for organisational activities. The importation of ideas from organisational sociology to the study of the policy process has its roots at least as far back as Selznick's classic study of the Tennessee Valley Authority, which was published in 1949. Even earlier, Barnard (1938) stressed the need to see policy decision making in its organisational context. This theme was picked up by Simon in his *Administrative Behaviour* (1957).

A distinction is made in much of the sociological work between 'organisations' and 'institutions'. Here Selznick is a key influence, arguing

> The term 'organization' thus suggests a certain bareness, a lean no-nonsense system of consciously coordinated activities. It refers to an expendable tool, a rational instrument engineered to do a job. An 'institution' on the other hand, is more nearly a natural product of social needs and pressures – a responsive adaptive organism.
>
> (Selznick, 1957, p. 5)

This distinction emphasises the social world within which organisations are created, drawing attention both to the impact of the external environment and to the way people bring their own needs and affiliations into organisations which then shape the social systems that develop there. Selznick describes this phenomenon very clearly in the following observations:

> All formal organizations are moulded by forces tangential to their rationally ordered structures and stated goals. Every formal organization – trade union, political party, army, corporation etcetera – attempts to mobilize human and technical resources as means for the achievement of its ends. However, the individuals within the system tend to resist being treated as means. They interact as wholes, bringing to bear their own special problems and purposes; moreover the organization is embedded in an institutional matrix and is therefore subject to pressure upon it from its environment, to which some general adjustment must be made. As a result, the organization may be significantly viewed as an adaptive social structure, facing problems which arise simply because it exists as an organization in an institutional environment, independently of the special (economic, military, political) goals which called it into being.
>
> (1949, p. 251)

Selznick's approach has been criticised as too deterministic, but the general thrust of his argument remains pertinent. Later work has emphasised the need to see institutions as 'cultural rules' (Meyer and Rowan, 1977). Such an approach follows Selznick in challenging the notion that an easy distinction can be drawn between formal and informal aspects of organised life; as DiMaggio and Powell put it

> Institutions are a phenomenological process by which certain social relationships and actions come to be taken for granted, that is they are conventions that take on a rule like status in social thought and action, which explains why sociologists find institutions everywhere from handshakes to marriages to strategic-planning departments.
>
> (1991, p. 5)

DiMaggio and Powell (1983) identify the way in which a process of 'structural isomorphism' occurs, which means that organisations working in similar 'fields' tend to develop similar characteristics. Another sociologist, Scott, writes about three 'pillars' of institutions:

- regulative, resting upon 'expedience' inasmuch as people recognise the coercive power of rule systems;
- normative, resting upon social obligations;
- cognitive, depending upon taken for granted cultural assumptions. (1995, p. 35).

This sociological work tackles the issues about the policy process from a rather different direction to that of the political scientists. It is not concerned with questions about how public policy develops but with how organisations work. But then policy processes are generally also organisational processes. Chapters 12, 13 and 14 will return to some of these themes from the sociology of organisations.

The Historical Approach

Another feature of the development of institutional analysis has been the recognition of the need to employ historical analysis, to trace the evolution of policy over a long period of time. Some of the key theorists have described themselves as 'historical institutionalists'. They see themselves as drawing inspiration from 'a long line of theorists in political science, economics and sociology including Polanyi, Veblen and Weber' (Thelen and Steinmo, 1992, p. 3). What is important about this approach to institutional analysis is that it does not see institutions as a source of inertia but rather as influences upon processes of change. It is appropriate to speak here of 'pathways', tracks which change processes are likely to follow. In fact most institutional theory implicitly, if not explicitly, has this characteristic. Of course exceptionally what is to be explained is a total block upon change, but more likely what the policy analyst is looking at is a change process that is marginal in nature (see the discussion of the Temporal Pattern Approach in Chapter 6) or in which the options for change are limited and influenced by what has been done before.

The Economics Approach

It is pertinent too to note some relevant work on the impact of institutional arrangements on decision making emerging from *economics*. To some extent this involves the development of classical economic theory to provide a foundation for the analysis of political life (a topic explored in Chapter 3). But it can also be seen in the recognition of the competitive advantages possessed by pioneer enterprises. The classic illustration is the dominance of Microsoft, having early secured a position in which the widespread dependence on the technologies it developed inhibited shifts to alternatives developed by competitors at later points in time. The concept applied to this is to speak of 'increasing returns dynamics':

> First, they pinpoint how the costs of switching from one alternative to another will, in certain social contexts, increase markedly over time. Second, and related, they draw attention to issues of timing and sequence, distinguishing formative moments or conjunctures from the periods that reinforce divergent paths. In an increasing returns process, it is not only a question of what happens but also of when it happens. Issues of temporality are at the heart of the analysis.
>
> (Pierson, 2000, p. 251)

Pierson goes on from the exploration of this phenomenon to suggest that features of political life make the reversal of institutional arrangements even more difficult than in economic life, where competitive processes may reward innovation.

Also relevant is the development within economics of an institutional perspective that challenged the relatively context-free way in which classical economics analysed market relationships, pointing out the importance of seeing these exchanges within structures with their own rules and expected practices (Coase, 1937; Williamson, 1975).

The various academic approaches discussed in this section stress aspects of the influence of institutions on the behaviour of political actors and, consequently, on the policy process and outputs. All authors agree that actors are 'embedded' in institutions and, at the same time, try to modify them. However, they use concepts of institutions that vary significantly across the disciplinary fields they come from. The definitions provided by various neo-institutionalist approaches are very broad and diverse, institutions being almost everything. This absence of parsimony is a major problem when we use institutional variables to explain policy process. We come back to this major issue in the concluding section of this chapter (see section on the garbage can model).

Institutional theory today

March and Olsen explain their view of the importance of the institutional approach as follows:

> Political democracy depends not only on economic and social conditions but also on the design of political institutions. The bureaucratic agency, the legislative committee, and the appellate court are arenas for contending social forces, but they are also collections of standard operating procedures and structures that define and defend interests. They are political actors in their own right.
>
> (March and Olsen, 1984, p. 738)

They draw attention to the work of Bachrach and Baratz, and by implication also to Lukes' and Hay's ideas (all discussed in Chapter 2), in arguing that operating procedures embody implicit assumptions of exclusion:

> Constitutions, laws, contracts, and customary rules of politics make many potential actions or considerations illegitimate or unnoticed; some alternatives are excluded from the agenda before politics begins . . . but these constraints are not imposed full blown by an external social system; they develop within the context of political institutions.
>
> (March and Olsen, 1984, p. 740)

A related point is made by Thelen and Steinmo, who argue that the use of class differences in explaining political behaviour needs to be supplemented by exploring 'the extent to which it is reinforced through state and societal institutions – party competition, union structures, and the like' (1992, p. 11). Hall makes a rather similar point in stressing the ways policy actors' behaviour is shaped:

> Institutional factors play two fundamental roles in this model. On the one hand, the organisation of policy-making affects the degree of power that any one set of actors has over the policy outcomes . . . On the other hand, organisational position also influences an actor's definition of his own interests, by establishing his institutional responsibilities and relationships to other actors. In this way, organizational factors affect both the degree of pressure an actor can bring to bear on policy and the likely direction of that pressure.
>
> (1986, p. 19)

Hall's approach involves stressing institutional influences outside the formal institutions of government. He asserts that he 'ranges more widely to consider the role of institutions located within society and the economy' (ibid., p. 20). His study of economic policy making in Britain and France pays considerable attention to the ways in which economic interests are formally represented in the political process. His perspective is very close, therefore, to that of the writers on policy communities discussed in the last chapter.

March and Olsen argue that 'programs adopted as a simple political compromise by a legislature become endowed with separate meaning and force by having an agency established to deal with them' (March and Olsen, 1984, p. 739, drawing here upon Skocpol and Finegold, 1982).

This may been seen in the work of Skocpol (1994) and her associates (Weir et al., 1988) which has used the institutional approach to good effect to explain the long-term evolution of social policy in the United States (see Box 5.3). They show how policy change at one point in time created institutions which served as a barrier to change at a later point.

Their analysis is taking a general point, which is quite often made, about the barriers to political change imposed by the United States constitution, and expanding it into an analysis of both barriers to and opportunities for policy change in a context in which one set of changes then sets the structure for future events (and thus perhaps for nondecision-making).

Box 5.3	The use of institutional analysis in the exploration of social policy in the United States by Skocpol and her associates

In the United States in the nineteenth century, democratic political institutions (only for white males, of course) predated the elaboration of public administration. This created a situation in which patronage practices were the main form of response to political demands as opposed to distributive policies using a state bureaucracy. For example, pension provisions for Civil War veterans were extended as political favours way beyond their original intentions. Political institutions were functioning to deliver benefits to some, but to limit the scope for more fundamental state-driven reform.

In the context of a federal constitution requiring complex alliances to secure social reform, policy change was difficult to achieve. Many promising movements for reform failed to put together winning coalitions. This remained the situation until an economic crisis in the 1930s enabled the leaders of the 'New Deal' to put together a coalition of the Northern urban working class with the whites of the rural and racist South which could initiate new policies and offer a brief challenge to the older interpretation of the constitution. But the changes achieved were limited because the President still had to carry a resistant legislature.

The legacy of the policy changes in the 1930s continued into the post-war period, and into the period when emergent black groups had some success in challenging the *status quo* and the constitution. But such social policy legislation as had been achieved in the 1930s had added the Northern white working class, who had gained through the development of social insurance pensions, to the coalition against more radical reform. This was then a source of resistance to more radical change, particularly change favouring black people.

This cuts both ways: there may be either barriers or opportunities, or of course both at the same time. Immergut (1993) has carried out a comparative basis, exploring the evolution of health policy in Switzerland, France and Sweden. She writes of a policy game being played within a set of institutional rules. In her study, other events, over a turbulent period in European history, had an influence on the 'rules'. These events had an impact in different ways in each country upon institutionalised 'veto' points (where those opposed to change, principally the medical profession, could successfully challenge it) and 'access' points (where agents for change could succeed). Box 5.4 illustrates some applications of this theme, with particular reference to policy cutbacks.

Box 5.4	Interest groups, institutional rules and policy change

Pierson (1994) explores the way in which pressure from interest groups inhibited the cutback aspirations of Ronald Reagan in the United States and Margaret Thatcher in the United Kingdom. Béland (2001) has addressed the same theme rather differently in a study of pension reform in France and the United States, showing that the extent to which group interests are institutionalised will have an impact. His contrast is between the influence of labour unions in the two countries. He argues that while union membership is actually proportionately lower in France than in the United States and the control over the pensions systems is in both cases firmly in the hands of the state, nevertheless, French unions have benefited from the fact that their right to be consulted about pension issues is formally embedded in the institutional arrangements. Taylor-Gooby (2001; 2002) similarly explores the impact of institutional arrangements upon social policy cuts in Europe.

There are questions here about the extent to which these institutions impose explicit constraints and the circumstances in which they are subject to change. As March and Olsen say, 'while institutions structure politics, they ordinarily do not determine political behaviour precisely' (1996, p. 252). If it is to work satisfactorily, the institutional approach must handle the relationship between structure and action. It is not enough just to emphasise institutional constraints. It is only too easy, as suggested above, to treat, for example, the United States' constitution as a straitjacket which effectively makes it impossible to get some issues on the agenda (see Skocpol, 1994, chapter 9). Yet the US constitution has been amended many times, and, perhaps even more importantly for the policy process, it has been subject to reinterpretation in ways that in the 1930s widened the scope for federal action and in the 1960s opened the door for the civil rights movement.

Political activity is not just a game played within rules, it also often involves efforts to renegotiate those rules. The revision or reinterpretation of those rules ('meta policy making') is important. The other point, which Skocpol's work particularly emphasises, is the way successful action then generates new constraints (rules or structures). Another way some writers talk about these processes is through the further exploration of pathways or path dependence. Here they are picking up the notion of 'increasing returns' outlined above in relation to perspectives devised from economics. In his analysis of this topic, Pierson stresses that pathways may be influenced by small incremental decisions as much as by big ones.

From a study of the development of Swedish labour market policy which examines the way trade union interests were built into the policy process, Rothstein suggests that 'In some, albeit probably rare, historical cases, people actually create the very institutional circumstances under which their own as well as others' future behavior will take place' (1992, p. 52). This approach, emphasising games about rules, is central to an approach to institutional theory, critical of some of the more rigid ways in which it is applied, set out in a book edited by Streeck and Thelen (2005). In their introductory essay the editors point out 'the enactment of a social rule is never perfect . . . there always is a gap between the ideal pattern of a rule and the real pattern of life under it' (p. 14). This theme – to which we return in discussions of rules and discretion in the implementation process later in the book – leads them to a distinctive approach to the analysis of institutional change.

Clearly, the institutional approach to the study of the policy process involves interpretation. It does not suggest that outcomes can be easily 'read off' from constitutional or institutional contexts. Immergut sets out her games analogy as follows: 'Institutions do not allow one to predict policy outcomes. But by establishing the rules of the game, they enable one to predict the ways in which policy conflicts will be played out' (1992, p. 63). In this way, modern institutional theory embodies 'cognitive and normative frames' which 'construct "mental maps"' and 'determine practices and behaviours' (Surel, 2000, p. 498).

Hall argues that:

> politicians, officials, the spokesmen for social interests, and policy experts all operate within the terms of political discourse that are current in the nation at a given time, and the terms of political discourse generally have a specific configuration that lends representative legitimacy to some social interests more than others, delineates the accepted boundaries of state action, associates contemporary political developments with particular interpretations of national history and defines the context in which many issues will be understood.
>
> (1993, p. 289)

However, these comments indicate that a problem remains that institutional analysis may need to lay so strong an emphasis upon specific configurations of institutional situations and actors (including ideas) that all it can offer is an account of past events, from which little generalisation is possible. Hence the next section examines efforts to apply institutional theory to the explanation of change.

Institutional theory and the explanation of change

Institutional theory faces a problem that confronts all theories that emphasise structure: they are better at explaining stability than change. If we go back to classical Marxist theory we see this difficulty being tackled with a sort of evolutionary theory which argues that contradictions within systems accumulate to the point where they force change – in that case, of course, revolutionary change. But of course institutional theory is not suggesting that change is impossible, nor is it simply taking us back to the sorts of functionalist theories that saw social change as going down some pre-determined pathways. Rather it is emphasising constraints on change and pathways that change may follow. But that still leaves a problem about identifying either when those constraints are least likely to apply or when there will be shifts from apparently pre-determined pathways.

We find a variety of efforts to deal with this problem. There have been attempts to do this using concepts like 'critical junctures' (Collier and Collier, 1991) or 'performance crises' (March and Olsen, 1989). A more fully argued through exploration of this issue uses the concept of 'punctuated equilibrium' (Baumgartner and Jones, 1993; Krasner, 1984). Baumgartner and Jones explore the way in which feedback from policy decisions builds up critical problems over time, hence accelerating the process of movement from stability to crisis (see the further discussion in Chapter 9). This has a parallel in economic theory in terms of notions that firms with oligopolistic advantages deriving from 'increasing returns' decline in efficiency to a point at which rivals can compete with them.

Surel argues that it is necessary to see exogenous influences as important for change processes. For him, 'transformations of economic conditions, and/ or a serious crisis' are crucial (Surel, 2000, p. 503). It is also possible to identify exogenous political changes (for example, the impact of the evolution of the EU on non-members such as Switzerland). Environmental changes may also be relevant, forcing the reconsideration of environmental policies. This approach still poses problems about the identification of crises and shocks (we return to this in Chapter 9). One cannot simply 'read off' policy change from such an event without placing it in context.

Another approach to the issue of the relationship between structuration and change involves the use of biological analogies. This occurs in the work of both Kingdon and John. Kingdon (whose very careful analysis of agenda setting in the policy process will be explored further in Chapter 9) sees the flowing together of forces for policy innovation into an equivalent of 'primeval soup' in which they combine together to produce change (1995).

Warning that evolutionary theory seems to carry with it a Darwinian notion of progress and the survival of the fittest, John points out that contemporary analyses of evolution (as in the work of Dawkins, 1976) do not contain these elements. Hence he sees it as feasible to see policy change as a process in which the elements of policy systems continually interact over time. Combinations of ideas and interests constantly seek to dominate decision making and to interact with institutions, patterns of interest groups and socio-economic processes which are also slowly changing and evolving over time. The notion is that some ideas are successful in this context, but that change defines the nature of modern public policy (John, 1998, p. 195).

Approaches to institutional explanation that explore differences in the extent to which institutional arrangements are 'embedded', that is, reinforced by ideological paradigms (Hall, 1993), offer another approach to the problem of explaining change. Hall explores the rise and fall of Keynesian economic dominance in government, seeing constraints not so much in structures as in dominant ideologies and charting how these change over time (Hall, 1986). Hall presents Keynesian economic theory and then monetarist theory as successive dominant paradigms. Hence he sets out to explain a 'paradigm shift' in which the emergence of new policy options required an ideological shift, facilitated in the British case by the victory of a government disposed to encourage that. In using notions of dominant ideas or paradigms, institutional theorists face questions about the extent to which these shifts can be explained independently of other phenomena. To go back to Hall's study, were Keynesian ideas and notions of public provision so universally discredited by economic changes and related crises, or was there not perhaps a form of contagious ideological change to which we need to turn to explain what happened? In other words, surely there was a new set of ideas waiting in the wings for the opportunity to replace Keynesianism (we may note not merely that the key exponents of 'new Right' ideologies, above all Hayek, had expounded their views long before but also that much that they had to say drew upon pre-Keynesian economics). Then also, what about the political actors who had adopted monetarist ideas in their programmes? It is this sort of objection to simple reliance on institutional explanations that has led theorists to stress the need to incorporate 'ideas' and 'agency' into institutionalist theory (see Peters et al., 2005, for a good exposition of this point of view).

There is an issue here about whether an emphasis on the importance of ideas is an extension to institutional theory or whether it provides the basis for a critique of it. Béland argues that 'institutional scholarship can pay greater attention to ideational processes without abandoning its core assumptions' (2005, p. 1), offering an approach that is superior to more pluralist related accounts of ideas that subsume them within interests. Lieberman, more cautiously, argues that 'institutional accounts of politics . . . challenge the tendency of institutional theories to take the interests and aims of political actors as given' (2002, p. 698). However, he points out that Marxist and other structuralist theories are even more limited in this respect, seeing ideas as consequences of material arrangements, and he goes on in the same article to explore ways to fuse institutional and ideational theories arguing that 'change arises out of "friction" among mismatched institutional and ideational patterns' (ibid., p. 697).

This throws the problem of explaining change onto changes in the structure of ideas, or the dominant paradigms. Béland (drawing on the work of Blyth, 2002) thus suggests that ideas have an impact upon political decisions in three ways:

- 'as "cognitive locks" that help reproduce existing institutions and policies over time' (as in Hall's policy paradigms perspective),
- 'as policy blueprints that provide political actors with a model for reform',
- 'as powerful ideological weapons' that allow actors to challenge existing policies (Béland, 2007, p. 125).

But that still leaves problems about explaining how ideas affect policy change. In Béland's article quoted here the case of ideas about 'social exclusion' are explored to show how they are used both to challenge existing policy paradigms (in France) and to support the dominant neo-liberal discourse (in the UK).

A related problem here is about clarity with respect to the concept of change. Streeck and Thelen (2005, p. 8; see also Kay, 2011) introduce two analytical considerations to try to deal with this. First, they argue that 'we must avoid being caught in a conceptual schema that provides only for either incremental change supporting institutional continuity through reproductive adaption, or disruptive change causing institutional breakdown and innovation and thereby resulting in discontinuity'. This leads them:

- to make a distinction between 'incremental' and 'abrupt' change;
- to suggest alternative 'results of change' including the subsequent restoration of continuity but also incremental change as a gradual process (Streeck and Thelen, 2005, p. 9).

Second, their emphasis on the incomplete nature of institutional arrangements leads them on to suggest a range of ways in which incremental change may occur:

- *Displacement*: the 'slowly rising salience of subordinate relative to dominant institutions'.
- *Layering*: 'new elements attached to existing institutions change their status and structure'.
- *Drift*: 'neglect of institutional maintenance resulting in slippage of institutional practice on the ground'.
- *Conversion*: 'redeployment of old institutions to new purposes'.
- *Exhaustion*: 'gradual breakdown . . . of institutions over time' (ibid, p. 31).

Pollitt and Bouckaert (2009, p. 18) build on these ideas to develop the classification of types of change set out in Table 5.1.

Table 5.1 Types of change

	Result of change	
	Within path (incremental)	**Radical/transformation**
Gradual change	A. Classic incrementalism TORTOISE	B. Gradual eventually fundamental STALACTITE
Abrupt change	C. Radical conservatism BOOMERANG	D. Sudden radical EARTHQUAKE

Based on Pollitt and Bouckaert, 2009, Table 1.1 p. 18.

However, what this highlights is the extent to which what is likely to be involved is the analysis of change *after* it has occurred. From an interpretative point of view, institutional theory is of value. But its predictive value is severely limited. If, exceptionally, an *earthquake* is occurring that may be evident right now, but if a *stalactite* is growing we will only be able to measure it in time to come.

From institutional theory to garbage cans

The previous section has demonstrated how there has been extensive effort to deal with the problem of explaining change within institutional theory. Clearly some approaches to the concept of change and to the factors that generate it are more sophisticated than others. Yet despite the sophistication the theory still has difficulty doing anything other than explaining change with the benefit of hindsight. Emphases on dramatic events and exogenous changes to which the political system needs to respond offer by contrast some bases for prediction. Yet even they offer us little that helps to explain the form political change takes. For example, changes in the world economy in the 1970s forced policy change, but it was not self-evident that those responses would take the neo-liberal form they did. More recent economic 'shocks' are similarly leading some to urge the need now to abandon neo-liberal and austerity policies. The battle of ideas goes on! These observations lead us to consider, therefore, forms of institutional theory that are much more sceptical about the feasibility of using the theory to explain events.

This is the direction in which some of the things March and Olsen had to say about the institutional approach seem to be heading:

> the new institutionalism is probably better viewed as a search for alternative ideas that simplify the subtleties of empirical wisdom in a theoretically useful way. The institutionalism we have considered is neither a theory nor a coherent critique of one. It is simply an argument that the organisation of political life makes a difference.
>
> (1984, p. 747)

There are two parts to this problem. One is that institutional theory brackets together a very wide range of potential constraints, from constitutions and laws, through institutional self-interest and standard operating procedures to dominant ideologies or paradigms. To some extent this mixing of the formal and the informal is justifiable. Sociologists have rightly warned us against treating constraints built into rule books as if they are necessarily firmer than custom and practice, particularly when the latter have penetrated into our language. But in analysing policy constraints we do need to make some distinctions in order to explore what a breach of those constraints may involve.

The way in which some of the institutional theorists go far beyond emphasis on the structuring provided by formal governmental arrangements to include accepted rules, norms and even ideologies has been described as 'the big tent theory of institutions', which implies that 'today we are all institutionalists' (Frederickson and Smith, 2003, p. 69). While such a development is compatible with the usages by sociologists it has been criticised, in much the same way as network theory has been (see Chapter 4), for encompassing so much that it explains little or nothing. John argues:

> The main problem with the new institutionalist approach is its definition of what counts as institutional. By incorporating values and norms as part of institutions, they include too many aspects of political life under one category. The resulting amalgam of processes appears to explain change under the rubric of institutions, but in reality it disguises the variety of interactions and causal mechanisms that occur between the contrasting elements of the political system.
>
> (1998, p. 64)

Thelen and Steinmo echo that, saying: 'institutions explain everything until they explain nothing' (1992, p. 15). They go on to argue that their concept of 'institutional dynamism' addresses the problem by identifying situations 'in which we can observe variability in the impact of institutions over time but within countries' (ibid., p. 16). The problem remains, however, that work from this school involves the interpretation of case studies where the reader is invited to share the writer's understanding of events.

As noted above, if the object is to try to achieve theoretical parsimony, this extension of institutional influences to include ideas and ideologies may be a weakness. However, its strength is that it recognises the soft and pliable nature of institutional systems. Fischer (2003), who welcomes modern institutional theory for the attention it gives to discourses, highlights the need to see institutions in the following way:

> A political system ... is a linguistic concept discursively invented and employed to describe a set of relationships that we can only partly experience – one goes to the voting booth, appears as a witness in a court case, visits parliament, speaks with a political representative, and so on. But no one ever sees an entire political system. While we can directly encounter parts of a political system or discover its effects, the system

itself remains a set of formal and informal relationships that can be constructed and discussed only through language.

(2003, p. 45)

Going even further down this problematical path, March and Olsen have given us, from their work with Cohen, a memorable expression to typify an extreme version of the institutional approach: 'the garbage can model'. In this notion, institutions are more or less conceived as places where chance contingencies occur. Cohen, March and Olsen say, almost as if distancing themselves from their own idea, that '[i]n the form most commonly discussed in the literature, the garbage-can model assumes that problems, solutions, decision makers, and choice opportunities are independent, exogenous streams flowing through a system' (Cohen et al., 1972). Additionally,

> [t]hey come together in a manner determined by their arrival times. Thus, solutions are linked to problems primarily by their simultaneity, relatively few problems are solved, and choices are made for the most part either before any problems are connected to them (oversight) or after the problems have abandoned one choice to associate themselves with another (flight.)
> (March and Olsen, 1984, p. 746; see also March and Olsen, 1989)

There is a problem that once any attempt to generalise is left behind in this way, the student of the policy process is being required to take a position like that of a purist atheoretical historian, determined to let the facts speak for themselves without any principles to help organise selection of those 'facts' or lessons to draw from the study. Or is he or she being urged to look to psychology to offer some organising principles? Certainly, there has been a whole range of policy analysis literature which suggests the need to draw upon psychology. Not surprisingly it has been particularly evident where individual decision making is very evident or likely to be personalised (as for example in foreign policy, see Alden and Aran, 2012, pp. 19–25). There is obviously no objection to this. However, except in some forms of social psychology which are very closely linked to organisational sociology, in endeavouring to explain how structures influence attitudes and thus actions, the problem is that much of this literature does no more than tell us that individual attitudes, emotions, etc. will influence decisions. Parsons makes this point well about Young's (1977) essay on the 'assumptive worlds' of policy actors:

> The problem is . . . how can we students of public policy actually study this 'assumptive world?' . . . Surface, observable forms of politics are somewhat straightforward as compared with 'values', 'beliefs', 'assumptions', and the 'subconscious aspects of policy-making'.
> (Parsons, 1995, p. 379)

There is obviously a need to be sensitive to unique juxtapositions of events and the unique responses of individual actors, but if we are sitting in the 'garbage can' watching the latter deal with the former, we can do little but describe what happens on each unique occasion.

But there is, perhaps, one other way forward by way of comparative analysis. Peters et al. speak of modern institutional theory as adopting an 'explicitly comparative focus' (2005, p. 1280). If propositions about 'pathways' or 'critical junctures' etc. are to stand up as more than observations – generally with the benefit of hindsight – about what has gone on in the 'garbage can' etc., then observations about differences in different institutional structures are needed. These may be observations about different points of time in the same country, hence the importance of historical institutionalism. In this respect there have been efforts to find a middle way between the emphasis on relatively predictable pathways discussed above and the unpredictability of the 'garbage can' model by exploring 'policy sequencing', seeing how policy changes 'are firmly based or rooted in previous events and thinking as related structural processes of both negative and positive feedback affect actor behaviour' (quotation from a review of relevant literature by Howlett, 2009, p. 252). It may also be that comparisons between different places (which normally means comparisons between nation states) can offer ways to address this problem. The next chapter explores this option, and shows that there have been various efforts to categorise nations in terms of differences in institutional configurations, which may have an impact on their responsiveness to the forces and ideas that trigger policy change.

CONCLUSIONS

Institutionalist writers offer a critique of other approaches to policy analysis. Inasmuch as they stress that pre-existing institutional configurations matter, they have points in common with the more structuralist theorists (discussed in Chapter 2). But they depart from the comparative inflexibility of most theory of that kind. They assert that 'the organisation of political life makes a difference' but require that statement to be contextualised by other things that make a difference. They see policy activity as kinds of 'games' with rules, but also recognise that they may be at the same time meta-games about changing those rules. They leave us with an impression of continuity in the policy process, of policy change following pathways. The explanation of more dramatic change then involves attention to exogenous factors, to the build up of internal contradictions and to ideas and ideologies.

Comparative work – looking at differences over time, between policies or between countries – can help with the examination of the connections between institutional arrangements and policies, and perhaps explain policy change. The next chapter is thus dedicated to comparative policy studies. But there remain difficulties in arriving at anything more than the retrospective explanation of policy processes. Institutions matter for policy analysis, but it is far from clear how they matter.

6 Comparative policy process studies

SYNOPSIS

It is implicit to the concerns of this book that generalisations about the policy process aim to apply across countries, and that therefore questions must be explored, through comparative studies, about the extent to which this is in fact the case. This is particularly so for many of the institutional theories considered in Chapter 5, with the further implication that if countries differ because of their particular institutional configurations, then their policy processes and policy outputs are likely to differ as well. Whilst it is easier to show that political systems diverge rather than converge, there is, nevertheless, a sense in which institutional theory, at the very least, needs comparison to demonstrate how divergence occurs. This chapter therefore aims at briefly presenting comparative approaches that examine policy differences and suggest how institutional differences may help to explain these.

The testing of hypotheses about policy process using the experimental methods favoured by natural scientists are largely ruled out for the study of the policy process, where researchers cannot control the variables and political processes themselves make experimentation inappropriate (see Lijphart, 1971). Then, as Durkheim argued in his classic book on comparison in the social sciences

> We have only one way of demonstrating that one phenomenon is the cause of another. That is to compare the cases where they are both simultaneously present or absent, so as to discover whether the variations they display in these different combinations of circumstances provide evidence that one depends on the other.
>
> (1982, p. 141)

Comparative methods, observing contrasts in policies or policy contexts (including particularly national variations), offer an alternative approach to testing theories. The classical response of political scientists to this has been to develop multi-variate quantitative studies using the statistical techniques particularly developed in the physical sciences and medicine using probabilistic assumptions and seeking to identify the best predictors of outputs and outcomes. The applications of this approach face a number of problems. Numbers of cases are often low and key variables are hard to quantify, particularly as continuous variables. The 'best' predictors identified are often at a fairly low level of probability, and indeed the use of probability theory is challengeable where the cases compared are not strictly speaking a 'sample' of a wide universe.

All of these problems are clearly identifiable when the 'cases' in question are nation states, or even regional and local units within them. Whilst these problems have led some scholars to engage in purely qualitative descriptive work, new techniques have emerged to facilitate systematic comparisons. A generic term 'qualitative comparative analysis' (QCA) has been developed, a label that may be at times slightly misleading as such techniques do not explicitly eschew quantification but rather recognise its limitations and recognise it may be necessary to reduce comparisons to single pairs of cases. The key theorist for the development of QCA is Ragin (see 1987 for his pioneering work).

The effective contribution of comparative policy studies for the exploration of the institutional perspective will depend upon the quality of the research design adopted. A policy scholar may combine different types of comparisons (e.g. across international regimes, countries and policy sectors, and over time as well) and – depending upon the developed research design – will face specific methodological challenges such as:

- How many cases are to be included in the comparison?
- Should the comparison focus on most similar or most different cases?
- How should one make causal inferences about the impact of institutional versus actor-based variables on policy processes and outputs?
- How should one address the trade-off between internal validity (accuracy of causal links) and external validity (generalisation beyond the cases) of the empirical findings?

Several recent handbooks on comparative politics (Powell et al., 2012; Caramani, 2014) and comparative policy studies (Engeli and Rothmayr Allison, 2014) discuss these conceptual and methodological issues in depth and are strongly recommended as further readings. In this chapter we do not go further into the methodological debates, but offer an introduction to comparative policy studies influenced by contemporary efforts to apply new analytical techniques influenced by QCA. We basically focus on the development of a 'compound research design' influence that was originally proposed by Levi-Faur (2004; 2006a; 2006b) and then further elaborated by van der Heijden (2014). This type of research design is appropriate to show how different explanatory variables and theoretical hypotheses can be combined in a comparative empirical study.

Compound research design: theories, combination and iteration

A compound research design has two main components. First, it implies the combination of different theoretical perspectives, which concentrate on alternative independent variables to explain policy processes and outputs. Concretely, Levi-Faur (2004; 2006a) distinguishes between the national pattern approach, the policy sector approach, the international regime approach and the temporal pattern approach. Even if they propose rival hypotheses on the factors explaining policy processes and outputs, these four approaches are not always mutually exclusive. On the contrary, they need to be combined in a compound research design. Second, the comparison involves an iterative strategy and a stepwise inferential process. The same research question is going to be successively asked for different policy sectors, national contexts, international regimes and periods of time, in order to stimulate as many pair-wise comparisons as possible. To address these two constitutive elements of a compound research design, the following sections present the four theoretical approaches, and then look at how they can be combined with an iterative comparison strategy.

Four theoretical approaches: nations, sectors, international regimes and time

The National Pattern Approach

The *National Pattern Approach (NPA)* puts the emphasis on institutional features, at the national level, that potentially exert a major impact on public policies. Such characteristics include for instance constitutional elements (e.g. central state versus federal state), the type of relations between interest groups and the state (e.g. pluralism versus neo-corporatism; see Chapters 2 and 4), the system of political parties and government (e.g. majority and opposition versus grand coalition; Lijphart, 1999), the media system (e.g. polarised pluralist, liberal versus democratic corporatist; see Hallin and Mancini, 2004) the dependence between state and church (e.g. religious versus secular world; see Engeli et al., 2012), etc. The overall kind of hypothesis embodied in the NPA stipulates that countries differ regarding specific institutional features and, as a consequence, countries will formulate and implement different policies.

Perhaps the most relevant comparative and holistic work of the NPA is that of Lijphart (1984; 1999). He argues that definitions of democracy raise the fundamental question of 'who will do the governing and to whose interests should the government be responsive when the people are in disagreement and have divergent preferences?' (Lijphart, 1999, p. 1). Lijphart goes on to contrast two answers to that question: 'the majority of the people' (i.e. the so-called '*Westminster* or *majoritarian* model'; typically the United Kingdom or New Zealand) and 'as many people as possible' (i.e. the '*consensus* model'; as illustrated by Switzerland or Belgium). His comparative analysis also examines variations along another dimension: that between strong federalism at one extreme and high degrees of unification at the other.

This theory was initially developed to explain the survival of divided societies with several languages, religions, ethnic groups, regional interests, etc. Lijphart is thus clearly engaged in a very bold attempt to produce what Lane and Ersson call 'grand social theory' (2000, p. 224). He treats the state as a rather passive entity, with a fixed set of institutions to which organised interests can relate. Furthermore, Lijphart's analysis and efforts to generalise about state power may be taken on to help to address issues about the conditions under which policy processes will occur. It may be suggested that in the consensual democracies, policy change will be slower and more subject to 'veto' by organised interests. In addition, Lijphart also suggests that consensual democracies are not only more inclusive – often operating through corporatist policy-making processes – but also more effective and implicitly more responsive. Concretely, he argues that consensus democracies are 'kindlier, gentler democracies in the sense that their welfare policies with regard to unemployment, disability, illness and old age permit people to maintain decent living standards independent of pure market forces' (Lijphart, 1999, p. 294). This seminal hypothesis has been tested in different policy domains and countries. For example, Lewin et al. (2008) analysed the disability policies implemented in Sweden and gave good reasons to doubt that consensus democracy always promotes more generous policies. The causal links needed for the distinction between a Westminster model and a consensus democracy, the openness and inclusiveness of the policy process, and the final policy outputs remain much more complex than postulated in Lijphart's holistic approach.

Other authors have also developed typologies of countries to contribute to the study of the way policy processes and outputs vary from country to country. It is in the field of 'welfare state' that most comparative work has been done. This is partly because variations in levels of social policy expenditure and the way in which social policy institutions have developed are particularly salient across the more economically developed nations, with questions about whether welfare states are boons or banes being particularly prominent in ideological debates. But it must also be partly attributable to the fact that social policy expenditure is a large item in the budgets of many states, and that its ingredients and implications are widely measured and reported in a variety of international databases which facilitate relatively accurate comparisons between countries.

The most influential comparative study of this kind is Esping-Andersen's *Three Worlds of Welfare Capitalism* (1990). He analyses aspects of the characteristics of social policy systems in terms of their contributions to social solidarity. Esping-Andersen's starting point was a view that 'politics matters', using an essentially neo-pluralist perspective emphasising variations in the representation of class interests within politics. This leads him to identify three regime types: (1) the *liberal* welfare state, in which 'means-tested assistance, modest universal transfers, or modest social-insurance plans predominate' (e.g. Australia, the United States, New Zealand, Canada, Ireland and the United Kingdom); (2) the conservative and strongly *corporatist* welfare states include Italy, Japan, France, Germany, Finland, Switzerland, Austria, Belgium and the Netherlands. In such nations, 'the preservation of status differentials' predominates and the granting to social rights is still attached to social class; (3) finally, Denmark, Norway and Sweden belong to the *social-democratic* type of welfare states, 'in which the principles of universalism and decommodification of social rights was extended also to the middle classes' (Esping-Andersen, 1990, pp. 26–8). Esping-Andersen's work has been widely criticised yet the regime concept remains dominant in comparative work on social policy. Most criticisms merely lead to reformulations of the regime model (Arts and Gelissen, 2002; Hill, 2006, chapter 2; Ferragina and Seelieb-Kaiser, 2011). However, a more fundamental objection by Walker and Wong (2004) suggests that the whole regime approach embodies 'Western' ethno-centric assumptions about the role of the state and about welfare development as a product of what has been described above as 'the truce' between capital and labour. Hence there is a need for caution about using it in societies, like those of East Asia, with very different experiences.

Building on Esping-Andersen's work, Pierson's contribution (1993; 2001) is particularly important in this respect since it uses institutional theory much more explicitly, with two key features. One is that it equates regimes with institutional configurations that will channel new policy initiatives. The other is that it suggests that the relative success of interest groups will depend upon institutional arrangements, such as the presence or absence of institutionalised 'access points' and 'veto points' in different societies (Immergut, 1993; see also Chapter 5). In general, a variety of scholars suggest that particular institutional approaches set up 'pathways' which influence future developments. Path-dependencies seem to be particularly important in income maintenance systems, where pension schemes imply long-run expectations (a theme to be explored further in Chapter 9) and often embody social insurance arrangements, which themselves build very strong, long-run political expectations and therefore obligations.

A third major theory in the NPA category is 'Varieties of Capitalism'. Hall and Soskice (2001) propose a classification of varieties of capitalism to make explicit connections between policy outputs and national institutional arrangements. They distinguish between 'liberal market economies' (e.g. the United States, the United Kingdom, New Zealand, Canada or Ireland) and 'coordinated market economies' (e.g. Germany, Switzerland, Japan, Belgium, the Netherlands or France). In the former, private firms mainly coordinate their activities via competitive market arrangements; by contrast, the state is crucially a more active partner in the latter, linking with a range of interest groups whose autonomy governments of the liberal market economies are more likely to respect.

It makes sense to see a connection between types of capitalist economy, the broad institutional configurations of different states and the type of policies implemented in specific domains (e.g. labour and wage policies, education policies, social policies, etc.). However, this dichotomy has been challenged by several authors. Schmidt (2002) prefers to distinguish between market capitalism (e.g. the United States or the United Kingdom), 'state enhanced' capitalism (e.g. France or Spain) and 'managed capitalism' (e.g. Germany or Japan). In addition, these diverging classifications of capitalisms bring with them explanatory problems. How stable are the observed connections between national institutions, economy and public policies? Can political action change national systems? And, are we not, as some globalism theorists strongly suggest (see the 'International Regime Approach' below), seeing shifts towards the dominance of liberal market systems as capitalism becomes more independent of nation states? In that respect, Thatcher (2004) offers some empirical evidence on the limits of the 'varieties of capitalism' theory to explain the major transformations of the telecommunications sector in Europe. Empirically, he compares the evolution from the 1960s onwards of the telecommunication market in Britain, Germany, Italy and France. Despite the fact that these four countries obviously belong to different types of capitalism (see the theoretical classifications above), they obviously converge towards the same sector-specific model, which is characterised by a privatisation of the previous public utility, the creation of an independent regulatory agency, and the predominance of competition rules. This convergence invalidates the hypothesis, embodied in the original varieties of capitalism theory, that technological changes, trade liberalisation, international capital flows, etc. will not necessarily lead to institutional and policy convergence (see Hall and Soskice, 2001, pp. 54–60).

Finally, we mention a last attempt to classify countries by relying conceptually on 'national policy styles'. In his pioneer volume, Richardson (1982) defines the policy style of a country along two dimensions. On one hand, decision makers may anticipate the social problems to be addressed by public policies or they may react to them. On the other hand, decision makers may try to seek a consensus with the policy stakeholders or they may impose their solutions and policy decisions. By crossing both analytical dimensions, four national policy styles emerge: anticipatory and consensus-seeking (e.g. the Netherlands or Spain), reactive and consensus-seeking (e.g. Germany or Sweden), anticipatory and imposing (e.g. the United Kingdom) and, reactive and imposing (e.g. Spain). However, at the end of his edited book, in which this basic model is explored through case studies, Richardson remains cautious about labelling countries in terms of policy styles. Nevertheless, Bovens et al., in their *Success and Failure in Public Governance* (2001, pp. 18–19, 645–7), offer expected 'styles' for the six countries they studied. However, they qualify their prediction by offering an alternative prediction that they may see 'roughly similar governance in each of the sectors [to be studied], and major differences between sectors even between cases set in the same country' (ibid., p. 18). Hence, we see suggestions that different national policy styles affect how policy is formulated, but then this is interestingly qualified by Bovens and his colleagues with suggestions that this may very much depend upon policy area. In practice, then, they have done little more than identify variations without adding any useful approaches to their explanation. In sum, within this literature, policy styles are seen as varied, not merely on account of national differences, but also because of differences in the policy issues at stake. This focus on the specificities of each policy domain lies at the core of the second generic approach identified by Levi-Faur (2004; 2006a; 2006b) to be mentioned next.

The Policy Sector Approach

The *Policy Sector Approach (PSA)* suggests that different policy styles may be manifested in different policy sectors, even within the same country, let alone between countries. Freeman (1985, p. 486) summarises this with two fundamental propositions: 'the style of policy making and the nature of political conflicts in a country will vary significantly from sector to sector . . . (and) . . . policy making in a particular sector will exhibit strong similarities, whatever its national context'. This approach claims that autonomous and generic characteristics of a specific policy sector are more influential than constitutional institutions and national patterns to explain policy processes and outputs. Comparative policy studies should thus focus on the types of policy issues at stake (according to the seminal argument made initially by Lowi, 1972; see Chapter 8 this volume), the network of policy stakeholders (e.g. closed policy communities or open issue network), and the technological and economic context impacting on the sector as well. These basic assumptions of the PSA are common to different theoretical frameworks, among which the *policy network* approach has already been discussed in Chapter 4.

Here we concentrate on a variant of this approach: the *Advocacy Coalition Framework (ACF)*. It was outlined in Chapter 4, here the concern is to explore how it has been advanced as a theory which may be used in comparative analysis. According to Sabatier and Jenkins-Smith the appropriate unit of analysis is a 'subsystem' defined as 'the set of actors who are involved in dealing with a policy problem' (1993, p. 24). Over decades, these stakeholders regularly seek to influence policy decisions within a specific subsystem such as Swedish nuclear energy policy (Nohrstedt, 2010; 2014), California Marine Protected Area policy (Weible, 2007) or Swiss drug policy (Kübler, 2001) for example. In the ACF approach, the outputs of a given policy-making process do not depend on individual action, but on the interactions between actors' coalitions. More concretely, the policy process is seen as a fierce competition between coalitions of actors who advocate beliefs about policy problems and solutions. Actors are said to build 'advocacy coalitions' independently of their organisational allegiances or institutional functions. The glue between the members of an advocacy coalition, which can include legislators, executive agencies, interest groups, political parties, academic researchers, journalists, etc., is their shared 'belief system'.

Three levels of beliefs are distinguished and measured. The 'deep core beliefs' involve ontological assumptions such as basic values or criteria of distributive justice. These fundamental axioms are part of the personal philosophy and remain stable over time. The 'policy core beliefs' represent the normative image of what the specific policy subsystem should be (policy goals) and provide the vision that guides a coalition's strategic behavior. Finally, the 'secondary aspects' of the belief system are preferences related to specific instruments and policy proposals. Whilst coalition members may differ in secondary preferences, they tend to agree on core beliefs.

The goal of each advocacy coalition is to successfully translate its belief system into a concrete policy programme, i.e. to become dominant or even hegemonic in the subsystem. Doing so, a coalition will find itself in conflict with other advocacy coalitions with different belief systems, which are also trying to have an influence on the policy programme (for example, pro- versus contra-nuclear power coalitions). 'Policy brokers' typically intervene in situations of high conflict between coalitions. Their role is to search for stability in the subsystem, and to mediate between the opponents in order to make compromise solutions feasible (Ingold and Varone, 2012).

Last but not least, 'policy oriented learning' by the dominant advocacy coalition is an important mechanism leading to minor policy changes: it principally concerns the level of secondary aspects of the belief system (Sabatier, 1988, p. 134; Weible, 2007). By contrast, major policy changes are only expected when a new advocacy coalition is able to take the power in the subsystem, for instance after an external shock (e.g. the catastrophic nuclear accidents in Chernobyl in 1986 or in Fukushima in 2011). Paradigmatic policy changes respond thus to larger and external factors and struggles for power.

Various other theoretical approaches that will be further discussed below (Hall, 1993; Baumgartner and Jones, 1993) reach similar conclusions about the importance of external factors that are not controlled by the members of the subsystem, to explain paradigmatic policy changes.

Although the ACF was developed in the specific policy-making environment of the United States its application in European countries and corporatist political systems can be observed over the last decade (see Weible et al., 2009, for an overview of empirical studies applying the ACF). As a consequence of these wider applications, the authors adapted some concepts to make the ACF better suited to different institutional contexts where consensual decision making is the rule (Sabatier and Weible, 2007), where political parties are also key players (Nohrstedt, 2009; Weible, 2007) or where the political system is less pluralist than the American one. Sabatier and Weible (2007) consider, as variables influencing policy making in a subsystem, both the openness of the political system and the degree of consensus needed for policy change. In short, the institutional rules inherent in a political system modify the 'political opportunity structure' that each coalition may strategically exploit to promote – or even to impose – its beliefs and policy preferences. The authors do not, however, formulate an explicit hypothesis regarding the expected effects of 'political opportunity structures' (which varies significantly between countries and amongst policy subsystems) on the behaviour of advocacy coalitions, or on the specific role of policy brokers (see also Weible et al., 2009, pp. 129, 132 and 134–5). So the ACF is still marked by an underdevelopment when it comes to clarifying the complex interactions of subsystems (at the policy level), the institutional rules constraining the decision-making process (at the polity level), and the political actors with the formal authority to make binding decisions in all policy fields. Therefore, it could make sense to cross-fertilise the ACF with other theories insisting on institutional variables at the national level (NPA). For instance, Ingold and Varone (2012) have demonstrated that policy brokers have a strong intermediation power and policy influence in situations where the advocacy coalitions in competition can (threaten to) use an institutionalised veto point (e.g. launching an optional referendum against a parliamentary law in Switzerland) to oppose any policy development. In addition, the ACF also has to integrate the fact that many policy sectors are characterised by multi-level governance, beyond the nation state. This dimension is central to the next approach to policy processes and outputs.

The International Regime Approach

The *International Regime Approach (IRA)* is the third category of theories considered by Levi-Faur. It is uncontroversial that policy making takes place in a globalised context and that interdependences between countries, as well as between nation states and supranational institutions (e.g. the European Union), have major impacts on domestic policy process and outputs (see Chapters 2 and 14). The question is no longer whether or to what extent multi-level governance (MLG) is a reality, but how MLG should be organised to be accountable, democratic, and efficient in problem solving (Hooghe and Marks, 2003, p. 233). In MLG and internationalised policies, the power of decision making is dispersed across multiple jurisdictions. For example, the European integration has clearly impacted domestic policies and politics, thereby challenging the central level of member states. Empirical studies have shown that the Europeanisation of public policies does not lead to a unilateral strengthening or weakening of one level of government at the expense of all the others. They do show, however, that this Europeanisation process results in new and more complex forms of shared governance and networks of policy actors.

To disentangle this complexity, Holzinger and Knill (2005) identify four main mechanisms behind internationalisation (see also Chapter 10 and Table 10.3):

1. 'Imposition' or coercion occurs when a supranational actor forces domestic policy makers to adopt a given policy. For example, a country which applies for formal EU membership has to adopt the whole '*community acquis*', i.e. all the accumulated legislative and regulatory acts and court decisions that constitute the body of EU law. The International Monetary Fund conditionality imposed on countries that receive a financial support for their development strategy is another emblematic case in point.

2. By contrast, 'harmonization' corresponds to the voluntary engagement of countries within an international negotiation and cooperation. This

translates into bilateral or multilateral agreements on specific policies such as tax exemption, climate change, management of an international water basin, etc.

3. The third mechanism is labelled 'regulatory competition' and presupposes a strong economic interdependency of various countries facing similar competitive pressures. The policy adopted by one country can cause direct or indirect negative externalities in another country. For example, if a country prohibits research on embryonic stem cells (e.g. in Germany), then national researchers and biotech firms will switch their activities to a more permissive country (e.g. the United Kingdom). This kind of competition between countries leads eventually to an international race towards the most permissive regulation (a 'race-to-the-bottom') in order to maintain the capacity for scientific innovation and commercial production. However, some authors also argue and demonstrate empirically that stricter regulations, which are decided by important countries and implemented in attractive markets, may influence the subsequent adoption of similar (i.e. strict) policies by other countries. This is especially the case in countries which have strong economic interdependence with the first-mover country. For example, when the USA adopted strict energy efficiency standards for household appliances (in 1987), several provinces of Canada (i.e. Ontario in 1988, British Columbia in 1990 and Québec in 1991) and eventually the federal government of Canada (in 1992) followed the USA; they formulated new laws and regulations to require higher energy performance for household appliances in their own provincial and national markets. The aim was to avoid a situation in which US appliances with the worst energy efficiency were sold in Canada (as they could not be marketed anymore in the USA). Furthermore, these new Canadian norms aimed to encourage Canadian producers to invest in technological innovations and to compete on the US market (Varone and Aebischer, 2001). This phenomenon is often qualified as the 'California effect' (Vogel, 1995).

4. Finally, the broad term 'transnational communication' encompasses various mechanisms of lessons-drawing, learning and emulation across countries. According to Dolowitz and Marsh (2000, p. 5), such a transfer mechanism consists of a 'process by which knowledge about policies, administrative arrangements, institutions and ideas in one political system (past or present) is used in the development of policies, administrative arrangements, institutions and ideas in another political system' (see also Chapter 10).

It is always necessary, as emphasised by Howlett and Ramesh (2002), to analyse these mechanisms of internationalisation and their effect on domestic policies by observing how new actors, new ideas or new institutional venues influence the pre-existing network of policy makers. And how this differentiated empowering of various policy makers causes a modification of the goals, instruments and implementation settings of a domestic policy. Policies are not homeostatic systems that automatically adapt to changes in the international context. On the contrary, agency has to be demonstrated and the empirical analysis has to identify the group of actors that uses the new international events and/or rules to promote their own interests and ideas.

The Temporal Pattern Approach

Finally, the last perspective that can be combined in a compound research design is the *Temporal Pattern Approach (TPA)*. This approach involves policy scholars investigating the evolution of a public policy over time and trying to find out regularities about policy dynamics. Longitudinal policy studies have long been dominated by the incrementalism paradigm inspired by Lindblom's article *The Science of Muddling Through* (published in 1959 and then revised in 1979). The incrementalism concept rapidly gained prominence in the policy-making literature (see Rothmayr Allison and Saint-Martin, 2011, for an historical overview).

This analytical vision of policy making in general, and patterns of policy change in particular, insists on the following elements. Decision making is not rational-comprehensive in the sense that all possible policy options are systematically assessed. In the real world, decision makers have a bounded rationality (Simon, 1945) and the dichotomy between facts and values, or between ends and means, remains an illusion. Therefore, past and familiar (policy) experiences have a major impact on the subsequent design of new policy alternatives. Policy making proceeds thus mainly through sequences of (revised) trial-and-error. Last but not least, decision making always involves 'partisan mutual adjustment', negotiation and bargaining among policy stakeholders (Lindblom, 1965). Incremental policy changes have the major advantage of reducing the risks of major conflicts and political stalemate. In essence, Lindblom assumes that policy changes are basically marginal increments from the status quo. However, incrementalism can also result in more fundamental change, through a sequence of small but cumulative policy changes (applications of incrementalism are explored further in Chapters 9 and 10).

Then Hall (1989; 1993) and other scholars challenged the dominant incremental interpretation of policy changes. In doing so, Hall defined three orders or layers of policy changes. First order changes are the most frequent ones and relate to the modifications of the settings of policy instruments (e.g. the level of an environmental tax). Second order changes refer to situations when the policy goals remain the same, but the policy instruments implemented to attain them are revised (e.g. implementation of an environmental tax instead of the prohibition of polluting activities). Third order changes are the least frequent and entail the simultaneous modification of policy goals (e.g. preventing climate change instead of controlling sectoral pollution), policy instruments and settings of these instruments. Even if they represent distinct types of policy changes, each order is linked to the other hierarchically (Hall, 1993, p. 293). This also means that a policy may change at different rates, with frequent but *incremental* and small scale changes (i.e. first and second orders), and rarer but large-scale and *paradig-matic* changes (i.e. third order). Furthermore, Hall linked each change process and outcome to different causes and agents (ibid., pp. 287–8). First and second order changes correspond to 'social learning processes' in which policy experts, specialised interests and civil servants are the key actors. By contrast, a shift of the whole policy paradigm occurs beyond the narrow frontiers of the policy subsystem, and involves political parties, the media and the whole society. As mentioned above, such an interpretation of policy dynamics is similar to that of the Advocacy Coalition Framework which also insists on the influence of policy learning upon incremental changes and of external factors for major changes.

In addition, it is worth noting that, to some extent at least, the *Punctuated Equilibrium model* (Baumgartner and Jones, 1993; further explored in Chapter 9) also proposes a quite similar definition of policy changes and change processes. Policy dynamics are characterised by long periods of stability (i.e. equilibrium with minor changes) and periods of instability (i.e. policy punctuations) during which the 'monopoly of policy actors' within the subsystem, the dominant 'policy image' and the traditional 'institutional venue' are challenged, resulting in a major policy change.

Howlett and Migone (2011) argue that a new orthodoxy in the comparative studies of policy dynamics predominates. This post-incrementalist 'Temporal Pattern Approach' is based on four main propositions (Howlett and Cashore, 2014, pp. 26–7):

1. 'Any analysis of policy development must be historical in nature and cover periods of years or even decades or more' (ibid., p. 26). This methodological recommendation has been explicitly formulated within the Advocacy Coalition Framework (Sabatier and Jenkins-Smith, 1993). Of course, investigating a long period of time is an (implicit) precondition for policy scholars applying the Punctuated Equilibrium model (Baumgartner and Jones, 1993) and for historical institutionalism (Thelen and Steinmo, 1992; Pierson, 1993).

2. 'Political institutions and their embedded policy subsystems act as the primary mechanisms of policy reproduction' (Howlett and Cashore, 2014, p. 27).

3. However, 'paradigmatic change, a process in which there is a fundamental realignment of most aspects of policy development, is generally understood to occur rarely, and in the absence of such processes policy changes are expected to follow incremental patterns' (ibid.).

4. Finally, 'paradigmatic transformations or punctuations themselves usually occur due to the effect of external perturbations that cause widespread disruptions in existing policy ideas, beliefs, actors, institutions and practices rather than due to endogenous causes, although this is also possible through processes such as policy learning.' (ibid.).

All in all, longitudinal studies are required to assess the empirical validity of these theoretical hypotheses.

Following on this brief presentation of (a selection of) theories belonging to the national pattern approach (NPA), the policy sector approach (PSA), the international regimes approach (IRA) and the temporal pattern approach (TPA), the next section provides a purposive combination of all of these approaches.

Comparing the regulation of biotechnology in Europe and North America

The major aim of combining various theoretical approaches is to overcome the shortcomings inherent in each approach. In other words, what is needed is a comparative research design that increases the number and type of (potential) variables that explain policy processes and outputs. Some combinations are more evident and frequently applied than others. For example, a classical study on regulatory reforms by Vogel (1996) combines the national pattern approach with the policy sector approach: it compares the regulation of telecommunications and financial sector in Japan and the United Kingdom. In his seminal book on the post-war transformation of industrialised countries, Castles (1998) applies a very ambitious compound research design, by combining the temporal pattern approach, the policy sector approach and the national pattern approach. He compares the evolution over time (1960–90) of 12 policy areas and their related outcomes (e.g. social security, health and education expenditures, unemployment, home ownership and fertility) in 21 countries that – with the notable exception of Japan and Switzerland – are all categorised in four 'families of nations' (his variation of Esping-Andersen's regime model): the English-speaking family (the USA, the United Kingdom, Canada, etc.), the Nordic family (Denmark, Finland, Norway and Sweden), the Continental Western European family (France, Germany, Italy, etc.) and the Southern European family (Greece, Portugal and Spain).

Rather than attempting to generalise across different studies we will illustrate how a combination of approaches towards comparative research designs can be brought together to further policy process analysis by summarising conclusions from empirical studies focusing on the same policy issue: the regulation of biotechnology in Europe and North America. We summarise the major findings of empirical studies that one of the authors has conducted with several European and Canadian colleagues, and which have been published in an edited volume (Montpetit et al., 2007) and journal articles (Varone and Schiffino, 2004; Varone et al., 2006; Schiffino et al., 2009).

The recent scientific developments of biotechnology and their application in the environmental, agriculture and food sectors, and in veterinary and human medicine as well, have been vividly discussed in the media and have become a salient issue on the political agenda (Durant et al., 1998; Gaskell and Bauer, 2001; Bauer and Gaskell, 2002). Two policy issues in particular have attracted the attention of elected policy makers, private firms, public interest groups, political parties, scientific experts and public administrations: on the one hand, *genetically modified organisms in the agro-food sector (GMOs)* and, on the other hand, *Assisted Reproductive Technologies (ART)* such as *in-vitro* fertilisation, pre-implantation diagnostics, genetic screening and engineering, as well as research on embryos and stem cells, and therapeutic and reproductive cloning. Both biotechnology fields raise a number of economic, social and ethical questions in terms of expected benefits (e.g. higher productivity in agriculture, new therapies for degenerative diseases) and potential risks (e.g. genetic pollution, commoditisation of life), which have produced varying degrees of controversy during policy-making processes in Europe and North America.

As a matter of fact, most advanced democracies have passed national legislation in response to these debates on red (ART) and green (GMOs) biotechnology, and several supra- and international institutions have adopted their own norms as well. In 1997, the UNESCO adopted a 'Universal Declaration on the Human Genome and Human Rights' to balance the freedom of science in biomedicine and the human dignity. The Cartagena Protocol on Biosafety (2000) is an additional protocol to the UN Convention on Biosafety, which aims at balancing international trade and the protection on the environment (based on the precautionary principle). At the European level, also relevant are the 'Convention on Human Rights and Biomedicine' adopted by the Council of Europe and that came into force in 1999, and several Directives and Regulations on GMOs (since 1990) and ART (since 1998) decided by the European Union. Agriculture and food are also well-established topics of international (trade) debates. For instance, the World Trade Organization implements the 'Agreements on Technical Barriers to Trade' and the 'Agreement on the Application of Sanitary and Phytosanitary Measures' that are highly relevant for GMOs. The later Agreement is closely linked to the non-binding 'Codex Alimentarium' jointly managed by the World Health Organization and the UN Food and Agriculture Organization. In sum, various international regimes define more or less binding and competing norms that can be strategically activated by policy makers at the various levels of government.

Furthermore, the substantive contents of the biotechnology policies in force diverge significantly across countries. In the biomedical sector, Germany can be classified as having a restrictive regulation of ART (Embryo Protection Law, 1990), while the UK's regulation is permissive (Human and Embryo Fertilisation Act, 1990), and France can be regarded as an intermediate case (Laws on Bioethics and ART, 1994). In respect of the public regulation of GMO concerns, the USA have promoted a permissive policy while, in sharp contrast, Switzerland follows a very restrictive path: a popular initiative introducing a five-year moratorium on the use of genetically modified plants, seeds and animals in Swiss agriculture was accepted by the Swiss people in November 2005. In a nutshell, the public regulation of biotechnology represents a promising empirical field to investigate 'how' and 'why' governments pursue particular courses of action or inaction (Heidenheimer et al., 1990), and thus to contribute to the cumulative development of comparative policy analysis.

The policy variable to be explained is the regulatory content of biotechnology policies. Varone et al. (2007) have categorised the real world, complex situations within three ideal-types of substantive policy designs: a permissive biopolicy, an intermediate biopolicy and a restrictive biopolicy. These ideal-types are not found directly in reality, but they constitute a theoretical abstraction for coding and distinguishing the biopolicies implemented in various sectors and countries. According to Max Weber (1947), ideal-types of a social phenomenon (as for example the content of a public policy) are useful to distinguish between occurrences, which otherwise might be difficult to recognise in a complex reality.

The three ideal-types of design for ART policies are distinct with respect to how strongly they protect the embryo *in vitro* and to what extent they adhere to a traditional notion of the family defined by genetic kinship and civil status. With respect to ART, a country with a permissive ideal-type design would typically not limit research possibilities and allow for the creation of embryos for research purposes. Furthermore, the selection of embryos through pre-implantation diagnostics is permitted, embryo and gamete donation are not restricted, and access to ART treatment is not restricted by civil status and sexual orientation. The reverse ideal-type of biopolicy, the restrictive design, to the contrary, severely limits embryo research by prohibiting the derivation of stem-cells, therapeutic cloning, and all type of invasive research. This restrictive design is also likely to prohibit the selection of embryos *in vitro*, prohibit embryo and gamete donation, and limit the access to ART treatment to married and heterosexual couples with some exceptions on a case-to-case basis. The intermediate design limits research to leftover embryos. It ties genetic screening and gametes donation to specific requirements and allows only stable couples to have access to ART treatment.

The three ideal types of designs for GMOs in the agro-food sector vary with respect to how strongly the state intervenes into research, production, commercialisation and distribution and, hence, how strongly the state adheres to the protection of conventional or organic farming. In the permissive ideal-type, the deliberative release of GMOs for research and production, as well as the commercialisation of products containing GMOs (called 'novel-food' in EU communications), are generally allowed. The traceability and labelling of these products are not mandatory. The intermediate type of design requires authorisation on a case-to-case basis for releases, research and production, and for the commercialisation of novel-food. Traceability and labelling are mandatory in order to guarantee a choice between products from biotech-agriculture and conventional or organic farming. In the case of the restrictive type, the release, production, commercialisation and distribution of GMOs are *de jure* forbidden or *de facto* not taking place because the respective authorisations are regularly refused.

In summary, if a country adopts a permissive policy design in a biotechnology sector, then everything is allowed with some exceptions. On the contrary, a restrictive policy means that everything is forbidden, with some exceptions. Finally, several things are allowed under strict conditions under an intermediate policy design. If one applies these three ideal-types of policy designs to measures the biopolicies adopted around the mid-2000s by various European and North American Countries in the GMO and ART sectors, then we observe many divergences across sectors, countries and between Europe and North America (see Table 6.1).

Table 6.1 shows that five countries regulate both the ART and GMO sectors in a similar way (i.e. restrictive biopolicies in Switzerland and Germany, intermediate biopolicies in France and the Netherlands, permissive biopolicies in the United States of America). This first empirical finding could be compatible with the 'national policy style' hypothesis presented above (see Richardson, 1982; Bovens et al., 2001). However, four countries from the empirical sample seem not to be 'consistent' across biotechnology sectors (i.e. Canada, Belgium, Sweden and the United Kingdom): for instance, the United Kingdom is restrictive on GMOs and, at the same time, permissive on ART. This second empirical evidence offers support for the 'policy sector style' hypothesis formulated by Freeman (1985). Furthermore, an Atlantic divide apparently exists in the public regulation of GMOs: the United States of America and Canada adopted a permissive policy, while all European countries follow a more interventionist path. This could be potentially explained by EU binding decisions, and thus provides support for the 'International Regime' approach. Nevertheless, this hypothesis is of little use for explaining the differences between EU countries (i.e. restrictive GMO policy in Germany, Sweden and the United Kingdom versus intermediate policy in Belgium, France and the Netherlands). In addition, the international regime approach hypothesis is not verified at all for the ART sector, as there are no systematic differences between North American and European countries. In one word, the different variables and hypotheses proposed by the national pattern approach, the policy sector approach, the international

Table 6.1 Biotechnology policies in nine countries and two sectors (as in 2005)

		Assisted Reproductive Technology (ART)		
		Restrictive Policy	Intermediate Policy	Permissive policy
Agri-food Genetic Engineering (GMOs)	Restrictive policy	Germany Switzerland (consistent cases)	Sweden	United Kingdom
	Intermediate policy		France The Netherlands (consistent cases)	Belgium
	Permissive policy		Canada	United States of America (consistent cases)

Source: Adaptation from Montpetit et al., 2007, p. 267.

regime approach and the temporal pattern approach need to be combined to explain (the variances) between all observed cases.

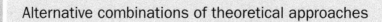

Alternative combinations of theoretical approaches

For illustrative purposes, we present in this section four empirical applications of alternative comparative research designs.

'One sector in many countries' design

Varone et al. (2006) compare the policy design processes and the resulting outputs of ART-policies implemented by eleven countries (adding Italy, Norway and Spain to the sample presented above, but not considering Sweden). Their theoretical framework is inspired by the 'actor-centred institutionalism' as developed by Scharpf (1997). It focuses on the policy preferences of key actors (e.g. political parties, medical physicians and researchers, religious groups and patients associations) and the institutional rules influencing the game theses actors concretely play. The authors look, on the one hand, at the number of policy-making arenas where ART-regulation is actually elaborated (divided powers or unitary states?) and, on the other hand, at the type of decision-making rules (lax rules for power-sharing or tight majority rule?). Both institutional dimensions are strongly inspired by the seminal typology of Lijphart (1999) that was discussed above. The main conclusion of this empirical study is that both policy preferences and institutional rules need to be considered conjointly. The conventional classification of democracies is of no help to explain why three ideal-typical 'consensus democracies' adopted radically different policies (i.e. permissive ART policy in Belgium, intermediate ART policy in the Netherlands and restrictive ART policy in Switzerland). In other words, the institutional 'frame of the game' (i.e. polity) does not have a greater influence than the policy positions advocated by key players. Party politics, self-regulation by physicians and the mobilisation of opponents to ART are crucial variables to explain the decision-making process and the final policy outputs. For instance, a strong polarisation between the most resourceful actors (such as the medical profession or the governmental parties) translates into a policy-making process that is labelled as 'designing by non-decisions' and leads to a permissive ART policy (e.g. in Belgium or Italy). By contrast, the 'designing by elites' process characterises a situation where the beliefs and interests of the major actors are congruent, and where few institutional venues are eventually mobilised (e.g. in France or Spain). All in all, this study suggests that to capture adequately the policy-making process and outputs, institutions- and actors-based variables need to be combined, beyond the conventional typologies of countries or institutional rules proposed by the national pattern approach. This finding also supports our claim (see Chapter 2) that both 'structure' and 'agency' need to be balanced in policy process studies.

'Two sectors in one country' design

The second research design compares how Belgium regulates the ART sector versus the GMO (Varone and Schiffino, 2004). Belgium is a very interesting case to investigate for two reasons. First, the country is a pioneer in both ART and GMO innovation. The scientific community attributes the development of the Intra-Cytoplasmic Sperm Injection (i.e. a new technique for *in-vitro* fertilisation first developed experimentally in 1992) to the Vrije Universiteit Brussels, and the first genetically modified plant to the University of Gent in 1983. This pioneering status in the development of red and green biotechnology could lead one to expect that there is a convergence of their respective biopolicies. Yet this is absolutely not the case. The regulation of ART is among the most permissive in the world, and Belgium is often described as a 'bioethical paradise' for medical physicians and researchers. On the contrary, the more interventionist regulation of GMOs imposes numerous conditions on the contained use and deliberate release of GMOs, as well as on the labelling of (food containing) GMOs. How can we explain that the same country adopted two different types of regulation for new biotechnologies? After conducting two in-depth case-studies in the ART and GMO sectors, and after realising a formal analysis of two actors' networks, the authors concluded that the structuring of the policy actors, at the sector level, lies at the heart of the explanation. The two policy networks in the ART and GMO sectors are located at the opposing ends of the continuum discussed in Chapter 4 (see Table 4.1). On one hand, the ART-network looks very much like a 'policy community' with a limited number of (nine very influential) actors, who all represent the interests of medical physicians and researchers, who have frequent and consensual interactions, and who share a common expertise. On the other hand, the GMO-network corresponds to an 'issue network' with a large number of actors, who are very diverse in nature (i.e. private firms, environmentalist groups, consumer associations, scientific researchers, political entrepreneurs from the green parties and administrative agencies), who represent a broad range of competing interests, and who have only sporadic and mostly conflictual contacts.

As rightly argued by Dowding (1995), one cannot conclude that various types of actors' network lead automatically to various policy-making processes and outputs, because 'the explanation lies in the characteristics of the actors' (ibid., 1995, p. 142). In the ART sector, the dominant actors were the medical physicians, who engaged in cooperative search for solution and eventually proposed (permissive) self-regulation. Such a problem-solving strategy (Scharpf, 1997) solution was not possible in the GMO sector. The private firms (e.g. Bayers crop science, Monsanto) and the sector-wide business associations (e.g. Europabio) were not able to self-organise; furthermore, they faced a strong mobilisation of environmental (e.g. Greenpeace, Nature & Progrès) and consumers groups (e.g. Test-Achat). The state agencies and elected politicians then played the role of a referee between two 'advocacy coalitions' and they finally adopted an intermediate regulation. As already underlined by the previous study on ART policies in eleven countries, agency seems to be the key explanatory factor, beyond institutions and structures.

'Two countries over time' design

The next empirical study briefly summarised here (Schiffino et al., 2009) also highlights the decisive impact of policy actors (political parties in this case) on the policy process and outputs. It applies the temporal pattern approach in combination with the national patterns approach. Concretely, the research design compares the evolution of ART-policies over more than three decades in Italy and Belgium. These two countries were consociational 'partitocracies'. We mean by this that party leaders were the key actors in the policy-making process and were present in all institutional arenas, such as the Parliament, the Government, the administration and the judiciary; decision making was closed, elite-steered and top-down, with a strong influence of Christian Democratic parties and/or the Catholic Church (see De Winter et al., 1996). In addition, both countries shared in common the fact that their respective ART sector was advanced in terms of technology, and were almost not regulated in the 1980s. At that time, Belgium was depicted as a 'bioethical paradise', while Italy was internationally labelled as the 'far west' of ART. Two common factors explain the reluctance to adopt a comprehensive and restrictive regulation in the 1980s. First, the polarised political party system, the fragile governmental coalitions and the internally divided parties made it difficult to adopt a coherent policy design. In particular, the cleavage between Catholicism and secularism tended to cut across right-left divisions and rendered thus compromise between parties difficult if not impossible. Second, the medical community engaged in a proactive self-regulation to pre-empt any state intervention. All in all, very few and mostly permissive regulations had been implemented in both countries in the 1980s.

However, the picture changed dramatically during the next decades and the policy path followed by Italy and Belgium in the 2000s started to diverge greatly. In Belgium, a new secular coalition (i.e. without the Christian Democrats) was in power in 1999–2007 and passed new ART legislations in 2003 and 2007 to reinforce the permissiveness of the ART policy. This development corresponded to a minor or *incremental* policy change. In sharp contrast, we observe a major policy change or *punctuation* in Italy after 2001. The new centre-right dominated legislature and government eventually adopted in 2004 a law prohibiting ART with donated gametes and research on embryos. This very restrictive law reflected the point of view of the Catholic Church, whose lobby efforts towards elected officials were highly influential. Medical physicians and other advocates of a permissive ART policy tried to launch an abrogative referendum against the 2004 law. However, they were unsuccessful and could not overturn the major policy change. In a nutshell, Schiffino et al. (2009) conclude that the policy punctuation of the Italian ART policy confirms the logic of the punctuated equilibrium model (Baumgartner and Jones, 1993; see also Chapter 9): a major policy change was possible as a new policy image (i.e. protection of the human embryo and defence of the traditional family) was promoted by a strong policy entrepreneur (i.e. the Catholic Church) in a new policy venue (i.e. homogenous coalition of centre-right parties). By contrast, we do not observe a major transformation of the policy image (i.e. freedom of research) in Belgium that could have led to a paradigmatic change. Comparing two countries over time was thus a good comparative strategy to assess how cognitive factors, policy actors and institutional venues conjointly influence the policy process and content.

'Two sectors in many countries and across international regimes' design

Last but not least, the study by Montpetit et al. (2007) compares the regulation of GMOs and ART in six member states of the European Union (France, Great Britain, Germany, the Netherlands, Sweden and Belgium), two North-American countries (USA and Canada), and one European but non-EU-member state (Switzerland). The study aims at identifying the differences and commonalities for these eighteen sector- and country-specific biotechnology policies (see Table 6.1 above). Such an ambitious design allows for the cumulative test of the national pattern approach (nine countries), the policy sector approach (two sectors) and the international regime approach (European Union versus non-European Union). Of course, the methodological challenges of comparing eighteen cases are rather complex. Therefore, the authors apply the Qualitative Comparative Analysis (QCA) tools developed by Ragin (1987) to identify patterns of 'multiple conjunctural causations'. The empirical findings of this QCA reveal that countries with restrictive policies share three explanatory factors. Restrictive biotechnology policies in the ART and the GMO sectors were adopted where opponents and actors concerned with biotechnology joined efforts in an 'issue network' (i.e. Policy Sector Approach), where administrative preferences matched the preferences of groups opposing or concerned about biotechnology (e.g. Ministry of Environment for GMOs, Ministry of Justice for ART) and where governance was not concentrated (i.e. National Pattern Approach). In the case of GMOs, the use of international rules (mainly EU regulations) by opponents to biotechnology also contributed to the restrictive output (International Regime Approach). At the same time, the presence of a conservative government, or control of key ministerial positions by parties with restrictive preferences (e.g. Green for GMOs, Christian Democrats for ART), is not an essential condition for adopting restrictive policies.

These findings are partly consistent with existing analyses of biotechnology policy development presented above or in the previous literature. Toke and Marsh (2003) also argue that issue networks and administrative preferences can contribute to increasing the restrictiveness of biotechnology policy (see also Box 4.3). Bernauer and Meins' (2003) institutional analysis suggesting that multiple access points to policy makers help actors pressing for policy restrictions also find echo in the finding that concentrated governance prevents the adoption of restrictive biotechnology policies. Likewise, Young's (2003) argument that international rules contribute to increased restrictiveness, an argument that appears counterintuitive in light of the globalisation discourse, matches the observations of Montpetit et al. (2007) in the GMO area. In fact, as Vogel (2004) argues, we can observe a shift in EU regulatory policies on food safety over the last decades towards the application of the precautionary principle and risk adverse policies. In sum, Montpetit et al. (2007) note that to fully capture the complex policy-making process, comparative policy studies should draw their explanatory variables from several complementary theoretical perspectives such as the four we have used here. To do so, one could increase the number of policy sectors, countries, international regimes and time periods compared in the empirical study. Such a research strategy is probably ideal; but it soon reaches its limits and, in most situations, is simply not feasible due to resources constraints. Therefore, the proponents of a compound research design suggest implementing an iterative strategy in the selection of empirical cases.

Iterative strategy

As argued at the beginning of this chapter, comparative policy studies require flexible approaches not limited by classical statistical techniques. A stepwise comparative and inferential process constitutes the crucial element for a compound research design. According to Levi-Faur (2006b), there is a need to adopt a 'Sherlock Holmesian style of inference' (ibid., p. 60). The main idea underlying such an iterative strategy is quite simple: the investigator asks the same research question again and again, repeats the empirical tests of theoretical hypotheses, and examines the internal and external validity against different kinds of empirical cases. This can be done by engaging in successive pairwise comparisons.

Concretely, if we take into account the four levels of comparisons presented above (i.e. policy sectors, national patterns, international regimes and temporal era), it makes sense to initially select cases which vary on at least two of the four levels, and to test causal hypotheses across these levels. The iteration proceeds in two steps. In the first step, the researcher increases the number of (most similar) primary cases to improve the internal validity or accuracy of the causal analyses. The second step focuses then on the external validity or (moderate) generalisability of the empirical findings across the (most different) cases. The causal relations that were found to be valid during the first step are examined once again in secondary or even tertiary cases. Levi-Faur (2006b, p. 64) provides a brief example of how this heuristic of stepwise comparison works in a study starting with two sectors and two countries. During the first step,

> both sectors and nations are selected according to the 'most similar system design' principle of minimising variations in the control variables across the cases. The number of sectoral cases is four and the number of national cases is two. One can compare the two countries; then one can compare the two sectors in the same country, move to the same two sectors in the other country, continue with a comparison of the same sector in the two

countries, and finally compare the second sector in the two countries. One can move farther still, and add a temporal dimension to the analysis to compare sectors and nations before and after a critical event or a turning point. This can be done at the level of the sector or the nation as well as the international; for example the creation of a new regime and the formalisation of new international commitments. Indeed, the number of possible pairwise comparisons is given by the formula n (n-1)/2, where *n* is the number of cases in the study. Thus, for four sectoral cases the maximum number of pairwise comparisons is six {[4(4-1)]/2}. If one distinguishes between old and new regimes in each of the sectors the number of cases doubles to eight, and the number of possible pairwise comparisons reaches 21. Only a small number of these possible comparative pairs might be used, but whatever the number the aim at this stage is to increase internal validity.

(Levi-Faur 2006b, p. 64)

During the second step of the iteration,

the argument or the relations between variables or aspects of the cases that were established in the first stage are then examined against most different cases, so case selection in this case involves an increase in the type of sectors and the countries. . . . The analysis at this stage . . . examines the robustness of the relations that were defined in the first stage; the aim is to explain system-level variations, thereby to determine if the relations are determined by national or sectoral characteristics.

(Ibid.)

Such an iterative inferential process has many advantages for comparative policy studies (ibid., pp. 64–5). First, the research design is very explicit and very transparent, and allows thus for constructive criticism and cumulative knowledge development. Second, it offers a good guidance for the (gradual) development of a research design. The initial selection of primary cases and the increases of the cases (secondary or tertiary cases) are clearly controlled. A clever cases' selection improves the validity of the empirical findings, and helps thus to reduce the number of cases needed for a strong comparative research. Finally, the iterative strategy might also help in better balancing the (to some extent) conflicting requirements of internal versus external validity.

CONCLUSIONS

This chapter first explored four approaches to the comparative study of the policy process all influenced by institutional theory (see Chapter 5). These

(*continued*)

approaches, described in the work of Levi-Faur (2004; 2006a; 2006b) are the National Pattern Approach, the Policy Sector Approach, the International Regime Approach and the Temporal Pattern Approach. All have been used in comparative studies. While they seem to offer competing hypotheses they are not always mutually exclusive. On the contrary, it is argued that they need to be combined in any effort to enhance the understanding of the policy process through comparative studies.

Ways of effecting this combination are explored through the use of material from comparative studies of policy developments with respect to two fields of bio-technology: assisted reproductive technology and genetically modified organisms in the agro-food sector. It is shown that no single approach offers a satisfactory explanation of the various quite marked differences between countries in policy development in these areas. Insights may be gained however by mixing the approaches used. But even this is not straightforward. It is then argued that the best results are achieved through an iterative strategy repeating the empirical tests of the various hypotheses. This is an invitation for policy scholars to work like Sherlock Holmes and to hope that (the art of conducting) successive investigations will help to solve the puzzle.

7 Integrating theoretical approaches

SYNOPSIS

This short chapter revisits the simple representation of the main approaches to the description of the policy process provided in Table 2.1 and suggests ways that they may be updated on the basis of the developments in theory set out previously in Chapters 2–6. This includes observations on ways in which they may, to some extent, be integrated with each other. This discussion introduces some of the key themes to be explored further in the rest of the book.

Introduction

Earlier chapters have reviewed a wide range of theoretical approaches to the public policy process, pointing out the strengths and weaknesses of each (Chapters 2–6). Where does that leave readers? Should they just make their own choices bearing in mind these points but guided by their own ideological predispositions? The answer is 'yes, up to a point'.

However, it is important to recognise that what has been described is a succession of ideas developed over a long period of time, in the course of which some degree of consensus has developed about which are most helpful for our understanding of the policy process and which are less so. In the rest of the book connections will be made back to these theories, highlighting their usefulness where applicable. This book does not reject altogether the social-scientific search for truth, at least in the form of the view that some explanations are better than others. So it is reasonable to expect us to 'get off the fence' and indicate our views of the validity of various perspectives.

Contrasting perspectives on the policy process revisited

In Chapter 2 a simple table (Table 2.1) was presented to sum up the key dimensions along which accounts of the policy process differ. Two dimensions were used: about the distribution of power and about the extent to which it is structured. In respect of both of these dimensions there has been convergence. A revised version of that figure is inserted here identifying the key aspects of this. The optimistic pluralism of the early work of Dahl and his followers (cell 2 of Figure 7.1) has been succeeded by a recognition of the salience of power inequalities (Chapter 2). There are disagreements about how much these matter, but rather less about their existence. Chapter 3 seems to offer the development of pluralist thinking, since rational choice theory is concerned with the impact of interests upon policy making. However, as was observed at the end of the chapter, quoting Hay, the aspiration of rational choice theorists to develop a predictive theory in which self-interest is central tends to give this approach a determinist emphasis very different to pluralist theory.

Otherwise, in many respects, differences are matters of emphasis, about the relative openness of decision-making systems. The original pluralist analysis has been enhanced by the recognition that interests may be aggregated in various ways, through the formation of networks and policy communities or even through incorporation into government (Chapter 4). It is interesting to note that in some of the more optimistic forms of corporatist theory this is seen, as in the original pluralism, as rescuing democracy by facilitating the organisation of countervailing power (as for example in trade unions). But then, conversely, the formation of policy communities is seen as ensuring secure control over policy by vested interests. Significantly if we turn then to the story in respect of structuration we find that the determinism of much early theory – particularly Marxist theory – has been discarded.

Figure 7.1   The simplified approach (see Table 2.1) reformulated

1. The institutions of government are important, but must be regarded with scepticism. The discourses and ideologies that surround them may be more important than their formal characteristics.	2. There is extensive competition between groups to influence government and this is likely to be organised in networks in which the interests of those inside government will be involved as well as those outside.
3. Power is distributed unequally both inside and outside government, having an impact as much upon what is on the agenda and the context in which decisions are taken as on the decision process itself.	4. There is a great deal of confusion and incoherence in the policy process, but nevertheless we can identify choices made by actors, who are influenced by ideas and may be able to learn from earlier events and choices.

But we then have instead a variety of approaches which argue that aspects of structure have a strong, but not necessarily, determining impact upon policy choice. Attention was paid to various versions of this point of view. In particular, globalist theory suggests problematical implications for explanations of the policy process which rest heavily on being able to identify the governments of nation states as autonomous actors. Clearly in the analysis of many policy-making situations propositions are encountered in which the decision takers are argued to have no alternative. It is this sense that we explore briefly in the next section the extent to which it may be possible to speak of a 'post-pluralist settlement'.

A post-pluralist settlement?

Is there now a consensus around what might be called a post-pluralist settlement? While this may be seen a particular preoccupation of those who seek radical social change, and therefore a topic that takes us beyond the examination of the policy process, it merits some attention inasmuch as it suggests limits to policy innovation.

The pluralist perspective theorising was associated with the notion that there was a general political accommodation around notions of a positive state, broadly supported by both sides of industry. This occurred across the thirty years or so after the Second World War when it was suggested that there was a relative consensus around Keynesian economic policies and welfare state oriented social policy. This was seen as a response to the crisis of capitalism in the inter-war period. Gamble's summary (echoing arguments developed by Karl Polanyi, 1944) sums up the way this development was perceived:

> Setting economic activity free had led to huge inequalities and suffering in society, and in time had produced strong political reaction. Social movements on both right and left arose to demand greater security, the imposition of minimum levels of income and welfare, and the control of the capitalist business cycle. Gradually the new collectivism won through, imposing new priorities on the enormously powerful capitalist economy, setting out new priorities and taming the market.
>
> (Gamble, 2009, p. 52)

The critique of pluralism indicated that these views of the shift of power were exaggerated, but what then made that critique more pertinent was the evidence of the way in which it was reversed after the 1970s. A vast literature has emerged exploring this, showing how capitalist dominance was re-established. The explanation of the change may be partly attributable to the emergence of increasing difficulties with Keynesian approaches to the management of the economy, but there is little doubt that there was a great ideational shift in which free market philosophies that had been given little attention in the heyday of Keynesianism became dominant again. This has been seen as a 'paradigm shift' in dominant ideas on economic policy (Hall, 1986, as explored in Chapter 5).

In respect of the United States, Hacker and Pierson have noted how strongly business is now able to influence the behaviour of both political parties. A potential countervailing force (see Galbraith, 1963) in mid-twentieth-century America, the trade union movement, has been seriously weakened. Large powerful businesses are the paymasters of the parties and dominate the agenda, nearly as much in the Democratic Party as in the Republican one (Hacker and Pierson, 2010). Generalising beyond the United States, Crouch observes how analyses of state/market relationships today need to take account of powerful 'firms', often multi-national in character:

> From the perspective of pluralist political theory, firms constitute 'lobbies' . . . But the role of today's global giants cannot be subsumed under the concept of lobbying . . . . [they] are not in the lobby, outside the real decision-making space of government at all. They are right inside the room of political decision-making. They set standards, establish private regulatory systems, act as consultants to government, even have staff seconded to ministers' offices'.
>
> (Crouch, 2011, p. 131)

While it remains difficult to explain how so substantial a shift in economic power has occurred, the evidence that its consequences have been massive increases in inequality, particularly in the United States and the United Kingdom, has been so strong that it has stimulated expressions of concern about it from some quite unlikely sources (note for example work by Fukuyama, 2011 and 2014, cited in Chapter 2). Inequality has become one of the most salient topics in many advanced democracies (Atkinson, 2015). Christine Lagarde, Managing Director of the International Monetary Fund, argued in a speech in May 2014:

> One of the leading economic stories of our time is rising income inequality, and the dark shadow it casts across the global economy. The facts are familiar. Since 1980, the richest 1 percent increased their share of income in 24 out of 26 countries for which we have data. In the US, the share of income taken home by the top one percent more than doubled since the 1980s, returning to where it was on the eve of the Great Depression. In the UK, France, and Germany, the share of private capital in national income is now back to levels last seen almost a century ago. With facts like these, it is no wonder that rising inequality has risen to the top of the agenda—not only among groups normally focused on social justice, but also increasingly among politicians, central bankers, and business leaders.
>
> (IMF handout)

Amongst Lagarde's sources there would seem to be Thomas Piketty's book *Capital* (2014). His analysis of trends since the nineteenth century in income and capital distribution in France, the United States and the United Kingdom shows that inequalities only diminished significantly in the periods of very high taxation around and after the two World Wars (particularly the latter) and there is now a very strong trend towards increased inequalities in both incomes and assets. Moreover he shows that periods of low growth such as at present tend to generate substantial increases in assets relative to incomes.

The particular point about highlighting these issues here is to ask is there in fact a new pluralist 'settlement' that is inherently unequal? And: is this inevitable? The evidence suggests scope for a massive egalitarian political movement, yet in most respects the policy process examined in this book is the politics of the status quo. Piketty has been hailed by some as the 'new Marx', but his analysis does not come reinforced by a theory about the destabilising impact of the trend he has observed.

Streeck (2014) offers an argument here, which does owe much to Marxist theory, that – with the acceptance of the imperatives of the needs of capitalist development (embodied in the triumph of the Hayekian view of the importance of minimal state intervention if economic growth is required) – capitalism and democracy are becoming incompatible. Is this a structuralist view or a plea for states to return to the interventionalist stances of the immediate post–Second Word War period? The structuralism lies in pessimism about its possibility. That pessimism is reinforced by considerations about global developments. That may be the case, but it depends upon political movements taking action.

Is there an implicit determinist logic here? Do the circumstances supporting the existing order come together so strongly that they might just as well be seen as deterministic? Those advocating change, in particular democratic socialists, are inhibited by four considerations.

First, while the socialism that failed in the Soviet empire was in no way democratic socialism what it left behind was a fear that too strong a challenge to pluralism leads to autocracy. In that respect the new Right, drawing also on evidence of inefficiency in state run enterprises, has been able to trump the case for more equality by suggestions of threats to liberty.

Second, there is a fear of 'killing the goose that lays the golden egg'. Social democrats (note for example a classic British text by Anthony Crosland, 1956) have laid great stress on the notion that redistribution can be most easily achieved when there are increments of economic growth to distribute. They are fearful of being labelled 'tax and spend' parties. Securing economic growth has become an obsession. Moreover this obsession often pays little attention to whether some forms of growth will bring little social benefit. If then, as economic analyses like Piketty's suggest, low growth is inevitable little can be done.

Third, the problems about low growth in advanced capitalist countries are consequent upon global economic changes in which countries in the hitherto disadvantaged parts of the world (particularly of course China) are increasingly important producers and engines of worldwide growth.

Fourth, there is simply a lack of support for democratic change. Political parties read the opinion evidence very carefully, and are led by it into advocacy of minor adjustments around the status quo (appealing to the median voter – see Chapter 3). Low political participation by the disadvantaged reinforces this. Moreover note again the points made above about trade union decline and the influence of money and the media on politics.

Limitations of generalisations about the 'settlement'

A great deal of the most compelling evidence for what we have described as a post-pluralist settlement comes from the United States and the United Kingdom. These have been seen as quintessential liberal 'market economies' by theorists who have identified 'varieties of capitalism' (Hall and Soskice, 2001). On the other hand, the evidence so far on the impact of the 2008 economic crisis suggests that then a market crisis did not lead to a reconsideration of the balance of power. From the neo-Marxist perspective the crisis seemed briefly to offer opportunities for change. Yet instead states rushed to the defence of markets. A market crisis was seen – certainly in the European Union countries – as requiring a combination of state support for banks and new austerities for the public sector.

In the discussion of the evolution of institutionalist theory in Chapter 5 issues about ideas and ideologies were raised, suggesting it is important to recognise a distinction between choices that are heavily constrained, by situations and particularly by the power of others, and choices that can literally be said to be pre-determined. However, the discussion (in Chapter 6) of comparative work on the policy process considers further the case for recognising that variation in politics 'matters', providing warnings against transforming generalisation about shared trends into determinist statements. If changing ideas were crucial for the paradigm shift from Keynesianism to the new Right then maybe currently expressed anxieties about market power and consequent inequalities are the harbingers of new ideological changes.

Institutional theory and comparative work highlighting policy choice

While the notion of 'the post-positivist settlement' may overstate the case, the perspective of this book involves a bringing together of issues about structuration and inequalities, as particularly identified in cell 3 of Figure 7.1. The policy process is seen as certainly very different from the naïve propositions emphasising 'representative government' (cell 1 in the original Table 2.1), yet not as an open process as presumed by the American pluralists of the 1950s (cell 2 in that chart).

Institutional theory observes policy making as taking place in an institutional context which tends to structure choice. The image of pathways is useful here, after all literally speaking we often follow pathways whilst still having some capacity to diverge from them when we think they are taking us the wrong way. The concept of paradigm shift is useful here in relation to the identification of situations in which such divergence is likely to occur.

The distinction between the new cells 3 and 4 is then important: just how important are choices, and to what extent are they based on sophisticated analysis of the issues at stake. As noted in the use of the concept of the 'garbage can' by Cohen, March and Olsen (1972) – it is recognised that at times policy processes can be seen as incoherent and perhaps impossible to explain (cell 4 of Figure 7.1). In the same way it is appropriate to note how many accounts of policy processes by politicians and journalists stress individual choice and the personalities of key actors. But to focus on regularities within the policy process, as is the case with most other perspectives, is not to deny these influences but rather to stress – as is needed for the systematic study of social processes – regularities and factors about which generalisation may be possible.

In various places there has been an emphasis on policy choice. It is, as noted above, relevant for the rejection of the more structurally determinist positions, embedded in some theoretical propositions. A view that there is both a measure of chaos and elements of choice in the policy system does not contradict the emphasis on power. The chaos benefits some more than others (particularly the defenders of the status quo), and some actors have more opportunities to choose or to influence choice than others.

There is a potential contradiction between emphasising the factors that contribute to stability in the system and emphasising the uncertainties and points at which choice is fundamental. But this is no more than a version of the difficulties involved in reconciling the evidence of stability and the evidence of change that lie at the heart of social science discourse (we will return to the question of policy stability versus policy change in Chapter 9 when presenting the Punctuated Equilibrium model). Under the influence of the sociologist Giddens, perhaps the most popular contemporary exploration of this uses the terms 'structure' and 'agency' (as discussed in Chapter 2). Hence the issues about relating these two are well expressed by Farnsworth (2007, p. 100), with particular reference to pluralist theory, as follows:

> The biggest shift made by pluralists, in accepting the privileged interest thesis, was their recognition of the importance of structural power to business influence on policy outcomes. Structural power (the power to influence without taking direct action) is derived from the ownership and control of capital and the uneven dependence of states and employees on capitalists. Agency power, upon which most analysis of business power tends to focus, is exercised through the actions of individual business people, firms or business associations (which themselves organise at different levels). The problem with focusing purely on agency, as classical pluralists found, is that it underplays the importance of political and

economic structures, which favour some interests above others, determine the nature and extent of agency engagement and shape the expressed views and opinions of actors.

(p. 100)

We may speak here of 'vested interests', using a concept of analytical value to understand the dynamics between stability and change, and the inter-actions between institutions and actors, or between structure and agency. Terry M. Moe (2015) argues that each institution, being a formal structure of the state or a concrete policy programme, generates inevitably social groups receiving (material, direct and concentrated) benefits. For example, pharma-ceutical firms have vested interests in the national health care system, as their research activities, economic growth and financial benefits will depend upon the reimbursement scheme for drugs that is implemented by the State. Beyond these private business actors (which are perceived as the usual suspects), various patients groups will also have vested interests, as they directly benefit from specific health services (e.g. senior citizens, low-income families). Even public employees working in public hospital or agencies deliv-ering health care have vested interests: the implemented health policy provides them a job, an income and a professional career. While these various actors reap very different benefits for the same institution, they share in common very strong incentives to protect 'their' institution (stability), to support only marginal change to the status quo, and to oppose any major reform. Furthermore, Moe (2015) argues that vested interests will even support institutions that perform badly: *'(A)ll institutions contain the seed of their own stability.* They all generate vested interests, and they all stand to be protected and stabilized by whatever power the vested interests can bring to bear in politics when major reform becomes a threat' (Moe, 2015, p. 293). In sum, vested interests are a universal phenomenon that can be found in all countries, in all policy areas and in all historical periods. Nevertheless, most theories of the policy process presented in Chapters 2–6 rarely stress this 'vested' aspect. This is particularly true for the institutional theories, which face major challenges in explaining the impact of institutional factors on policy process and outputs. Institutional scholars should thus focus on 'vested interests' as these precisely arise from the institutions whose stability, change and influence on policy process they want to explain.

The propositions explored here have tended to concentrate on influences from within the nation state. But there is a need not to forget the complexity of modern *governance*. This means that the institutions of government may be international, that groups may be organised outside and across individual states, that issues about inequalities of power need to be analysed globally, and that choices are made by actors who are increasingly conscious that they are playing on an international stage (see Chapter 14).

The ideas summarised here will be kept in mind during the discussion in the rest of this book. There are various shades of difference of emphasis between writers on our subject. It will also be the case that there are differ-ences between countries, or between different points in time in the same country, or even between different policy areas, in the extent to which each of the points is relevant. Power may be more unequal, or institutional constraints may be greater, or networks may be more important, or decision processes may be more coherent, in some places or situations than in others. In this sense readers may find it helpful to explore issues by contrasting the strengths and weaknesses of different perspectives along the lines mentioned previously (Chapter 1), where reference was made to Allison's use of contrasting lenses (see also Box 8.2). But in Chapter 6 we suggest it is possible to go further than that. Chapter 6 observes how efforts have been made to test theories, of the kind explored in Chapters 2 to 5. In doing so it suggests that rather than treating theories as simply opposing interpretations of reality it may be possible to combine them. This is the way in which it becomes possible to move from the simple oppositions noted in Table 2.1 to the more complex ones set out in Figure 7.1.

The goal then is obviously to move towards better theories. But as noted in Chapter 1, ours is a subject in which making the sort of progress embodied in the scientific model provided by the physical sciences is very difficult. Chapter 3 explored and criticised approaches to this subject which have endeavoured to build theory using deductive approaches. Howlett and Ramesh appropriately warn us that 'many deductive-oriented researchers often seem to forget the contingent nature of their hypotheses and the need to constantly test and refine their assumptions against empirical evidence' (2003, pp. 46–7). But in contrasting deduction with induction we do not argue for an approach to the explanation of events that makes no effort to build on efforts to theorise, wherever these come from. In Chapter 3 a model of 'iterative induction' was introduced, and that same notion of iteration is given further attention in Chapter 6.

However, there is much to be done to further advance our subject. The stance taken here, accepting the undesirability of imposing an assumed model of the physical sciences on the study of public policy and acknowledging the very tentative nature of most generalisations on offer, means that a very pragmatic perspective will be a key influence on the discussion that follows. In an effort to provide as balanced an account of the policy process as we can, we are inevitably influenced by ideas and approaches that we find plausible.

In using the 'catalogue' of explanations on offer different analyses are likely to apply to different issues. In Chapter 1 definitions of policy were explored and a contrast drawn between very general ones (policies as stances) and much more specific ones (policies as interrelated decisions). That obviously influences the specific policy analyses. A second influence concerns the extent to which the policy process is a contested one. There may be virtual consensus about a new policy, in which case translating it into action may be little more than a quest for the best way of fitting it into an existing institutional framework (Box 1 in Figure 7.1). Beyond that we may draw a contrast between what is contested territory in a very narrow, comparatively uncontroversial sense (even with scope for what seems to be an amicable compromise between interests) and one of the core areas of conflict in contemporary politics.

However, regardless of the policy issue the examination of the policy process involves:

- issues about how matters get on the agenda;
- issues about their progress once on the agenda;
- issues about implementation;
- issues about how accountability for outputs and outcomes work in practice.

The rest of this book looks as these issues; the theories explored in this section offer a variety of overall approaches to their examination.

Part 2

Analysis of the policy process

8 Policy and politics

SYNOPSIS

While it is obvious that studying the policy process means investigating the making of policy, we noted in Chapter 1 that policy is by no means a simple phenomenon. Furthermore, since different policies have substantive contents it must be expected that policy will be made manifest in many different ways and will affect various categories of actors. This chapter presents three approaches to handling this problem: the first uses policy typologies; the second distinguishes between the winners and losers from policy initiatives; and the third divides the policy cycle into discrete stages.

The first approach starts with an exploration of the characteristics of various policy issues and a brief discussion of Lowi's (1972) policy typology and Matland's (1995) emphasis upon the need to relate policy ambiguity and policy conflict. This shows how Lowi's contribution puts the emphasis on the need to explore the relationship between policy issues and politics.

The second approach takes up the commonplace but important observations that politics is about 'who gets what' (Lasswell, 1936) and that participation in the policy process is likely to be about the advancement or protection of vested interests.

This key theme is explored through the elaboration of a simple model (set out in Figure 8.1) which sees the policy process as interactions between political and administrative decision makers and two potentially antagonistic groups of citizens: winners and losers from policy initiatives. That elaboration requires a recognition that there may be 'third parties' who are indirect winners or losers, and that the notions of direct and indirect impacts merge into each other in complicated ways. It then adds to that the fact that – as set out in various ways earlier in the book the political and administrative decision makers will themselves have interests that may come into play. This model is then applied briefly to various policy areas, highlighting some of the ways in which it can apply and also some situations in which it is hard to apply.

The chapter ends with an examination of the stages model of the policy process, showing why it has been given attention and outlining its strengths and weaknesses. While this is a necessary prelude to the rest of the book, set out in this chapter since that is the logical place to put it, it may seem to take the discussion in a rather different direction to the rest of the chapter. However, the presentation here of the main critique of this third approach – that there is no simple linear process from political initiation to action – serves to emphasise something important for all that is to come: that politics in the widest sense infuses the whole process.

Policy types

There are obviously divisions in the literature in respect of policy content, often with distinct areas of scholarship in respect of foreign policy, economic policy, social policy, environmental policy, defence policy and so on. These areas are further sub-divided: hence, for example, within social policy we find specialists on health policy, education policy, housing policy, income maintenance and so on. Prima facie, there are good grounds for arguing that what we have here are very different policy 'contents' and that these will have an influence on the characteristics of the policy process.

Furthermore policy scholars interested in the public regulation of so-called morality issues (e.g. abortion, euthanasia, research on embryos, same-sex marriage, gambling, prostitution, tobacco smoking, death penalty, etc.) claim that morality policies are very different from all other policy areas (Engeli and Varone, 2011). These scholars highlight three key features of morality issues, which have a major impact on the making of morality policies. First, morality issues are highly salient to the general public. Everyone is directly confronted by these issues and, thus, has an opinion about how to regulate them. Second, these issues are technically simple and the frequent use of popular images and symbols (e.g. the 'sinful gambler', the 'mad scientists', the 'irresponsible smoker', etc.) contributes to the popular reduction of their complexity. Third, they address fundamental moral and social values, which are not divisible and on which political compromise is usually not possible. The conjunction of these three peculiarities leads to vivid public debates and intense conflict during the policy-making process. For instance, the evidence on the public regulation of assisted reproductive technology (see Chapter 6) clearly shows how political parties, private pressure groups, citizen associations and religious organisations mobilise their members and activate different institutional venues (i.e. government, parliament, courts, media, etc.) to influence the policy process and output. Similar political conflicts are typical of other morality issues such as the right to die. In sum, policy scholars expect that morality issues always lead to contentious politics (Mooney, 2001; Tribe, 1990; Meier, 1994).

In the light of these differences between policy areas can the relationships between policy content and policy process be organised using policy typologies? The most influential approach to this has been the typology originally developed by Lowi, who argues that 'policy may determine politics' (1972, p. 298) and goes on to specify four kinds of policy:

1. *Distributive policy*: the distribution of new resources;
2. *Redistributive policy*: changing the distribution of existing resources;
3. *Regulatory policy*: regulating activities;
4. *Constituent policy*: establishing or reorganising institutions.

While many textbooks on policy analysis present Lowi's typology, many policies have no obvious place in one of the four (exclusive) categories of the typology. For example, inasmuch as it is a state-provided or state-supported service it is difficult to specify the role of education policy in respect of Lowi's categories. Providing education gives social advantages, and education policies may be (but are also often not) designed to redistribute advantages by enhancing social mobility. Education policy also involves a great deal of regulation of both public and private actors. In some respects regulation is one of the functions of education. Children are required to be sent to school where they have to be taught effectively by (normally) qualified persons.

Income maintenance seems to be an example of redistributive policy but may also involve regulatory policy. Much of it is not redistributive, inasmuch as social insurance is premised – to varying degrees – upon the idea of forced saving. Pollution control policy is obviously regulatory but has a variety of redistributive effects as the ban of polluting industrial activities has different impacts on private firms. Constituent policy may also have redistributive effects, complex questions arising about who gains or loses from health service reorganisation.

Furthermore, there is a logical problem with Lowi's concept of 'distributive policy'. The notion of policies being distributive without having any redistributive effects is problematical inasmuch as expenditure has to be funded and any advantages conferred on one person implicitly confer disadvantages on another. Lowi's typology was explicitly developed to elucidate the extent to which policy initiatives encounter resistance. He was thus directly concerned with the issues about winners and losers. It is a crucial point about the politics of policy that a great deal depends upon whether these people (and particularly losers) can identify themselves and are organised to do something about it. What then we are left with, given the difficulties about the application of the typology to real policy examples, is the notion that, whilst we cannot necessarily develop a typology based on these differences, policy differences matter for the way in which policy actors mobilise and the policy process works.

Before we leave this point entirely it is appropriate to mention one theorist who addresses issues about policy differences, albeit in a much simpler way. Matland suggests two distinguishing features of policies: the extent to which they are ambiguous and the extent to which they provoke conflict. In doing this he is trying to theorise about implementation, but equally this distinction may be as much an underlying feature of a whole policy area as a specific feature of any policy as enacted (Matland's model is explored further in Chapter 11). Where you put policy activities on his two dimensions depends, however, upon some very complex questions. In general, while Matland, like

Lowi before him, helps to sensitise us to issues about differences between policy processes, he does not progress this subject very much.

The most important point to be derived from Lowi's analysis is his observation that policies may determine politics. He deliberately argues for a need to see the relationship that way round against the perhaps more conventional view that politics determines policy. But this relationship must be examined both ways round.

Policy and power

In the first section of this book it was made very clear that the study of the policy process has to be directly related to the study of power. Therefore here, taking as our starting point the first part of Lasswell's (1936) definition of politics (quoted in Chapter 1) as about 'who gets what . . .', it is appropriate to ask to what extent the political games associated with various policy areas can be analysed in these terms. Of course there will be claims, made by key policy-making actors, in perhaps many cases that all will benefit from new policies. Of course it may exceptionally be true that losers are absent, or insignificant. Lowi (1972) uses the example of the land distribution policy in the nineteenth-century United States to explain his notion of distributive policy, as distinguishable from re-distributive policy. But that is an extraordinary view that surely Native Americans would dispute. Even in this case such distribution as occurred will have favoured some more than others. Ripley and Franklin (1982), who use Lowi's typology, rest their version of the distributive/re-distributive divide on the extent to which the losers can readily identify themselves. Significantly, Ripley and Franklin partly acknowledge the illogicality of this by indicating that they confine their redistributive concept to shifts of resources from advantaged to disadvantaged groups, whilst acknowledging that the reverse does apply. They justify this in terms of ideological perceptions in the United States (perhaps better put as the 'dominant ideology').

In any case as far as the policy process is concerned policies that cause little or no controversy are not particularly significant topics for study. The issues that concern policy analysts are policies whose impact generates 'winners' and 'losers'. This basic point take us back to the central concern of the classic pluralist theorists, examining 'interests' and attempting, as in Dahl's (1961) New Haven study, to find ways to assess their impact on policy. The recognition of biases in interest systems does not detract from that essential point. It is similarly appropriate to have regard to the way in which public choice theory directs our attention to 'the political marketplace'. Note here the title of Buchanan and Tullock's book *The Calculus of Consent* (1962); even though there are many problems about identifying and aggregating interests (on which more will be said below) this is still a useful starting point for much policy process analysis.

Identifying winners and losers

Knoepfel and his colleagues (2007) explore the impact of the policy process in terms of implications for 'beneficiary groups' and 'target groups'. The simpler terms 'winners' and 'losers' are preferred here. They go on to use the notion of 'a triangle of policy actors' (ibid., pp. 56–61), the basic components of which are winners and losers together with 'political administrative authorities that develop and implement policy' at the apex (see Figure 8.1).

This simple model claims that the political-administrative actors, who are formally in charge of a public policy, select and then implement various policy instruments (mixes) to modify the behaviour of target groups (or losers), with the aim of improving the personal situation of the end beneficiaries (or winners) of the policy. For example, the ministry of environment introduces a carbon tax to reduce the pollutant emissions generated by industries (losers) and, consequently, to improve the quality of the environment for human beings, fauna and flora (winners). According to this approach, every public policy imposes costs on the target groups and grants privileges to end beneficiaries. Generally public policies are thus intrinsically redistributive in nature and Knoepfel et al. (2007, p. 60) argues that the aims of policy analysis should be to investigate these redistributive effects and, ultimately, to answer the classical question: who gets what, when, how (see Lasswell, 1936) and from whom.

This basic actors' triangle then needs to be made more complicated. As far as winners and losers are concerned there are also 'positively' and 'negatively' affected third parties. If we expand the example discussed above, then 'eco-business' firms, which develop new and less polluting technologies, will indirectly benefit from a strict pollution policy: they can sell their innovative technologies to the polluting firms and constitute thus a positively affected third party. By contrast, consumers may be negatively affected by this policy:

Figure 8.1   The triangle of policy actors

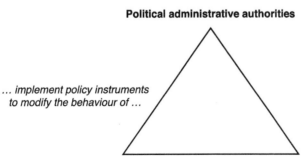

Political administrative authorities

*... implement policy instruments
to modify the behaviour of ...*

Target groups / losers   **End beneficiaries / winners**

*... with the aim of improving
the situation of ...*

they may end up paying more for the products delivered by the polluting industries which have to pay the carbon tax and/or to buy new technologies to reduce their pollutant emissions.

However, the distinction between directly affected actors and these so-called third parties can be a difficult one. In legal contexts, for example in relation to planning issues, third parties are defined as people who are deemed to be likely to be affected by a development. They are then given a direct right to provide evidence on the impact of that development. But from a political point of view assigning others to the weaker status of third parties may be contestable. Consider for example the indirect effects of a new road upon people whose property remains intact but who experience more noise and other nuisances (there may of course also be winners who experience less). So while it is useful to bear in mind here the notion of 'third parties' it is probably more useful to talk about indirect winners and losers, who may spread across a spectrum from the situations in which these are very clear to ones where those gains and losses are indirect, very diluted and obscure.

Wilson (1973), for example, has distinguished between 'concentrated' and 'dispersed' costs and benefits, with the blocking of policy least likely where there is a broad distribution of both. The issues about dispersed costs – even hidden costs – seem particularly important here. Much public policy involves costs which fall on a collective exchequer – often that of the nation state. Incremental addition to benefits for specific groups, that may be readily identifiable, may involve additional costs that are very widely spread so that they are small or even unidentifiable to those that pay them. In Swiss agricultural policy, the so-called 'direct payments' are a policy tool that concentrates benefits on very few actors and spreads costs on all taxpayers. No less than 2.5 billion a year are given to Swiss farmers as compensation for the ecological services they provide, such as the protection of biodiversity in agricultural areas, the reduction of fertilisers' use, the promotion of animal-friendly conditions for livestock or the sustainable use of summer pastures. This important remuneration of farmers is funded through the general budget of the federal authorities and is thus not noticed by most citizens. This aspect of policy, of course, also featured earlier (in Chapter 3) as an aspect of public choice analysis of the real costs of public policy, where reference was made to the fact that politicians may endeavour to make clear who are winners and hide the evidence on who are the losers.

Hogwood (1987) on the same theme suggests issues about the extent to which policy benefits can be distinguished will be relevant. Relevant here too are 'policy instruments'. This term is used 'to encompass the myriad techniques at the disposal of governments to implement their public policy objectives. Sometimes referred to as "governing instruments", these techniques range in complexity and age' (Howlett, 1991, p. 2).

Issues about the choice of instruments have been seen to be influenced by concerns about costs and benefits. Hence, Howlett suggests, 'instrument choice, from this perspective, is public policymaking' (ibid.). However, instrument choice – while influenced by the policy issue at stake – is much more about the selection of means to achieve policy objectives. As such it is discussed further in the context of policy formulation in Chapter 10.

Another complication for any analysis in respect of winners and losers is that policies may involve choices between alternative winners and losers. Take the example of a new airport, where a choice is made between alternative venues. Depending upon interest configurations there may be both winners and losers in the chosen area. One of the authors lives in the vicinity of the London (Gatwick) Airport. This has only one runway and the addition of a second one features amongst the possible proposals for expanding London's airports. Local press coverage of efforts to influence the decision has included strong expressions of both hostility from environmental protection groups and support from those who see expansion as a potential source of economic benefits. Moreover the intensity of involvement in the controversy, on both sides, depends upon situational factors such as position in relation to proposed flight paths and the nature of economic activity. The winners/losers model may be extended to cover decisions like this, but it is stretching it a little. It is another reminder of the complexity of the policy/politics relationship.

It is important, too, to make clear here something that is implicit in talking of 'winners' and 'losers' using plural forms, which is that there may be various groups or coalitions involved. In this respect various scholars have made use of the 'advocacy coalition framework' (see Chapters 4 and 6) to identify groupings of this kind, with 'dominant' groups probably influencing the policy process over a significant period of time until 'shocks' of some kind disturb the consensus.

A related point of importance about the identification of winners and losers is that it is necessary to give attention to the apex of the triangle in Figure 8.1: the political administrative authorities. We explored theoretical perspectives that indicate that the bodies that make policy have vested interests too. It was suggested (in Chapter 4) that we may find them in the networks and policy communities to which the organisations that represent the public also belong. It also indicated that there may be competing networks, with different parts of the government machine potentially in conflict with each other (e.g. in relation to anti-pollution policy, the ministry of environment and the ministry of industry may have very different opinions about the relevance and the effectiveness of a carbon tax). We reinforced that perspective by indicating that there is a need to recognise institutional configurations with their own commitments, expectations and standard operating procedures (Chapter 5). Then we added the public choice perspective with its strong emphasis on the likelihood that public officials will pursue their own interests (Chapter 3). So it is important to add this group of 'actors' as not necessarily impartial initiators, formulators and implementers of public policy but also as people who may see themselves and their departments as winners or losers, and who may be drawn into collaboration with winners and losers amongst the general public.

Social constructions and policy narratives

An extension of these ideas involves the use of a 'narrative policy framework' that distinguishes between different categories of actors who are directly or indirectly concerned by a public problem and the related distribution of costs and benefits. To identify these categories of actors, (so-called post-positivist) policy scholars analyse the stories or narratives that people tell about the policy issue at stake. These policy narratives always have four core components: (1) a *setting*, consisting in a policy problem and context; (2) *characters*, such as victims, villains and heroes; (3) a *plot*, situating the characters in the policy setting; and (4) a *moral*, corresponding to the proposed policy solution. The categories of victims, who are harmed by the public problem, of villains, who do the harm and cause the problem, and of heroes, who provide relief from the harm and solve the problem, are socially constructed (Jones et al., 2014, pp. 6–7; McBeth et al., 2014, p. 228).

Such a deliberate portrayal of groups is also present in the analytical approach suggested by Knoepfel et al. (2007) and discussed above. While the labels used are obviously different, the underlying concepts are quite similar: the 'end beneficiaries' of a policy are the 'victims', the 'target groups' are the villains, and the heroes correspond to the public or private actors implementing the policy solution. Furthermore, both approaches assume that the social construction of groups is crucial to understand how policy actors give a meaning to a policy problem and solution; and that competing actors or advocacy coalitions strategically use alternative policy narratives to influence the policy process and outputs.

Box 8.1 presents competing policy narratives about climate change (as originally depicted by Jones, 2014). The casts of the characters vary across the narratives and, consequently, the policy solutions are very different.

| Box 8.1 | Three policy narratives about climate change (Jones, 2014, p. 652) |

Profligacy: 'The cause of global warming is overconsumption. . . . Selfishness has driven the environment to the brink of destruction. The villains of this story are profit-driven corporations, governments that facilitate these corporations, and any group that supports the status quo. The heroes . . . are groups like Ecodefense and Earth First! that seek the elimination of greenhouse gasses and advocate for fundamental changes in the human relationship with nature. The setting . . . is a fragile world where humans have overstepped their bounds, while the moral of the story is that humankind is doomed if it does not correct for past mistakes. The profligacy story favours renewable resources to deal with greenhouse gas emissions (GHGs).'

Lack of Global Planning: '(This) story depicts the cause of climate change as runaway markets that have led to excessive economic and population growth. The setting is a world where humans have not properly managed economic and societal systems to allow for growth at a responsible pace that the climate can tolerate. The heroes . . . are groups like the Club of Rome, impartial scientists, and the governments that employ them. Hierarchs advocate for increased scientific management and governmental intervention to curtail climate change. The hierarchical story favours expert-driven solutions like nuclear energy to solve the problem of GHGs.'

Business as Usual: '(The) story's heroes are groups such as the Cato Institute and organizations like the *Wall Street Journal*. The cause of global climate change for these groups is generally naïve but dangerous idealists (egalitarians) and self-interested government representatives (hierarchs) that have fabricated the story. Should they admit climate change is reality, they will argue the cause is irrelevant. The only solution for climate change is to allow market forces to move naturally as individuals compete and innovate to create new technologies that reduce carbon emissions and allow adaptation. The moral of the story is that markets must operate with minimal interference. Thus, individualists are likely to be more sympathetic to market solutions such as a cap-and-trade on GHGs.'

Both Knoepfel et al. (2007) and the narrative policy framework approach claim that the framing of a policy problem involves the distribution of blame (for target groups or villains), innocence (for beneficiaries or victims) and praise (for heroes as fixers of the policy solution) across different social groups. Such categories are always socially constructed and, eventually, legitimated by elected officials. However, these constructed categories can be observed by analysing empirically the constitutive elements of policy narratives. As explicitly formulated by Radaelli et al. (2013, p. 501), 'Narratives are representations of policy created by social actors, and thus have an inter-subjective nature, that can be examined empirically using an objective epistemology'.

This moderate constructivism is a useful approach to understand and explain how problems are framed and then gain access to the political agenda (see Chapter 9); and how decision makers select instruments to modify the behaviour of the politically designated target groups (see in particular the section devoted to 'social constructions and policy design' in Chapter 10).

Winners and losers in relation to the policy areas

With these considerations in mind various policy areas will be discussed, in an order starting from the one where the process of identifying winners and losers may be easiest. The aim is to contrast the policies about which a clear open political competition is possible with those where this is likely to be much more obscure. We do not discuss here the issues raised above about morality policies, it is implicit to what we noted there that a perspective about 'winners' and 'losers' may be inadequate where political participants compete in respect of views of 'right' and 'wrong' irrespective of whether they have material interests at stake.

Income maintenance policy is explicitly about benefits, and debate about policy change is likely to take the form of claims about winners and losers. However, even here the debate may be complicated. It is generally true that where benefits are funded from taxation and directly applied to the relief of poverty, through means tests for example, winners and losers will be identifiable. However, even here the complexity of taxation can obscure exactly where the costs will fall. Social insurance is even more complicated, implicit within it is collectivisation of risks, but there is a compromise made between actual re-distribution (from those more likely to be sick or unemployed to those less likely to be so) and a process in which we contribute at some stages in our lives and receive benefits at others. This is particularly true of pensions, where in fact the greater longevity of the better off may make them long-term winners at the expense of poorer contributors. Calculating actual re-distributive effects is a scholarly activity which will not be discussed here. However, the ultimate obscurity of outcomes does not prevent much political debate around social insurance being conducted on the assumption that a re-distribution process from rich to poor is occurring.

In the discussion of *anti-pollution policy*, much was made of both externalities and the global nature of some key problems. In that sense the winners from pollution control are us all. However, what is central to much pollution control is the curbing of economic activities with costs to be met by polluters. In that sense the losers' side of the equation is very explicit, and often losers are immediately evident and winners obscure. However, even in the context of a general gain from pollution control there are likely to be differences in gains, as a consequence for example of relative proximity to the nuisance to be curbed. Not surprisingly the politics of pollution control is often fiercely fought out. Potential losers are likely to be powerful, able to remind politicians of their economic importance. Potential winners are either economically weak (workers living close to factories) or not particularly aware of their possible gains.

Many *education and health policy* changes are likely to be presented by policy makers as involving general benefits. In this respect – take for example the extension of higher education – the critical political debate is about the cost side of the equation. However, in relation to both of these policy areas there is a salient debate about the reduction of inequalities. This obviously implies an identifiable group of potential winners. Except at a time of rapid social advance, upward mobility is likely to have to be balanced by downward mobility; it may be observed that political actors find it difficult to come to terms with the fact that redressing inequalities implies that there will be losers too.

In relation to services like education the point made above, about choices between places (using the airport example), can be important. The allocation of new resources generates winners and losers inasmuch as only some secure scarce benefits. Issues about the extension of, or correction of, inequalities may be evident in this area of policy. We see here decisions in Lowi's (1972) 'constituent policy' category which may have important re-distributional consequences.

In respect of both health and education policy making there are actors within the system – teachers, doctors, etc. – who may be (indirect) winners or losers from policy change. The key point here is that much policy change in health and education is explicitly about how professional staff are to be organised, deployed and rewarded. In fact we often see (positively or negatively) affected staff as salient protagonists in debates about policy changes with patients observing this rather passively on the sidelines. The complexity of the issues contributes to this. But in addition a peculiarity of health politics is that while we almost all need health care sometime in our lives those who are most intimately affected at any point in time are probably also – as a consequence of their infirmities – unlikely to engage with the policy process.

So far four policy areas have been explored, in all of which there is likely – in a democratic state – to be fairly active public participation (directly or through interest groups) affected by considerations about gains and losses likely to be consequent on policy change. In the last two policy areas addressed here – making war and controlling the economy – the policy process seems to be rather different. In both, the issues about winners and losers are perhaps rather peculiar.

We will not detain us here with a discussion of whether there are ever real winners from a war. What is clear is that the case for *war* is made by politicians in terms of general benefit, at least to their own nation state and perhaps for the world as a whole. There are then obvious losers and modern politicians are very sensitive to the impact on public opinion of repatriated bodies. There are also good reasons why those who 'profit' from conflict are likely to want to evade identification.

The discussion of the issues about waging war also highlight the way in which participation in decision making before action may be limited. It is also pertinent to note the high speed with which actual decisions are made. There are then strong efforts to try to maximise support once conflicts start, manipulating notions of loyalty and patriotism. However, citizens frequently oppose the involvement of their own country into armed conflicts. The anti-Vietnam war movement on various American campuses is the reference case. More recently, there were also very large street demonstrations, in many countries around the world, against the (so called pre-emptive) invasion of Iraq in 2003. While the US and UK governments claimed that this war aimed at preventing the use of weapons of mass destruction by Saddam Hussein, many Western citizens believed that the war was more about accessing the oil reserves in Iraq than about effectively dealing with (non-existent) weapons of mass destruction. Citizen movements thus promoted a non-violent, diplomatic solution to the conflict in Iraq. Moral arguments against the war were much more important than national interests such as homeland security or economic growth. This example illustrates how difficult it can be, for the policy analysts, to clearly disentangle arguments based on moral values versus those on material self-interests.

The *management of the economy* is seen as something done for the general good. There is little dissent from the view that it should be about securing growth without excessive inflation or unemployment. But then exactly how that should be done takes us right to the heart of political controversy. That would seem to take us into forms of democratic debate any bit as explicit as the debates over social security. Yet somehow it does not always do so.

In looking at the twenty-first-century world it may be the case that now the parameters for any debate are set globally – by the economic relationships between nations and the international capitalist institutions. As this piece is being written, week after week the news is full of the complex problem of solving a crisis for the Euro posed particularly by the contrast between nations with high levels of public debt (particularly Greece) and those in securer circumstances (particularly Germany). There are evident problems here about relationships between nations, highlighted by German unhappiness about getting into a role as a rescuer of weaker economies. But solutions lie as much within the politics of the individual countries as in the development of better ways to manage the economic relationships between nations. Within Greece, for example, what has been said above about winners and losers is only too evident in respect of solutions to the problem that focus on the need for massive public expenditure cuts. It is all very well for external commentators to point to overpaid or unnecessary civil servants or to the need for the elimination of tax evasion. But those who gained from the previous status quo can hardly be expected to cheerfully give up those gains in the national interest, particularly when it is people from other countries who lecture them on the need to do so. A similar point may be made about expectations of political leaders; delivering unpopular cuts is not a good strategy for re-election. Not surprisingly the politics of response to an economic crisis is complicated and fraught; meanwhile the journalists criticise and the financiers speculate!

Significantly both the making of war and the management of the economy (the latter in a rather weak sense) predate the democratic era as state activities. Some writers have described them as 'high politics', to refer to the way in which they are the particular concerns of political elites with little wider participation in decision making, but with (potentially) strong *ex post* reactions by citizens (as illustrated by the massive street demonstrations against the Iraq war or against austerity policies in Southern EU countries). In the UK context, John reports that Bulpitt (1983) argued that during the twentieth century 'British statecraft separated decisions between central and local government, in particular distinguishing between the "high politics" of managing external relations and economic management and the "low politics" of delivering public services' (John, 2001, p. 30). However, drawing a distinction between high and low seems to carry an ideologically and politically loaded tone in which those who have been in a position to devolve power have a distinct view about what they regard as important. It may also be argued to be out of date inasmuch as there has been a tendency for modern British national politicians to want to try to extend their grasp to issues that their predecessors would have regarded as beneath their concern (those issues that Bulpitt saw as belonging to local government such as much social policy). Hence the labels 'high' and 'low' add little to our analytical understanding of the nature of the policy issues, and the use of them by Bulpitt is no more than a prescription about how to separate the role of different layers of government (see also Chapter 14 on vertical coordination).

In what other ways may these two last named policy areas be distinguished? Are these issues where the need for a rapid response means that the policy-making process is rather different, in particularly precluding the competition between interests? This seems sometimes to be the case but there are several problems about developing generalisations based upon that. While there does seem to have been a tendency in the past for efforts to keep foreign policy issues out of the democratic process (and there is some evidence on the lack of public interest in such matters – though surely not in respect of issues about war), this cannot now be seen to justify the scholarly separation of the foreign policy from other forms of policy analysis. One other approach to foreign policy decision making that may be noted is Putnam's (1988) notion of a 'two-level game': a domestic level operating with recognisable rules and an anarchic international level. But that surely over stresses regularity at the first level and disregards the increasing structuring of the second level, a topic to which the discussion of governance beyond the nation state returns (see Chapter 14).

Allison's (1971) comparison of models (see Box 8.2) of the process in his study of the Cuban missile crisis illustrates nicely that while events may be explained in terms of a low visibility chess game played by the two political leaders they may equally be explained by a bureaucratic politics that has much in common with other policy processes. In general, when we look at the making of war, attention can be given to elaborate preparatory events that only differ from other policy-making activities inasmuch as efforts are made to keep them obscure and minimise public participation in debates about them.

Box 8.2	Allison's (1971) analysis of the Cuban missile crisis, using three models

The so-called Cuban missile crisis (October 1962) refers to the major conflict between the United States of America (John F. Kennedy) and the Soviet Union (Nikita Khrushchev) over the deployment of Soviet missiles in Cuba (Fidel Castro). After much deliberation between the three countries to avoid an escalation towards a nuclear war, the American government agreed to remove its missiles set in southern Italy and in Turkey against the USSR, in exchange for the Soviet removal of their missiles in Cuba.

(continued)

Allison (1971) has applied three different theoretical lenses to interpret this key episode of the Cold War between the USA and USSR.

- The 'rational actor model' which sees actions as being formed by purposeful agents with certain goals and objectives. These agents have to choose between alternative courses of action in order to achieve their goals. Alternatives are assumed to have a set of consequences attached, and rational choice consists of selecting the best alternative in these terms. This version of the story highlights the roles of the two national leaders, Kennedy and Khrushchev, as decision makers, as do most popular accounts of the crisis.

- The organisational process model which sees action not as rational choice but as the output of organisational behaviour. This behaviour is largely the enactment of established routines in which sequential attention is given to goals and standard operating procedures are adopted. The concern here is with how the decision systems worked in the two countries, a topic on which there is of course much better evidence from the United States than from Russia.

- The bureaucratic politics model, seeing action as neither choice nor output but as the result of bargaining between groups and individuals in the political system. Here questions are raised about the interests of the key actors in the crisis. Crucial here is the power of the military. Accounts of events in the United States suggest that Kennedy came under enormous pressure from the 'hawks' within the military, who wanted to bomb Cuba, but resisted with the support of the more cautious State Department (see also Dallek, 2003, chapter 16).

Then when we look at aspects of economic policy making we see side by side rapid responses, where again there may be preparatory moves obscured by efforts to avoid giving advance notice which will influence speculative activity. But then, for example, a rapid response to an economic crisis, as in 2008, spawns a mass of issues about public and private indebtedness and about control over banking which become very much matters of public participation. The final point here is that there are issues in other policy areas where there is a need for a rapid response, probably combined with efforts to restrict the range of participants in decision making. Environmental disasters (e.g. the Fukushima nuclear disaster in March 2011), disease outbreaks (e.g. the Ebola epidemic in West Africa in 2014) or refugees' flows as a direct consequence of civil wars (e.g. refugees escaping from Syria, through the Mediterranean Sea, to Europe in 2015) probably come into this category. Nevertheless, and as already argued above, citizen groups may react to policy decisions taken behind closed doors, and demonstrate on the street to change the policy course decided by the political elite (e.g. environmental groups asking for a nuclear phasing out, humanitarian groups asking for a more generous asylum policy).

There is a point to be made here – highlighted by use of the notion of high politics to focus upon issues that are central to the lives of key politicians – about the way in which the real world of policy making is one in which elaborate efforts at policy problem solving are going on side by side with rapid responses to events. This is well explored in Rhodes' (2011) study of 'everyday life' at the top of a government department, a contribution discussed further (see the concept of 'departmental court' introduced in Chapter 10).

Those events may require decisions of fundamental importance or they may be the day-to-day trivia of the hothouse politics of operating in a 24/7 media environment (Raynsford, 2007). There are some issues here about the relationship between policy and politics which are confusing inasmuch as plenty that is written about the latter, particularly by the media, features the exceptional and the short term. Here then we particularly see the need to turn Lowi's emphasis on the impact of policy on politics around the other way. McConnell, in a book about policy success, argues that it is important to have regard to the extent to which what is being sought in the policy process is 'political success': 'If public policy is broadly what governments choose to do (or not do), then government does not just "do" processes or programmes, it also does politics' (McConnell, 2010, p. 25).

While McConnell's work is explicitly concerned with examining 'success' claims, in doing so he explores a wide range of ways in which political concerns influence policy choices. The discussion of evaluation in Chapter 15 returns to aspects of his approach. Chapter 9 picks up some relevant points on this theme with the examination of Kingdon's (1995) exploration of how problems, policies and politics interact in determining the policy agenda.

McConnell stresses the work of writers who have seen 'political symbolism' as important for political life and, therefore, for understanding the policy process from the politician's point of view (Edelman, 1984; Stone, 2002). He makes an interesting comment on what have been called 'wicked issues' by Head and Alford (2008), calling these issues 'complex problems without clear solutions' (McConnell, 2010, p. 79), where politicians experience strong pressure to do something with accordingly '. . . a placebo or symbolic dimension to many of the programmes designed to tackle' them (ibid.).

We have here a relationship between policy and politics that may be compared with a piece of music in which the use of a clear theme is complicated by a mass of cross-cutting distracting alternatives, which may or may not harmonise with the theme. At the heart of the literature on the policy process are questions about how feasible a rational policy process is in the context of all the political 'noise'.

Policy stages

The next topic in this chapter, policy stages, may seem to involve a distinct change of emphasis. But it has important connections with the preceding discussion of the relationship between policy and politics in two respects. First, the theory of representative democracy sees expressions of the popular will as an 'input' into the political system leading through various processing stages to a policy outcome as an 'output'. In that sense there is an assumption that policy should start with politics. Second, implicit in that theory is the notion of a linear process of realising political goals. In that, 'losers' in the initial political battles might be expected to drop out – as in a knockout tournament in sport. Both of these assumptions have been challenged.

The propagation of the stages model, not just to describe the policy process but also as an ideal for rational administration, has its roots in an influential nineteenth-century essay which stressed a need for a clear distinction between politics and administration (Wilson, 1887). The case for this is also made in arguments about the rule of law as well as in arguments for representative democracy. Implicit in the latter concept is the notion that citizens should be able to predict the impact of the actions of the state upon themselves and secure redress when affected by illegitimate actions, hence what this implies is a coherent law-making process that then binds the subsequent actions of state officials (whether or not that process is democratic).

The development of the stages or policy cycle model may be seen, in part, as an elaboration of these concerns. The systems approach outlined by David Easton (1953; 1965a; 1965b) is seen as a key source for the stages model. Easton argues that political activity can be analysed in terms of a system containing a number of processes which must remain in balance if the activity is to survive. The main merit of systems theory is that it provides a way of conceptualising what are often complex political phenomena. In emphasising processes as opposed to institutions or structures, the approach is also useful in disaggregating the policy process into a number of different stages, each of which becomes amenable to more detailed analysis. For all of these reasons, stripped of the biological emphasis in Easton's work, the systems model is of value, and this no doubt helps to account for its prominence in the literature. Other writers who do not necessarily share Easton's systems framework have also used the idea of stages in the policy process for the purposes of analysis (see Box 8.3).

| Box 8.3 | Variations on Easton's systems model of stages |

Jenkins (1978, p. 17) elaborates the Easton model considerably, recognising complex feedback flows and identifying the following stages:

- Initiation
- Information
- Consideration
- Decision

- Implementation
- Evaluation
- Termination.

Hogwood and Gunn (1984, p. 4) offer a more complex model in which they identify the following:

- Deciding to decide
- Deciding how to decide
- Issue definition
- Forecasting
- Setting objectives and priorities
- Options analysis
- Policy implementation, monitoring and control
- Evaluation and review
- Policy maintenance, succession and termination.

The advantage of a stages model is that it offers a way of chopping up, if only for the purposes of analysis, a complex and elaborate process. It is useful as a heuristic device but potentially misleading about what actually happens (Parsons, 1995, pp. 79–81). As noted above, it is important to recognise the extent to which both the systems model and the stages 'discourse' rest upon a model of the representative democratic policy process in which politicians make decisions, senior civil servants help to translate them into specific legislation, and junior civil servants implement them. This is a widely held view of what 'should' happen. From the standpoint of this book the most important problem with this perspective is that the use of the stages model imposes upon the analysis of what actually happens a potentially distorting framework wherever what really happens is radically different from this.

From an empirical perspective, policy processes are in many respects continuous processes of evolution in which a realistic starting point may be far back in history. It was noted in considering the definitions of the term 'policy' that it is inappropriate to get into a model of the way policy processes occur which might only apply to a newly annexed desert island where nothing had been done before. Inasmuch, therefore, as it is possible to identify policy 'initiation', it may start anywhere in the system. Whilst there are grounds for seeing the stages as involving the progressive concretisation of policy (or involving a nesting of decisions in which some are logically prior to others), this offers no basis for prediction about how much will occur at any stage (in other words, whilst some policies may be formulated in very explicit terms early in the process, others may gradually manifest themselves as they are implemented).

Stages are not insulated from each other and there may be a succession of feedback loops between them – often the same actors are involved at different stages and the policy games they play will be carried on through different parts of the process (this remark is particularly applicable to the policy-making/implementation distinction). Friedrich summed up this alternative perspective long ago when he argued that 'public policy is being formed as it is being executed and it is likewise executed as it is being formed' (1940, p. 6).

The stages model has been discussed here because it is still widely used. This discussion has suggested, however, that its use can mislead. The problem – as John, one of the model's severest critics, has recognised – is that there is a pragmatic case for the model as it 'imposes some order on the research process' (1998, p. 36). What had to be recognised in shaping this book was that if every process is continuously seen as interacting with every other process, there is no way to divide up discussion into separate chapters or sections. Hence, limited use is made of the stages model by recognising rather that there are somewhat different things to say about agenda setting, policy formulation, implementation and evaluation respectively. At the same time, interactions are regularly stressed.

Relating the stages approach to actual policy issues

As far as the stages approach to policy analysis is concerned, there are some significant contrasts to be made. It is quite obvious that if a country has to manage a crisis situation, then the stages model is of very little use to explain policy decisions and actions. In 2015, the sudden and massive flows of refugees escaping Syria, Middle East (e.g. Afghanistan) and sub-Saharan countries (e.g. Eritrea, Somalia, Nigeria), and trying to join the EU, are the most important people displacements since the Second World War. Millions of people have been fleeing their home countries due to war or persecution. These refugees' flows lead to chaotic and uncoordinated actions in EU countries. The European Union seems unable (up to the time of writing) to handle this issue at a global scale, and to 'allocate' fair shares of refugees across EU member states. Nobody knows (yet) how refugees are going to be resettled across Europe. Some countries follow their own strategy and try to prevent refugees reaching their territory, or transitting towards rich EU countries (e.g. Germany) over their own land (e.g. Hungary). Humanitarian groups and international organisations strongly criticise this attitude, whereas nationalist and populist parties ask for an even more restrictive asylum policy. In a nutshell, the classical policy cycle model, with its clear-cut distinction of successive phases, is not very useful to describe and understand how politics and policy interact in such emergency situations.

If we return here to some of the substantive policy examples used above and apply the stage heuristics to these more conventional situations, then two extremes are perhaps economic policy and income maintenance policy. In the case of *economic policy*, in the use of the key instruments of influence in the modern world – the exchange rate and the rate of interest – there really is no staged process at all. Specific actions or specific decisions are often made and implemented simultaneously (by the Central Banks). There will of course be some sort of agenda-setting process. Inasmuch as this may be expected to involve a public debate, political leaders may be reluctant to have one, since a debate about impending economic measures generates anticipatory actions by those likely to be affected.

As far as the device of leaving interest rate setting to a partly autonomous bank or committee is concerned, it may be argued that such a body is merely an implementing agency working within strict parameters defined by 'policy'. But that is really playing with words, thereby illustrating the problematical nature of the policy formulation/implementation distinction. The decisions in question may have been quite closely pre-programmed, but their impact can be such that it seems inappropriate to describe them as 'merely' implementation. The Swiss National Bank is largely independent from elected officials. For instance, the Swiss National Bank introduced autonomously a minimum exchange rate of CHF 1.20 per euro during a period of exceptional overvaluation of the Swiss franc and uncertainty in financial markets (in 2014). This policy decision had major impacts on the economic activity of private firms in Switzerland, but also on unemployment, fiscal revenues and thus public finances. Contrastingly, while the UK seemed to be following that model after 1997, the 2008 crisis appears to have brought to an end a process in which the Bank of England simply reacted to the inflation rate without consulting the government.

In the case of *income maintenance policy*, there is likely to be not merely a prolonged, but almost certainly a public, agenda-setting process in which stages are evident. During its later stages that agenda setting will generally take the form of the presentation of proposals to a legislature, which will then be debated and perhaps amended. Once that stage is completed (or nearing completion, as these parts of the process will overlap) work will be done to translate legislation into a rule structure that will enable individual entitlements to be identified. Once that is done the legislation will be brought into action in a form in which very explicit instructions will be given to implementers. Inasmuch as the legislation gives individuals rights, the concerns in the implementation process will be about managerial control and about ways in which people may ensure they secure those rights. Of course, discretion may be enshrined within the rules, but these will tend to be tightly structured by the legislation. Feedbacks will occur, but primarily in the interaction between legislation and more detailed formulation. Here simultaneous work on both will tend to save governments the embarrassment of having to introduce amending legislation soon after the initial legislation. Furthermore, as is the case in the UK, with what is known as the use of 'delegated legislation', flexibility for amendments based upon later experience will be built into the primary legislation. Feedbacks can often be seen as a clearly structured part of a structured process.

Another but similar process is at work in federalist countries, between layers of government. The federal level formulates some framework legislation that is then adapted to local circumstances by decentralised entities. Experiences made in the 'federalist laboratory' are then evaluated, lessons about what works are drawn, and the primary legislation may eventually be revised.

The only exceptions to these propositions about income maintenance policy will be some forms of means-tested benefits (with characteristics not dissimilar to the 'poor laws' of earlier ages), where high levels of policy choice have been delegated downwards (Eardley et al., 1996). On the other hand, in the cases of education policy and pollution control policy, the delegation of policy choice is likely to be much more evident. Furthermore, in these two areas notions that are crucial for the characteristics of the policy are likely to be left to be settled at later stages. The UK National Curriculum for schools offers a good illustration. Beyond the specification of subjects to be studied, most of the detail of what should go into a specific curriculum has been left to officials within the education system, and even then the resulting documents leave many areas of choice for teachers. Occasionally, politicians or the media have raised certain issues for national debate – such as the extent to which the history that is taught should be national history – but on the whole the detail is settled 'lower down' the system.

The equivalent to this in pollution control policy is the range of issues discussed above about different options for use of the planning system, about co-production and doctrines like 'best practical means'. These too need to be seen as matters not just for any particular level in a staged system but as the subject of interactions between the systems. A good approach to the exploration of these interactions involves seeing one level as engaged in 'mandating' others (May, 1993). An interesting characteristic of pollution control is the extent to which there is expectation of a tightening of control over time, using targets to be reached incrementally. Such targets even appear in international agreements. Hence there is an interesting contrast between the macro-politics of target setting (often involving supra-national bodies) and the very specific (and more local) micro-politics of determining implementation arrangements. If a stages model is used in this field of policy then it is at best going to be one in which feedback is particularly important.

Turning now to the making of war, here there is clearly a prolonged process which can be traced over time. But does it make any sense at all to describe, for example, the Vietnam War as involving agenda setting, formulation and then implementation, let alone to follow any even more elaborate version of the stages model? What was described above in relation to all the examples given was indeed agenda-setting processes, in which public participation was unwelcome and political elites sought (not necessarily successfully) to keep strong control over events. An interesting feature of the relationship between agenda setting and policy formulation is the fact that nations do not declare war until they have prepared for it. To what extent does preparing for war make war inevitable? The evidence on the Cuban missile crisis suggests there can be a negative answer to that question, but that was a very closely run thing.

Going to war is therefore, perhaps, a very strong example of *implementation as policy making*. A great deal of the detail is settled incrementally in action. What makes this implementation very different from most of the examples of implementation discussed in the texts on this subject is the very high involvement of the 'top' of the political and administrative systems in the process. Once a war is in progress, policy change processes, affected by local intelligence and by local action, are likely to continue. It is an interesting paradox about military action that, whilst there is a high stress upon top-down authority and discipline, much of this is actually designed to pre-programme highly discretionary actions in situations in which those at the front have to react to unpredictable situations.

There are clearly other policy issues where a 'crisis' (in reality or as defined by the government) that requires rapid executive action creates a policy process in which separating the stages is problematical. That is very evident in the refugee crisis described above. A different, and less complicated example is provided by Taylor's (2003a) study of the response to the outbreak of foot and mouth disease amongst animals in the UK in 2001 that provides a good example of this. What was involved was action that the prime minister and other politicians initiated quickly to supplement or replace an existing policy framework. In this case an animal disease emerged, for which there was already an apparently coherent policy on the statute book, but the problem was that the disease had not manifested itself for nearly 40 years and in that time the organisation of both agriculture and the regulatory system had changed dramatically. Policy therefore had to be made 'on the hoof', as Taylor puns in his article, in a context in which very activist politicians needed quick results when a general election was pending (see Box 8.4).

Box 8.4	Taylor's (2003a) account of the handling of the 2001 foot and mouth disease outbreak in the UK

The last serious outbreak of foot and mouth disease occurred in 1967–68. A sequence of recommendations was adopted after that to involve the rapid diagnosis, slaughter and disposal of all animals that might have been exposed to the disease. The problem in 2001 was that agricultural and marketing arrangements had changed significantly, with very much more movement of animals around the country, hence the potential rate of spread of the disease was much increased. After such a long, almost disease free, period, few experts had any familiarity with the disease. Furthermore, there had been substantial changes to the veterinary service at the disposal of the government, so that it was very difficult to get services into action quickly. Evidence that the disease was likely to be located in several different parts of

(continued)

the country and that very large numbers of animals might have been exposed to it (in all, once the picture became clear, about 2000 cases were confirmed and four million animals needed to be slaughtered) made it difficult to implement the standard policy. The government was seen by some as acting too slowly, by others of making unnecessarily draconian decisions about slaughter and about the movement of both people and animals. 'From a policy-making and implementation perspective, the notion of "policy on the hoof" is appropriate because that was the way in which policy proceeded during the crisis' (Taylor, 2003a, p. 544). This is illustrated by:

> the proposal to vaccinate and the decision to base culling on contiguous contact culling rather than contiguous premises, the decisions to reprieve Phoenix [a pet calf featured in newspaper stories] . . ., bury instead of burn carcasses, make use of retired veterinary surgeons after initially rejecting the proposal, use the army later rather than immediately and transfer major decision making to . . . [the Prime Minister's office].
>
> (ibid.)

The use of a stages approach: just a pragmatic matter or something more?

The chapters in the rest of this book have labels and contents that broadly follow the specifications of the stages model. The matter could be left there, using the pragmatic case for this approach. There are however two threads in the case for the stages model that are regarded as important. One, to which only brief attention is appropriate (the main case has been made above) is that, while this book is an exercise in descriptive analysis rather than prescription, the prescriptive importance of the stages model (embodied in the model of representative democracy and of the rule of law) suggests that it is important to be aware of the extent to which processes are staged in the real world. This is particularly important for the democratic legitimacy and the legality of policies regulating individual rights.

The other justification is a matter of logic. This was explored in terms of a journey earlier (Chapter 1) where it was suggested that there will be three or four separable elements: deciding where we want to go to (agenda setting), deciding how to get there (formulation) and going (implementation). There may even be a fourth stage: evaluating what we did and how we did it. But it was pointed out that people may change their mind about where they want to go or how they want to get to somewhere during a journey. The point about this mundane example is then that if we want to analyse a purposive act it is surely logical to assume, but not take for granted, some kind of sequencing.

The journey example here involves a single actor but its logic can be extended to multiple actor situations more typical of the policy process.

Here of course the conventional prescriptive position implies some sort of hierarchy, and particularly a distinction between who decides where to go and who goes on the journey. The position to be adopted here is that who does what should be regarded as an empirical question.

But, as institutional theory stresses (see Chapter 5), earlier decisions tend to structure subsequent ones. In this respect, Kiser and Ostrom's (1982) notion of three related but distinct levels of analysis is useful. They thus separate decisions taken at the constitutional level, which structure the design of the context within which choices are made, from the collective choice level, at which key decisions about the management of policy are made, and the operational level, which explains the world of action. There is a 'nesting' process in which some kinds of decisions have a particularly strong impact upon the context for later ones, hence the idea of constitutional level and collective choice level decisions. Hill and Hupe (2006) have adapted this idea for the examination of the implementation process arguing that there is a need to separate the fact that there are different decision levels from the exploration of the actual layers of organisation of governance.

CONCLUSIONS

This chapter has argued that, while Lowi is right that policy characteristics influence the politics of the policy process, there is no easy way to generalise about that through a typology. Rather it is important to take that observation as a cue to recognise the importance of conflicts of interest. If that is done then it leads on to attention to the fact that there are winners and losers from policies, and that it is the configuration of these that may determine what is done.

The chapter ends with an exploration of the use of, and limitations of, the stages model of the policy process. It shows that the limitations of it rest upon the fact that in one sense or another politics continues as policy is translated into action. Losers at one stage in the process fight on, and in doing so may contribute to feedback processes or even complete re-starts.

Finally, there are some observations indicating that, while the structure of the discussion in the rest of the book loosely follows the stages model, and is justified in pragmatic terms, some of the notions embedded within the stages model of the policy process can be used in the analysis of the process so long as they are only seen as relating to the logical sequencing of activities, and the impact of early decisions on later ones.

9 Agenda setting

SYNOPSIS

After a brief comment on the difficulties about separating a distinct 'agenda setting' stage in the policy process, the starting point for the discussion of that will be a sociological analysis of the way in which public problems emerge. This points us in a very different direction to the prescriptive literature's concern about how policies should be made. The first challenge to the prescriptive so-called 'rational model' came from a literature that suggested that most decision making is 'incremental' in nature. The incrementalist perspective will thus be examined.

This will be followed by considering an approach to this topic which can be said to come out of incrementalism but goes considerably further, in stressing more strongly the relative absence of a consistent or 'rational' process. This is Kingdon's model of the agenda-setting process. The strengths and weaknesses of that model are then examined.

Finally, the chapter presents the 'punctuated equilibrium' approach, a theoretical development that owes much to Kingdon's pioneeering work (1995), as one example of the new orthodoxy of policy dynamics that was already discussed in Chapter 6 (see 'Temporal pattern approach' section). This approach explains how and why long periods of policy stability, that are characterised by low issue saliency and minor changes (i.e. equilibrium or incrementalism), alternate with rare episodes of increasing issue attention and major changes (i.e. punctuations).

Introduction

In the previous chapter the commonplace idea of a journey was used both to illustrate the logic of the stages model and to indicate problems about that approach. This chapter and the next two separate the analysis of the policy process along the lines suggested by the journey metaphor. This chapter is about deciding where to go (agenda setting), the next about deciding how to get there (formulation or policy programming) and the third about going (implementation). We start therefore not merely with a warning about seeing policy-making stages as neatly separable in these terms but also with the observation that readers are likely to note ways in which – in order to provide a coherent account of relevant ideas and theories – the authors will have to depart from the divisions implied by the chapter headings.

The agenda setting/formulation distinction is a particularly difficult one to make, since in the modern world we very rarely see an issue that is entirely new appearing on the agenda. Moreover, where this does happen there is often a very strong and complex interaction between the initial stages of that process and those that immediately follow it as it is translated into a more concrete form. It is also important to bear in mind that in some circumstances policy may be initiated and changed without formal legislation. In Chapter 8, the examples from foreign policy and economic policy both largely fell into this category.

In looking at agenda setting we are clearly being taken back to Chapter 5 where the theoretical issues about explaining change in a context of institutional continuity were explored. There we briefly examined Baumgartner and Jones' (1993) concept of 'punctuated equilibrium' suggesting that feedback from policy decisions generates change which builds up critical problems over time, Streeck and Thelen's (2005) distinction between 'incremental' and 'abrupt' change and Pollitt and Bouckaert's (2009) exploration of the relationship between the extent of change and the type of change. While we will see a tendency for the agenda-setting literature to be concerned with more clear-cut change there are, even in the most stable administrative systems, processes of change occurring all the while.

Sometimes agenda-setting processes and further policy formulation can be distinguished, and sometimes not. Various policy examples presented in the previous chapters of this book illustrate this very clearly. For instance, the right to roam policy (see Chapter 1) can easily be examined in terms of a specific policy commitment (put on the agenda by a political manifesto) and subsequent rather detailed work that had to be done to translate that into action. By contrast, the reduction of child poverty policy (see Chapter 1) required a whole range of detailed decisions about tax rates, minimum wage legislation, social benefit rules and so on.

What is a policy issue or problem?

It is appropriate to start examining agenda setting by taking a step back to ask: where do the issues or problems that get on the political agenda come from? No objective fact constitutes a problem in itself (Cobb and Elder, 1983, p. 172; Dery, 1984, p. xi). The – social and then political – definition of a matter that needs attention always represents a collective construction directly linked to the individual perceptions, social representations, material interests and moral values of the actors concerned. It always depends on persons directly affected by the problem and/or those whose behaviour may need to change to solve it.

There is a need here to recognise that there are issues that may be regarded as private concerns or problems for specific individuals. These may be quite specific to the individuals themselves, or they may be problems shared with others. If we take the issue of poverty, there are two separate but related questions: (a) is that condition shared with others and (b) inasmuch as it is shared is it seen as appropriate to try to take collective action to deal with the problem? From an examination of the history of concerns about poverty we may note evidence that it is more than an isolated problem, but also a widely propagated view that it is an individual problem (explicable in terms of the moral incapacities of the individuals concerned and their lack of efforts to remedy the situation). The latter can then be observed to have been challenged ideologically by arguments that the causes of poverty lie in phenomena other than individual culpability, and practically by social movements to attack those causes. We thereby may see the translation of individual issues into social problems.

That analysis can then be taken a stage further. Gusfield (1981) makes a distinction between 'social problems' and 'public problems', noting that all social problems do not necessarily become public problems: that is objects of political controversy. Hence, public problems represent an extension of social problems to the extent that, having emerged within civil society, they are debated within an emerging political arena. In this sense, the definition of a public problem is essentially political in nature. In other words, a problem becomes public by being put on the political agenda. At this stage of the definitional process, public actors (for example, the administration, government, parliament) recognise the need to consider a possible state solution, and thus a concrete public policy, to the identified problem.

The transfer of a problem or issue from the social sphere to the public sphere involves public actors as orchestrators or 'policy entrepreneurs' of the agenda-setting process (Kingdon, 1995, p. 225). Modern political history can be seen as involving the enlargement of the public agenda in this way. While this attributes a proactive role to the public actors, it must, however, be stressed that the passage of a public problem is neither linear nor inevitable. Many issues on the agenda today were not on it in the past. But equally there are issues that are not on the agenda that could be on it.

It is interesting to observe, for example, that whilst public policy today is less concerned about issues about people's private sexual behaviour it seems to be becoming more concerned about what (or how much) we eat and drink. Questions about whether it is appropriate for certain issues to be on the agenda lie at the centre of ideological conflict in societies and are linked to the evolution of social values. From an analytical point of view, it is worth investigating how policy issues that reach the political agenda are socially constructed and politically framed; and framing social problems as 'morality issues' is more conducive to attract political attention and thus to get (high) on the political agenda (see below the example of the death penalty in US). As already mentioned in Chapter 8, a morality issue displays three typical features: it is salient to the overall population as many people experience in person the problematic situation (e.g. tobacco or alcohol consumption, obesity, etc.); most people have an opinion on the issue because it is perceived as technically simple; finally, it concerns fundamental moral and social values (e.g. individual responsibility for health problems versus solidarity between healthy and sick persons). In addition, all problems framed as morality issues are also very divisive: once a problem definition is dominant on the political agenda, then a new set of values gets the official state's stamp of approval (Haider-Markel and Meier, 1996, p. 333), whereas an old set of values clearly loses. In other words, political agenda setting is here no less than the political validation of what is seen as morally right or wrong (Mooney, 1999, p. 675).

While putting specific (morality) issues on the political agenda may be attractive for various policy actors, it should not be forgotten that, contrary to the pluralistic vision of democracy which assumes that every actor may access the decision-making arena to thematicise a particular problem, Bachrach and Baratz (1970) and Lukes (1974; 2005) assert that a specific form of public power consists precisely in the possibility of keeping certain social problems off the public agenda (see Chapter 2).

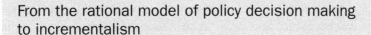

From the rational model of policy decision making to incrementalism

The need for a political analysis of the way in which issues get onto the agenda developed out of a disquiet with earlier models of the policy process. Here we encounter one of those issues (explored in Chapter 1), about distinguishing between a prescriptive and a descriptive approach to policy analysis. King and Crewe's *The Blunders of Our Governments* (2013) provides, as its title suggests, a recent example of the traditional prescriptive approach to policy problem solving using a rational model essentially rooted in a view of what *should* happen. Since the very beginnings of attempts to develop an academic approach to administration, efforts have been made to formulate guidance on how to secure the 'best' decisions. At the heart of this lies a perspective that does not recognise the complex relationship between problem identification and action described above. That perspective requires problem-solving behaviour to be unsullied by politics: an impartial search for the best solution. The contemporary emphasis upon 'evidence based policy' (see Davies et al., 2000, for a discussion of this) seems to sum up this aspiration. Yet insightful prescriptive policy analysis recognises the problems about achieving this. Perhaps the most influential figure in this respect has been Herbert Simon (1957) who, while he is often presented as the exponent of the so-called 'rational model' of policy making, in fact recognises the 'limits' upon the achievement of that ideal. Much of what he says on this belongs (in terms of what has already been acknowledged as an obscure boundary between agenda setting and policy formulation) rather more to the next chapter than to this one, so we return to that there. Hence aspects of a long-standing debate about decision making, driven by prescriptive concerns but inevitably spilling over into questions about what actually happens, will be split between this chapter and the next.

The concern here is with the way in which the rational model was challenged by an argument that goes further than Simon in seeing it as an unrealistic view of how policy decisions are made. The key protagonist here was Charles Lindblom. His work is confusing because he revised his position several times.

Lindblom is critical of the rational-comprehensive method prescribed for decision making. In its place, he sets out an approach he calls 'successive limited comparisons' which starts from the existing situation and involves changing policy incrementally. In describing decision making by successive limited comparisons, Braybrooke and Lindblom (1963) note eight ways in which the rational-comprehensive model fails to adapt to the real world of policy decision making (set out in Box 9.1).

Consequently, Braybrooke and Lindblom argue, decision making in practice proceeds by successive limited comparisons. This simplifies the decision-making process not only by limiting the number of alternatives considered to those that differ in small degrees from existing policies, but also by ignoring the consequences of some possible policies. Further, deciding through successive limited comparisons involves simultaneous analysis of facts and values, means and ends. As Lindblom states, 'one chooses among values and among policies at one and the same time' (1959, p. 82). That is, instead of specifying objectives and then assessing what policies would fulfil these objectives, the decision maker reaches decisions by comparing specific policies and the extent to which these policies will result in the attainment of objectives.

Box 9.1	Braybrooke and Lindblom's eight reasons why the rational approach fails to deal with real-world decision making

- limited human problem-solving capacities;
- situations where there is inadequacy of information;
- the costliness of analysis;
- failures in constructing a satisfactory evaluative method;
- the closeness of observed relationships between fact and value in policy making;
- the openness of the system of variables with which it contends;
- the analyst's need for strategic sequences of analytical moves;
- the diverse forms in which policy problems actually arise.

Source: Summarised from Braybrooke and Lindblom (1963).

Lindblom argues that incrementalism is both a good description of how policies are actually made, and a model for how decisions should be made. Prescriptively, one of the claimed advantages of what he calls 'muddling through' is that serious mistakes can be avoided if only incremental changes are made. By testing the water the decision maker can assess the wisdom of the moves he or she is undertaking and can decide whether to make further progress or to change direction. This is developed at some length by Lindblom and his collaborators. In *A Strategy of Decision* (1963), David Braybrooke and Lindblom describe in detail the strategy of disjointed incrementalism, which is a refinement of the successive limited comparisons method. That of course takes us back into the prescriptive debate, hence its features are merely summarised in Box 9.2.

Box 9.2	Disjointed incrementalism as a decision strategy

Disjointed incrementalism involves examining policies which differ from each other incrementally, and which differ incrementally from the status quo. Analysis is not comprehensive but is limited to comparisons of marginal differences in expected consequences. Using disjointed incrementalism, the decision maker keeps on returning to problems, and attempts to ameliorate those problems rather than to achieve some ideal future state. What is more, decision makers adjust objectives to available means instead of striving for a fixed set of objectives. Braybrooke and Lindblom note that disjointed incrementalism is characteristic of the United States, where 'policy-making proceeds through a series of approximations. A policy is directed at a problem; it is tried, altered, tried in its altered form, altered again, and so forth' (Braybrooke and Lindblom, 1963, p. 73).

This theme of coordination is taken up in Lindblom's *The Intelligence of Democracy* (1965). 'Partisan mutual adjustment' is the concept Lindblom develops to describe how coordination will be achieved in the absence of a central coordinator. Partisan mutual adjustment is the process by which independent decision makers coordinate their behaviour. It involves adaptive adjustments 'in which a decision-maker simply adapts to decisions around him', and manipulated adjustments 'in which he seeks to enlist a response desired from the other decision-maker' (ibid., p. 33). Each of these forms of adjustment is further divided into a variety of more specific behaviour, including negotiation and bargaining. In a later article, Lindblom (1979) notes that although there is no necessary connection between partisan mutual adjustment and political change by small steps, in practice the two are usually closely linked. This has been shown (by Harrison et al., 1990, pp. 8–13) to be a weakness in Lindblom's argument since a sequence of essentially incremental changes may well occur in a context in which certain parties are dominating and therefore 'mutual adjustment' is not occurring. This, they contend, has been characteristic of change in British health policy, where until recently medical interests have dominated.

Lindblom accepts, in his later work, that partisan mutual adjustment is only active on ordinary questions of policy. Certain grand issues such as the existence of private enterprise and private property and the distribution of income and wealth are not resolved through adjustment. Rather, because of 'a high degree of homogeneity of opinion' (Lindblom, 1979, p. 523) grand issues are not included on the agenda. Lindblom adds that this homogeneity of opinion is heavily indoctrinated, and in *Politics and Markets* he explores the operation of ideology. Lindblom's argument is that in any stable society there is a unifying set of beliefs which are communicated to the population through the church, the media, the schools and other mechanisms (1977, chapter 15). These beliefs appear to be spontaneous because they are so much taken for granted, but they favour, and to some extent emanate from, dominant social groups.

There is thus a shift in Lindblom's position from one in which bargaining is seen as inevitable (and desirable) to one in which ideology is seen to play a role, though essentially the latter has a limited influence upon the range of actors and options going into the bargaining process.

The rationalism/incrementalism debate may be beside the point when it is party-political commitment or ideology rather than either rational planning or 'partisan mutual adjustment' that drives the policy debate. The following scenario is surely by no means unlikely:

1. A problem arises in which it is difficult for government to develop an effective response – its causes are unknown, or beyond the reach of government action, or are phenomena with which the government is reluctant to deal (for example, economic influences upon crime or sudden flows of refugees asking for asylum).

2. Nevertheless, the key policy actors want to be seen to be 'in control', or at least doing something (they have made claims that they can manage the economy, combat crime or solve international conflicts).

3. In addition, some of the actors are driven by strong ideologies (particularly important as far as politicians are concerned) and partisan strategies (e.g. the populist rhetoric of nationalist parties).

4. The result is a series of actions that are presented as problem solving but which may equally be the thrashing around of a system that needs to be seen as active but does not really know what to do (in these circumstances it is important not to be deceived by the rational action language politicians are likely to use).

It is also vital to see agenda-setting processes in their institutional contexts. Such constraints make both 'rational' policy planning and 'partisan mutual adjustment' difficult. March and Olsen argue that 'insofar as political actors act by making choices, they act within definitions of alternatives, consequences, preferences (interests), and strategic options that are strongly affected by the institutional context in which the actors find themselves' (March and Olsen, 1996, p. 251). We also saw that in some of their work March and Olsen seem to go even further, seeing the way policies emerge as being similar to the way rubbish accumulates in a 'garbage can' (see Chapter 5). An alternative, institutional theory-linked approach to this issue which picks up on all the points emphasised in this paragraph is Kingdon's analysis of agenda setting.

Kingdon's multiple streams approach to the exploration of the agenda-setting process

Kingdon originally set out his approach in a book published in 1984. He updated that book in 1995 and 2013. Kingdon's work is a study of policy agenda setting in the United States. Kingdon describes his approach to the analysis of agenda setting as follows:

> Comprehensive, rational policy making is portrayed as impractical for the most part, although there are occasions where it is found. Incrementalism describes parts of the process, particularly the gradual evolution of proposals or policy changes, but does not describe the more discontinuous or sudden agenda change. Instead of these approaches, we use a revised version of the Cohen–March–Olsen garbage can model of organisational choice to understand agenda setting and alternative generation. We conceive of three process streams flowing through the system – streams of problems, policies, and politics. They are largely independent of one another, and each develops according to its own dynamics and rules. But at some critical junctures the three streams are joined, and the greatest policy changes grow out of that coupling of problems, policy proposals, and politics.
>
> (Kingdon, 1995, p. 19)

It is important to note the way in which Kingdon associates his analysis with the garbage can model (see Chapter 5). He thus dissociates himself from traditional positivist American political science, which searches for universal testable propositions. He sees the policy process instead as in many respects chaotic and unpredictable. In that sense the use of the term model is open to challenge by those who prefer to apply that term to something rather more precise (see Sabatier, 2007, p. 6). However, Kingdon aims to offer an approach that helps us to understand what goes on even if we cannot easily predict outcomes.

An aspect of Kingdon's approach that is widely quoted is his alternative metaphor to the garbage can, 'primeval soup'. This is a reference to the way in which modern explanations of the early stages of biological evolution see change occurring because genetic combinations occurred in the shapeless, soup-like environment, in which only some of them proved successful and thus led on to subsequent developments. But this is just an analogy, and one which should be treated with caution.

What is more important for his theory is the notion that in the soup-like environment that is the modern policy process there are three streams: problems, policies and politics. Simpler explanations of the policy process have seen policies as designed to solve problems, but the weakness of such approaches is that problems themselves are socially constructed (Berger and Luckman, 1975). Kingdon suggests it can often be the case that there are policies looking for problems: things key actors want to do that need justifications. He identifies the presence of what he calls 'policy entrepreneurs' who do this. These people may be politicians or civil servants or pressure group leaders with issues they want to put on the public agenda. They are, he says, like 'surfers waiting for the big wave' (Kingdon, 1995, p. 225), on the look out for a combination of public concern about a problem and political interest in doing something about it.

Kingdon's primeval soup image is intended to convey the way in which the policy process environment is forever changing, hence opportunities for agenda setting come and go with shifting attention to issues, influenced by the short attention span of the media and the changing needs of politicians in the course of the electoral cycle. This observation echoes earlier work by Downs suggesting that there is an 'issue-attention cycle' in politics (1972, p. 38). Kingdon shifts into yet another image here, of *windows (of opportunity)* that open briefly and then close. He recognises the importance of feedback from existing policies into the agenda-setting process. He also identifies what he calls 'spillovers', the impact of one policy change on other policies. These two elements – feedback and spillovers – may be important for the problem identified with regard to both network theory and institutional theory: that despite evidence of the existence of strong forces towards stability in the policy process, there are spells of quite intense change in many systems. What may appear to involve marginal change can have major consequences.

It has been mentioned that Kingdon's book is only about the United States (and in practice only about the federal government). It is full of illustrations from recent policy history in the US, and the 2013 edition contains an appendix applying the model to health policy reform. Nevertheless it seems amazing that a book that offers a general approach to the analysis of agenda setting should have no references whatsoever to the process outside the United States. But his approach has been applied to other situations (see Cairney and Jones' review of the theory, 2016). Particularly interesting in this respect is Zahariadis' use of it in challenging the interpretation of European Union policy making which explains 'policy outputs as a function of the rational design of institutions'. Zahariadis stresses the vitality of the three streams and the dynamic coupling processes that occur making 'ambiguity . . . an integral part of EU policy making' (2008, p. 527).

Another interesting application of Kingdon's model is Marchildon's (2014) examination of the early history of health reform in Canada where interactions between provincial and federal governments were essential, with politics at both levels playing a part and some provincial governments (particularly Saskatchewan) playing a crucial 'policy entrepreneur' role in respect of federal reform.

Developments of Kingdon's approach

Birkland's research on 'focusing events' offers support for Kingdon's perspective (see Box 9.3). When the 'big wave' comes, problems, policies and politics may be coupled to form the policy agenda. For example, terrorist attacks such as 9/11 in the USA opened a window of opportunity to reform the homeland security policies. In the energy sector, the Fukushima disaster in March 2011 was strategically exploited by environmental groups advocating a phasing out of nuclear power. However, this is not necessarily a simple process. Kingdon makes a distinction between 'agendas' and 'alternatives', recognising that there is competition at this time. As the carrying capacity of political agendas is limited, different policy issues are always in competition to attract the scarce attention of politicians. A more nuanced approach to focusing events is provided by Kodate's comparative study of health and social care scandals in Japan and Sweden showing that an understanding of 'formal governance arrangements' (Kodate, 2014, p. 114) is necessary for any explanation of responses.

Another approach to events which create opportunities for policy change involves an emphasis on *policy fiascos* (Bovens and 't Hart, 1996; Gray and 't Hart, 1998). Here, of course, the problems that force their attention on policy makers are the consequences of earlier, non-effective or even counterproductive, policies. For example, the regulation of the financial and banking sector was reformed after the economic crisis of 2008. In this case, then, we see feedback cycles in the policy process and also a variation on Kingdon's theme of the impact of 'feedback and spillovers' on the policy process.

A related concern is with the impact of crises. Bovens et al.'s (2001) comparative study emphasises ways in which crises force attention to be given to problems, looking then at different ways in which governments respond to problems. This also reminds us, as with the example of foot and mouth disease explored in Taylor's study (2003a) cited in the last chapter, that governments have to respond to problems even if there is a lack of policy ideas on the agenda and the need for that response disrupts their policy agendas.

Kingdon sees his approach to the agenda-setting process as building on incrementalist theory in its rejection of the 'rational' problem-solving model. But he argues that not all change is incremental and that incrementalist theory tends to disregard issues about the way streams join and policy windows open. He sees his approach as superior to a pluralist perspective inasmuch as he is interested in the way key actors both inside and outside government come together. Similarly, for him network theory and the work on policy communities neglect issues about coupling and about variations in the extent to which behaviour is unified. His perspective can be seen as institutionalist in approach, in the light of its emphasis on the significance of actors both inside and outside government and its recognition of the impact of earlier decisions on current ones. Indeed, in his second edition he recognises the parallels between his approach and that of Baumgartner and Jones (1993) in their analysis of punctuated equilibrium, a theoretical framework that will be discussed in depth below.

Box 9.3	Birkland's (1998) analysis of the impact of focusing events

Birkland studied the impact of disasters (hurricanes and earthquakes) and industrial accidents (oil spills and nuclear power disasters) on the policy agenda in the United States. Interestingly, he links Kingdon's analysis of 'problems' with the networks, policy communities and advocacy coalitions' perspective (explored in Chapter 4). He shows that focusing events may serve to bring attention to problems on the agenda, but that 'an event is more likely to be focal if an interest group or groups are available to exploit the event . . .' (Birkland, 1998, p. 72)

Kingdon's examination of the roles of policy entrepreneurs fits well with the modern developments in institutional theory and the so-called cognitive approaches of policy making that emphasise ideas. But this emphasis involves a very different perspective on the roles of experts in the policy process than that implied by those who call for more 'evidence-based policy'. That emphasis has led to a concern with the circumstances under which evidence is taken seriously, whilst Kingdon's emphasis on opening windows suggests a rather more haphazard linking of (a) political contingencies and (b) unsolved policy problems. Other writers go further in seeing this linking as very dependent upon power and ideology. There are issues here about the organisation of expert 'epistemic communities', which Haas describes as 'the transmission belts by which new knowledge is developed and transmitted to decision-makers' (2004, p. 587). Haas raises issues about the ideological compatibility between these communities and powerful political actors.

Applying Kingdon's model: does it underplay the ways in which agenda setting may be structured?

This section takes further the proposition, advanced above, that despite its apparent American ethnocentrism Kingdon's approach is of value for the analysis of agenda setting elsewhere, using a policy issue that is on the agenda in all developed countries: pensions. Exploration of policy agenda setting in respect of pensions illustrates the value of Kingdon's approach, but also enables the identification of some limitations.

In many countries (and particularly in Europe) there have been three phases in pension policy making:

- A first phase, in which, in most countries, relatively rudimentary public pensions were provided for only some groups in the population.
- A second phase of consolidation, involving either the development of comprehensive public schemes or the formation of combinations of public and private provisions.
- A third phase, in which, while development and consolidation issues are still on the agenda, a key policy preoccupation is with cutting public pension commitments and there are efforts to promote private pensions.

Tables 9.1 to 9.3 summarise the issues that influence the prospects of pension issues getting on the public policy agenda using Kingdon's key concepts.

The explanation given for the first phase in pension policy making (see Table 9.1) seems to offer a more political approach to agenda setting than there is in Kingdon's model. This seems to be dominant in historical accounts of the evolution of pension policies, though there are differences of view on the importance of the political Left (Ashford, 1986; Baldwin, 1990; Heclo,

Table 9.1 Phase 1: initial moves towards pension policies

Problems	An ageing population and increasing reluctance on the part of employers to keep older workers
Politics	The emergence of democracy, a readiness to see poverty in old age as not the fault of the individual
Policies	Either ideas derived from insurance or more universal models of public assistance for the elderly
Policy entrepreneurs	Politicians on the Left; friendly society leaders recognising increased problems with voluntary initiatives
Windows of opportunity	Electoral shifts to the Left

Table 9.2 Phase 2: pension policy consolidation

Problems	Poverty amongst those not in schemes; equity problems because of mixtures of different schemes; insolvency of some private schemes
Politics	Championing of universalist solutions by the political Left
Policies	Universal models; models involving public/private combinations
Policy entrepreneurs	Politicians of the Left; private companies eager to secure new business or protect existing business
Windows of opportunity	Electoral shifts to the Left; scandals about private schemes

1974). But the demographic aspect of the emergence of the problem has also been widely emphasised (Pampel and Williamson, 1989), and detailed accounts suggest the importance of policy entrepreneurs other than politicians (Baldwin, 1990; Gilbert, 1966). Furthermore, accounts of European developments make a great deal of the activities of one politician of the Right, Bismarck, who perceived an opportunity to tie the new industrial working class into the support of the state as the collector of their contributions and the guarantor of their pensions.

In the consolidation period (see Table 9.2) the divergences that are a key concern of modern comparative studies really emerged between those countries that adopted more or less universal public schemes (Sweden, Norway and Denmark, for example), those that developed a more divided version of the universalist approach (Germany and France, for example) and those that settled for provisions that were a mix of public and private (the UK and Australia, for example) (Esping-Andersen, 1990). The key explanatory variables were perhaps concerns about inconsistencies and a strong universalist drive from the Left of the political spectrum. But the emergence of a variety of private pension initiatives meant that the Left faced a rival agenda, with the more sophisticated of the advocates of the private model recognising the case for partnership (inasmuch as they were reluctant to take on the provision of pensions for low-income workers) and the need to secure private schemes against scandals that could discredit them.

The interesting thing about the third phase (see Table 9.3) is not so much successful agenda setting as considerable difficulties in getting cuts on the agenda (see Box 5.4 in Chapter 5; also Bonoli and Shinkawa, 2005; Ebbinghaus, 2011; Meyer et al., 2007) because of the strength of the support coalition for the status quo. A peculiarity of any pension scheme is that it embodies promises made to people a long while before they reach the age of entitlement. Furthermore, if a scheme is contributory, which it is in most countries with large comprehensive schemes, then those promises for the future are being paid for in the present. The problem that prompts action is very often an expected future one rather than a current one. Policy entrepreneurs have to persuade politicians, whose time frames are (as) short (as an electoral mandate), that they should worry about long-term trends. Here the so-called 'demographic time bomb' is a good example of a socially defined problem exaggerating the implications of demographic change (see Hill, 2007, chapter 6). Moreover, funded pension schemes, particularly if that funding is through investment in the

Table 9.3 Phase 3: pension cutting

Problems	Substantial increases in the elderly population; threats of insolvency for both public and private schemes
Politics	Championing of privatised solutions by the political Right
Policies	Cuts to promised entitlements; ways to increase prefunding
Policy entrepreneurs	Private pension providers: international organisations
Windows of opportunity	Electoral shifts to the Right; fiscal crises

stock market, themselves offer uncertain promises for the future. Nevertheless, a combination of the recognition of emergent fiscal problems by governments only too aware of difficulties in raising revenues, increased commitment to privatisation, and, perhaps above all, hard selling by private pension providers has succeeded in getting the case for changes onto the agenda.

This discussion has explored the issue in the group of countries that went into pension provision early in the twentieth century and consolidated schemes soon after the Second World War. The politics of pensions is very much more complicated in countries where pension provision or consolidation has only recently got onto the agenda. In these cases the conflict between the case for pension development and recognition of the strong case against open-ended and unfunded commitments made by bodies like the World Bank (1994) seriously complicates the agenda. We see here the influence of ideas, particularly the dominance of a belief in privatised market solutions to a problem like this.

In the UK, there has been a long conflict between a perspective which puts the main responsibility for pension provision on the state and an alternative view that, wherever possible, pensions should be provided by employers and probably involve investment of contributions in the money market. We see then efforts to reconcile the conflicting concerns articulated by policy entrepreneurs as set out in Box 9.4.

Box 9.4	Dimensions of the UK pensions policy debate

- the high levels of current pensioner poverty;
- the future balance between the generations;
- the recognition that the favourable situation of many contributors to good private pension schemes is one that should be shared more widely;
- the desire of the financial market to sell pensions;
- a recognition that some marketised pensions may not be a good buy for their contributors in the long run.

A more detailed examination of the British case highlights (Hill, 2007; see also Ebbinghaus, 2011, on the wider European picture) the following aspects of an agenda-setting process:

- the way in which current agendas emerge as consequences of past decisions;
- the incremental nature of change;
- the way alternative agendas come into conflict;
- the way those alternative agendas do not just arise out of conflicting interests and ideologies but also out of interrelated problems (in the UK case particularly the differences between the issues about current pensioner poverty and those about future comprehensive provisions).

Kingdon's model depicts the policy process as disorganised or haphazard. The pensions case discussed here suggests a need to question that. What has been suggested in the exploration of that issue is that it has been regularly on the agendas of many nations over a long period of time, that there has been a distinct 'politics' theme running through it and that there has been a comparative similarity, or at least a clustering, of ultimate policy responses. This politics has been analysed by a comparative study edited by Bonoli and Shinkawa (2005) that uses an approach to the analysis of that element in Kingdon's model which emphasises the significance of 'blame avoidance' by political actors (Weaver, 1986, p. 371). Hence it can be argued that the twin dilemmas for pension reform are that the funding of improvements will impose costs upon people who will not be immediate beneficiaries while the retrenchment necessary without those improvements 'forces tangible costs upon a limited number of people' (Shinkawa in Bonoli and Shinkawa, 2005, p. 165). The consequence is a search for approaches that yield benefits but hide costs (see Wilson's typology of policy issues presented in Chapter 8).

There is a case for caution about the emphasis on *politics* in the case chosen here. Pension policy is perhaps a rather 'mainstream' policy issue, bound to get considerable attention and to appear regularly on policy agendas. Nevertheless, there is a need to ask whether Kingdon's American perspective leads him to underemphasise the factors that may give agenda setting a rather clearer shape, bringing it closer to the notion of a rational search for solutions to problems that he has criticised. The view that there may be differences in the way the agenda is set is explored by Cobb et al. (1976), who distinguish between the 'outside initiation model' of liberal pluralist societies, the 'mobilisation model' of totalitarian regimes and the 'inside initiation model' where influential groups have easy access to decision makers. But that approach seems still to accept the relevance of the Kingdon model for open systems. It is important to consider whether the Kingdon model pays sufficient attention to institutional variations, in particular the different ways in which the political process is organised in different societies. Particular problems here are his treatment of the roles of politicians and his comments on the role of the media. The next section develops these points.

Kingdon's model makes no effort to weight the influence of the three streams of problems, policies and politics. They are broadly treated as equal. In analysing actual cases there are questions to be asked about this equality. The work discussed above on focusing events and on crises implies situations in which problems may be particularly important for the analysis, so does punctuated equilibrium theory (on which we say more below). The examination of power inequalities (Chapter 2) obviously suggests that a portrait of policy advocacy which implies a very equal competition may be misleading. On this theme it is interesting to note an article by Pralle (2009) which develops a prescriptive argument on how those concerned about getting policies to combat global warming on the agenda can use Kingdon's model. In effect her concern is to help advocates stress problems and seize political opportunities.

The impact of electoral mandates?

Perhaps the most important questions about parity between the streams take us back to the institutional context, and raise issues about the importance of politics. Essentially, the theory of representative democracy puts this first. It involves a model of the political process in which political parties compete to win elections, presenting manifestos between which the public may choose. There is then some expectation that the winners will implement the policy pledges set out in their manifestos, on the basis that they have a 'mandate' for those policies (Hofferbert and Budge, 1992; Klingemann et al., 1994; McDonald and Budge, 2005). Of course, studies of electoral behaviour suggest that our voting choices are largely not determined in the rational way embodied in that model, and that fact may give politicians an excuse to disregard their commitments. However, despite this, the 'mandate' model operates as an important influence upon the formation of the policy agenda.

There are, then, clearly differences in the extent to which a coherent mandate can be expected. It is in the division that exists in the United States between President and Congress, and in the relatively loose programmatic bonds within parties, that we may find the basis for the relative underplaying of 'politics' in the Kingdon model (and in the punctuated equilibrium model as well; see Walgrave and Varone, 2008). But within systems that are in formal terms more unified there may be another problem with identifying a coherent mandate: the fact that the government emerges not from the decisive victory of one party over another but from a compromise between more than one party. Notwithstanding this, it is interesting to note the continuing importance of the notion of a mandate in the very divided system in the Netherlands. A crucial stage in negotiations about the formation of a government there involves the drawing up of a *regeeraccoord* embodying an agreed policy programme. Similar 'coalition agreements' are also negotiated in Belgium and represent here the governmental 'policy bible'. Indeed, Walgrave et al. (2006) have demonstrated that electoral party manifestos and the negotiated coalition agreements are fairly good predictors of the legislative attention that various policy issues will receive during the governmental term.

Peter John and his colleagues (John et al., 2013) investigated the evolution of various British political agendas over the period 1945 to 2008. Empirically, they measured the proportion of attention that decision makers devoted to 21 categories of policies (e.g. economy, health, agriculture, labour, education, defence, etc.) in the Speeches from the Throne, in the acts of the Parliament and, in the public expenditures. These three agendas (speeches, legislation and budget) represent accurately the policy priorities of the British government. Overall, the longitudinal analysis of the shares of each policy topic on these agendas (e.g. evolution of the yearly percentage of laws dedicated to each policy topic) show that the relative importance of some issues rises over time (i.e. civil rights, law and crime, health), whereas other policy issues clearly decline (i.e. defence, territorial management and agriculture) or basically remain stable with some incremental changes (i.e. macroeconomics, housing and community development) (John et al., 2013, pp. 202–3). These changes in policy attention and prioritisation are explained by comparing political agendas with the evolution of public opinion, media coverage of social problems and party manifestos. The authors concluded that neither the disjointed incrementalism approach (i.e. series of small-scale adjustments and absence of radical change), nor the issue attention cycle approach (i.e. problems hitting the agenda, just after a crisis, but then declining rapidly) are sufficient to understand how British political agendas evolve. They build up on these previous approaches but propose a new heuristics that also includes the role of party politics. They summarise their 'focused adaptation' approach as follows:

1. A re-election-seeking government controls a mechanism that generates substantive attention to public policy topics in spite of significant pressure on the political agenda from the media and public opinion.

2. A landscape, or population, of policy problems exists and voters are concerned that government allocates attention to those policy problems, though not all problems impact all voters.

3. Government searches this problem landscape to learn its characteristics. This search includes assessing information about mass and elite views of the relative importance of particular problems.

4. Armed with that information, government adjusts its policy-making attention mechanism to reflect what it has learned to pursue its electoral goals (John et al., 2013, pp. 10–11).

This iteration of search and adjustment processes is able to describe the gradual transformations of the political agendas, even after major changes in government. All in all, pragmatism appears to be central to British agenda setting and policy making (John et al., 2013, pp. 38–40).

An observation of elections since 1997 by one of the authors (reported in the fourth edition of this book, 2005) suggests considerable variations in the relevance of mandates:

1. A party which had been out of power for a long while fighting an election on a rather specific mandate (1997), following it then in respect of a range of the more straightforward domestic issues.

2. Two elections (2001, 2005) where the application of the mandate of the winning party was more about its own unfinished business.

3. An election resulting in the formation of a coalition (2010) in which, rather like the Dutch or the Belgian, mandates formed a basis for inter-party negotiations, yet the realities of power after rather hasty discussions limited their real impact.

4. An election (2015) after which the dominant party in the previous coalition secured power on its own, implying a mixture of the new mandate model (1 above) and the unfinished business model (3).

5. Across the period decisions in matters of macro-economic policy (dealing with crises in particular) and foreign policy (interventions in Afghanistan, Iraq, Libya and Syria in particular) that cannot be realistically related back to mandates.

The impact of the media

Another issue here concerns the role of the media. Kingdon's book devotes a section to the media, within its consideration of policy entrepreneurs. However, Kingdon argues that the influence of the media on the agenda is less than might be expected, something he attributes partly to the way the media focuses attention on an issue for a while and then loses interest and moves onto something else. He argues that 'the media report what is going on in government . . . rather than having an independent effect *on* governmental agendas' (Kingdon, 1995, p. 59). He goes on to qualify that a little with three points about the media role:

- as communicators within policy communities;
- as magnifiers of movements that have occurred elsewhere;
- as agencies which some actors may particularly use.

Kingdon seems here to accept a portrayal of the media role which journalists themselves propagate: as the messengers rather than as the shapers of the message. Apart from repeating here the observation already made that Kingdon is of course only reporting on the United States, it is appropriate to challenge this view for its disregard of the second and third faces of power (see Chapter 2). This can be done with reference to all three of Kingdon's trilogy of problems, policy proposals and politics.

As far as 'problems' are concerned the media's limited and changing attention span is more relevant than Kingdon suggests. It is very easy to find examples every day of news value judgements about whose accidents and disasters merit attention and whose do not. Deaths of American and British soldiers in Iraq and Afghanistan get attention, more or less one by one, the much greater numbers of deaths of Iraqis and Afghans secure occasional references, often quoting challengeable estimates. When a natural disaster occurs in a foreign country the media tends to highlight cases where its own nationals are involved. In any case, reporting of the consequences of these disasters tends to be heavy for a short time, after which they disappear from the media. Murders get more attention than accidents and some accidents (for example affecting planes as opposed to cars) get much more attention than others. Since this is not a book of media analysis the object here is neither to expose these issues fully, nor to examine the obvious journalistic defences of these cases of selective reporting. There are two points here:

- that when and how problems are reported affects the political attention they get;
- that media priorities are both their own priorities and reflections of what they expect public priorities to be, which can mean in both cases reinforcements of the dominant views (see Parsons, 1995, pp. 89–92 for some case study illustrations of this).

Turning then to policies, Kingdon's interpretation of the transmission role of the media is just too facile. The media tend to simplify the policies on the agenda and often highlight the simpler rather than the more complex ideas. This remark applies as much to the so-called serious press as to the mass circulation newspapers, and above all to television which works with communicable sound bites, pictures and dichotomies that can engender lively controversies. In relation to the example of pensions policy discussed above, issues about demographic change and about funding are often presented in very simplified (and often exaggerated) forms (Hill, 2007).

The general point illustrated in the last paragraph is that the media shape ideas on the policy agenda in a way that promotes some perspectives and excludes others (see McCombs and Shaw, 1972, for a classic influential presentation of this view). This is particularly the case in respect of economic ideas where conventional wisdom shapes political thinking and journalists are important for the packaging of that wisdom, given the busy lives and limited attention spans of the key political actors. In this sense, notions about the relatively serious consequences of on the one hand rising inflation and on the other rising unemployment or about the need to limit public spending and avoid tax increases are as much the clichés of contemporary journalism as the shibboleths of contemporary politics.

It was suggested earlier that inasmuch as rational choice theory has been taken seriously it has had a certain self-fulfilling effect. Journalists surely have had a role in propagating the simplistic generalisations of rational choice theory (see Chapter 3) as universal truths contributing to:

- perceptions of politicians themselves as essentially self-interested actors;
- inculcating distrust of bureaucrats, as similarly simply self-interested;
- propagating through things like the 'median voter theorem' the view that political strategies that alienate 'middle England' (or wherever) are inherently risky.

Of course this is not agenda setting, but what it is doing is contributing to the constraints upon the agenda: discouraging innovation and political or administrative risk-taking.

That brings us to the third item in Kingdon's trilogy: 'politics'. The media are themselves part of the political process, not just influences upon it. Accounts of contemporary politics draw attention to key figures amongst the ownership of the media, above all Rupert Murdoch and his family with their massive newspaper and television interests around the world. The views such figures take about what should or should not be on the political agenda are important, since they have the capacity to use the media to this end (see

Kuhn, 2007, on Blair's efforts to influence the media magnates). Again here the emphasis needs to be on the negative rather than the positive, counter-balancing Kingdon's stress on the pushing forward of ideas. While mass circulation newspapers may be wary about campaigning against a political party that is rising in popularity that does not contradict the proposition here about their influence on ideas (Dean, 2011).

But any account of the media *in politics* would be limited if it simply drew attention to the big figures with ownership powers. Journalists themselves need to be seen as members of an occupational community with views about what they should and should not do. Political journalists live their lives close to political elites, with privileged access to the powerful (which can be taken away if they are seen to go beyond the bounds of what the latter see as acceptable behaviour).

Recent studies have focused on the colonisation of the (commercial) media logic into the policy-making sphere (see Chapter 2) and, furthermore, on the autonomous agenda-setting power of the media. However, the findings of these studies are not crystal-clear. On the one hand, studies relying on hard behavioural data and quantitative time-series analysis investigate to what extent agenda-setting activities of MPs (e.g. questions to the government, private bills) in a given policy domain are preceded in time by media articles about the same issue. The empirical evidence shows that the media impact seems to remain rather modest. On the other hand, studies relying on MPs survey lead to a very different picture. No less than two-thirds of MPs participating to a survey in Belgium, Denmark, Sweden and the Netherlands self-reported, according to their subjective perceptions, that media set the parliamentary agenda more than party politics. In a nutshell, different methods of policy analysis lead to contradictory and confusing results. This contradiction can probably be explained by the fact that elected politicians and media interact in a very complex way, as underlined above: politicians may attribute a strong agenda-setting power to media even when the initial agenda setter are not journalists *per se* but other politicians who had a big impact on the media coverage of a policy topic at a previous point in time (van Aelst and Walgrave, 2011).

The chicken and egg problem is not solved yet. Actually, it is even more complex if we look at the (causal) relationships between media and policy making over the subsequent stages of the policy cycle (see Chapter 8). Tresch and her colleagues (Tresch et al., 2013) showed that the correspondence of policy issue attention between media and political agendas varies across the initiation, preparatory, parliamentary, and referendum phases of the Swiss decision-making process. Furthermore, media and political agendas are both concentrated on fewer issues in the initiation phase, indicating that a naïve pluralist view of agenda setting does not hold. In addition, the media and political agendas are less correlated (i.e. different issues addressed by politicians versus in the media) in the initiation phase than in the following phases. In sum, the effects of the media on agenda setting is contingent upon many factors such as the types and characteristics of political parties (e.g. majority versus opposition), policy issues (e.g. conflictual versus consensual), media channels (e.g. print versus audio) and stages of the policy cycle as well.

The qualifications to Kingdon's approach set out in this section and the previous one consist essentially, notwithstanding the apparent radicalism of his approach, of suggesting that his valuable account of the dynamics of agenda setting is still too wedded to a pluralist view of the political process in which interests clash in a relatively unstructured arena. This leads him to neglect the way in which political actors can control the agenda and above all to underplay the complex role of the media in the policy process.

The punctuated equilibrium approach

Kingdon's contribution may be seen as not so much a 'theory' that can contribute to hypothesis testing as 'a work of art' offering 'flexibility to scholars ... when they engage in case study-based empirical work' (Cairney and Jones, 2016). The punctuated equilibrium model was directly influenced by the work of Kingdon, who also suggested to the authors the use of the punctuated equilibrium language (Jones, 2015, p. 4). It was developed by Frank Baumgartner and Bryan Jones (Baumgartner and Jones, 1993; Jones and Baumgartner, 2005) to offer another approach to agenda setting, connecting the issues about how agendas are set with the concerns (explored in Chapter 5) about the relationship between stability and change.

In each political system, the number of policy issues that compete for consideration by elected politicians is potentially infinite. In other words, there is clearly an oversupply of public problems to be addressed by policy-makers and institutions, which have a very limited carrying capacity (Hilgartner and Bosk, 1988). The government and parliament can only deal with a restricted number of issues at a time. A governmental meeting or a parliamentary session is obviously limited, and issues have thus to be prioritised. Some problems are given attention, while other problems are simply left out of the political agenda. Similar constraints can also be seen in relation to other agendas such as the media (i.e. very few stories on the front-pages of newspapers) or the party manifestos (i.e. concentration on some slogans during an electoral campaign).

In sum, *political attention* is probably the most scare resource in the agenda-setting process. If a political agenda is the set of policy issues considered for debate (Cobb and Elder, 1983, p. 14), then it depicts how attention is distributed among different issues at a given point in time. This allocation of political attention across issues on a given agenda represents a zero-sum situation: devoting attention to one issue (e.g. economy) restricts, by definition, the attention that could be given to other issues (e.g. environment, education). Tracing the rise and falls of policy issues from political agendas becomes essential because the definition of public priorities through political agendas can be understood as the 'conflict of conflicts' (Schattschneider, 1960, p. 68).

While tracing public policies across several decades in the United States, Baumgartner and Jones (1993) discovered that long periods of *policy continuity* were interrupted by a few radical shifts (*punctuations*). They additionally noted that political attention across issues followed a similar pattern: long periods of low saliency contrasted with a few, short but dramatic peaks in political attention. Interestingly, these periods of high political attention were congruent with the occurrence of major policy changes. Consequently, the authors conclude that policies are most of the time in equilibrium, responding to environmental pressures only with marginal adaptations (as predicted by the 'disjointed incrementalism' approach presented in Box 9.2). However, such equilibrium is only partial as it can be strongly altered by bursts of political attention. These attention peaks induce major policy changes that give rise to new partial equilibria. Borrowing from evolutionary biology (Prindle, 2012), Baumgartner and Jones (1993) consider that policies follow a *punctuated equilibrium* pattern across time, where long periods of stability are interrupted by major policy changes.

Policy continuity is associated with a stable configuration of actors in the concerned policy domain. In policy making during normal times, dominant actors exert a policy monopoly: they define the framing of the issue at stake and they control the access to the institutional venue in which the policy is primarily discussed (Baumgartner and Jones, 1993, pp. 4–9). Issue attention remains thus essentially confined to the boundaries of policy subsystems, and policy change is expected to be marginal at most.

In order to depart from this policy status quo, pro-change actors seek to attract the attention of politicians who do not belong to the closed policy subsystem. They expand the scope of the political conflict, promoting aware-ness of the policy issue outside the original community of policy insiders. When following such a conflict expansion strategy (Schattschneider, 1960), change advocates aim at gaining the support for alternative framing of the policy issue. Major policy change becomes more likely if challenging frames displace established ones, becoming the new dominant lenses through which both the policy problem and the policy solution are understood. According to the punctuated equilibrium approach, this often results from the shifting of the institutional setting in which new information about the issue is processed. All in all, we should expect a major policy change when non-subsystem actors get involved in the political debates, when the issue is treated in alternative venues, and when a challenging frame receives increasing levels of attention (Baumgartner and Jones, 1993, pp. 25–30). Box 9.5 summarises these core elements of the punctuated equilibrium model, while the next section presents two empirical applications of this framework.

Box 9.5	The punctuated equilibrium approach

Agenda setting and policy process	Normal phase (equilibrium)	Critical phase (punctuations)
Issue attention and political agenda	Low saliency; issue is out of the radar of political actors	High saliency; issue is a high priority on the agenda of all political actors
Actors' configuration, policy image and institutional venue	Policy monopoly: a small policy community, organised at the subsystem level, controls the framing of the issue, and the dominant venue of policy making	Policy entrepreneurs successfully propose a new frame of the policy issue at stake, and shop for an alternative venue of policy making
Policy change	Status quo or incremental change: negative feedbacks to external pressure	Punctuation or major change: Positive feedbacks and over-proportional reactions to the increasing issue attention

Applying Baumgartner and Jones' framework

Roy Gava (2014) applies the punctuated equilibrium approach and methodology to describe and understand how the public regulation of the banking sector has evolved in Switzerland. He compares different issues that were put on the political agenda (e.g. money laundering, tax evasion, dormant accounts or deposit protection) and that eventually generated minor or major regulatory changes. Empirically, he identifies an alternation between periods of policy stability and punctuations, as predicted by the framework of Baumgartner and Jones. An emblematic example of a major policy change is the 2009–2013 reform of the Swiss banking secrecy and tax evasion policy.

Box 9.6	Swiss banking secrecy (Gava, 2014, pp. 179–83)

Swiss banks have been very successful in attracting off-shore assets. This is partially due to the secrecy rules that were formally enacted in the 1934 Banking Act. According to this formal regulation, any bank representative who discloses a customer's information to third parties, without the explicit customer's consent, may face imprisonment or a fine. For decades, the non-disclosure of customers' information to foreign authorities (also in presumed cases of tax evasion) was thus the legitimate Swiss policy. Although such a practice is not unique to Switzerland, the country became the target of many international pressures after the 2007–09 financial crisis. Strongly concerned by their fiscal deficits, various European governments searched for new fiscal revenues and put the Swiss banking sector and authorities under pressure. For instance, Peter Steinbrück, the German finance minister, declared a 'war against European tax havens' and frontally accused Swiss banks of helping German citizens to evade taxes at home.

The initial position of the Swiss government was to maintain the status quo. In other words, the finance ministers argued that banking secrecy is 'not negotiable' and even claimed before the Swiss Parliament that 'those who attack banking secrecy will break their teeth'. That was the situation in March 2008.

However, the EU commission, and then the OECD, joined the international crusade against tax evasion. Consequently, Switzerland was designated as a potential candidate for the OECD blacklist of countries actively promoting tax evasion. In addition, former UBS bankers became whistle-blowers in the United States of America. They deliberately explained to the American administration how Swiss banks have helped wealthy US citizens to evade taxes. Swiss bankers were then 'invited' to testify before the US congress and to recognise that they had violated US rules since years. These new international fronts of the war against tax havens made it impossible for the Swiss government to further defend the policy status quo.

In March 2009 (on Friday the 13th, a day that will stay in all Swiss bankers' memories), the Swiss government announced that it will adopt the OECD standards. This concretely means that the Swiss banking secrecy can no longer be invoked to deny the disclosure of banking information for tax matters. Swiss authorities will provide this information to foreign tax authorities upon request. This major policy change (i.e. the death of the Swiss banking secrecy) was then concretised by the signature of several international double taxation agreements with many OECD countries. Later Switzerland also expanded its new 'white money' policy by implementing a withholding tax to regularise previously untaxed assets and to anonymously tax future income of non-residents (so-called 'Rubik project'), and by refusing undeclared money in Swiss banks.

Gava's case study (2014, pp. 179–83) described in Box 9.6 shows how this policy punctuation was induced by the uninterrupted international pressures, which put this policy issue very high on the media and political agendas. The broadening of the debate led to open divergences among Swiss bankers (private banks versus big banks, domestic versus international-ised banks), within the policy subsystem. At a more general level, it also generated clashes between bankers and elected officials from the political Right, who were until then traditional supporters of the banking secrecy. Gava observes thus a clear departure from the previous self-regulation policy, that was not under the public scrutiny and below the political radar, and that was dominated by few actors of the banking industry. By contrast, high profile policy entrepreneurs, who did not belong to the narrow (banking) policy domain, entered the political debate after 2008. Consequently, the previous (pro status quo) coalition of bankers and political elites broke down. In parallel, new institutional venues were activated, both at the national (e.g. Parliament) and international levels (e.g. OECD, EU commission). Swiss bankers completely lost the control over the arenas activated during the decision-making process. Last, but not least, a new policy frame (i.e. the moral duty to fight against international tax evasion) replaced the old conception of the Swiss banking secrecy (i.e. the absolute protection of customers' privacy) and the non-criminalisation of tax fraud. This case study illustrates how changes in actors' configuration, 'venue shopping' across different levels of government, and a new issue framing are three phenomena reinforcing each other and, eventually, triggering a major policy change.

Frank Baumgartner and his colleagues (Baumgartner et al., 2008) conducted another fascinating case study showing the analytical utility of the punctuated equilibrium approach. They trace back the changing framing of policy with regard to the death penalty in the United States of America since 1960. Capital punishment is a very sensitive issue and stories of wrongly convicted innocents, who are sent to death row for a crime they did not commit, but who are finally freed after a new trial, make the newspapers' headlines. Anthony Ray Hinton is one recent example of a black man who spent more than half his life on death row. He was wrongly convicted of two murders perpetuated in 1985, without any eyewitness, fingerprints or other physical evidence. After three decades of insisting he was innocent and desperately asking for a fair trial, Hinton was eventually freed on April 15, 2015.

This dramatic story happened during a period of change in the US death penalty policy. Baumgartner et al. (2008, chapter 4) observe that, since the end of the 1990s a new 'innocence frame' is displacing the traditional 'morality frame' relating to capital punishment. The authors come to this overall conclusion after investigating how the media have covered death penalty issues since 1960. They identified and coded almost 4,000 articles published in the *New York Times* about the death penalty. They identified which arguments and frames were mobilised to discuss the death penalty issue, and the tone of the article (i.e. pro versus-contra capital punishment) as well. This longitudinal analysis reveals that the media coverage of the death penalty issue reaches its highest peak in the 2000s. In addition, this recent period is very unbalanced as a net anti-death penalty tone is observed. By contrast, previous periods were characterised by a relative balance of pro- versus anti-capital punishment articles. More importantly, the *New York Times* articles published in the 2000s framed the issue of the death penalty very differently. Constitutionality and morality arguments have been prominent over time, for both proponents or opponents of capital punishment (e.g. 'eye for eye' versus 'vengeance is wrong, even when performed by the State'; 'the victim's family deserves justice' versus 'the victim's family is opposed to death penalty'; 'the death penalty is the will of the US people' versus 'other countries denounce death penalty', etc.). However, since the end of the 1990s, a new innocence frame has arisen and fully transformed the public and policy debate: the new dominating arguments focus on errors, mistakes and the unacceptable possibility that wrong people are executed (e.g. 'death penalty proceedings are fair' versus 'proceedings are racist and classist'; 'defendants denied sufficient access to evidence, e.g. DNA test'; 'human-run system cannot avoiding making some mistakes', etc.).

The impressive rise of the innocence frame, within the media, has also very important effects on the implementation of capital punishment at the state level. Baumgartner et al. (2008, chapter 7) show that the innocence frame has challenged the behaviour of judges and popular juries who have to pronounce death sentences. They ran sophisticated statistical models to assess if and to what extend a change in issue framing has a major impact on the annual number of death sentences handed down across the US (i.e. policy outputs), when other key explanatory factors (e.g. evolution of public opinion, rate of homicides) are controlled for. Their empirical findings support the idea of an 'attention cascade': the rise of the innocence frame and anti-death penalty tone in the media articles has translated into less annual death sentences since the 2000s. This change in issue framing and sentencing practice represents a major punctuation in the implementation of the US capital punishment policy to the extent that, bearing in mind the arguments in this book about the drawing of the policy-making/implementation distinction, it may reasonably be called a policy agenda change.

It is worth noting that Baumgartner et al. (2008, chapter 6) investigate the direct effect of media framing on death sentencing, and its indirect effects (i.e. over a change in public opinion) as well. Their various statistical models show that the tone of media articles using the 'innocence frame' had both direct and indirect impacts. Furthermore, the substantive effect of a burst shift of attention in the media is greater than the slowly shifting nature of public opinion. Finally, the authors argue that this media and framing effect is not a journalistic bias; it reflects how legal professionals discuss this policy issue in their communities. All in all, the robust conclusion from this empirical study is that media coverage of the death penalty issue affects public opinion and jury behaviour, and not vice versa.

Two more general lessons can be drawn from the Swiss banking secrecy and US death penalty examples. First, the framing of an issue is always a key element in agenda-setting dynamics. If the political attention dedicated to a specific issue suddenly rises, then this is probably linked to the strategic use (by policy entrepreneurs) of a new issue framing (in alternative institutional venues). However, policy scholars always need to remain very cautious when they interpret media data: the causal relationships between real-world events, agenda-setting activities by political actors, public opinion and media coverage are not easy to disentangle. Second, the fact that one and the same policy issue can be framed in very different ways, over time and across policy agendas, is inherently also a very strong argument against effort to develop definitive typologies of policies (as discussed in Chapter 8). As shown above, the Swiss banking policy seems to be increasingly framed as a morality issue, whereas the US death penalty policy is rather experiencing a de-moralisation process. Several policy examples that were discussed in the previous chapter are also multi-faceted (e.g. war, reduction of poverty, immigration) and this multi-dimensionality allows for concurrent policy frames promoted by various policy actors (Engeli and Varone, 2011).

CONCLUSIONS

While the starting point for any consideration of agenda setting needs to be the social processes that translate individual problems into social problems and then into political problems, efforts by policy analysts to theorise about agenda setting have their origins in efforts to prescribe how policy agendas should be set, using a 'rational' problem-solving model. But that model offers not so much an approach that helps us interpret how policy is actually made but rather an 'ideal type' against which more realistic models may be measured. The dominant approach to this realism is 'incrementalism', offered as an account of what is, but also as a more 'democratic' model for the messy world of pluralistic politics. However, that is both still probably too rational and does not address the issues about the circumstances in which more fragmented shifts in the agenda occur. Hence the importance of analyses that get away from the prescriptive preoccupations of the rationalism/incrementalism debate. The main contributions to this are Kingdon's 'multiple streams approach' and the 'punctuated equilibrium model' developed by Baumgartner and Jones.

Kingdon is not a dogmatic theorist. He speaks of himself as aiming to make progress 'in understanding . . . vague and imprecise phenomena', but finding that 'vision is still obscured' (1995, p. 208) and says that he is 'trying to weave a rich tapestry' (ibid., p. 230). In this sense the fact that he gives no attention to agenda setting anywhere other than in the US federal government should not be held against him. Rather, he has given us an approach – we may even say a 'toolkit' – which we can use to explore agenda setting anywhere.

Embodied in Kingdon's notion that three streams – problems, policies and politics – mingle in the 'soup' is an interesting challenge to do two related things. These are to ask questions about the extent to which agenda setting may be stabilised in practice. The discussion above, conducted by means of the example of pensions policy, where in some respects stability or shaping comes from the long-run continuity of the 'problem', has suggested that 'politics' makes a difference to national responses. That leads us to look at the role of politics as a source of agenda shaping in societies that are less institutionally fragmented than the United States.

Where Kingdon's work remains to some extent embedded in the pluralist concern to explain the multiple influences on policy making, Baumgartner and Jones address the wider issues (identified briefly in Chapter 5) about the need to explain the combination of continuity on the one hand and change on the other that characterises much of the policy process. The discussion of their work delineated their model and explored two examples, one their own account of the changing debate about capital punishment in the United States the other the modification of bank secrecy policy in Switzerland.

The four approaches to the exploration of policy formulation – the rational model of decision making, incrementalism, Kingdon's multiple streams approach and Baumgartner and Jones' punctuated equilibrium model reflect different policy process theories. The rational model has much in common with the traditional approach to representative government, seeing policy formulation as a systematic response to authoritatively set goals. While there is not much discussion of how these may be set, the presumption is that they emerge from the democratic political process. Incrementalism's links with pluralist thinking are very evident in the writings of Lindblom. Furthermore, Lindblom's shift in perspective through his career can be seen as a response to the challenge posed to pluralism by those who stressed power inequalities. Then, the way in which Kingdon was influenced by March and Olsen's emphasis upon system unpredictability in an institutional context shows itself in his explicit use of the concept of the 'garbage can'. Furthermore, the challenge to Kingdon's model offered by evidence that systems may be more organised than he suggests emphasises institutional arrangements and the stability of some policy networks and communities. However, there then remains the need to provide an account of the policy process that both acknowledges that stability and explores the way it may be undermined, offers potential for comparative work. Baumgartner and Jones' punctuated equilibrium theory responds to that need.

Chapter 5 mentioned the contributions of various developments of institutional theory which try to handle issues about change, notably Surel's discussion of the influence of exogenous and endogenous factors and Streeck and Thelen's distinctions between gradual change and dramatic change. The explanations of policy agenda-setting here brings us back to these ideas. Modern theories, particularly punctuated equilibrium theory, take us a long way from the apparently tightly controlled policy change processes implied by the early approaches to this subject. But there remain questions to be answered about variation in respect of the models on offer. These may be seen as variations in respect of issue, place and time as explored in Chapter 6 in terms of the national pattern approach, the policy sector approach, the international regime approach and the temporal pattern approach.

Variation from place to place has been suggested by recognition of the institutional arrangements that tend to structure the agenda setting process

(continued)

through mandates. A few comparative studies have explored the extent to which the equilibrium of policy systems may vary from country to country (see for instance Baumgartner et al., 2009; Jones et al., 2009; Green-Pedersen and Walgrave, 2014).

Variation over time is particularly addressed by punctuated equilibrium theory. It raises questions about the extent to which established policies become undermined by changes to the demographic and economic contexts in which they were established. Analyses of the post–Second World War welfare state settlement provide examples of this (see, discussions of this in *inter alia* Taylor-Gooby, 2013). But there are issues here about the extent to which policies themselves contain what may be seen as 'the seeds of their own destruction', features that make them particularly subject to disequilibrium. The international scene provides illustrations of this, notably the way in which the efforts to construct an international order after the First World War continue to have repercussions after nearly 100 years (MacMillan, 2001; Barr, 2011).

These observations could take us into a neo-Marxist discussion of inherent contradictions in society (see for example Streeck, 2014), or to questions about whether disequilibrium in policy is increasing. The point at which we need to stop here is to acknowledge that discussions of policy agenda setting have been taken, particularly by Kingdon and by Baumgartner and Jones, a long way from a simple social problem solving perspective.

10 Policy formulation

SYNOPSIS

There is a great deal of policy-making work that sits between successful agenda setting and implementation. The term 'policy formulation' is used to describe this, though an alternative perspective on this as 'policy programming' is also seen to be useful.

A policy example, where policy formulation might be expected to be quite simple, is used to illustrate the importance of this part of the process. That is followed by consideration of some policy process theory that focuses on 'instrument choice' – the fact that there are alternative ways of attempting to achieve policy goals. Choosing the right instrument is a key condition to achieve policy objectives, but also to foster the participation of the target populations affected by the policy. While some approaches clearly focus on the substantive aims of a policy and on instruments' effectiveness (How can the state solve public problems?), others rather emphasise the indirect impacts of policy instruments on the identity and political attitudes of target groups, and eventually, on democracy (What messages are sent by the state to citizens?).

The discussion of policy formulation leads on to a consideration of the literature on the power of civil servants, people who are likely to be particularly involved in this part of the policy process. While recognising the potential significance of wider propositions about the extent to which civil servants may be seen as the makers of policy, it will be suggested that a more plausible scenario is that civil servants will be very involved in the detailed programming of policy but that they may do this (as Page and Jenkins' 2005 study of British civil servants suggests) in a context in which they are guided by politicians' expectations or values.

Introduction

In the last chapter the distinction between it and this one was set out simplistically in terms of the distinction between deciding where to go (agenda setting) and working out how to get there (formulation or policy programming). But it was noted that the agenda-setting/formulation distinction is a difficult one, with a strong interaction between the two very likely. Nevertheless it is worthwhile to make the distinction and to emphasise its significance through the use of two separate chapters because the extensive range of policy-making activities that must follow on an initial policy commitment is often overlooked. A realistic approach to the study of the policy process must involve a recognition that if policies are to have real effects a great deal of detailed work has to be done. It has been suggested that much policy making is merely 'symbolic' (Edelman, 1971; 1977) consisting of gestures by politicians aimed to convince the electorate that they care and are doing things when little is in practice being achieved. Detailed policy formulation is fundamental to the making of what may perhaps be called *real* as opposed to symbolic policy.

Attention to policy formulation is also important to avoid falling into the dichotomisation of the policy process in which just two stages are highlighted: one in which politicians *make* policy and the other in which civil servants merely *implement* it.

Note how the two examples of the stages model by British authors, featured in Box 8.3 included, in Jenkins' formulation 'information', 'consideration' and 'decision' after 'initiation' and even more, namely 'deciding how to decide', 'issue definition', 'forecasting', 'setting objectives and priorities' and 'options analysis' after 'deciding to decide' in Hogwood and Gunn's version. We thus see these authors clustering a number of activities around agenda setting but not making the distinction between that and formulation as used in this book. Their approach takes us back to something mentioned in the chapter on agenda setting: the 'rational' approach seen as using an unrealistic view of how policy decisions are made but providing a starting point for the more realistic agenda-setting model used by the incrementalists and by Kingdon. Simon argues, in his formulation of the rational approach:

> It has not been commonly recognized that a theory of administration should be concerned with the processes of decision as well as with the processes of action. This neglect perhaps stems from the notion that decision making is confined to the formulation of overall policy. On the contrary, the process of decision does not come to an end when the general purpose of an organization has been determined. The task of 'deciding' pervades the entire administrative organization quite as much as the task of 'doing' – indeed, it is integrally tied up with the latter.
>
> (1957, p. 1)

Simon attacks the notion of decision taking as external to administration, the notion that decisions are taken by politicians leaving administrators to put those decisions into 'action'. He points out that administration involves continual decision taking. Such decisions can be seen as organised in a hierarchy, minor decisions being consequent upon major ones.

Simon presents decision making not as a process of 'maximising', as in economic theory, but as a process in which individual rationality is limited:

> The central concern of administrative theory is with the boundary between the rational and the non-rational aspects of human social behaviour. Administrative theory is peculiarly the theory of intended and bounded rationality – of the behaviour of human beings who *satisfice* because they have not the wit to *maximise*.
>
> (Ibid., p. xxiv)

New insights from behavioural sciences and (social) psychology have recurrently demonstrated that people always make imperfect decisions. Consequently, conventional policy approaches that are based on the neo-classical assumption of rationality are of little help to explain the (human) behaviour of policy actors. In addition, they are of no use for designing effective policies: opting for instruments that should work if people were perfectly rational (see the section on 'nudging' below).

Simon pays particular attention to the fact that decisions are based upon premises and that these premises will involve both factual and value elements. He recognises that it is often difficult to separate these elements but suggests that in ordering the hierarchy of decisions, deciding which decisions are the key ones which should form the premises for lower-order decisions, administrators should try to give priority to value premises. While from his prescriptive position he argues that the value premises should come from politicians, who are democratically elected and accountable to citizens, he explores the difficulties about making the fact/value distinction in real situations.

Simon's treatment of this issue then leads on to questions about who does this sort of work. Is it easy to make a distinction between what politicians do and what civil servants do (bearing in mind that this topic is often approached prescriptively in terms of propositions about what each should do)? Or have we here a range of activity within which that distinction is very likely to be blurred?

The relevance here of the incrementalist challenge to Simon (discussed in the previous chapter) lies in the extent to which, however policy goals are selected, detailed policy formulation is a piecemeal activity too. Institutional theory, and particularly its emphasis upon pathways, suggests that this will be the case. There are moreover some activities, involving the adjustment of policy over time, that seem particularly likely to take that form. A good example here is the budgetary process. There have been various studies of the budgeting process outlining the ways in which government departments negotiate with the central finance department (including notably a classic study of the UK by Heclo and Wildavsky called significantly *The Private Government of Public Money*, 1981). To understand what is involved simply bear in mind what happens in voluntary organisations, large and small. On a regular basis, probably once a year, expenditure plans and income sources are reviewed. That review seldom involves wholesale reconsideration of activities. Rather the expectation is that existing activities will continue, and the existing revenue stream will remain. The questions that then get considered are about small variations in activities and small adjustments in, for example, subscriptions. Changes upwards or downwards will be *incremental*. Most governmental budgetary review processes are similar, merely just more complex. Public budgets are highly incremental in all countries and at all levels of government; only rarely punctuated by large changes (see Jones et al., 2009, for a comparative analysis).

Key aspects of policy formulation

We start therefore with an examination of what policy formulation is likely to involve. This is a topic that is quite difficult to address in general terms. Hence the more abstract discussion of the topic will be illustrated with explicit examples. In this respect it needs to be remembered that the distinctions between the various formal policy formulation activities will vary from country to country (see the 'National Pattern Approach' presented in Chapter 6).

Knoepfel and Weidner use the term 'policy programming' (1982; see also Knoepfel et al., 2007, chapter 8) rather than formulation to address this issue and use a model that sees the detail of a policy as forming a series of layers around a policy core. These will include:

- More precise definitions of policy objectives. It was noted in relation to anti-poverty policy in Chapter 1 that the adoption of such a policy must imply a stance on the definition of poverty.
- Operational elements, which include the 'instruments' to be used to make the policy effective, a topic discussed further below.
- 'Political-administrative arrangements', which involve the specification of the authorities whose duty it will be to implement the policy, the notion that such authorities need money and other resources to do that follows self-evidently from that point.
- Procedural elements, namely the rules to be used in the implementation of the policy.

Box 10.1 illustrates these points with reference to the already used example of the 'right to roam' policy in England and Wales. What that example suggests is that even with a relatively simple example of a public policy, the policy formulation process may be of considerable complexity. This simple Act translating a policy objective into action runs to 22 pages. It deals with important questions about the overall definition of the 'right of access', of related rights and duties, of administering authorities and their tasks, of exceptions and of appeals.

Box 10.1	The legislation to enact the 'right to roam' policy in England and Wales

The relevant legislation is the Countryside and Rights of Way Act of 2000, of which this measure forms the principle part (Part 1). Part 1 of the Act, however, runs to 48 sections across 22 pages. Within it can be found:

- 'Principal definitions' including the meaning of 'access land' in the sections to come.
- Rights of the public in respect of access land, including some rules about things they may not do.
- A duty given to a public agency to prepare maps, and some specifications about how those maps should be prepared.
- Liabilities of owners of access land.
- Specification of responsibilities of 'access authorities' – the public bodies required to administer the legislation – including powers to enable them to employ wardens.
- Conditions under which the general right of access may be withdrawn in exceptional circumstances.
- Rules about how access land can be 'accessed' – about fencing, gates, etc.
- Appeal rules in respect of various provisions.

The Countryside and Rights of Way Act 2000 is a British Act of Parliament. In this sense the policy formulation responsibility seems to be right where it should be in a system of representative government: with the legislature. But of course when we consider how detailed it is we must ask two questions: where did that detail come from, and how fully did the legislature scrutinise it? The answer – without going into what actually happened in this case – is that those 22 pages contain a great deal of material that was prepared by the executive assisted by unelected civil servants and that the actual legislative scrutiny will have been quite abbreviated. We will return to this below.

However, within the Act there are other things that point to policy formulation that is likely to occur outside the legislature. The Act contains in various places a power to make further regulations. For example it lists nine more specific issues in respect of the making of definitive maps (their form and scale, how the public shall be informed about them, how appeals about them should be handled) for which regulations may be made. There is also one more fundamental supplementary power 'the Secretary of State (as respects England) or the Welsh Assembly (as respects Wales) may by order amend the definition of "open country" . . . so as to include a reference to coastal land' (clause 3). Interestingly in this case the government subsequently decided that further substantive legislation was necessary and passed the Marine and Coastal Access Act in 2009. Since then, the translation of that into action remains a long drawn out process.

In British law Acts of Parliament regularly involve the granting of power to make subsequent 'regulations'. The procedures relating to these are complex. Technically they have to be 'laid before Parliament' but in practice there are so many regulations that only a minute quantity get any detailed scrutiny. Once through that technical law-making process they form a substantive addition to the Act. In the past this form of law making, called 'delegated legislation', has been attacked by administrative lawyers as involving the taking of arbitrary powers by the government. The consensus today is that it would be impossible to deal with detailed amplification of legislation without some sort of power of this kind. For example, social security payment rates are changed regularly to allow for movements in the cost of living, Parliament would be overwhelmed if all changes of this kind needed new Acts of Parliament. On the other hand there is an implicit – but difficult – distinction to be made between detailed adjustments of policies and clauses that enable fundamental policy change without Parliamentary scrutiny.

There are other clauses in the Countryside and Rights of Way Act that delegate more limited policy formulation responsibilities without even the notional requirement to involve the legislature. A central government 'agency', the Countryside Agency, has a variety of duties under the Act, including the giving of guidance to other authorities. Then lower down the system the various 'access authorities', generally local governments, may make their own arrangements about how to carry out their responsibilities. Note for example that they have 'powers' not 'duties' to employ wardens.

Readers who are neither British citizens nor irresistibly attracted by a walk in the countryside will easily find other empirical examples, depicting very similar situations all around the world. For instance, ocean beaches are central to most Californians and waves' surfing is part of their identity. It is thus not surprising that the public access to beaches is guaranteed in the state Constitution (Section 4 of Article X). It is further regulated by the – no less than 146 pages long – California Coastal Act (Public Resource Code, Division 20). In addition, a state agency, the California Coastal Commission, is in charge of monitoring the beach access by the public. Despite this very dense policy program, conflicts recurrently emerge between landowners and surfers. The scenario is well known. Landowners lock the gate across 'their' private road to the beach. However, surfers ignore the no access warnings, go around the locked gate and jump into the ocean. When they come out of the water, they are arrested by the Sheriff's Office deputies. The case is then adjudicated by the Coastal Commission (since the law modification in June 2014) or ends up in a court after the private landowner and/or the 'Surfrider Foundation' having filed different judicial suits. In a nutshell, an apparently simple problem has generated an impressive number of constitutional and legislatives norms, rule-making procedures by the Coastal Commissions and judgments by courts. This example also suggests that implementation decisions by an executive agency may have an impact on the re-formulation of the policy over time.

As noted above, it is difficult to address the subject of policy formulation without the use of examples that may be dismissed as specific to individual countries. The argument here is not that legislation in other countries will have the legal shape described for the UK or the Californian case, but that it may reasonably be predicted that they will have a structure that will contain most if not all of the following elements:

■ Basic laws with clauses enabling later amendment.

■ Provisions to make more detailed rules within the overarching legislative framework.

■ Systems under which central responsible ministries will give more detailed instructions and/or advice to lower-tier agencies (including local governments).

■ Adaptation of legislative rules and regulatory decisions after court's rulings.

To these may be added, in respect of forms of privatisation, the specification of much detail in contracts to non-public agencies expected to perform public functions.

This detailed formulation process involves the making of choices about ways to enact policy. This is the concern of the next section. It is followed by a section on a topic given considerable attention in the literature since the last years of the twentieth century, policy transfer, involving learning from other countries. Since that learning mostly involves formulation issues once a policy issue is on the agenda, it is included here rather than in the previous chapter.

Instrument choice

Knoepfel and Weidner's model of the policy formulation process has been noted as including 'instruments' within the list of operational elements (1982). The issues about instrument choice may be very important. Howlett goes so far as to suggest that 'instrument choice . . . is public policymaking' (1991, p. 2).

Efforts to specify the key instruments have involved the provision of a list that is often quite extensive. As an appendix to his article, Howlett (1991) provides a list from other work, which contains 63 items. However, in the textbook he produced with Ramesh (Howlett and Ramesh, 2003; third edition published in 2009) he commends an approach to the delineation of policy instruments based upon Hood's listing of 'tools of government'. Hood (1986) classifies these in terms of

■ 'nodality' – meaning the use of information;

■ 'authority' – meaning the legal power used;

- 'treasure' – that is the use of money;
- 'organisation' – the use of formal organisational arrangements.

It is unfortunate that Hood's fondness for acronyms leads him to use this rather odd terminology (added together they make NATO), but his approach is helpful. Howlett and Ramesh (2003) go on from this starting point to a valuable discussion of the strengths and weaknesses of various policy instruments. Key issues from their analyses are summarised in Box 10.2.

Policy making involves choices about instrument use. Linder and Peters (1991) see policy instruments as in principle substitutable. They argue that in practice the choice of instruments depends upon

- resource intensiveness;
- the extent to which precise targeting of policies is required;
- levels of political risk;
- constraints on state activity.

Box 10.2	Howlett and Ramesh's (2003) analysis of policy instruments

It is argued that instruments can be seen as within a spectrum involving increased levels of state involvement from low (at the voluntary instruments end) to high (at the compulsory instruments end). Decisions about instrument use will be influenced by the likelihood of resistance. Hence there will tend to be a preference for using low state involvement options. However, choices will be affected by the resources (as specified in Hood's list of tools) available to governments.

Howlett and Ramesh specify the following instruments (2003, p. 195):

Voluntary Instruments

Family and community

Voluntary organisation

Private markets.

Mixed Instruments

Information and exhortation

Subsidies

Auction of property rights

Tax and user charges.

Compulsory Instruments

Regulation

Public enterprise

Direct provision.

Earlier in their book they offer an even more complex formulation of this typology (p. 92).

This 'policy design' approach clearly stresses the political essence of instrument choice. For example, to promote energy-efficient household appliances, office equipment or cars (as objectives of the energy policy), different policy tools can be alternatively implemented by the government: information campaigns for consumers, education programmes for retailers, quality labels indicating the energy performance of products, minimum standards to be reached by producers, tax on products with a low energy-efficiency, subsidy for high energy-efficiency products, etc. While these different instruments can be considered as functionally equivalent from a technical point of view, they are absolutely not substitutable from a political point of view. Indeed, each policy instrument is inextricably linked to specific administrative resources, implementing agencies, target groups, etc. In other words, each instrument generates its own 'political economy' (Varone, 1998; Landry and Varone, 2005).

A comparative study has systematically applied the four instrument attributes suggested by Linder and Peters (1991) to investigate the formulation of energy-efficiency policies in Canada, Denmark, the United States, Sweden and Switzerland since 1973 (Varone, 1998; Varone and Aebischer, 2001). This study shows the explanatory power of the four factors and demonstrates that a policy instrument is eventually adopted by decision makers:

- If a specialised administrative agency already exists, which helps to minimise the financial costs of implementation (e.g. in Denmark, the creation of a new Energy Ministry in 1979 – only after the second oil-shock – was a precondition for adopting a mandatory labelling program in 1982).

- If the groups which are directly targeted by the instrument are not opposed to it (e.g. in Switzerland, manufacturers of office equipment were strongly opposed to any mandatory standards and only supported voluntary target-values in 1990).

- If other political jurisdictions have already applied this instrument with success and thus reduced the political costs of a potential policy failure (e.g. Canada adopted in 1992 the product standards that were first experienced in 1987 in the USA).

- If the degree of coercion inherent in the instrument is compatible with the party ideology of the ruling majority (e.g. in the American case, Democrats adopted regulatory standards while Republicans only supported voluntary labels).

Finally, the comparative study of energy-efficiency policies also suggests that the choice of an instrument always implies some trade-offs: it is impossible for decision makers to find an instrument that cumulatively has a low resource intensity, is fully supported by its target groups, has absolutely no uncertain outcome and is perfectly compatible with the pro-market versus pro-State ideology of the ruling majority. On the contrary, choosing an instrument or an instruments' mix necessarily implies prioritising some element over the other (e.g. to accept higher implementation cost of subsidies that are accepted by target groups).

Doern also insists on the political nature of instrument choice and sees it as essentially ideological, but with governments choosing the least coercive instrument. In his work with Phidd (Doern and Phidd, 1983, p. 134) he portrays instruments along a continuum rather like that provided in Box 10.2, from 'exhortation' through 'expenditure' and 'regulation' to 'public ownership'. More recent writing on policy instruments also emphasises the ideological dimension. Lascoumes and Le Galès argue, '[p]ublic policy instrumentation . . . reveals a (fairly explicit) theorisation of the relationship between the governing and the governed: every instrument constitutes a condensed form of knowledge about social control and ways of exercising it' (2007, p. 3). They go on to say that 'instruments that work are not neutral devices: they produce specific effects, independently of the objective pursued (the aims ascribed to them), which structure public policy according to their own logic' (ibid.).

This view treats the issues about instrument choice as much more than a pragmatic matter of deciding the best way of achieving an objective. It will be influenced by views about the right way to govern, and then – as suggested by institutional theory – chosen instruments will then give characteristics to policy that are likely to influence future decisions about the best way to carry it forward.

What the literature on instruments has made very clear is that the factors that influence instrument choice are complex. Policy type comes into play here and the issues about resistance to policy, but we may also see ideology influencing choice. In each specific case much depends on what is available, what has been done before, or what is already in use in a closely related policy area. Howlett argues that it is not feasible to 'develop a general theory of policy instrument types' (1991, p. 1). Rather, he suggests that issues of instrument choice need to be linked up with issues about national policy styles (see the 'National Pattern Approach' in Chapter 6):

> There are several areas in which much more work remains to be done. First, the relationship between policy styles and policy instruments needs to be elaborated more precisely. This involves not only additional work conceptualising and clarifying theories of policy instrument choice, but also work clarifying the concept of national policy styles. Second, much more comparative work needs to be done to add to the number of cases of instrument choice available, thus contributing to the development of studies of national styles, whether these turn out to be truly national or sectoral in nature.
>
> (Ibid., p. 16)

These questions about instrument choice connect up with another theme in the discussion of the policy process, one which is widely used in association with analyses of modern approaches to public management and to governance. Various writers have developed typologies for the analysis of policy processes, stimulated by the issues on the agenda about the use of market mechanisms. Government has been seen to have choices between leaving matters to the market or imposing hierarchical systems. Then, with the development of network theory (see Chapter 4), it has been suggested that networks offer a third alternative. Hence Thompson et al. (1991) speak of hierarchies, markets and networks as three general models of social coordination, while Ouchi (1980) distinguishes between bureaucracies, markets and clans. Bradach and Eccles (1991) and Colebatch and Larmour (1993) examine the organisation of policy action in terms of hierarchic authority (bureaucracy), individual exchanges (markets) and group activities (community). In a classic exploration of authority within organisations Etzioni (1961) outlined three ways of securing compliance, which he called 'coercive', 'utilitarian' and 'normative'. Hood colloquially calls these 'sticks', 'carrots' and sermons' (2007, p. 138; see also Bemelmans-Videc et al., 2003).

Hill and Hupe's version of these alternatives is to propose the following distinctions for policy processes:

- 'authority' – where rules are laid down in advance;
- 'transaction' – where certain outputs are expected, often as specified in contracts;
- 'persuasion' – where the essential mode of operation involves collaboration or what may be called 'co-production' (Hill and Hupe, 2014, pp. 186–8).

Table 10.1 sets out the kinds of activities for which the different modes of governance and accountability may be appropriate. In the second row of Table 10.1 the alternative perspectives on the management of implementation draw a distinction between top-down authority in the first column, issues about the extent to which there has been conformity with a contract in the second one, and a very mixed mode of accountability in the third column called 'co-production'. In the final row the way the actual management of the system is likely to be carried out is highlighted. This is seen in the 'Authority' column as particularly concerned with inputs, that is, questions about the extent to which resources have been appropriately applied to the performance of a task. In the 'Transaction' column it is suggested that crucial for this mode is a concern with outputs – have contractual obligations been fulfilled? By contrast with these two, the concern within the 'Persuasion' mode is with success in achieving shared goals – health or education improvement, for example – where it is real results as opposed to formally specified outputs that is crucial. There are then questions about choices between the alternatives (just as explored in the policy instruments literature). These will depend on:

- considerations about the 'best' ways to organise any specific policy delivery process;
- the extent to which the relationship between inputs, outputs and outcomes is complicated;
- the ideologies of those who make the crucial choices (for example the strong preference for markets amongst many politicians of the liberal Right).

Table 10.1   Three kinds of governance

	Authority	Transaction	Persuasion
Core activity of government	Imposing Regulating Delivering goods and services	Creating frameworks Assessing results	Inviting participation Showing direction
Appropriate perspective on managing implementation	Enforcement	Performance	Co-production
Management via	Inputs	Outputs	Outcomes as shared results

Simplified model based upon Hill and Hupe, 2014, Table 8.6, p. 187.

There are some issues of importance for modern governance about the distinctions made in the last row of Table 10.1. Where traditional bureaucratic governance depended upon clearly specified inputs we now see the specification of expected outputs or outcomes as important. How these are specified and measured will naturally be influential. Behind this is a broad sociological point about how the development of statistical measures may influence policy discourse (Desrosières, 2002). There is considerable controversy (for example about the applicability of measures of performance in schools, hospitals and so on), and about the ways this data is published and used for future decision making (see Pollitt, 2003). Much of this focuses upon output measures that are often rather crude. All gets much more complicated if attention is shifted to outcome measures (think for example of debates about inequalities of health, social mobility or what crime measures can tell us about the state of our society). This may seem to take us a long way from pragmatic questions about instrument choice; however, data outputs from policy feed back into subsequent decisions. These feedbacks are very important for both policy effectiveness and policy legitimacy, particularly where outcomes are clearly identified objectives. The next two sections address these topics.

Insights from behavioural sciences: nudging

Some policy scholars argue that the design of policy instruments should integrate more accurate knowledge about how and why people really make (always imperfect) decisions. This convincing appeal to develop behaviourally informed policy is called 'nudging'. It can be defined as designing 'any aspect of the choice architecture that alters people's behaviour in a predictable way without forbidding any options or significantly changing their economic incentives' (Thaler and Sunstein, 2008, p. 6). Three major findings of behavioural research are particularly relevant for policy makers who want to engage in a nudging strategy (Sibony and Alemano, 2015, pp. 3–4).

First, human beings have a natural propensity to accept their environment as a given; they try to avoid major change of the status quo. Due to this strong inertia, they prefer to stick to the so-called *default options* (or the status quo). Hence the definition of the policy default option is important. Let's take the example of organ donation: the rate of organ donors among the overall population is much higher in countries where the policy default option is a 'presumed consent' (e.g. France, Belgium, Italy, Austria, Spain, Norway, Sweden, etc.), than in countries where it is an 'informed consent' (e.g. the UK, the Netherlands, Germany, Switzerland, Denmark, Japan, Canada, etc.). In the first case ('opt-out' policy), everyone is a donor as long as they did not ask not to be one. In the second case ('opt-in' policy), one can become a donor only if one registers on a donor list. To increase the rate of organ donors and thus to reach a higher policy effectiveness, shifting the default option to the 'presumed consent' (opt-out; everyone is a donor) makes sense (see also G. Smith et al., 2011, pp. 95–110).

The second lesson of behavioural sciences is that a human choice between various options depends also a lot about how these options are formulated (i.e. a *framing effect*). For example, people accept surgery more frequently if told that the survival rate is about 90 percent, than if told that the mortality is rate is about 10 percent. Consequently, how target groups are informed about the content of the policy will affect its reception. In addition, information that is concrete has a greater impact on behaviour than information that is abstract. This has been demonstrated for the prevention of tobacco consumption: pictorial warnings on tobacco products are much more persuasive than a text warning. The state needs to use adequate framing techniques (a strategy that private advertisers and marketers have been exploiting since decades!).

Third, the behaviour of others has a big influence on human decisions. The third nudging strategy relies thus on the appeals of *social norms*. Social psychologists and behavioural economists argue that people benchmark their achievements using the performances of others. Furthermore, everyone has a tendency to fear being worse than average. So direct evidence on how others behave may influence behaviour. For example, therefore we find where 'information' is chosen as a policy instrument the use of comparative material that suggests we use fuel extravagantly, or consume more calories than others.

These three basic elements of a 'nudging' approach to instrument choice show how the state may regulate the behaviour of private actors and eventually achieve its policy objectives. Policy makers are 'architects of individual choice' when they steer people towards decisions by organising the context and process of individual decision making. To do so, they need to capitalise on how citizens really behave (e.g. findings of experiences in behavioural sciences), and not on how they are theoretically supposed to behave (according to pure neoclassical economics' assumptions or normative statements; see Chapter 3).

The American and British governments, amongst others, have given attention to these ideas. The UK Treasury set up a 'Behavioural Insights Team', which became colloquially known as 'the nudge unit' in 2010 and subsequently privatised it. On September 15, 2015, the US President Barack Obama adopted the 'Behavioural Science Insight Policy Directive'. This Executive Order urges American executive departments and agencies to design their policies and programmes 'to reflect our best understanding of how people engage with, participate in, use, and respond to those policies and programs'. The aim is to expand the experimentation and evaluation of nudging mechanisms that have already proven to be effective in the past, such as the automatic enrolment and automatic escalation in retirement saving plans or the streamlining of the application process for financial aids granted to college students.

This discussion obviously tends to take us into the territory of analysis 'for policy' (see Chapter 1) inasmuch as nudging is advocated in order to 'improve' the policy process. The point here is that instrument choice may be influenced by considerations about the way policy is likely to be received. The assumption about nudging, at least in Thaler and Sunstein's original work (op. cit.), where they called it 'libertarian paternalism', is an absence of compulsion. But there is a potential conflict between those terms, 'whether or not one is influenced by a nudge is voluntary . . . is sometimes difficult to guarantee' (Oliver, 2013, p. 686). It has been embraced in areas of public policy – particularly health promotion policy – where there is a fine line between nudging and 'shoving' (Local Government Association UK, 2013) and it has been seen as one 'step' in a 'ladder of intervention' (Nuffield Council on Bioethics, 2007) in which the provision of information and the enabling of choice represent elements at the bottom and the use of disincentives or the restriction/elimination of choice the upper steps with nudging somewhere in between. This clearly brings us back to Doern's point about concerns to use the least coercive policy instrument. That, however, begs questions about who is to be coerced, taking us to a development of the arguments about power within the 'triangle of policy actors' discussed in Chapter 8. This is explored further in the next section.

Social constructions and policy design

Anne. L Schneider and Helen Ingram have developed a constructivist approach to policy formulation (Schneider and Ingram, 1997) which highlights how the 'design' of a substantive policy content is always based on the social construction and political power of target groups. This resonates with the narrative policy framework (see Chapter 8), which also focuses on how groups are portrayed (as victims, villains or heroes) during policy debates.

When formulating a policy solution, decisions makers usually may choose among different target populations. For example, to reduce drunk driving and the related damages, a public policy can focus on repeat offenders (e.g. severe sanctions), on persons under the legal age of buying alcohol (e.g. education and prevention), on those who sell alcohol (e.g. regulation of opening hours), on the liquor industry (e.g. higher taxes on beverages), etc. Implicit in policy design is likely to be the formal designation of the primary target groups of a policy. This decision is highly political and normative inasmuch as the selected target groups are politically designated as responsible of – or even guilty for – the public problem to be solved. In Chapter 8 we argued that issues about who gains and who loses from policies loom large in policy process analysis. Then in this chapter we have argued that similar considerations apply to the adoption of policy instruments. Schneider and Ingram's constructivist approach then directs attention to the issues about the extent to which what is specifically involved in respect of what we earlier loosely called 'losers' is the extent to which the policy makes them a target group whose behaviour is to be modified. To do this many options are on the table, from very soft instruments, such as information campaigns or financial incentives, to very constraining instruments, such as licence withdrawal or sentences to prison.

Schneider and Ingram (1997) claim that the selection of both the target group and the instrument (mix) is not a technical, value-neutral exercise. On the contrary, decision makers will opt for an instrument targeting a specific group according to their own assumptions and biases about how this target group behaves. Two dimensions are particularly important here to assess a target group: its social construction, as a deserving versus undeserving group; and its strong versus weak political power. A matrix crossing the two basic dimensions allow a distinction between four ideal-types of target groups, as summarised in Table 10.2: (1) 'advantaged' groups, with a positive image and a high amount of power; (2) 'contenders', who suffer from a negative social perception, but are nevertheless powerful; (3) 'dependents', groups with a positive image but no power attributes; and, finally, (4) 'deviant' groups that have a negative image and, at the same time, are powerless.

Furthermore, these different target groups are expected to receive disproportionate shares of either policy benefits or policy burdens. Ingram et al.

Table 10.2 Types of target groups and choice of policy instruments

Types of target group and corresponding policy instruments		Social construction of target group as. . .	
		Deserving	Undeserving
Political power of target groups is . . .	Strong	'Advantaged' (e.g. business, farmers, military): self-regulation or entitlements	'Contenders' (e.g. gun owners, Wall street bankers): regulatory instruments
	Weak	'Dependents' (e.g. mothers, children): income-tested subsidies and persuasion	'Deviants' (e.g. criminals, homeless, terrorists, drug addicts): sanctions and punishment

Source: Free adaptation from Schneider and Ingram, 1997, pp. 109 and 130.

(2016, pp. 15–20) provide illustrative examples from US policies that we briefly summarise here. Homeowners obviously constitutes an *advantaged* group. Consequently, they are offered a number of policy benefits, such as mortgage-interest deduction. The yearly costs to the US Treasury of these tax deductions amount to about $175 million (i.e. more than the sum of the discretionary budgets of the departments for Education, Homeland security, Energy and Agriculture). After the 2008 financial crisis, bankers were socially perceived and politically constructed as *contenders*. Nevertheless, no limit on executive pay and bonuses have been adopted so far, and the major Dodd-Frank banking reform has been implemented with important delays and regulatory setbacks. In sharp opposition, policies targeting *deviant* groups generally apply coercive tools and involve sanctions, force or even death. The incarceration of prisoners in Guantanamo, without a fair trial and clear convictions, is an emblematic example of how the state may treat undeserving and powerless people. Finally, policy designs which aim at modifying the behaviour of *dependents* frequently include income-tested subsidies. Eligible persons have to apply to receive state aid, for instance as disabled person, unemployed, student without resources, etc. In a nutshell, it is argued that different patterns of instrument choice exist, and that they vary with the social constructions and power of target groups.

Beyond this strong analytical proposition, which has been tested empirically in many policy domains and countries (Pierce et al., 2014), the social construction approach also suggests that the differentiated treatment of target groups, through more or less biased policy designs, has enduring effects. The way target populations concretely experience public policies (e.g. contact with welfare agencies versus with criminal justice) has a crucial impact on their identity, and on their political attitudes and participation as well. The presence of so-called 'feed-forward effects' (Pierce et al., 2014, p. 5) is a core proposition of the approach that establishes a link between (the design of) public policies, politics and democracy. The key assumption can be summarised as follows:

> At each stage in the policy cycle, the discourse in policy formulation, the provisions in legislation and rules, the ways laws are implemented and policy impact all carry powerful messages about who matters, and whom governments serves and punishes. These messages teach citizens whether or not their problems are public problems related to welfare or are their own to solve. It tells them whether they are to be treated with respect, ignored or punished. They teach whether participation matters or whether government is something to be avoided. . . . Thus, some people are strongly and successfully motivated by policy to participate in politics. Other are sidelined and repelled by policy. The system is degenerative because the next round of policy making reproduces the same pathologies that become even more entrenched in the policy processes and institutions of the society. Instead of a self-correcting system of governance, as the pluralists thought, the problems build themselves.
>
> (Ingram et al., 2015, p. 186)

Policy designs and instrument choices tend thus to reproduce the stereotypes and stigma on which they are based. This leads to a vicious circle. People who are perpetually portrayed as undeserving and who have negative experiences with biased policy designs are gradually alienated as citizens. They do not trust state institutions and democracy anymore. This, however is contested, inasmuch as policies that emphasise a process from welfare to work are seen as establishing a virtuous circle. Some policy messages and benefits' allocation decisions do foster civic participation. The long standing debate in social policy studies, particularly in the UK, between the advocacy of benefit targeting and the rejection of this in favour of universalism focuses upon the implications of these issues for citizenship (Dwyer, 2010).

This approach reminds us that the relationships between policy and politics explored in Chapter 8 is complex, that the identified interaction extends beyond the agenda setting process explored in Chapter 9 into the policy formation process examined in this chapter, and will (it must be added) go on to be evident in the chapters on implementation to follow. Ingram et al. (2015) thus urge policy scholars to devote attention to the impact of policy designs on democracy and citizens' engagement. They argue that scholars should adopt a 'democracy-centered approach to policy analysis' (p. 10), and renew the research programme that was originally initiated by Harold Lasswell who founded the field (see Farr et al., 2006, describing Lasswell as 'the policy scientist of democracy').

Policy interdependences

It is quite obvious that, nowadays, policy formulation occurs in a context of interdependence. Decision makers in one jurisdiction are influenced by the decisions and actions taken by public authorities in other cities, subnational entities, countries and, inter- or supranational organisations.

Some scholars have suggested a case for 'policy transfer theory' as a distinct 'framework of' policy analysis (see Dolowitz and Marsh, 1996 and 2000; Dolowitz et al., 2000) and separate contribution to the study of the policy process. One aspect of globalist theory (see Chapter 2) that is fairly self-evident is that in the modern world a great deal of effort is put into policy transfer. Not only do national policy makers look around at what is occurring elsewhere when they design their own policy, but it is also the case that there are a number of international organisations that are explicitly in the business of offering policy prescriptions – notably the various United Nations agencies, the World Bank and the Organization for Economic Co-operation and Development.

Yet since attempts to transfer policies are so widespread, a theory of 'policy transfer' can have either a slightly banal quality or tend to invest too much importance in the migration of ideas as a driver of policy change. Is it merely the case that 'just as individuals open their umbrellas simultaneously during a rainstorm, governments may decide to change their policies in the presence of tax evasion, environmental pressures, such as air pollution, or an ageing population' (Holzinger and Knill, 2005, p. 786).

An exploration of contemporary developments in policies for long-term care by Theobald and Kern (2011) illustrates how there has been extensive policy transfer yet at the same time there are great variations between societies to the extent that they regard internal factors as crucial for any explanation of actual decisions.

A feature of much of the policy transfer literature has been to explore problems associated with uncritical policy transfer (see particularly the work of Dolowitz cited above). There are obviously some important issues to raise about the conditions under which policy transfer occurs. There are clearly problems that arise from uncritical policy transfer. Governments faced with new policy problems send delegations off to other countries in search of ideas. These movements not unnaturally follow linguistic and cultural lines. These may lead to the adoption of ideas that do not easily fit in a very different institutional framework. There are policy entrepreneurs (see Chapter 9) who play active roles in the transfer process; not surprisingly many of these come from the United States. Given what we know about the distribution of power and the funding of policy entrepreneurs it is not surprising that the interests of business and market models for the operation of the policy process are propagated though these channels.

The transfer approach, which builds on Rose's (1991; 1993) work on 'policy learning', leaves questions unanswered about how decisions are made to accept or reject ideas from elsewhere (see Box 10.3 for some of the key critical points made by James and Lodge, 2003, p. 179).

Box 10.3	James and Lodge's critique of theories of lesson drawing and policy transfer

First, can they be defined as distinctive forms of policy making separate from other, more conventional forms? 'Lesson drawing' is very similar to conventional accounts of 'rational' policy making, and it is very difficult to define 'policy transfer' distinctly from many other forms of policy making. Second, why do 'lesson drawing' and 'policy transfer' occur rather than some other form of policy making? The proponents of 'policy transfer' put a set of diverse and conflicting theories under a common framework, obscuring differences between them. Third, what are the effects of 'lesson drawing' and 'policy transfer' on policy making and how do they compare to other processes?

International organisations play important roles in respect of policy transfer, particularly to developing nations and economies in need of aid. Here obviously transfer may be more compulsory, explicitly or implicitly, inasmuch as aid depends upon it. While again models from the United States are salient, and much advice comes packaged in terms of pro-market economic theory, there are sometimes rival sources of advice. This is explored further in Chapter 14.

Bulmer and Padgett describe the relationship between the European Union and the individual nation states as involving three distinctive forms of governance:

> Hierarchical governance is prevalent in policy areas like the single market where EU institutions exercise supranational authority leading to coercive forms of transfer. A second form of governance occurs where the European Union seeks to agree common rules or norms by common (or majority) consent. It is not uncommon to find norms modelled on those of one or more member state(s) in a form of transfer by negotiation. Finally, where member states retain sovereignty but coordinate policy via EU institutions (as in Justice and Home Affairs), policy transfer will take the form of unilateral voluntary exchange facilitated by the European Union.
>
> (2004, p. 104)

These observations suggest that it is unsatisfactory to encapsulate all these developments within what is labelled policy transfer theory. It is preferable to speak of a variety of interdependencies (hence the title for this section). Comparative policy scholars have distinguished three different concepts to capture these interdependences (Gilardi, 2014, pp. 187–8):

- *Policy transfer* describes the *process* by which decision makers use the policy implemented in another political system to formulate their own policy. This transfer process is generally investigated with qualitative methods (e.g. process tracing).

- *Policy diffusion* occurs when a *policy change* adopted in a given political system is systematically conditioned by prior policy choices made in other political systems. This phenomenon is very similar to policy transfer. However, the focus is here on the substantive policy change rather than on the process, and quantitative methods (e.g. spatial regression or dyadic approach) are generally applied to model policy diffusion.

- *Policy convergence* is something different and basically means that the policies adopted by different political systems become *similar* over time. The convergence of policy *outcomes* can be the result of transfer or diffusion, of course; but it can also be linked to common external pressures, without any horizontal interactions between the political systems.

As highlighted by Gilardi (2014), all three literatures have in common the quest for causal mechanisms underlying a transfer process, policy diffusion or outcomes' convergence. Many explanatory possibilities have been made between simple copying and stronger influences. Table 10.3 reproduces Holzinger and Knill's identification of the various influences on the transfer process ranging from strong ones that follow from wide, possibly supranational

Table 10.3   Causal mechanisms in policy interdependence

Mechanism	Stimulus	Response
Imposition	Political demand or pressure	Submission
International harmonisation	Legal obligation through international law	Compliance
Regulatory competition	Competitive pressure	Mutual adjustment
Transnational communication		
Lesson drawing	Problem pressure	Transfer of model found elsewhere
Transnational problem solving	Parallel problem pressure	Adoption of commonly developed model
Emulation	Desire for conformity	Copying of widely used model
International policy promotion	Legitimacy pressure	Adoption of a recommended model
Independent problem solving	Parallel problem pressure	Independent similar response

Based on Holzinger and Knill, 2005, Table 3, p. 780.

pressures, through weaker ones where a shared 'problem pressure' is evident (see also the 'International Regime Approach' presented in Chapter 6).

It may be questioned whether the term 'interdependence' is the right one for the first of those forms of governance (it is pertinent to note that other analysts of this phenomenon have described it as 'implementation'). However, the other two are pertinent to the discussion of agenda setting and policy formulation. With the second we see a negotiated form of the model set out by Kingdon, but with more complicated institutional arrangements. The third, on the other hand, can be seen as an important exogenous influence on policy processes largely contained within nation states. Chapter 14 will give some attention to the strong pressures, and to the roles of global and other international organisations.

Civil servants and policy formulation: the debate about the power of civil servants

We saw in Chapter 4 that a combination of politicians, civil servants and interest group representatives is implicit in the policy networks and policy communities theories. Much of the discussion of the roles of civil servants outside that framework, however, has tended to involve seeing them as alternative, even subversive, decision makers to politicians rather than as partners in a shared system. The published diaries of one politician, Richard Crossman (1975; 1976; 1977), dealt particularly fully with his relationships with civil servants and inspired a comedy series on TV, 'Yes, Minister'. That series reversed Crossman's (predictable?) picture of his success in securing dominance in the face of manipulative civil servants and represented the minister as the hapless dupe of the top civil servant. We have noted that such a perspective has been strongly influenced by the traditional preoccupation with the relationship between politics and administration. This discussion will start from that issue but aim to move away from it to a more balanced account of how these two groups interact in the policy process. In doing so it will consider, first, some of the issues about the respective roles of politicians and civil servants and then some of the issues about the compatibility of values, or ideologies, between them.

If permanent civil servants play a key role in the policy process they may tend to give continuity to the policy agenda, pursuing a departmental line regardless of political leadership. The power of the civil service and the importance of departmental agendas was emphasised in many past studies of British public administration. The 'Whitehall model' has been seen as firmly established in Britain. Even though, as will be shown below, they suggest change is occurring, Campbell and Wilson say:

> politicians in few countries place as much faith in bureaucrats as do the British. The British system contrasts not only with the patronage system at the top of the executive branch in the United States but also with the continental European practice (as in Germany) of placing senior civil servants in temporary retirement if a governing party loses power. . . . [t]he dependence of elected politicians on the non-partisan, permanent civil service was the core of the system that has been exported to other countries and admired by many non-British scholars.
>
> (1995, p. 293)

Nevertheless, we see similar features in some other European systems. In Switzerland, for instance, civil servants play a key role during the pre-parliamentary phase of the decision-making process. They usually draft the bill proposal, organise consultation procedures with policy stakeholders and promote the horizontal coordination between ministerial departments. Even if this pre-parliamentary phase seems to be less important today than it used to be three decades ago (Kriesi, 1980), civil servants still assume crucial functions when preparing policy decisions. Furthermore, 'bureaucratic policy-making' (Sciarini, 2015) is even stronger in policy processes that are Europeanised (e.g. formal agreements between Switzerland and the European Union on the free-movement of persons, taxation of savings or participation to Schengen-Dublin). As predicted by Moravcsik (1994), the executive power in general, and high civil servants in particular, are clearly strengthened in internationalised policy processes (Fischer and Sciarini, 2013). In the Netherlands, Anderweg and Irwin's (2002) account of policy making suggests the importance of departmental agendas, with civil servants as the key advisers for their ministers. In respect of France, Knapp and Wright speak of 'the colonisation by the civil service of areas beyond the confines of mere administration' (2001, p. 276). Knapp and Wright's discussion of this phenomenon indicates that this has come under attack but that the situation has not been changed significantly.

Obviously there will be differences between societies in how these roles are distributed. Dyson's (1980) analysis of 'strong' and 'weak' states suggests that in the 'strong' state civil servants are carriers of a tradition of service to the state, which is seen as providing a context for the more temporary concerns of politicians. Much depends here upon other aspects of the constitution. If electoral systems tend to produce unified programmatic parties then there is a potential tension between the two elements in the policy-making process. Here differences between the early (agenda setting) and later parts of the policy process are likely to be relevant. But much will depend upon the extent to which either one political party is largely dominant (as in Sweden until recently) or where there is a relatively low level of conflict between the parties (as in Germany). France is an interesting case because the constitution of the Fifth Republic gives administrators considerable autonomy. Commentators on France suggest that the period in which Mitterrand came to presidential power (i.e. the early 1980s) with innovatory socialist policies but was then forced first to water them down and then to accept 'cohabitation' with a prime minister of a different political persuasion was a crucial testing time for French democracy (Knapp and Wright, 2001).

An alternative perspective is supplied by those states where multi-party systems dominate or have dominated (the Netherlands, Belgium, the French Fourth Republic). In these the party-political input is largely seen very early in the policy process – in the issues that are contested in elections and in the compromises that occur between the elements in a coalition (see the discussion on party politics and coalition agreements in Chapter 9) – after which a kind of administrator/politician accommodation seems to apply.

One of the reasons for the preoccupation in much earlier literature with questions about whether politicians or administrators dominate in the policy process arises from a concern that civil servants 'subvert' policy because they do not share the ideologies or value commitments of democratically elected politicians. One possible way of dealing with this concern, the idea that civil servants should be 'representative' in a social sense, is explored in Box 10.4. The extent to which it is seen as a problem is influenced by the extent to which there are significant political or ideological divisions with regard to the policy agenda. Earlier writers on the British civil service (for example, Chapman, 1970) suggest that civil servants in Britain have strong reservations about party politics while at the same time possessing commitments to particular policies. The implication is that these officials find changes in their political masters easy to adjust to so long as they do not involve violent ideological shifts. Officials can operate most easily in a situation of political consensus. Where consensus does not exist, however, their role may become one of trying to create it. Graham Wallas sums this up most neatly:

> The real 'Second Chamber', the real 'constitutional check' in England, is provided, not by the House of Lords or the Monarchy, but by the existence of a permanent Civil Service, appointed on a system independent of the opinion or desires of any politician and holding office during good behaviour.
>
> (1948, p. 262)

Box 10.4	Representative bureaucracy

One response to ideological differences between politicians and civil servants has been to argue that civil servants should be, as far as possible, representative of the societies from which they are drawn. Kingsley's (1944) pioneering work on this topic looked at the British civil service, arguing that it was transformed from an aristocratic into a bourgeois organisation during that period in the nineteenth century when the commercial middle class were becoming politically dominant. The British bureaucracy was thus made representative of the dominant political class, but not, of course, of the people as a whole. To work effectively the democratic state requires a 'representative bureaucracy', Kingsley argues, thus taking up the theme, developed also by Friedrich (1940), that the power of the civil service is such that formal constitutional controls upon its activities are insufficient. Kingsley sees the recruitment of the civil service from all sectors of the population as one means of ensuring that it is a 'responsible bureaucracy'.

This issue has traditionally been explored very much in class terms (see Aberbach et al., 1981). More recent work has added attention to issues about gender and about ethnic, regional or religious origins or background (Meier et al., 1991; Selden, 1997). Much of this new work is concerned with the behaviour of 'street-level bureaucrats' (and will be discussed in Chapter 13).

In the 1960s, discontent developed on the political Left in the UK about this comfortable consensual doctrine. A response to it was to appoint temporary political advisers to ministers. But it was on the political Right that the most robust response developed during the governments led by Margaret Thatcher in the 1980s. As a consequence, Campbell and Wilson suggest that the traditional 'Whitehall model' is being destroyed by:

- the breaking of the monopoly of the civil service as advisers to ministers;
- the development of systems to help the Prime Minister contest civil service advice;
- most importantly, 'whole generations of bureaucrats and politicians have been socialised since the 1970s into very different professional norms . . . enthusiasm for government policies has been rewarded more than honest criticism' (Campbell and Wilson, 1995, p. 296);
- 'the erosion of the belief that the civil service is an established profession, like all professions delineated from society as a whole by clear boundaries' (ibid., p. 297).

That argument was developed before Tony Blair came to power in 1997. His obsessive desire to control policy and to control the way policy was presented has done much to further these developments. This led to a rather different attitude to the organisation of the upper reaches of the civil service, with more temporary civil servants being recruited and more attention being paid to the commitments of candidates for top jobs.

Campbell and Wilson chart some similar developments in other systems close to the 'Whitehall model' in Australia, New Zealand and Canada. In Australia, Pusey, however, raises a rather different issue. He explores the way in which a new ideological agenda has been pursued from within the civil service. He argues that alternative ways of managing the economy have been advanced systematically by 'economic rationalisers' who have come to dominate key roles within the civil service (Pusey, 1991). An interesting ambiguity in Pusey's analysis concerns the extent to which this has been tacitly encouraged by elected politicians, on the Labor side as much as the Liberal. A similar phenomenon has been observed in New Zealand, where a determined group of 'economic rationalisers' closely linked with the Treasury secured the support of first a Labour finance minister and later a National Party one. In respect of this case, Wallis writes of a 'conspiracy', in which the change of the agenda depended upon a concerted effort to win support in the civil service and the political parties (1997).

The evidence marshalled by Pusey and Wallis suggests that there may be a need, alongside interest in the way in which the relationship between political values and a permanent administration is managed, to look at how new ideological consensuses may be developed within a ruling elite. If, in fact, it is the case in the more unified systems, particularly those following the Westminster model, that the policy process is more controlled than Kingdon's analysis suggests, it may be beside the point to ask whether this control comes from the politicians' agenda or from a civil service-dominated policy agenda. We may, particularly when one party is in government for a long while or when the differences between the two parties are quite slight or when political changes often involve slight shifts within a coalition, be looking at control over the agenda exercised by a relatively unified community of politicians and civil servants. In many respects this is the picture painted by Rhodes (2011) on the basis of a qualitative study which particularly focused on politician/civil servant relationships in the UK between 2001 and 2005. He refutes the oppositional ('Yes, Minister') view and does not support the view that the importation of outsiders has transformed the traditional civil service.

There are some interesting points to raise about the use of 'outsiders'. In respect of developments in the UK, Gains and Stoker draw upon a Parliamentary Select Committee investigation to identify three kinds of role:

- an explicitly political one 'to keep the politics in policy' (2011, p. 493);
- a role advancing a specific minister's personal agenda;
- the provision of 'independently authoritative' advice (ibid.).

There seems good reason to suggest that these get very muddled together in practice. Much depends upon the relationship between ideology and expertise.

There is one other group of special advisers, introduced into UK government since 1999, colloquially called 'tsars' (Smith, 2011). They are neither direct recruits to the civil service nor political appointees in a party political sense but experts in specific policy areas. Their roles involve a combination of concern with policy formulation and with effective implementation. The development of such roles needs to be understood in the context of the shift away from traditional notions of hierarchy in administration. What is entailed here is the giving of a measure of responsibility for solutions to a policy problem to an expert (note that many of the UK initiatives involve medical experts), placing them outside a hierarchy but expecting them to have the capacity to secure support from key actors (notably the minister) within it. These may be seen as rather more specific replications of a long-standing and more general approach to the use of expertise *within* the civil service hierarchy in respect of medical, scientific and professional expertise.

Gains and Stoker, seeing advisers (probably excluding the 'tsars', whose roles they do not explore) in Kingdon's terms as 'policy entrepreneurs' further follow his approach to write of them as operating in:

> The messy interplay of problematisation, policy and politics streams in the primeval soup of policy making . . . the role of special advisers should be understood as playing a 'brokering' role, acting as 'middlemen' between the social science, bureaucrat and political decision-making worlds.
>
> (2011, p. 495)

In respect of the introduction of 'expertise', this is an optimistic view that others do not share. In the last chapter Haas' comments on the significance of ideological compatibility (or the lack of it) between the views of expert 'epistemic communities' and those of powerful political actors were noted. Stevens, summing up his evidence on the marginalised roles of experts argues:

> It has been shown that there is little conclusive evidence available for policy-makers in the vast mass of information that is available to them. A certain group of policy-makers chose some of this information as evidence to tell stories. They selected evidence that fitted with the stories that have previously constructed their unquestioned concept of public value. This arose ideologically from the extant distribution of power, which structured their capability to take part in policy decisions. They used evidence to tell stories that were likely to be accepted within a thought world that favoured certainty over accuracy and action over contradiction. They attempted to transform issues of ethical value into questions of financial value.
>
> (Stevens, 2011, p. 252)

This perspective is also that of Smith (2007) who explored the issue of health inequalities in the UK. The change of government in 1997 led to a policy environment in which a case for attention to health inequalities was, in general terms, on the agenda. However, the experts Smith interviewed found it difficult to extend their engagement further into the policy process.

Inasmuch as they were successful it was in respect of one interpretation of the causes of health inequalities – that root them in individual behaviour – that is least challenging to the political status quo. The creditability of experts seemed to rest upon factors not necessarily related to their expertise. Smith says, cautiously, 'the factors influencing an individual's credibility in policy circles are likely to be different to, and may potentially conflict with, the factors affecting credibility in academic circles' (2007, p. 1447).

These contributions focus upon issues about the introduction of expertise. The attack upon civil service values associated with the Left in the 1960s perhaps took what was, from their point of view, an optimistic view of the prospects of fusing expertise, ideology and political commitment. It is important to bear in mind that political parties may not be the driving forces with regard to the injection of ideological elements into the political process. Furthermore, when ideologies become dominant they may fuse all aspects of the policy process. Many writers at the end of the twentieth century gave attention to the way in which economic belief systems, stressing a need to restore market processes to a more central position in the determination of policy, secured acceptance beyond the ranks of the political 'new Right'. The case of New Zealand has attracted particular attention in this respect, since there it was a Labour government that took the crucial first steps (Kelsey, 1995; Massey, 1995). It was noted above that Wallis (1997) describes the New Zealand case as involving a 'conspiracy', inasmuch as 'an exclusive social network of policy participants' worked together to change policy (p. 1).

Clearly, where 'policy communities' are able to dominate the policy process, shared ideologies may be important for this domination and alternative ideologies will be marginalised. In addition, it may be important to see interest groups as part of this organised community. This refers to the concept of 'policy monopoly', which explains policy stability according to the punctuated equilibrium framework (see Chapter 9): a small and very cohesive community of actors controls the policy image and the dominant institutional venue in which authoritative policy decisions are made.

The implication of the above discussion is that it may be inappropriate to polarise the distinction between politician and civil service domination. Evidence from 'experts', who had expected to work with politicians who would be active innovators but had found themselves marginalised, may not be very reliable. There is another picture of the world of politician/civil service interaction, as in the account from Rhodes quoted in the next section, in which a shared concern with short-run expediency was likely to lead to this marginalisation. Another kind of outsider introduced to deal with the media or with party-political management is more useful to politicians in this context.

Important for the continuing primacy of the traditional civil service may be a commitment to collaborative working in government regardless of ideology. The political system of the Netherlands has been seen as characterised by 'consociational democracy' (Lijphart, 1975) with extensive collaboration between opposed social 'pillars' (Catholic, Protestant, secular liberal and social democratic) in both politics and administration. While there is extensive evidence that the era of pillarisation has passed (see Anderweg and Irwin, 2002), neo-corporatist characteristics remain very persistent in the Netherlands. Success in dealing with the need for industrial restructuring has been seen as attributable to the continuation of a weak form of neo-corporatism which has been called the 'polder model' (Visser and Hemerijk, 1997). The question about whether it is better to have a stable traditional civil service, sceptical about ideology, or alternatively for politicians to be able to stir the government machine with enthusiasm for new ideas takes us beyond this effort to explore the roles of the various actors in the policy formulation process.

Civil servants and policy formulation: does the traditional debate miss the point?

Beyond this recognition of the prominence of the civil service role in general, a great deal of the discussion of the roles of civil servants seems to have been locked into the dated debate about the possibility of distinguishing policy making from administration. The position that has been taken in the first part of this chapter has been partly to challenge that directly but primarily to argue that it involves a very simplistic view of policy making, disregarding the complexity of the policy formulation task. But there is still much modern writing that reverts in one way or another to simplifications about policy-making roles. Huber and Shipan's *Deliberate Discretion?* (2002) explores why 'politicians sometimes allow substantial discretion and at other times tell bureaucrats precisely what to do' (p. 9). But the problem is that such an approach is still searching for an easy way to dichotomise roles, in this case treating rule making as what politicians do and disregarding the complexity of this task (as illustrated above, for example, with the 'right to roam' legislation) which surely calls for some combination of roles. Campbell and Wilson's analysis of the changing role of the UK civil service seems similarly to miss the point when they write of 'civil servants increasingly defining their role as policy implementers rather than policy analysts' (1995, p. 60) disregarding tasks between agenda setting and implementation. The same is true of an account of the changing civil service by someone with long experience of observing British government, Anthony King, heading a chapter 'Mandarins as managers' and surely – again because of disregard of detailed work – exaggerating the extent to which senior civil servants are shifting from policy-making activity to the management of implementation (2007, chapter 9).

A study of the work of middle-ranking civil servants by Page and Jenkins (2005) supports the account of the policy formulation process set out in this chapter. It shows how civil servants, often well below the leading grades in the British civil service, play crucial roles in the formulation of policy. At the same time it challenges the view that this in any respect involves subversion of political roles. It points instead to a team-like activity in which there are close working relationships between civil servants and ministers. In some respects civil servants can be seen as paying attention to Simon's values/facts distinction, showing sensitivity to issues that might concern the politicians. They identify a variety of 'cues' used for this:

- the perceived thrust of government policy;
- experience from frequent interaction with ministers;
- departmental priorities;
- reference to documents;
- 'Consensus mongering' (ibid., p. 134) implying a sensitivity to contested issues.

Another crucial concept here is the notion of a 'steer', described as 'not a command' (ibid., p. 136), and allowing for the possibility of questioning. Page and Jenkins say '. . . its general legitimacy as a guide to developing policy comes because it is directly or indirectly an expression of a minister's wishes' (ibid., p. 137). This study supplements an earlier one by Page in which attention was paid to the specific roles played by civil servants during the legislative process (Box 10.5 summarises the findings from this).

Page and Jenkins sum up by saying:

> Politicians are clearly at the apex of the executive structure. In comparison with the full range of tasks they oversee, ministers can at best take a close interest only in a small proportion of the decisions taken in their name. They are highly dependent upon officials working within the policy bureaucracy who work hard to fashion policies in ways they think their ministers will like.
>
> (Ibid., p. 184)

Box 10.5	Page's (2003) examination of the role of the British 'civil servant as legislator'

British civil servants are drafted into 'bill teams' to work on the preparation of legislation. Such teams are typically led by civil servants drawn from the lowest grade of the 'senior' civil service. The teams tend to be formed early in the process of preparing a new policy, before it has been agreed that there will be a place for legislation in the parliamentary timetable. The decision to legislate will be a political one. However, Page shows the identification of a need for legislation may be as much a civil service activity as a political one.

Once a decision to legislate is made, teams will work on the detailed drafting of legislation. Drafting will involve the team, joined or assisted by lawyers employed by the civil service. Before being put before Parliament a draft bill will be submitted to the relevant minister or ministers, who will be responsible for steering the legislation through Parliament. To assist ministers, large briefing documents will be compiled. During the legislation process any suggested amendments will be carefully scrutinised by the team. Many will be the product of further thoughts about the legislation from within the department. Some will be inspired by pressure groups and some will come from within Parliament, but very often the aim will be to accept these in principle and secure their withdrawal so that they can be replaced by amendments compatible with the bill as a whole. Once the legislation has been steered through Parliament, the bill team is likely to move on to drafting implementing amendments and guidance on the legislation.

Rhodes' account of life at that 'apex' (2007) indirectly reinforces that picture. He says: 'I saw . . . little policy analysis. It is simply not done in the departmental court [the term Rhodes uses for arena he observed] but in the Directorates General by middle-ranking officials' (2011, p. 186). But what is distinctive about his research is the picture it presents of the untidy life at the top where day-to-day events continually confuse policy making, administrative machine management and responses to political and media pressure. While then what he is describing is neither policy making nor policy formulation as such it offers a correction to any simplistic view of relationships between politicians and civil servants:

> Distinctions between policy and management, politician and civil servant, are meaningless when confronted with the imperative to cope and survive. Both minister and permanent secretary are political-administrators, dependent on one another and, in many of their everyday tasks, interchangeable.
>
> (Rhodes, 2011, p. 163)

Interestingly, while Rhodes' picture has been reinforced in a British TV comedy series *The Thick of it*, showing chaotic obscenity laced interactions between a group of politicians, civil servants and advisers, a more sensitive and nuanced picture has been provided by a Danish TV account of life at this level, *Borgen* (available with English sub-titles). There is obviously an issue here about the extent to which the above conclusions only apply to the UK. Page and Jenkins consider this issue and indicate that there are parallels in the systems used in other European countries. In Switzerland, for example, there are specific Legislation Units in the Ministry of Justice and Police, whose main task is to supervise the quality of legislative projects. These units review the legal merits of constitutional amendments, primary and secondary legislation, executive decrees, etc. proposed by other agencies. They check if the legislative project has a sufficient legal basis, if it is logically structured and worded in an understandable manner, or if inherent inconsistencies or superfluous provisions remain.

There are evidently variations in the extent to which outsiders are brought in to play key roles close to ministers (particularly in respect of legislation). Page and Jenkins acknowledge the likelihood of differences in the United States with the separation between executive and legislature, and the fact that accordingly key roles are played by staff working for members of Congress.

The long-standing concern to distinguish politics (or policy making) from administration, though it has its roots in an obvious issue about representative democracy, manifests itself often as a naïve demand to take politics out of medicine, or education, or whatever. In practice, these issues matter too much either for politicians to be prepared to leave them alone or for the 'administrators' (including many professional staff, a point we return to in Chapter 13) to abdicate what they see as their responsibilities for doing the right thing. Hence there are large parts of the policy process in which political and administrative roles are inextricably mixed.

This discussion of administrative roles in the policy formulation process involves an exploration of what is perhaps the most ambiguous part of the initial policy process. It is certainly the most difficult to research, because so much of the action is private (in the UK there is a wait of 30 years for the publication of official papers, and even then some items are protected for longer, some are purged, and many were never committed to paper records in the first place). The fact that there have been so many attempts to draw the politics/administration distinction or to delimit the political roles and interests of permanent officials indicates the complexity of this issue. The achievement of the aspiration that civil servants should be just 'managers' or just concerned with 'means' is fraught with difficulty.

Dunleavy and O'Leary refer to the 'professionalisation' of government to suggest that in areas where expertise is important, issues are pulled out of the general political arena into the more private politics of 'policy communities':

> In the professionalized state the grassroots implementation of policy, and major shifts in the overall climate of debate in each issue area, are both influenced chiefly by individual occupational groups. Professional communities act as a key forum for developing and testing knowledge, setting standards and policing the behaviour of individual policy-makers and policy implementers. Knowledge elites are crucial sources of innovations in public policy-making . . . in areas where professions directly control service delivery the whole policy formulation process may be 'implementation skewed'.
>
> (1987, pp. 302–3)

A modern twist to all the issues about the way the politician/administrator boundary is organised comes with two approaches to government which, while they have echoes in the past and particularly in pre-democratic regimes, are currently assuming increasing importance: public/private partnerships and the delegation of public tasks to quasi-independent or independent organisations. In many respects this is a subject for the discussion of implementation (see for example the discussion of 'Independent Regulatory Agencies' in Chapters 11 and 15). Certainly this is how governments tend to present these developments – emphasising Woodrow Wilson's politics/administration distinction or stressing that 'we' still make the 'policy', 'they' are responsible for 'operations'. Invoking the already criticised Wilson distinction indicates that this should be viewed with caution. Sonia Exley, in her study of 'think tanks' in English education (2014), writes of them being 'rebranded as "do tanks" turning ideas into concrete entrepreneurial action' (p. 184), with a movement of individuals from pressure groups into government and then into organisations and companies competing to be providers of new initiatives in education. In a context of increasing liberalisation and privatisation there are issues here about the potentiality for corruption. Invoking the Woodrow Wilson perspective here reminds us that a key objective of the civil service reform movements in the UK and the USA in the late nineteenth century arose from a concern to create a civil service independent both of politics and of private interests.

Any 'agent' with responsibilities to implement a policy is likely to develop very real concerns about the way in which the policy it operates is constructed. If confronted with something unexpectedly expensive or something unworkable, the agent is likely to lobby (probably covertly) for policy change. The 'agent' with a contract to carry out a specific task with a specific sum of money is a politically interested party (a new actor in the bargaining part of the game), and perhaps particularly likely to behave in the way predicted by public choice theory. At the end of a book of case studies from various countries Colebatch et al. (2010) bring together a series of observations of the diffuse nature of what they call 'policy work'. Their starting point is an observation pertinent to some of the puzzles that have been addressed in this chapter:

> There are two very distinct approaches to thinking about policy practice. One is *teleological*, outcome-focused: the activity is about making policy, and focus of attention is on the problem being addressed and how the measures proposed would contribute to its solution. The alternative approach might be termed *relational*, or process focused: policy activity is a continuing but variable flow of attention among a large and diverse array of participants, who have overlapping agendas, different interpretations of the problem, and varying levels of concern about its resolution.
>
> (Ibid., p. 228)

They go on to indicate that they have been particularly concerned to outline the implications of the second approach. In doing so they engage very much with the issue of the extent to which decision making occurs in the context of complex 'governance'. But their observations are pertinent to the next of the boundaries between chapters in this book: the formulation/implementation one.

The policy formulation/implementation relationship

There may be situations in which much of the activity that creates the policy actually experienced (see the discussion of the meaning of policy in Chapter 1) occurs during what is generally perceived as the implementation process. To return briefly to the metaphor of a journey: we may change our route during it. It is appropriate to supplement that with another 'homely' metaphor, the cooking of a meal. This is done in Box 10.6.

In the world of public policy we find a similar range of options to those set out in Box 10.6, with – as noted at the end of the box – many complications because of the existence of multiple actors. The first three options listed correspond with three degrees of high discretion in implementation contexts. In the more extreme cases this makes the implementer responsible for matters that in the other two options are seen as agenda setting or policy formulation. The situation of following a recipe book fits well with the classical staged model. The recipe book has identified dishes (policies) and formulated rules about how to make them, implementation consists of judgements around the aspects of the recipe that are not (and perhaps cannot be) easily specified. But in the last example in the box there is action, based on previous prescriptions, but also reference back towards someone who may be seen here as in a somewhat equivalent role to those concerned with the earlier stages of the policy process. The parallel here is with one task identified by the civil servants who Page and Jenkins (2005) studied: giving advice on the interpretation of policy to implementers.

The point here is that much of the literature on implementation is about the various degrees of discretion accorded to those close to, or actually at, the delivery point for policy, but that means that issues inevitably arise about how the agenda-setting/policy formulation/implementation distinctions have been made, or are worked out in practice. We will find that the implementation literature, like so much else in the literature on which this book has to draw, is very influenced by efforts to prescribe how those boundaries should be drawn; and of course the politics/administration distinction raises its head again.

Box 10.6	Alternative ways in which discretionary elements occur in the policy process: a homely example

Imagine a two-person household in which one person undertakes to cook a meal to be shared with the other. There are then a variety of possibilities, of which the following are the main ones:

- That the cook is quite free to choose what to do.

■ That the cook is free to choose what to do within constraints such as the size of the budget, the availability of ingredients, the amount of time available and some knowledge of the likes and dislikes of the other.

■ That the ingredients were chosen in advance but that the cook then still has considerable latitude about how to use them.

■ That the recipe was chosen in advance, which means that what is to be done is closely prescribed (but following a recipe may still involve judgements about when elements are sufficiently well cooked, about seasoning 'to taste', etc.). A particularly problematic example here occurs with the making of a sauce, where adjustments in the course of action may be essential.

■ Variants of the above but with negotiations during the process – 'Would you like this?', 'How do you think I should deal with that?', 'Taste this and tell me what you think of it' and so on.

In the authors' own households versions of all those five options occur, with the last very common. But of course, as many students who have lived in communal households will know, decision making may be much more complicated than the two person interaction described here.

CONCLUSIONS

This chapter has been concerned with the fact that, whilst agenda setting and policy formulation are closely connected, it is very clear that the translation of policy objectives into instructions for action is an extensive task often given insufficient attention in discussions of the policy process.

Various aspects of policy formulation have been identified. Particularly important are the issues posed by policy instrument theory, which see choices between alternative ways of seeking policy objectives as salient in much policy decision making and influenced by concerns about both feasibility and acceptability. Social constructions of those affected by policies are significant influences on the ways policies are framed. It is also noted that there is a great deal of policy interdependence – between jurisdictions, territories, countries and international organisations – phenomena often characterised in terms of policy transfer and policy learning but which go beyond those concepts.

A recognition that much attention needs to be given to detail inevitably leads to an examination of the roles of those who do such work. It is suggested that in the British system and in many other administrative systems such work falls to full-time officials rather than to politicians or their immediate impermanent assistants. That leads the chapter into a discussion of the power of

(continued)

the civil service, even though much of that literature goes much wider than a concern with detailed policy formulation to postulate that civil servants often *make* policy in the strong sense of that term. Page and Jenkins' careful work on actual civil service roles brings us back to the suggestion that this postulate over-simplifies a complex team-like relationship. A fuller discussion of these relationships requires attention to implementation as well as policy formulation, the concern of the next chapter.

11 Implementation: an overview

SYNOPSIS

This chapter starts by noting how a very distinctive vein of 'implementation' studies developed towards the end of the twentieth century. It goes on to explore briefly how that work was concerned to make a clear distinction between policy formulation and implementation, and suggests that this is now a source of difficulties. This leads naturally into a consideration of the 'top-down' studies that particularly emphasised that distinction. It is followed by an exposition of the 'bottom-up' evaluation of these studies. The next section, headed 'Beyond the top-down/bottom-up debate', provides an approach which then dominates the rest of the chapter. It suggests a need for an awareness that there is a complex mix of issues to be understood about the different ways actual policies are developed, about how they may best be studied, and about the normative arguments about who should be in charge which often dominate (and obscure) discussions about implementation. Subsequent sections then highlight issues about variations in the 'policy rule framework' and about 'variations in the administrative system'.

    In this chapter the focus will be very much upon introducing issues about what happens during the implementation process. The chapters that follow it explore aspects of the organisation of the policy process that need to be looked at in any account of that process as a whole, but in which issues about implementation loom large.

Introduction

Issues about implementation as a process are as old as collective human endeavour, particularly since the development of political arrangements in which some actors expected to make decisions that others would put into operation. But the systematic academic study of implementation has a much shorter history. In the United States in the early 1970s and in Europe later in that decade there emerged a wave of studies examining the implementation of public policy. Their rationale was that there had been, in the study of public policy, a 'missing link' (Hargrove, 1975) between concern with policy making and the evaluation of policy outcomes. We should perhaps be wary when academics claim to have discovered a new topic or a 'missing link', as they are very good at dressing up old concerns in new language and thereby claiming originality. The absence of theory and literature on implementation before Pressman and Wildavsky's seminal work (1973) on that topic has been exaggerated: for example, many organisational studies are de facto concerned with this phenomenon. Furthermore, a concern with the relationship between policy making and administration, in many ways implementation by another name, is as old as democratic politics (Wilson, 1887). Nevertheless, as empirical research in political science developed in the first half of the twentieth century there was perhaps a relative neglect of the study of the processes by which policies are translated into action. They were regarded as mundane and taken for granted. As Gunn (1978) argues, 'academics have often seemed obsessed with policy formation while leaving the "practical details" of policy implementation to administrators' (p. 169).

The explosion of implementation studies therefore represents an important advance in policy analysis. Yet, like so many paradigm shifts in the social sciences, this new intellectual development has come to be seen to have its own limitations. At various places already in this book warnings have been sounded about the stages model of the policy process. At the end of the previous chapter problems were examined about the distinction between policy formulation (often, indeed, called 'making') and implementation, a division particularly highlighted in stagist approaches to policy analysis.

The case for stressing the importance of implementation as distinct from the policy formulation process, and as deserving of attention in its own right, has tended to lead to an overemphasis on the distinctiveness of the two processes. There has been a tendency to treat policies as clear-cut, uncontroversial entities whose implementation can be studied quite separately. This has raised both methodological problems and problems about the extent to which the very practical concerns of implementation studies may involve, explicitly or implicitly, identification with some actors' views of what should happen.

This difficulty has been compounded by the extent to which policy actors and scholars regard it as important to make this distinction. We have here an argument that may be taken in two possible directions. One is to say that inasmuch as policy makers regard a distinction as important, then in all sorts of respects it will be evident in their activities, and the empirical study of their activities must have regard to that. The other is to say that there is a need to be sceptical about a distinction that is so widely used in policy rhetoric, closely linked as it is with the notion that some actors have responsibilities to be leading decision makers (a notion often embedded in versions of democratic theory) whilst others have duties to carry out the policies of their 'masters'. There is in this latter case a situation in which there will be powerful decision makers who want us to believe that the reality corresponds with the rhetoric, or will want to blame the 'implementers' when events do not correspond with their original expectations. Some theoretical frameworks clearly emphasise this distinction. For example, the principal-agent approach, which was summarised in Chapter 3, postulates that the self-interests of a principal (i.e. elected official, who formulates the policy programme and then delegates implementation tasks) and his or her agent (i.e. bureaucrat, who implements the policy programme and fulfils the delegated tasks) are potentially divergent. If the policy objectives are not fully achieved, then the principal blames the agent for not implementing the decision correctly. However, it could also be the case that the policy did not deliver the expected outcomes because the law was badly formulated (i.e. failure in programme design), and not because there was an implementation deficit. It is often very difficult to know if a policy failure is due to a poor policy formulation, to an imperfect policy implementation or to a subtle mix of both elements.

In this book the aim is to try to have it both ways – that is, both to reflect the importance of the formulation/implementation distinction in the policy process, and to be aware of how confused it may be in practice.

The top-down model for the study of implementation

In the course of the evolution of work on implementation in the later part of the twentieth century, a debate developed between the 'top-down' and the 'bottom-up' perspectives. As in all such debates, a later resolution has been reached in which most scholars will want to avoid taking either of the extreme positions, and 'the gradual silencing of the protracted and unproductive debate between top-down and bottom-up scholars' (Saetren, 2014, p. 95) may reasonably be welcomed. Nevertheless it is helpful, in a text like this, to examine this debate for the insights it gives us into some of the key issues about the study of implementation. Furthermore, that debate particularly focuses on judgements about the policy process that are widespread in observations by politicians and journalists, as well as still many academics, expressed in terms of the achievement of previously expressed goals. As Hupe puts it, 'The assumption is that once one knows the good intentions as laid down in a law or official policy document, one can infer the results-to-be-realized from it' (Hupe, 2014, p. 176).

The top-down perspective is thus deeply rooted in the stages model, and involves making a clear distinction between policy formulation and policy implementation. Thus Pressman and Wildavsky argue:

> Implementation to us, means just what [dictionary definitions] . . . say it does: to carry out, accomplish, fulfil, produce, complete. But what is it being implemented? A policy, naturally. There must be something out

there prior to implementation; otherwise there would be nothing to move towards in the process of implementation. A verb like 'implement' must have an object like 'policy'. But policies normally contain both goals and the means for achieving them. How, then, do we distinguish between a policy and its implementation?

(Pressman and Wildavsky, 1973; 1984 edition, p. xxi)

Pressman and Wildavsky thus highlight a question that is for them of more than linguistic relevance:

We can work neither with a definition of policy that excludes any implementation nor one that includes all implementation. There must be a starting point. If no action is begun, implementation cannot take place. There must be also an end point. Implementation cannot succeed or fail without a goal against which to judge it.

(Ibid., p. xxii)

There is an issue of logic here. The act of 'implementation' presupposes a prior act, particularly the act of formulating and deciding what needs to be done. Various questions follow from this: Who is the formulator? Who is the decision maker? Who is the implementer? If they are not integrated as a single actor, there is a need to identify the variety of actors involved. Then there are questions about whether the formulator or decision maker has more power, or a role that is more legitimised, than the implementer. The act of formulation and decision making may take place anywhere in the policy process. There is no necessary assumption that formulators are always at the 'top' in a political or hierarchical sense, but there is embodied in this perspective a view of the prior nature of the formulation process. This may be called the *'implementation follows formulation and decision theorem'* (Hill and Hupe, 2014, p. 4).

The pioneering implementation studies therefore highlighted the need to examine the process of putting policy into action. Their concern was to challenge those who, at that time, took it for granted that this process would be smooth and straightforward. Hence Pressman and Wildavsky gave their book a very long and often quoted subtitle: *'How Great Expectations in Washington are Dashed in Oakland; or Why It's Amazing that Federal Programs Work At All, This Being a Saga of the Economic Development Administration as told by Two Sympathetic Observers who Seek to Build Morals on a Foundation of Ruined Hopes'.*

One senses in that title some of the frustration felt by many Americans about the failure, or limited success, of the war on poverty and the great society programmes of the late 1960s. Pressman and Wildavsky were not the first to observe this apparent gap between federal aspirations and local reality: there was a similar body of literature on the limitations of Roosevelt's reformist interventions in American society in the 1930s (see, in particular, Selznick, 1949). An important preoccupation in this work is clearly the concern with the problem of intervention from the top of a federal system;

it comes through similarly in other analyses of American social policy which have less of an emphasis on implementation *per se* (see Marris and Rein, 1967; Moynihan, 1969).

However, the focus on American federalism does not destroy the value of this approach for the study of implementation in other societies. Indeed, if analysed in this manner it raises important questions about the ways in which policy transmission occurs, or fails to occur, through multi-government systems. Certainly, a great deal of the analysis in Pressman and Wildavsky's book is concerned with the extent to which successful implementation depends upon linkages between different organisations and departments at the local level. They argue that if action depends upon a number of links in an implementation chain, then the degree of cooperation required between agencies to make those links has to be very close to 100 percent if a situation is not to occur in which a number of small deficits cumulatively create a large shortfall. They thus introduce the idea of 'implementation deficit' and suggest that implementation may be analysed mathematically in this way. This is an important idea, but it is perhaps stated too strongly in this formulation. Bowen (1982) points out that such a formulation disregards the extent to which the interactions between these actors occur in contexts in which they rarely concern simply 'one-off' affairs; rather, these interactions are repeated and accompanied by others, in which case it can be seen that collaboration becomes much more likely. In that sense the 'chain' metaphor is perhaps misleading. Smith and his colleagues suggest instead the notion of 'fields of action as . . . constituted structures of social relations within which agents and their social positions are located' (Smith et al., 2011, p. 979).

The notion of cumulative deficit if cooperation is less than perfect has similarities to the approach to the study of administration developed in Britain by Hood (1976). He suggests:

> One way of analysing implementation problems is to begin by thinking about what 'perfect administration' would be like, comparable to the way in which economists employ the model of perfect competition. Perfect administration could be defined as a condition in which 'external' elements of resource availability and political acceptability combine with 'administration' to produce perfect policy implementation.
>
> (Hood, 1976, p. 6)

Hood goes on to develop an argument about the 'limits of administration' (his book title) which focuses not so much on the political processes that occur within the administrative system as on the inherent limits to control in complex systems. This is similarly the concern of a two-volume contribution to the subject by another British writer, Andrew Dunsire (1978a, 1978b). Hood and Dunsire, although they use examples from real situations, are concerned to link organisation theory with the study of implementation to provide an abstract model of the problems to be faced by persons attempting top-down control over the administrative system.

Criticisms of the top-down approach

The argument in this section will be complicated, since there are a number of different kinds of criticism of the top-down approach which apply differently to different representatives of that school of thought. Broadly, the arguments separate out into those about the nature of policy, those about the interrelationship between policy formulation and the implementation process, and those about the normative stance adopted by students of implementation (particularly when this is implicit rather than explicit).

Pressman and Wildavsky were quoted earlier as approaching their definition of implementation by asserting that 'implement' is a verb that must have an object: policy. In arguing in this way they surely ran the risk of catching themselves in a linguistic trap of their own making. As was recognised in the third edition of their book (1984), published after Pressman's death, it is dangerous to regard it as self-evident that implementers are working with a recognisable entity that may be called a policy. In Chapter 1, and in various other places in this book, it has been shown that policy is an extremely slippery concept. It may really only emerge through an elaborate process that is likely to include those stages that are conventionally described as implementation.

The definitions of policy quoted in Chapter 1 referred to its different characteristics. Two particularly different approaches to identifying policy described there – as a general stance and a rather more concrete formulation – both entail problems for implementation studies, however. These problems are, in a sense, mirror images of each other. Policies as defined as stances (Friend et al., 1974) may be relatively clear-cut, political commitments to specific action. The difficulty is that they are made much more complex as they are translated into action. Policies as defined in more concrete terms are, as the definitions of Easton (1953) and Jenkins (1978) suggest, often so complex that we are unlikely to be able to identify simple goals within them. Friend's definition is really closer to the concept of policy as used in everyday speech. It refers to the goals embodied in the 'Queen's speeches' or the President's 'messages to Congress', not to the complex phenomena that emerge at the end of the legislative process. Yet it is surely the latter with which most students of implementation work.

The argument so far has been that implementation studies face problems in identifying what is being implemented because policies are complex phenomena. This needs now to be taken a stage further. Perhaps policies are quite deliberately made complex, obscure, ambiguous or even meaningless. In the most extreme case the policies that are the concern of politicians may be no more than symbolic, formulated without any intention to secure implementation (Easton, 1953). Politicians may want to be seen to be in favour of certain ideals or goals while actually doing nothing about them. Any system in which policy making and implementation are clearly separated, either by a division between legislature and executive (as in the United

States) or by a division between levels of government or ministries and implementing agencies (present in most systems but most clear in federal ones), provides opportunities for the promulgation of symbolic policies. In Britain, for example, many regulatory policies require parliamentary enactment but local authority implementation. Parliament may relatively easily pass laws allowing the control of certain activities or the provision of certain services whilst not providing the resources to make action possible. Relatively small teams of local environmental health officials, for example, have to cope with a mountain of legislation designed to protect the public from many potential health hazards in restaurants, shops, etc. Boxes 11.1 and 11.2 set out examples where local discretion is evident, something that many will regard as desirable but others may condemn it as involving 'symbolic' legislation.

Even when policies are not simply symbolic it is important to recognise that the phenomena upon which action must be based are products of negotiation and compromise. Hence, as Barrett and Hill (1981) argue, many policies:

- represent compromises between conflicting values;
- involve compromises with key interests within the implementation structure;
- involve compromises with key interests upon whom implementation will have an impact;
- are framed without attention being given to the way in which underlying forces (particularly economic ones) will undermine them (Barrett and Hill, 1981, p. 89).

Box 11.1	Local government and litter in England

In England there are laws to enable local governments to prosecute those who drop litter. In 2008 a television programme drew attention to the considerable variations in the extent to which prosecutions occur; whilst some authorities bring many actions, many others do not prosecute at all. In defence of the inactive authorities attention was drawn to the complexity of the law and the difficulty in achieving prosecutions. Nevertheless some authorities spent considerable sums to overcome these.

In many other areas of policy, central government exercises pressures to compel local authorities to act in matters like this. A particularly important device here is requirements for statistical returns on performance. Clearly, for example, numbers of prosecutions for litter offences could be added to the list of required performance indicators. On the other hand, there are important distinctions to be drawn between litter offences, running across a continuum from casual droppings of a single item to organised disposal of rubbish (so-called 'fly tipping'). Performance indicators could easily be manipulated, with perverse effects on actual behaviour (see also Chapters 13

(continued)

and 15). It may be argued that it is best for local authorities to organise their own approaches to this problem, depending on local circumstances. Even further than that it is arguable that this is a localised problem where local choice about action is most appropriate. But alternatively, as the TV programme suggested, this may be seen as an issue on which the government has been content to provide the legislation which facilitates action, without addressing the issues about making it effective.

A similar situation is also observable in federalist countries where implementation by federal delegation is the predominant model (i.e. so-called 'executive federalism' or 'Vollzugsfoederalismus' in Germany or Switzerland). Here, the policy responsibilities are functionally divided between the levels of power: the federal government formulates legislations and regulations, while the federated entities (e.g. German *Laender* or Swiss cantons) implement them. This functional division of tasks frequently leads to differences in implementation across space (see Box 11.2).

Box 11.2   Swiss cantons and the acquisition of real estate by foreigners

In Switzerland, the cantonal implementation of the federal legislation regulating the acquisition of real estate by foreigners is a classic example of how 'executive federalism' produces very different outputs across cantons. In the 1960s, nationalist movements successfully pushed for the adoption of federal regulations restricting the acquisition of houses by foreign owners. According to this new national policy, the cantons had to deliver sale permits to foreigners in a very restricted way. The federal regulations were gradually tightened in the 1970s. Furthermore, the federal government was granted a right to appeal against cantonal authorisations to buy a real estate that are too generously given by the cantons to foreigners. Nevertheless, the global number of real estates sold to foreigners increased over time. This is notably due to the fact that, whereas some cantons implement the federal regulations, other cantons (i.e. typically Alpine cantons with a strong tourism sector) fully use their room of manoeuvre to develop their local touristic projects with foreign capital. In the canton of Lucerne, the implementation even led to a relaxation of the previously strict practice of real estate permits. In sum, the implementation does neither translate into uniform results nor contributes to policy effectiveness (Delley et al., 1982).

It must, then, be recognised, first, that compromise is not a once-and-for-all process but one that may continue throughout the history of the translation of that policy into action. Second, the initial 'policy makers' may be happy to let this occur as it enables them to evade decision problems (the so-called 'buck passing' strategy). If, then, the implementers are distanced from the original policy-framing process, and indeed perhaps even belong to separate, 'subordinate' organisations, they may be perceived as responsible for problems and inconsistencies and for unpopular resolutions of these.

A further complication for the analysis of policies is that many government actions do not involve the promulgation of explicit programmes requiring new activities. They involve adjustments to the way existing activities are to be carried out. The most common and obvious interventions of this kind are increases or decreases in the resources available for specific activities. In this way programmes are stimulated or allowed to wither away. What, however, makes implementation studies even more complex is that the relationship between resource adjustment and substantive programmes may be an indirect one. This is particularly a feature of central local government relations in the UK where, generally, central government does not explicitly fund programmes but makes resources available to multi-purpose authorities. In some policy fields – notably education and social care – central government has become increasingly explicit about what it expects local governments to do, and has been prepared to apply sanctions to authorities considered to be ineffective implementers. Hence, whilst local authorities may still appear to have expenditure choices, these are very constrained in practice.

The opposite situation is also possible. There are many policy domains in which the financial resources allocated by the central government to achieve an explicit and specific policy objective are not used towards this end at the local level. In Switzerland, the central government gave impressive funding to promote the construction, by municipalities, of anti-nuclear shelters (i.e. civil protection policy against war or natural disasters). This policy proved to be highly effective as shelters were made available to 90 percent of the population. Some municipalities even show a protection over 100 percent. A closer look at the infrastructures built at the local level shows that federal subsidies have been occasionally 'instrumentalised' by local authorities to build multi-purpose gyms and entertainments centres (i.e. sport and cultural policies) with some shelters in the basements. Such a 'non-compliance' has not been sanctioned by the federal authorities, even if the federal subsidies were gradually reduced over time (Knoepfel et al., 2007, p. 194).

Adjustments to the context in which decisions are made do not only come in the form of resource change, they may also come in the form of structure change. These structure changes may or may not carry implications for substantive outputs. Hence services may be transferred from one agency to another, new rules may be made on how services are to be administered, or new arrangements may be made for policy delivery (e.g. introduction of service contracts and performance indicators as key instruments of the New Public Management). These changes are common top-down interventions in public policy, but the analysis of their effects must rest upon an elaborate study of the way in which the balance of power is changed within the implementation system. In purposive language they are concerned with means, not ends, therefore explicit goals cannot be identified, yet they may be of fundamental importance for outcomes and may embody implicit goals. Developments (discussed further in Chapter 14) that are transforming the way policies are delivered – replacing large, bureaucratic departments by hived-off agencies, units that are placed in a quasi-market situation, or even private organisations operating as contractors for public services – must be seen not merely as restructuring the policy delivery system but also as often transforming the policies themselves.

Examples are particularly salient in the reforms aiming to transform welfare into an instrument of activation. Benefit recipients should be induced, via 'making work pay' programmes, to quickly reintegrate in the labour market. Local agents are to act as intermediaries towards such quick and possibly long-lasting professional reinsertion. At the same time, New Public Management (see further discussion in Chapter 15) has been a driving force in the setting up of contractualisation practices in the public sector. A 'service contract' is negotiated between the political authorities and an administrative unit or a private provider. The terms of such a contract defines performance indicators about the quantity and quality of administrative outputs to be delivered by the local agents, and about the speed of the job-seeker's return to the labour market as well. In return, political authorities grant the administrative unit a budget allocation, giving it freedom over production processes and management tools (i.e. a lump sum budget). Both reforms – activation of job seekers and incentives for civil servants – are combined in the active labour market policies introduced in Switzerland. Service contracts were thus negotiated between the various actors in charge of implementing the Swiss law on unemployment insurance, namely between the Confederation and the cantons and between the cantons and the third sector organisations responsible for active labour market policies. Despite the apparent room of manoeuvre delegated to local agents, the performance indicators led to a strong standardisation of the implementation practices by the cantons, as the federal government uses performance indicators to compare the cantons' practice (i.e. comparative benchmarking) and to softly impose best practices:

> This is particularly prominent in the case of local agents and beneficiaries, where the logic of contractualism is used with a view to checking more efficiently their behaviour and enforcing compliance with administratively defined objectives.
>
> (Bonvin and Moachon, 2007, p. 411; see also Bonvin and Moachon, 2013)

The last chapter looked at the importance of the policy formulation process and ended by pointing out the difficulties in determining where policy formulation stops and implementation begins. The concretisation of policy continues way beyond the legislative process. There is something of a seamless web here, though it may be that it is possible to identify some decisions that are more fundamental for determining the major 'policy' issues than others. There is, however, no reason why we should always expect to find such decisions, nor is it the case that these decisions, when they exist, are invariably taken during what we conventionally define as the policy formulation process. There are, on the contrary, a number of reasons why they may be left to the implementation process, of which the following is by no means an exhaustive list:

- because conflicts cannot be resolved during the policy formulation stage;
- because it is regarded as necessary to let key decisions be made when all the facts are available to implementers;
- because it is believed that implementers (professionals, for example) are better equipped to make the key decisions than anyone else;
- because little is known in advance about the actual impact of the new measures;
- because it is recognised that day-to-day decisions will have to involve negotiation and compromise with powerful groups;
- because it is considered politically inexpedient to try to resolve the conflicts early in the policy process.

Considerations of this kind must lead us to regard the policy-making process as something which often continues during the so-called implementation phase. It may involve continuing flexibility, it may involve the concretisation of policy in action, or it may involve a process of movement back and forth between policy and action. Barrett and Fudge (1981) have stressed the need, therefore, 'to consider implementation as a policy/action continuum in which an interactive and negotiative process is taking place over time between those seeking to put policy into effect and those upon whom action depends' (p. 25). The study by Smith and his colleagues, mentioned above, which stresses 'fields of action' rather than implementation 'chains', explores how a 'top-down' initiative encountered this issue; it is featured in Box 11.3.

Box 11.3	Implementation as an interactive and negotiative process: Smith et al.'s (2011) study of government initiatives on street crime and anti-social behaviour

This study examines the local impact of policies where the government clearly aspired to achieve top-down control. A mechanism was created by the Blair government (the Prime Minister's Delivery Unit) to give particular attention to implementation: 'extending the traditional empiricism of British government beyond policy-making to policy-delivery' (p. 982). The study looks at two initiatives: one seeking to reduce street crime, the other setting up a system to impose 'anti-social behaviour orders' on minor offenders.

The verdict of a senior official on the local impact of the street crime initiative was that it 'ran out of steam', it 'worked when it had Prime Ministerial authority behind it, and the resources to act as incentives, but

(continued)

it had less long-term ability to impact on the behaviour at constabulary level' (p. 990).

In respect of the use of anti-social behaviour orders, the study concluded that there was considerable variation in local practice. It noted: 'Anti-social behaviour is not easily defined and it is clear that local authorities and police forces are focusing on different phenomena when tackling it' (p. 995).

The article stresses the 'relatively autonomous fields' (p. 996) in which local actors like police forces, local authorities and magistrates operate. Then when 'the problem is amorphous and there are multiple agencies involved in implementation, the ability to deliver can be severely compromised'.

In the same vein, Eugene Bardach (1977, p. 56) proposes a conceptual shift from top down implementation chains to an 'implementation game'. This game metaphor aims at attracting 'the attention of researchers to players, to what the latter considers at stake, to their strategies and their tactics, their way of entering into the game, the rules of the game (which stipulate the condition for winning) and the rules of 'fair-play' (which stipulate the limits beyond which you enter the domain of fraud and illegality)'.

Lane (1987) also highlights some of the key points here in a paper in which, amongst a variety of approaches to implementation, he identifies it as 'evolution' (p. 532; see also Majone and Wildavsky, 1978), as 'learning' (p. 534; see also Browne and Wildavsky, 1984), as 'coalition' (p. 539, with important references to the essentially collaborative implementation implicit in corporatist relationships), and as 'responsibility and trust' (p. 541, this is a theme which we will explore further in later chapters in relation to organisational life). All of these imply a system in which a close collaborative relationship characterises relations within the policy system, allowing policy to emerge in action.

To emphasise the overall thrust of the points being made here we need to return to our insistence, at various places in the book, that while the stages model has been used to structure our discussion it can lead to confusion in the analysis of the real world. In the case of implementation that problem is exacerbated by the very loose way in which that word is used. Some discussions of the policy process use it to include much that follows from a very early stage in agenda setting. An example of this can be found in Marsh and Rhodes' edited book *Implementing Thatcherite Policies* (1992). We accept the validity of this usage since we do not think that academics should attempt to appropriate words in everyday use and apply them in very specific ways, however we prefer to confine discussion of implementation to activities close to the point of delivery. But our stance does not solve the problem that, for the reasons outlined above, it is very difficult to determine a cut-off point where it can be said that agenda setting and formulation processes end and implementation ones begin. For those devising a research project on implementation there are problems to be solved that follow from this.

The proponents of a bottom-up approach argue that they can avoid the predetermining assumptions implicit in the top-down approach: about cause and effect, about hierarchical or any other structural relations between actors and agencies, and about what should be going on between them. The bottom-up approach is expounded forcefully by Hjern and his associates (Hjern and Hull, 1982; Hjern and Porter, 1981), who argue for a methodology in which researchers construct empirically the networks within which field-level, decision-making actors carry out their activities without predetermining assumptions about the structures within which these occur. But this is not just an argument about methodology:

> to understand the policy–action relationship we must get away from a single perspective of the process that reflects a normative administrative or managerial view of how the process should be, and try to find a conceptualisation that reflects better the empirical evidence of the complexity and dynamics of the interactions between individuals and groups seeking to put policy into effect, those upon whom action depends and those whose interests are affected when change is proposed. To do this, we have argued for an alternative perspective to be adopted – one that focuses on the actors and agencies themselves and their interactions, and for an action-centred or 'bottom-up' mode of analysis as a method of identifying more clearly who seems to be influencing what, how and why.
>
> (Barrett and Hill, 1981, p. 19)

This suggests a wider approach to the discussion of how implementation occurs than do those propositions rooted in a concern about how implementation should be controlled. What, in many respects, is being emphasised in this more action-centred mode of analysis is that the very things that top-down theorists urge must be controlled are the elements that are difficult to bring under control. The reality, therefore, is not of imperfect control but of action as a continuous process of interaction:

- with a changing and changeable policy;
- in a complex interaction structure;
- in an outside world which must interfere with implementation because government action does, and is designed to, impinge upon it;
- with implementing actors who are inherently difficult to control.

Analysis is best focused upon the levels at which this is occurring, since it is not so much creating implementation deficiency as recreating policy.

This emphasis, in the bottom-up critique, upon the complexities in the concept of policy and the way it is made also suggests that implementation may itself be an ambiguous concept. Lane has argued that there is some confusion in the implementation literature between 'implementation and successful implementation as an outcome, and the implementation process or how implementation comes about' (Lane, 1987, p. 528). The classical top-down studies are principally concerned with explaining why an expected

Table 11.1   Differences between the 'top-down' and 'bottom-up' visions of policy implementation

Implementation approaches	'Top-down' vision	'Bottom-up' vision
Starting point of analysis	Decisions taken by political and administrative authorities (laws, regulations, action plans)	Activities of actors participating to the implementation network at local level (actors' network)
Process for identifying the main actors	From the top and public sector down to the bottom and private sector	From the bottom ('street-level') to the top with simultaneous consideration of public and private actors
Criteria for evaluating the quality of policy implementation	• Regularity (conformity, legality) of implementation procedure • Effectiveness: extent of realisation of the formal policy objectives	• No *a priori* clearly defined evaluation criteria • Level of participation of actors involved • Degree of conflict in implementation
Basic question (for the conduct of public policies)	Which implementation modes (structures and procedures) must be adopted to ensure optimum possible achievement of official objectives?	Which interactions between the public and private actors of a policy network should be considered during implementation so that it will be accepted?

Source: Loose adaptation by Knoepfel et al. (2007, p. 196) of the comparison initially proposed by Sabatier (1986, p. 33).

outcome does or does not occur, and to do this they need clear goal statements to work with. These may be supplied by the policy makers or imputed by the researchers. Without such yardsticks we may still study processes, but our activity is rather different. Sabatier, in an attempt to fuse the best ideas from both top-down and bottom-up processes, rightly suggests that the presence or absence of a 'dominant piece of legislation structuring the situation' (1986, p. 37) may help to determine which approach is appropriate. However, that may involve starting with a question begging the assumption that this structuring has in fact occurred. One can obviously treat a piece of legislation as dominant, but if one does so the problems for explanation, in cases of implementation failure, tend to be either what others have done to subvert it, or what is wrong with it. As the arguments above suggest, both of these may be oversimplified questions about both policy and its implementation context, and particularly about the relationship between the two. The main features of the debate between these perspectives is summarised in table 11.1.

 ## Beyond the top-down/bottom-up debate

The methodological argument that surfaces in the discussion above can be resolved relatively simply. It may be possible to examine an implementation process in terms of what happens to goals proclaimed early in the policy process (or even in terms of imputed goals) and then look at what happened. It may also be possible to start at the output end and engage in 'backward mapping' (Elmore, 1980). Both approaches will have strengths and weaknesses; both may be biased by the prejudices of the actors, the researchers or the research funders; and choices between them need to be determined by empirical factors and contingencies. Mixed approaches, with triangulation between them, may be desirable.

Winter, in two reviews of this topic, has adopted a pragmatic response to the theoretical debate as far as implementation research is concerned (2003; 2006). He argues that 'looking for *the* overall and one for all implementation theory' is a 'utopian' objective which is not feasible, and may even inhibit the creativity that comes from diversity (2006, p. 158). He argues that we should look for partial rather than general implementation theories.

From that point of view Winter sees implementation research as able to address concrete issues, of a kind that an obsession with all-encompassing theories will tend to inhibit. He argues that there needs to be an emphasis on exploring the determinants of policy outputs: 'I suggest that we look for behavioural *output* variables to characterize the *performance* of implementers. . . . The first aim of implementation research then should be to explain variation in such performance' (ibid., p. 158). While this argument is framed in terms of choice about methodology, what it implies is a wider need to avoid the obsession with whether the 'goals' of policy designers are achieved that characterises top-down theory. Goals are contestable and change over time. Work that focuses upon goals gets into questions about what the 'real goals' in a policy process are, and often gets tangled up with debates about what they should be. Variation in performance can be identified without engaging with these issues.

The case for trying to ensure that normative preoccupations do not interfere with a clear analysis of the implementation process has been emphasised throughout the discussion. The issue, then, for discussion here about ways to move beyond the top-down/bottom-up debate is about recognising that there will be various ways in which actors will attempt to exercise prior control over the implementation process. The concern is with a variety of issues about the extent to which actors impose rules upon others. The other side of this is about how discretion is structured, about how easily actors can exercise autonomy.

Considerations discussed earlier about types of policy suggested various ways in which decisions may be structured. It also suggested that the quest for some simple policy typology that would help with the interpretation of when different structuring will occur has been fruitless. It was suggested however that Matland's (1995) use of 'ambiguity' and 'conflict' to typify different policy issues is helpful. Matland's amplification of that point, with examples added by the present authors, is provided in table 11.2. Ambiguity tends to make the delegation of discretion likely (the need to make judgements during the process highlighted in the cookery example in Box 10.6). In the absence of conflicting goals, experimentation will be feasible. Conflict,

Table 11.2   Matland's analysis of the impact of conflict and ambiguity upon implementation, illustrated with examples

	Low conflict	High conflict
Low ambiguity	1 Administrative Implementation	3 Political Implementation
	Example: a social insurance where there is general acceptance of the case for it and the qualification test is simple.	Example: contested reforms (health care change, or service privatisation) where, in the face of resistance, government can nevertheless still drive through change.
High ambiguity	2 Experimental Implementation	4 Symbolic Implementation
	Example: measures to try to reduce health inequalities where there is general acceptance of the case for action but uncertainty about what is effective.	Example: where there is both difficulty in specifying objectives and opposition to them, for example equal pay legislation involving complex comparisons and contested goals.

Source: Adapted from Matland, 1995, Table 4.1, p. 160.

on the other hand, implies a desire to control. Actors claiming hierarchical rights will seek to assert them, and this will be particularly evident in the absence of consensus. If low ambiguity is involved then rules will be formulated (the cookery book approach to implementation). High conflict and high ambiguity is a difficult combination. Matland, in his original analysis, called this 'symbolic implementation'. This puts it perhaps too strongly, inasmuch as symbolic implies no effort to implement whilst what is actually being highlighted is the level of difficulty. Nevertheless, of course, there may be situations in which those attempting to dictate policy want merely to claim to have tried.

Matland's approach is still rather static, however, and his model of conflict rather a simple dichotomy. The clarity of his two by two diagram masks the fact that both ambiguity and conflict are complex continuous variables. Many of the most controversial (and perhaps most interesting) implementation stories involve prolonged interactions in situations of considerable and very complicated multi-party conflicts.

This leads us on to two crucial issues for the examination of the implementation process:

- the fact that policy processes vary greatly in the extent to which there is an attempt to prescribe a rule framework;
- the importance of variations in the administrative framework within which the process occurs.

In the terms of the cooking analogy in Box 10.6, the issues can be said to be about the extent to which there is a cookbook containing clear prescriptions, and about the relational frameworks in which that will be used (not just two persons in a household but something much more complex).

Putting implementation in context

The issues Matland is struggling with are given attention in a rather different way in work that uses the notion of 'implementation regimes' (May and Jochim, 2013; May 2015). This approach argues for a focus on policy areas:

> Rather than starting with a policy, one starts with a particular set of problems – crime, environmental harm, illegal immigration, terrorism and so on – and seeks to depict the ideas, institutional arrangements, and interests that constitute the governing arrangements for dealing with the problem.
> (May and Jochim, 2013, p. 429)

A series of questions are then posed about those three organising concepts:

- Ideas: to what extent are there 'shared commitments concerning policy purpose'.
- Institutional structures and arrangements: the nature of 'structures of authority, attention, information and organizational arrangements'.
- Interests: what are the 'constituencies that provide interest, support and opposition' (quotes from Table 1 of May, 2015).

These questions are particularly pertinent to policies featuring in the 'high conflict' column in Matland's model. Thus May (2015) examines the implementation difficulties that Obama's Affordable Care Act has faced in these terms.

May and Jochim's approach resonates with many themes discussed already in this book. Their notions of problem clusters and communities organised around them picks up themes explored in Chapter 4 about policy network and communities, and about advocacy coalitions. There is a need for caution here, as explored in that chapter, about assumptions both about shared interests and about network stability. Issues from Chapter 5 about institutions and ideas need also to be highlighted.

This is also an approach that connects up policy formulation issues with implementation ones. Indeed, May's (2015) exploration of the Affordable Care Act includes consideration of the processes necessary to put the Act into operation, including negotiated arrangements with States that we would describe as continuing policy formulation. The next section explores this issue further.

The nature of the policy rule framework

Much attention was given in Chapter 10 to the ways in which details are formulated which will govern policy implementation. At the same time it was acknowledged that there will be differences in the extent to which this takes place, from policy to policy or policy subsystem to policy subsystem. Crucial then for the examination of implementation is the extent to which this concretisation of policy has occurred. Whilst some policies pass out of the legislative stages with very clear rule structures, enabling implementation deficits to be easily identified, others are much less fully formed. There are two considerations here, one is the nature of the policy issue, the other is the institutional context.

It can generally be argued that, in modern taxation, initiatives will reach the implementation stage with comparatively clear rule structures. Those rules have very clear target groups, may be hard to implement and may be the subject of formal disputes in the courts, hence implementation deficit may be analysed, but in most societies political and social forces have taken taxation a long way from the vague 'tax farming' that characterised such policies in early mediaeval societies when implementers were charged to bring in money – to profit if they were good at it and to be punished if they were not – by rulers who cared little about how it was done.

Similar points may be made about cash benefit systems. Many income maintenance systems have evolved a long way from the decentralised 'poor law', in which a great deal of discretion was vested in local 'boards of guardians', to a modern situation in which all the main benefit systems have strong rule-based structures which facilitate computerised calculation and the operation of formal appeal mechanisms.

However here institutional factors may apply. Cash benefit systems (amongst which are included what Americans call 'welfare') have been given attention by many implementation scholars. Systems of all kinds are likely to have rules to establish relevant contingencies (sickness, unemployment, old age, etc.). But then a contrast may be drawn between those where entitlement then depends upon past contributions, with clear rules in respect of ways of calculating the cumulative implications of these, and those that use means-tests to determine entitlement where rules may be more complex and forms of discretion may be given to administrative staff (see Eardley et al., 1996, for an international comparison). One of the authors wrote about a UK means-testing system on which he worked many years ago (Hill, 1969) where implementation involved the extensive delegation of discretion to implementing staff at 'street-level'. However, since that time the UK system has become much more rule based, and decision making rests more upon office-based scrutiny of forms completed by applicants as opposed to the face-to-face interviewing described in that article (Walker, 2015). Nevertheless, as Box 11.4 indicates, there are still interesting variations around this theme, interpreted in terms that make it in fact an application of the National Patterns Approach (see Chapter 6).

Box 11.4	Jewell's comparative analysis of the administration of social assistance (2007)

Jewell carried out case studies of social assistance officials in the United States (California), Germany (Bremen) and Sweden (Malmö). He shows that those in California work within a system with simple rules but minimal discretion, while in Bremen they are seen as the formally qualified operators of a complex legal structure and in Malmö they have high levels of discretion. There is a fascinating contrast in Jewell's book between the elaborate legal structure of the German system, where ironically high discretion emerges principally from the difficulties staff have in navigating through complex and ever changing rules, and the very loosely regulated Swedish system where high discretion is implicit and even administrative court decisions do not create precedents.

Jewell explores the impact of growth of caseloads and pressure of work upon the three systems. What he found was variation in all three systems arising from the impact of efforts to cut administrative costs, leading to staff shortages and staff turnover. The Swedish system seemed to be suffering least from these problems, but then it was from the outset the system in which most variation was likely. In the German case rule application seemed to have become more erratic, whilst in the American one it was 'corner cutting' by a system under great strain that was the principal source of diversity.

There are other areas of policy where there is a complex and dynamic relationship between rule structures and their interpretation. Here a substantive consideration is important: the extent to which it is accepted as undesirable to firm up policy options too much in advance. This may apply to complex service activities. This is not just an issue about the feasibility of controlling in advance how actors should behave at the point of delivery ('the street-level'; see Chapter 13). It will also apply where it is accepted that the structures of working arrangements are best determined close to that point (see for example two case-studies that illustrate this, an account by Virtanen [2014] of university reforms in Finland and one by Coleman et al. [2014] on changes to health service delivery arrangements in England). Similar issues arise in many areas of regulatory policy.

In this area of policy, alongside the problems of complexity, there may be other features which complicate implementation: in particular, the fact that the regulatee often understands the process better than the regulators, that there are difficult trade-off judgements to be made about the costs of compliance and that the ability of the regulatee to evade control puts willing compliance at a premium. This has led Hanf to see much regulatory activity as involving 'coproduction' between regulator and regulatee (Hanf, 1993). At its extreme – and this probably characterised much British pollution control until very recently – policy is essentially no more than the terms that the regulator is able to reach with the regulatee. In industrial air pollution control the statutory concept of the use of the 'best practicable means' to limit emissions had little meaning except in the context of such an agreement (Hill in Downing and Hanf, 1983). It certainly could not in any realistic sense be described as defined in the policy-making process. Since then, under pressure from the European Union for a more precise approach, this 'policy' has moved on a little, but the policy emphasis is still rather more upon ambient air quality targets than upon specific control over what goes up individual chimneys.

The co-production of regulatory outputs inherently bears the risk that the regulator is 'captured' by the regulatees (Stigler, 1971). Therefore, some authors ask for the creation of independent regulatory agencies or, at least, acknowledge positively the emergence of the 'regulatory state' in Europe (Majone, 1994). As a matter of fact, many independent agencies have been institutionalised since the 1980s, in various countries and economic sectors (e.g. banking, insurances, etc.) or liberalised network industries such as electricity, telecommunications, water or airlines (Thatcher, 2007; Gilardi, 2008; Jordana et al., 2011). If these regulatory agencies display a high level of independency from elected officials (e.g. no partisan nomination of agency staff) and from regulatees (e.g. no revolving doors between regulated industry and agency), then they probably are able to reduce problems of information asymmetries between regulators and regulatees, and to improve the quality, stability and credibility of their regulatory decisions. In these cases independent regulatory agencies are obviously more than just implementers of political decisions. They are autonomous decision- and rule-makers as long as they are able to make credible commitments over a period spanning several legislatures and governmental terms.

There are very important areas of policy where the policy/implementation distinction is even more blurred than in these examples from service provision and regulation. Oddly, these do not seem to have been given much attention in the implementation literature, perhaps because they concern issues at the very centre of national politics – economic and foreign policy.

If your primary aim is to understand the implementation process, a great deal is going to depend upon the activity in which you are interested. If you are looking at one in which there is a quite explicit 'top'-initiated, goal-directed activity, it may be justifiable to use a 'top-down' methodology and work with a notion such as 'implementation deficit'. This may be particularly the case where a quantifiable output is available and explicit inputs can be measured. Yet many other events in the policy process do not involve such clarity. Examples can be taken of complex and confusing cases where central goals were not nearly so clear, or where central goal statements should be received with great scepticism – in fields like social care, employment policy, urban renewal or the prevention of crime, for example. Furthermore, as suggested above, concern may be with an ongoing process where explicit change is not initiated from above, or where there are grounds for scepticism about whether efforts to bring about change will carry through to the 'bottom'.

The importance of variations in the administrative system

The discussion in the last section has drawn distinctions between situations in which rules for implementation are very much in evidence, situations in which implementation is very much a process of developing and elaborating initial policy frameworks and situations in which either we need to say that the implementation or regulation process *is* the policy-making process or to regard this distinction as meaningless.

This variation may, of course, be influenced by the characteristics of governmental systems and by political or administrative culture (see also Chapter 10). It is appropriate to emphasise federal government forms here. This has been highlighted in examples drawn from Switzerland in the discussion above (see in particular Box 11.2). It is perhaps not surprising that issues about the capacity of policy makers to influence implementation have been given particular attention in the United States, because of the ways in which federalism, the division of executive, legislative and judicial powers, regulatory politics and the written constitution complicate executive action. As suggested above, ever since the New Deal in the 1930s the exploration of ways to increase Washington's influence in Oakland, or wherever, has been a key preoccupation of those Americans who regard active federal government as important for their society. In the 1960s the struggle against racial segregation in the Deep South and the efforts to develop new initiatives in welfare policy and in urban policy offered particularly salient examples.

A major factor contributing to that complexity is the fact that often intervening levels, as layers in the political-administrative system, have a legitimate claim to engage in policy formulation and decision making: where does 'policy formation' end and 'implementation' begin? It is in recognition of this that Goggin et al. (1990) refer to federal 'messages' to states rather than to federal policies. Similarly, studies of the implementation of European Union policies (Knill and Lenschow, 1998; Lampinen and Uusikylä, 1998) indicate very distinct processes of re-formulations within individual nation states. What is called 'implementation' in those studies in fact may rather be seen as 'policy formulation'.

A realistic approach to the examination of implementation in its administrative context therefore needs to give attention to the facts:

- that implementation involves complex intra-organisational interactions;
- that the analysis of those interactions must take us into issues about negotiations between actors who are at least quasi-autonomous;

- that this autonomy may be linked with claims of legitimacy which render beside the point those analyses that emphasise recalcitrance, shortfalls and deficits;

- that these complexities need to be seen, as explored in Chapter 6, as contained within different national or transnational political systems which influence the games played and the legitimacies claimed.

These themes are explored further in later chapters.

Modelling the influences on implementation

The discussion of the importance of giving attention to variations in the form policy takes shifts the focus a long way from approaches to the topic which sees implementers simply as people who change the policy as it is put into action. It suggests that influences upon the implementation process extend from considerations about how policy is formulated through to factors that influence behaviour close to 'street-level'. They may be modelled in terms of six categories (this categorisation owes a great deal to Van Meter and Van Horn's 1975 original modelling of the implementation process):

- policy characteristics, including issues about the way in which these have been shaped by the formulation process;

- issues about 'layers' in the policy transfer process, or what may be called 'vertical public administration', that is the issues about the vertical inter-organisational relationship that so concerned Pressman and Wildavsky;

- horizontal inter-organisational relationships (relationships between parallel organisations required to collaborate in implementation);

- factors affecting the responses of implementation agencies (their organisation, their disposition, and so on) – these may be subdivided into issues about the overall characteristics of the agencies and issues about the behaviour of front-line (or street-level) staff;

- the impact of responses from those affected by the policy; and

- wider macro-environmental factors.

Theoretically it should be possible to try to sort out the respective impacts of these elements using, as a dependent variable (i.e. variable to be explained): policy outputs. Box 11.5 works through an example where this approach is feasible. In practice the feasibility of this depends upon a number of things. First, the extent to which distinct outputs can be identified. It is important here to bear in mind Winter's distinction between outputs and goals (see pp. 216–7). There has been a tendency for implementation studies to use goal statements made by actors with a distinct, but contestable, view on what *they* think should be achieved. Second, a policy may have various outputs (the complexity of policy hardly needs emphasising at this stage in the book). Third, policy outputs may be hard to identify let alone quantify. Fourth, an approach of this kind depends upon being able to separate implementers (different parts of a department or different local authorities for example) in order to tease out differences; this will often not be feasible.

| Box 11.5 | Studying implementation: an example involving comparison of the responses of English local authorities to a central government policy initiative |

In England there is a central government policy concerned with facilitating arrangements in which individuals in need of social care can be given direct payments of cash to purchase services for themselves instead of being provided with services commissioned by local authorities. Whilst some local authorities had been pioneers of this approach, central government adopted the policy and put pressure on local governments to implement it. However, local authorities vary significantly in their enthusiasm for the policy. Hence there is thus a relatively straightforward 'dependent variable' published in official statistics: numbers of payments made by each local authority over a period corrected to take into account variations in overall population size.

It is then possible to identify factors affecting implementation:

- Policy characteristics – features of the policy which affect implementation (such as rules about preventing the misuse of direct payments).

- Layers in the policy transfer process – the mechanisms that govern central/local government relationships (inspection, the collection of performance indictors, etc.).

- Horizontal inter-organisation relationships – social care direct payments may require liaison between local authorities and the health service and these vary from place to place.

- Factors affecting responses by implementing agencies – the enthusiasm of politicians and senior officials, whether there was a 'champion' who pushed the scheme at the local level, whether street-level workers found direct payments difficult to implement or felt that they upset standard operating procedures.

- Responses from those affected – was there a public demand or widespread suspicion of the measure? Were there local pressure groups in favour or against?

- Wider macro-environmental factors – since direct payments often involve the employment of service workers by individuals the local labour market may have an effect upon their availability.

Sources: Examples based upon work on this topic by Fernándes et al. (2007); Leece and Bornat (2006); and Vick et al. (2006).

CONCLUSIONS

This chapter started with the arguments between top-down and bottom-up approaches to the study of implementation. Like all such dialectical debates in the social sciences, this one is more important in illuminating the many facets of the subject than in leading the reader to a conclusion on one side or the other.

The aim in this discussion has been first to draw attention to the importance of the top-down school of implementation studies initiated by Pressman and Wildavsky, stressing their role in opening up the analysis of an important, and previously rather neglected, part of the policy process. But then, second, it has sought to demonstrate the blind spots in such a perspective – which may be corrected by considering the alternative bottom-up approach. Whether you favour one or the other approach, some combination of the two, or one that tries to avoid either, depends very much on what you are trying to do. Clearly, they can be integrated.

Any effort to develop implementation theory – once it moves away from the attempt to develop checklists of pitfalls for the implementation process in the way described and criticised above – must face the difficulty of becoming involved with the wide range of questions that have been raised in relation to policy making and in the study of organisations. If we substitute the word 'doing' for 'implementation' we see how we are confronted by an attempt to develop a 'theory of doing' – or of action. As Winter argues, that is not a very helpful way to proceed. Rather, it is hard to go beyond the identification of the key elements that must be analysed in the study of implementation, and the recognition of the overwhelming importance of the negotiation and bargaining that occur throughout the policy process:

> many so-called implementation problems arise precisely because there is a tension between the normative assumptions of government – what ought to be done and how it should happen – and the struggle and conflict between interests – the need to bargain and compromise – that represent the reality of the process by which power/influence is gained and held in order to pursue ideological goals.
>
> (Barrett and Hill, 1981, p. 145)

This general exploration of implementation – with its emphasis upon the significance of organisational complexity and upon the sources of variation in discretion in the implementation process – is now followed by chapters which look at some of these issues more fully.

12 Bureaucracy: organisational structures and processes

SYNOPSIS

The public policy process, particularly that part of it concerned with implementation, is very largely an organisational process. It involves work within (intra-) and between (inter-) organisations.

Public organisations are often described as bureaucracies. A brief discussion explores the implications of the use of the word 'bureaucracy' in light of the fact that it is often given a pejorative sense. This leads onto an examination of the most influential theoretical analysis of public bureaucracy, provided by the German sociologist Max Weber, and an exploration of the way his ideas have been used by others. A brief account is provided of some other key work on the sociology of organisations that is important for understanding public sector organisations. In the end this leads to the introduction of varieties of organisation theory that suggests that the classical theory exaggerates the significance of the unitary, closely regulated, formal organisation when the actual boundaries between aspects of human life, and therefore between organisations, can be quite fluid.

The section on 'rules and discretion' seems to involve a distinct change of emphasis, particularly as some of the important work analysing this has been done within academic law. However, the aim in that section, and the one that follows it on the treatment of the same theme in organisational sociology, is to show how issues about possibilities of and limits to control are of fundamental importance for understanding how the policy process is handled in many contexts.

The chapter ends with some consideration about comparative perspectives on public bureaucracies, examining how efforts to compare national administrative arrangements throw light upon differences in the way the issues discussed in the chapter manifest themselves in practice.

Organisation as bureaucracy

The emergence of extensive efforts by governments to make policy, in the twentieth century, is generally also seen as involving the creation of unitary bureaucratic states. Since the 1980s that model of public policy making and implementation has come under challenge. This was noted in Chapter 1 as involving a transition from government to governance. But of course we are talking here about partial changes and the unitary model remains of importance. In any case it needs to be seen as the starting point for its alternatives. Hence this chapter, and to a large extent the next one too, is about unitary bureaucratic government. The issues about governance are then explored further in Chapter 14.

In the first part of the book it was shown that some of the key theories of the state – particularly elitist theories, rational choice theories and institutional theories – concern themselves with issues about bureaucratic power, often seeing it as involving the domination of the policy process by those inside the organisational system. The word 'bureaucracy' is a neutral term used to describe a complex organisation and is therefore particularly likely to be applicable to a governmental one. But it is also used in a pejorative sense to denote an impenetrable, ponderous and unimaginative organisation.

In many discussions of the role of organisations in the modern world these complex 'bureaucracies' are seen as necessary evils. As Perrow puts it, 'Without this form of social technology, the industrialized countries of the West could not have reached the heights of extravagance, wealth and pollution that they currently enjoy' (Perrow, 1972, p. 5). The emphasis upon bureaucracy as a potentially problematical form of organisation, highlighted by the frequency with which the term is used pejoratively, has two separate key concerns which can be described simply as concerns about (a) accountability and (b) efficiency and effectiveness. One tendency of critiques of bureaucracy is to stress problems about making government organisations accountable to politicians and the people, as bureaucrats are appointed and cannot be dismissed by citizens through democratic elections. Another is to emphasise the extent to which they are unsatisfactory 'instruments' for the carrying out of policy – they are seen as increasing costs and distorting outputs, as bureaucrats generally operate in a public monopoly situation and are not sanctioned by market mechanisms. Accountability mechanisms in a New Public Management context will be further discussed in Chapter 15).

Protagonists at both ends of the political spectrum offer solutions to the alleged problem of 'bureaucracy' in public policy. For many on the 'Right' the solution is the allocation of goods and services by way of the market, with the role of government kept to a minimum. The market offers a mechanism which is allegedly accountable, because the public are then consumers and are able to make choices about what they purchase, and efficient, because providers are in continuous competition with each other. This solution has been applied in many so-called 'network industries' or public utility domains, which have been liberalised. Competition between (both public and private) operators has been introduced in previously monopolistic sectors such as telecommunication, electricity and gas, civil aviation, railways, postal services, water, etc. The libertarian 'Left' alternatively sees a world in which capitalist power is curbed or overthrown as offering the possibility of free collaboration between equal citizens in meeting their needs. Both extremes embody a utopian element – in the case of the 'Right', a belief in the feasibility of a really competitive market rather than an economy in which there is a tendency for monopoly to develop and for choices to be limited and manipulated; in the case of the 'Left', a world in which big government is as unnecessary as big capitalism.

The utopianism of the 'Right' is more important for the modern political agenda than that of the 'Left', partly because of the dominance of capitalist ideology and partly because the history of communism has offered so dramatic a betrayal of its idealistic roots. Yet nearer the centre of the political debate the idealistic assertions of both camps offer key poles for debate about public policy – concerning the extent to which there are problems about organising the public sector and regulating the market sector. This takes us back to Perrow's neat aphorism. Complex organisations are needed to meet the needs of modern society because governments are engaged in a complicated combination of direct service delivery (i.e. the state as provider) and market organisation and oversight (i.e. the state as a regulator of providers). Moreover, they have to cope with trade-offs between the two. In most of the twentieth century the tendency was for governments – at least in Western Europe – to see direct provision as preferable to regulation in many areas of social and economic life. This forced them to focus on issues about the control of their own large, bureaucratic organisations. In the final quarter of the century there was a reaction against this approach. But that heightens the need for attention to regulation, essentially an issue about the relationships between government organisations and private or quasi-autonomous ones. The worries about 'bureaucracy' have not been dispelled, as many within the 'neo-liberal Right' had hoped – rather, they take new forms, forcing us to reconceptualise bureaucracy in a more complex way. This reconceptualisation has been a key concern of work which sees late twentieth-century innovations in the public sector as a 'New Public Management' movement (Hood, 1991; Pollitt, 1990). New Public Management is discussed further in Chapter 15.

These normative and prescriptive arguments are not the main concerns of this book. However, some of them will emerge again in the analysis of the issues about accountability in Chapter 15. They have also coloured much theorising and research about organisational behaviour. And, as the last paragraph suggests, they have had an impact upon innovation in public policy and particularly on efforts to influence the implementation process.

Max Weber and the theory of bureaucracy

The work of a German theorist, Max Weber, active at the end of the nine-teenth century and in the early years of the twentieth, was particularly important for the development of the theory of organisations. Furthermore, it was the organisation of government in the modern state that particularly concerned him. He observed the development of a powerful unified civil service in Germany, recognising its potential as an instrument of govern-ment and worrying about its implications for democratic accountability.

Weber embedded his theory of bureaucracy in a wider theory of social power. His discussion of bureaucracy is linked to an analysis of types of authority. He postulates three basic authority types: charismatic, traditional and rational–legal (see Box 12.1). He sees the last-named as characteristic of the modern state.

Box 12.1	Max Weber's analysis of types of authority

Charismatic authority is based upon 'devotion to the specific and excep-tional sanctity, heroism or exemplary character of an individual person' (Weber, 1947, p. 328). Reference may be made here to key historical figures, both ones viewed positively like Mahatma Ghandi and Nelson Mandela and notable for their negative impact like Hitler. It is a transitory phenomenon associated with periods of social turmoil; the essentially personal nature of the relationship between leader and follower makes the development of permanent institutions impossible and accordingly it succumbs to processes of 'routinisation' which transform it into one of the other types of authority.

Traditional authority, on the other hand, rests upon 'an established belief in the sanctity of immemorial traditions and the legitimacy of the status of those exercising authority under them' (ibid.). Hereditary monarchs are thus seen as epitomal examples. While charismatic authority's weakness lies in its instability, the weakness of traditional authority is its static nature. It is thus argued to be the case that the rational–legal type of authority is superior to either of the other two types.

Weber states that rational–legal authority rests upon 'a belief in the legality of patterns of normative rules, and the right of those elevated to authority under such rules to issue commands' (ibid.). The maintenance of such a system of authority rests upon the development of a bureaucratic system of administration in which permanent officials administer, and are bound by, rules. The primacy of formal rules aims at avoiding arbitrary decisions and at securing predictability and legal certainty. These principles are crucial for the equal treatment of all citizens by bureaucrats producing policy outputs and delivering services.

Weber regards the development of bureaucratic administration as intimately associated with the evolution of modern industrialised society. Bureaucratisation is seen as a consequence of the development of complex economic and political systems, and also as a phenomenon that has helped to make these developments possible. In this sense he sees bureaucracy as the most efficient organisational form and therefore one that will inevitably become dominant due to the parallel modernisation of society, economy and the state.

Students of Weber have differed in the extent to which they regard him as a theorist who believed that bureaucracy can be subjected to democratic control. He was clearly ambivalent on that topic. Whilst the use of 'bureaucracy' as a pejorative term clearly predates Weber, he must be seen as the theorist who effectively poses the dilemma: here is an instrument that enables much to be done that could not otherwise be done, but there is a need to be concerned about how it is used, how it is controlled and who controls it (Albrow, 1970; Beetham, 1987).

The strength of the bureaucratic form of administration, according to Weber, rests upon its formal rationality, a notion which a number of modern students of organisations have equated with efficiency. This translation of Weber's concept has led to some useful discussions of the relationship between formalism and efficiency but has also given currency to a rather unsubtle characterisation of Weber's theory. Albrow (1970) shows how this confusion arose and provides the following clarification of Weber's position:

> The real relation between formal rationality and efficiency can best be understood by considering the means by which efficiency is commonly measured, through the calculation of cost in money terms, or in time, or in energy expended. Such calculations are formal procedures which do not in themselves guarantee efficiency, but are among the conditions for determining what level of efficiency has been reached. At the heart of Weber's idea of formal rationality was the idea of correct calculation, in either numerical terms, as with the accountant, or in logical terms, as with the lawyer. This was normally a necessary though not sufficient condition for the attainment of goals; it could even conflict with material rationality.
>
> (Albrow, 1970, p. 65)

Weber's theory is seen as providing a number of simple propositions about the formal structure of organisations, a misconception that has contributed to his usefulness to students of organisations but which does not do justice to the depth of his understanding of the critical issues in organisational sociology. As he outlines the characteristics of an organisational type that is important in complex societies because of its formal rationality, he naturally stresses the strength of that type rather than its weakness. Weber's work defines a widespread kind of organisation and explains why it grew in importance, offering thereby sociological analysis which may be separated from political polemic.

Weber lists a number of characteristics which, taken together, define 'bureaucracy' as an ideal-type of organisation. According to Weber, 'an ideal type is formed by the one-sided accentuation of one or more points of view and by the synthesis of a great many diffuse, discrete, more or less present and occasionally absent concrete individual phenomena, which are arranged according to those one-sidedly emphasised viewpoints into a unified analytical construct ("Gedankenbild"). In its conceptual purity, this mental construct cannot be found empirically anywhere in reality. It is a utopia. Historical research faces the task of determining in each individual case, the extent to which this ideal-construct approximates to or diverges from reality' (Weber, 1997, p. 90). The characteristics of the bureaucratic phenomenon are set out in Box 12.2. While Weber does not see these characteristics as prescriptions for organisation but as an analytical concept, many subsequent writers have seized upon their similarity to the model prescribed by others who were searching for the best way to organise.

Perhaps the most influential figure in the search for principles of organisation before the First World War was F.W. Taylor (1911). He was an American who tried to develop scientific principles for industrial management based upon a series of generalisations which he claimed to be of universal

---

Box 12.2	Max Weber's delineation of the characteristics of bureaucracy

1. A continuous organisation with a specified function, or functions, its operation bound by rules. Continuity and consistency within the organisation are ensured by the use of writing to record acts, decisions and rules.

2. The organisation of personnel is on the basis of hierarchy. The scope of authority within the hierarchy is clearly defined, and the rights and duties of the officials at each level are specified.

3. The staff are separated from ownership of the means of administration or production. They are personally free, 'subject to authority only with respect to their impersonal official obligations'.

4. Staff are appointed, not elected, on the basis of impersonal qualifications, and are promoted on the basis of merit.

5. Staff are paid fixed salaries and have fixed terms of employment. The salary scale is normally graded according to rank in the hierarchy. Employment is permanent with a certain security of tenure, and pensions are usually paid on retirement.

Source: Based on Weber, 1947, pp. 329–41.

application. His importance for this account is that he has been widely seen as the leading exponent of methods of organisation which rest upon treating human beings as units of labour to be used 'efficiently' without regard to their needs, attitudes and emotions (Braverman, 1974). Hence a great deal of the subsequent concern about human relations in organisations emerged from the exposure of the limitations of 'Taylorism'. Despite that exposure the influence of Taylorism lives on. Pollitt (1990) has described much modern managerialism in the public services as 'neo-Taylorism'. He argues:

> Taylorism was centrally concerned with the 'processes of determining and fixing effort levels' and can be seen as 'the bureaucratization of the structure of control but *not* the employment relationship' (Littler, 1978, pp. 199 and 185 respectively). It proceeded on the basis that . . . the work process could and should be measured by management, and then used as a basis for rewarding and controlling effort. . . . This is not far, in principle, from the recent epidemic of electronically-mediated public-service systems of performance indicators, individual performance review and merit pay.
>
> (Pollitt, 1990, p. 16)

Taylor was working for the Ford motor company, a pioneer in mass production methods. Hence other theorists have spoken of 'Fordism' (Sabel, 1982) to describe an approach to organisation in which Taylorist methods are used to try to reduce workers to commodities, performing limited tasks in tightly regulated conditions for the lowest possible rewards. At that time, H. Fayol, a French mining engineer, also proposed his own theory of 'general and industrial administration' (1949) and defined rules of scientific management to increase organisational efficiency (e.g. division of labour, delegation of authority and responsibility, clear chain of commands, etc.). It is worth noting then that three authors, with very different professional and cultural backgrounds and working on both public administration and on the management of private firms indeed share many ideas about the specialisation of functions and tasks, the formalisation of operating procedures, the hierarchical supervision of subordinates, etc. and claim that these principles are relevant for both the public and the private sector. Whilst public policy implementation is seen as less likely to embody circumstances in which mass production is feasible, Taylorism or Fordism can be seen to offer one model for the public bureaucracy (see Pollitt, 1990). It is one model, moreover, which may be seen as solving the dilemma of accountability – at least as far as routine tasks like social benefit administration are concerned – by ensuring a rigid adherence to hierarchically (and thus perhaps ultimately democratically) determined rules. This is an issue to which we will return below when we explore the relationship between rules and discretion later in the chapter.

But that is only one way to take the Weberian model, seeking to make it simply a compliant instrument. Other ways suggest that there are problems with this, and observe some of the tensions and contradictions between the characteristics of the 'ideal type'. In the 1920s and 1930s, management theory gradually began to move away from a concern with the development of formal prescriptions for organisational structure towards a better understanding of organisational life (see Box 12.3). This development, while still firmly preoccupied with the question of how to control subordinates within the industrial enterprise, nevertheless eventually contributed to a transformation of the way organisations are understood.

Box 12.3	The role of the Hawthorne research programme for an understanding of the importance of human relationships in organisational life

An important contribution to understanding the importance of human relationships in organisational life came from research carried out under Elton Mayo at the Hawthorne Works in Chicago during the late 1920s and early 1930s (Roethlisberger and Dickson, 1939). The researchers were influenced by research on morale carried out during the First World War, and by developments in social psychology and by Freudian psychology. The development of a more complex approach to social structure by sociologists and anthropologists also had an impact on their work.

The importance of the Hawthorne researchers lies in the way they shifted the emphasis in organisation theory from a mechanical concern to discover the 'one best way' to organise work tasks to a recognition of the importance of human relationships for organisational performance. The early research draws attention to the relevance of managerial interest in workers' activities for motivation and morale, while later work throws light upon relationships within the work group.

The Hawthorne researchers demonstrate the need to analyse organisations as living social structures. They indicate that to regard an organisation as merely a pattern of formal roles is likely to make it impossible to understand fully the determinants of behaviour, even formally prescribed behaviour, within that organisation.

The development of the sociology of organisations

As the social sciences began to grow in importance in the United States in the 1940s and 1950s, two developments in organisation theory – one stimulated by the work of Max Weber, the other influenced by the more obviously relevant findings of the Hawthorne research (see Box 12.3) – began to come together. Sociologists, using Weber's work (or their understanding of it) as their starting point, set out to show the importance of patterns of informal relationships alongside formal ones. Social psychologists, on the other hand, sought to explore the conflict between human needs and the apparent requirements of formal organisations. Drawing on this work, administrative theorists sought to update the old formal prescriptive models with more flexible propositions based upon this new understanding of organisational life (Argyris, 1964; Herzberg, 1966; McGregor, 1960).

Once Weber's work became available to sociologists in the United States in the 1940s and 1950s, it was applied to organisational studies as a kind of model against which real situations might be measured. By treating it in this way sociologists began to identify problems with the rational model of bureaucracy, often unjustly alleging that Weber had not been aware of them but nevertheless usefully advancing organisational theory.

In some of this work it is suggested that there is likely to be a conflict within a bureaucratic organisation between the principle of hierarchy and the need to maximise the use of expertise. Gouldner (1954) makes this point in the following way: 'Weber, then, thought of bureaucracy as a Janus-faced organisation, looking two ways at once. On the one side, it was administration based on expertise: while on the other, it was administration based on discipline' (Gouldner, 1954, p. 22). Bureaucratic organisation is founded upon the need to make the maximum use of the division of labour. Such division is based upon the need to subdivide a task either because of its size or because it is impossible for a single individual to master all its aspects. In fact, in most cases both of these reasons apply. The principle of hierarchy rests upon the notion of the delegation of responsibility to subordinates. If the superior could perform the whole of the task that is delegated, there would be no need to have subordinates. He or she will delegate part of the task either because of a lack of time to do it alone, or because he or she has neither the time nor the knowledge to perform certain parts of the task. Inasmuch as the latter is the case, it is obvious that in respect of at least part of the task the superior is less expert than the subordinate. But even in the former case this may also be true, since, particularly as far as tasks that require decision making are concerned, the subordinate will be in possession of detailed information which, in delegating responsibility, the superior has chosen not to receive. We are back here, of course, to the issues about the likelihood of discretion in action (explored in the cookery example in Box 10.6).

It is for these reasons that, as far as the detailed functioning of any organisation with complex tasks to perform is concerned, it must be recognised that expertise resides to a large extent in the lower ranks of a hierarchy. And it is for these reasons that it is inevitable that there tends to be conflict between authority based upon expertise and authority based upon hierarchy in bureaucratic organisations. Michel Crozier (1964), the father of the French sociology of organisations, analysed the conflict between expertise and hierarchy within various bureaucratic organisations. In particular, he investigated the development of parallel power relationships and informal rules-in-use, beyond the official organisation's chart and formalised rules. One of his seminal empirical studies focuses on the relationships between shop foremen, maintenance workers and production workers in the French tobacco monopoly (SEITA), at the end of the 1950s. Crozier observed that maintenance workers, who are located at a low level of the official organisation's chart, have in practice a disproportionate power. They seem to be even more powerful than shop foremen, who occupy a much higher hierarchical position. Crozier explains this paradoxical situation by the fact that maintenance workers benefit from an expertise (i.e. competences to repair the production machine when a technical problem arises) that is absolutely crucial for the whole SEITA enterprise. If maintenance workers do not (want to) fix the technical problem (rapidly), then production workers and shop foremen are blocked as well, and the SEITA cannot achieve its production goals. In other words, maintenance workers control a remaining 'zone of uncertainty' within the SEITA organisation.

Such a zone of uncertainty will always exist in bureaucratic organisations, despite the constant addition of impersonal and formal rules to prevent unpredictable events and/or the progressive centralisation of decision making to tightly control subordinates. Individuals or professional groups who control these remaining zones of uncertainty – thanks to their specific and non-substitutable expertise – will consequently wield a considerable amount of informal power. This can eventually translate into permanent parallel power structures, even in an organisation that perfectly corresponds to the Weberian ideal-type. In a nutshell, while Weber argues that formal rules and authority lead to a clear power structure and predictability of workers' behaviour, Crozier rather suggests that expertise – which is a consequence of the division of labour and the specialisation of functions – may lead to zones of uncertainty, unpredictable behaviour of workers with an expertise and, eventually, strategic power games within the organisation.

The apparent inconsistency in Weber's theory identified by Gouldner, Crozier and other sociologists of organisations has helped to provoke several valuable studies of conflict between experts and administrators within organisations. An allied topic that has also been explored is the conflict that exists for experts between professional orientation and organisational orientation in their attitudes to their work (Gouldner, 1957–58; Reissman, 1949).

A second important theme deriving from Weber's work concerns the relationship between rationality and rigidity. One of the earliest essays on this theme was Merton's (1957) discussion of bureaucratic structure and personality. This emphasis fits with the arguments about expertise within organisations. The implications of this point and the one in the previous paragraph for the behaviour of bureaucratic employees will be explored further in the next chapter.

All this sociological work led to an exploration of the relationship between organisational structure and organisational tasks. Thus, the question raised was whether the 'rational' structure may be well adapted to some tasks but ill adapted to others. Two British researchers, Burns and Stalker (1961), made an important contribution on this theme. They drew a distinction between 'mechanistic' and 'organic' management systems (see Box 12.4). Other sociologists began, however, to raise wider questions about the fit between organisational task and structure by examining a wide range of work situations. Some other British research played a seminal role in this

| Box 12.4 | Burns and Stalker's distinction between mechanistic and organic management systems |

Mechanistic systems, involving formal structures broadly comparable to the Weberian ideal-type of bureaucracy, are most suitable for stable, unchanging tasks. Organic ones are, by contrast, best:

> adapted to unstable conditions, when problems and requirements for action arise which cannot be broken down and distributed among specialist rules within a clearly defined hierarchy. Individuals have to perform their special tasks in the light of their knowledge of the tasks of the firm as a whole. Jobs lose much of their formal definition in terms of methods, duties, and powers, which have to be redefined continually by interaction with others participating in a task. Interaction runs laterally as much as vertically. Communication between people of different ranks tends to resemble lateral consultation rather than vertical command. Omniscience can no longer be imputed to the head of the concern.
>
> (Burns and Stalker, 1961, pp. 5–6)

development. First, Woodward (1965) developed a typology of industrial organisations based upon differences in technology. Then, later sociologists, notably a group working together at Aston University, began to argue that the varied and multi-dimensional nature of organisational arrangements is determined by a variety of 'contingencies' (see Greenwood et al., 1975, for an application of this work in public organisations). These include variables which are external to the organisation in its 'environment', variables determined by the power structure in which it operates, and variables which will depend upon 'ideology', or what Child (1972) describes as 'strategic choice'.

Organisations have thus to be recognised as being power systems in which structural features interact with, and are affected by, factors which make some participants within them more powerful than others. Hence Salaman argues:

> What occurs within organisations, the ways in which work is designed, control applied, rewards and deprivations distributed, decisions made, must be seen in terms of a constant conflict of interests, now apparent, now disguised, now overt, often implicit, which lies behind, and informs, the nature of work organisations within capitalist societies.
>
> (Salaman, 1979, p. 216; see also Clegg, 1990, and Clegg et al., 2006, for more on these contributions to organisational theory)

Beyond the single organisation perspective

These power relations within organisations are in various respects related to others outside the organisation. This issue was explored in the discussion of institutional theory in Chapter 5. Note there Selznick's concern to show how behaviour within organisations may be influenced by social life outside them, leading on to theoretical approaches that stress 'cultural rules'. A strong emphasis upon formal organisation structures sees behaviour as determined by rules belonging to the organisation. There are grounds for asking, as Gouldner (1954) does, who makes those rules, or in whose interests they operate; we return to that later in the chapter. The boundaries between organisations are social constructions that may vary and may be disputed. Knoke argues that 'boundaries maintained by organizational authorities or the participants themselves are more or less based on the type of organiza-tion' (1990, p. 86). Having noted 'total institutions' at one extreme, he goes on to say:

> Less rigid organizations, such as volunteer groups, maintain only informal boundaries; for example, the Red Cross counts as a member anyone who has ever donated blood [reference here is to the United States]. These porous boundaries are defined mainly by the members themselves, and the leaders have little power over them.
>
> (Ibid.)

The traditional emphasis on closure in respect of organisations implies a contractual obligation upon a paid employee, and in respect of state organisa-tions also other obligations embodied in codes of conduct (even perhaps the signing of a declaration to protect official secrets). The important question here then is about the extent to which more flexible forms of organisation in and around the public sector, involving networks and inter-organisational relationships, make it necessary to revise the formal model embodied in bureaucratic theory. This is one recurrent criticism addressed to the ideal-type of bureaucracy. The Weberian approach is basically static as it neglects the role of bureaucracies in policy-making processes and thus the direct interac-tions between bureaucrats and interest groups, political parties, the media, members of parliament, judges or other policy actors.

Issues about the policy process that can be seen as occurring within a single organisation and those that concern relationships between organisa-tions can in most respects be understood in common-sense terms. Distinctions between what goes on, for example, within a government department and between departments are often made, and need no explanation. However, at the margins it may be difficult to make this distinction. Boundaries may be permeable and changing. This issue has become more important in the modern world of governance, two of the characteristics of which are the abandonment of simple hierarchical arrangements and the creation of hybrid organisational forms in which tasks may be subcontracted and shared. Hence, individuals may work for more than one organisation and services may depend upon collaborative arrangements. Inasmuch as this is the case, the distinction drawn here may be a misleading one. Chapter 14 returns to this theme.

Rules and discretion

We need to return here to the topic of the relationship between rules, which specify the duties and obligations of officials, and discretion, which allows them freedom of choice of action. This topic, clearly very central to the accountability concerns of the top-down model of implementation, is, not surprisingly, also a preoccupation of a body of literature on public law. However, these legal preoccupations tend to involve an approach to these concepts which sees rules very much in a statutory context and discretionary actions as involving not so much individual choice of courses of action (which many will take for granted as inevitable) but as particular cases of legitimate departure from action prescribed by a legal rule structure.

Under the 'rule of law' principle, or what is called 'principe de la légalité' in French, it is seen as important for state legitimacy (and therefore implicit in the idea of the democratic state) that a civil servant needs a legal basis for his/her actions or decisions. Hence discretion will be embedded in a rule structure – at the very least in a form that will make it clear that only in a very specific set of circumstances can officials do what they like. Probably the laws which come nearest to this form are those that give certain officials very wide discretion to act in the interests of public safety. This embedded character of discretion leads to a rather confusing argument between those who use broad and those who use narrow definitions of the concept. Perhaps the most influential definition of discretion is Davis': 'A public officer has discretion wherever the effective limits on his power leave him free to make a choice among possible courses of action and inaction' (1969, p. 4). Others have used quite restrictive definitions, reserving the concept for only some of the phenomena embraced by Davis' definition. For example, Bull (1980) and Donnison (1977), in their separate discussions of social security discretion, draw a distinction between judgement, where the simple interpretation of rules is required, and discretion, where the rules give specific functionaries in particular situations the responsibility to make such decisions as they think fit. This seems to be drawing an unnecessary distinction. If all discretion is embedded to some extent in a rule structure (being what Dworkin has called 'the hole in the doughnut', 1977), then Bull and Donnison are merely drawing a distinction between more and less structured discretion, or between what Dworkin has called weak and strong forms (ibid., p. 31).

The approach in this book is to use the concept of discretion in the wide sense embodied in Davis' definition. This is partly influenced by a belief that social scientists should try to avoid imposing their own restrictive definitions of concepts used in everyday speech. But it is also justified by the fact that this discussion is concerned to see to what extent discretion is a useful concept with which to explore delegated decision-making processes.

The use of a wide definition like Davis' implies a concern with almost all decision-making situations since, as Jacques (1967) points out, almost all delegated tasks involve some degree of discretion. The study of discretion must involve, by implication, the study of rules, and may alternatively be defined as being concerned with the extent to which actions are determined by rules. This also means that students of discretion must be concerned with rule breaking since in real-life situations the interpretation of the extent to which rule following allows discretion merges imperceptibly into the witting or unwitting disregard of rules.

Davis' definition comes from a book in which he argues that any rule structure within which discretion is exercised should be drawn as tightly as possible. He argues: 'Our governmental and legal systems are saturated with excessive discretionary power which needs to be confined, structured and checked' (1969, p. 27). Later in the same book he argues that:

> we have to open our eyes to the reality that justice to individual parties is administered more outside courts than in them, and we have to penetrate the unpleasant areas of discretionary determinations by police and prosecutors and other administrators, where huge concentrations of injustice invite drastic reforms.
>
> (Ibid., p. 215)

Davis argues that citizens' rights to procedural justice can best be achieved through earlier and more elaborate administrative rule making and in better structuring and checking of discretionary power (ibid., p. 219). He thus has a prescriptive concern about the need for the public organisation to control the discretionary power of the individual public officer, and he feels this should be primarily attempted through rules that are open to public inspection.

In Britain, Jeffrey Jowell carried forward the kind of concern about discretion shown by Davis in the United States. Jowell's definition of discretion is similar to Davis'. He defines it as 'the room for decisional manoeuvre possessed by a decision maker' (Jowell, 1973, p. 179), and argues that the key need is to ensure that decision makers cannot make arbitrary decisions. However, Jowell lays a far greater stress than Davis upon difficulties with reducing administrative discretion. In particular, he shows how many of the considerations with which decisions must be concerned are inherently difficult to specify in rules. Legislators are concerned to prevent dangerous driving, for example, to ensure that food is pure, and that factories are safe. The provision of clear-cut rules to define what is safe or dangerous, pure or polluted, is often difficult. It may be that legislators need the help of the experts who are to enforce the law to provide some specific rules. In this sense discretion may be limited at a later date when experience of enforcement enables explicit rules to be devised. It may be that conflict over the legislation has led to a blurring of the issues, and that legislators have evaded their responsibility to make more explicit rules. But it may be the case that the translation of standards into explicit rules is so difficult as to be practically impossible.

Jowell provides a valuable discussion of the problems of fettering discretion where concern is with the enforcement of standards. He argues that standards may be rendered more precise by criteria, facts that are to be taken into account. However, he argues that 'the feature of standards that distinguishes them from rules is their flexibility and susceptibility to change over time' (Jowell, 1973, p. 204).

Jowell does not accept a simple dichotomy between rules and discretion as suggested by Davis, but rather argues that discretion 'is a matter of degree, and ranges along a continuum between high and low' (1973, p. 179). At first glance, rules may appear to abolish such discretion, 'but since rules are purposively devised . . . and because language is largely uncertain in its application to situations that cannot be foreseen, the applier of a rule will frequently be possessed of some degree of discretion to interpret its scope' (ibid., p. 201). This last comment suggests that any study of discretionary decision making requires a consideration of social processes internal to the organisation and a study of the attitudes and beliefs of those who have to interpret the rules.

Jowell's arguments suggest a need to relate any evaluation of discretion to the substantive issue involved. He suggests some reasons why discretion may be inevitable. Alongside complex difficulties about specifying standards are 'polycentric' issues where many factors interact (Baldwin, 1995, p. 29). This suggests a need to identify types of decision situations in which discretion is more likely.

These issues have been taken up in other legal writing on discretion – hence Dworkin's (1977) distinction between strong discretion, where the decision maker creates the standards, and weak discretion, where standards set by a prior authority have to be interpreted. Galligan (1986) is similarly concerned to analyse discretion in this way, pointing out that decision makers have to apply standards to the interpretation of facts. These distinctions may seem very academic, but they are important in administrative law for drawing distinctions between decisions that are within an official's powers and ones that are not, and therefore for determining whether intervention by an appeal body is appropriate.

Issues about conflicting facts arise where evidence is ambiguous, or where individuals present different versions of the same events. One of the surprising aspects of some of the less sophisticated attacks on discretionary administration by lawyers is that, while in practising their own profession they talk of facts and law and of proof and disproof, they very often require judges and juries to decide between conflicting evidence. The proper distinction to make here is not between the precision of judicial decision making and the imprecision of much administration, but between the extent to which procedural safeguards for the individual, or due process, exist in each situation. Here again Jowell's work is helpful since he distinguishes between two approaches to the control of discretion: 'legalisation', the 'process of subjecting official decisions to predetermined rules' and thus, of course, the elimination of discretion; and 'judicialisation', involving 'submitting official decisions to adjudicative procedures' (1973, p. 178). In that sense the issue is then about where ultimate decision-making power, or discretion, is to reside when there is conflict over official decisions. Many authors claim that constitutional and administrative courts are playing an increasing role in policy-making processes in general (see for example Horowitz, 1977; Rosenberg, 1991; Tate, 1995; Feeley and Rubin, 1998; McCann, 1998) and during policy implementation in particular (Shapiro, 1996, p. 121). This judicialisation phenomenon is obviously present in political regimes which have institutionalised 'checks and balances' between the executive, legislative and judiciary branches of power (e.g. in the USA). It is also at work in other countries with either a common law tradition (e.g. the UK, see Platt et al., 2010, for a study of its impact of this on English local government) or an administrative law system (e.g. Germany or France).

Rules and discretion in organisational sociology

All work, however closely controlled and supervised by administrative superiors, elected officials and/or judicial courts, involves some degree of discretion. Wherever work is delegated, the person who delegates it loses a certain amount of control. To approach the concept in this way is, of course, to examine it from the perspective of superordinate authority. Viewed the other way round, the equivalent phenomenon is rules which apparently guarantee benefits or services but nevertheless have to be interpreted by intermediaries. It is in the twin contexts of task complexity and the delegation of responsibility that the phenomenon of discretion becomes of salient importance. In complex organisational situations gaps readily emerge between intentions and outcomes. People running one-person businesses exercise discretion, of course, but the concern here is with it as a relational phenomenon. The problems about discretion are perceived, not surprisingly, as arising when one person's discretionary freedom may subvert the intentions of another.

Running through much organisation theory, and in particular through the work of those writers who are seeking to help those they see as in control of organisations to determine the right way to approach the delegation of tasks, is therefore a concern about the balance between rules and discretion, even when different words are used. Hence Simon, in his classic work *Administrative Behaviour* (1957), emphasises the importance of the various premises upon which decisions are based. Rule making and control within organisations is concerned with the specification of premises for subordinates. Simon argues:

> The behaviour of a rational person can be controlled, therefore, if the value and factual premises upon which he bases his decisions are specified

for him. This control can be complete or partial – all premises can be specified, or some can be left to his discretion. Influence, then, is exercised through control over the premises of decision.

(Simon, 1957, p. 223)

One reservation must be made about this statement (in addition to objecting to its gendered nature), namely that, as suggested above, the notion of total control in an organisational context is unrealistic. Otherwise this is a valuable statement of the place of discretion in a hierarchical relationship. Simon goes on to suggest that what occurs within an organisational system is that a series of areas of discretion are created in which individuals have freedom to interpret their tasks within general frameworks provided by their superiors. He quotes a military example relevant to the 'modern battlefield' (see Box 12.5), recognising the prevalence of discretion even in the most hierarchical and authoritarian of organisations.

Dunsire (1978a) has seized upon the interesting reference to the 'province' of the subordinate in this context. He portrays organisational activities as involving 'programmes within programmes'. In a hierarchy subordinate programmes are dependent upon superior ones, but they may involve very different kinds of activities. Dunsire elaborates an example of a railway closure

---

| **Box 12.5** | Simon's example of the rules/discretion relationship on a battlefield |

Simon writes:

> How does the authority of the commander extend to the soldiers in the ranks? How does he limit and guide their behaviour? He does this by specifying the general mission and objective of each unit on the next level below, and by determining such elements of time and place as will assure a proper coordination among units. The colonel assigns to each battalion in his regiment its task; the major, to each company in his battalion; the captain, to each platoon in his company. Beyond this, the officer does not ordinarily go. The internal arrangements of Army Field Services Regulations specify that 'an order should not trespass upon the province of a subordinate. It should contain everything beyond the independent authority of the subordinate, but nothing more'.

(Simon, 1957, p. 224)

This example shows how, in what is regarded as the most hierarchical of organisations, discretion is inevitable. The paradox here arises because in a war situation personnel at the lowest level may have to respond immediately to the unexpected. Hierarchical discipline is designed to try to make that response predictable, or at least compatible with strategy determined at higher levels. A similar point may be made about policing.

to show that while activities such as the rerouting of trains, the selling of railway property and, at the very end of the chain, the removal of ballast from abandoned tracks are necessarily dependent upon superior decisions about the closure of the line, the way they are carried out is not predetermined by the decisions taken at the top of the hierarchy. He argues that decisions at the higher level are of high generality, those at the bottom of high specificity. This does not mean, however, 'that a worker at a high specificity level necessarily has a smaller amount of discretion (in any of its senses) than a worker at a high generality level' (Dunsire, 1978a, p. 221). There are echoes here of Crozier's observations on 'zone of uncertainty' discussed above. This approach helps us to make sense of the use of the concept of discretion in relation to professional hierarchies such as education or medicine. The organisational or planning activities at the top of such hierarchies set contexts for, but do not necessarily predetermine, decision making at field level, where very different tasks are performed and very different problems have to be solved.

All the writers who have been concerned with the complexity of organisations have acknowledged that there are related problems of control, coordination and communication between these different 'provinces' and linking these programmes within programmes (see Dunsire, 1978b). Attention has been drawn to the interdependence involved, and therefore to the fact that in a hierarchical situation superiors may be dependent upon subordinates. This is taken further by Gouldner (1954), who shows that the top-down presentation of hierarchical relationships with superiors promulgating rules to restrict the discretion of subordinates may sometimes be turned on its head. He draws attention to the development of rules which limit the discretionary freedom of superiors in the interests of their subordinates. The classical discussion of this occurs in Gouldner's *Patterns of Industrial Bureaucracy* (1954), in which he shows the part that workers may play in securing rules to protect their interests. Overall his emphasis is upon the appeal to rules, by either party, in a situation in which a previously obtained relationship breaks down:

> Efforts are made to install new bureaucratic rules, or enforce old ones, when people in a given social position (i.e. management or workers) perceive those in a reciprocal position (i.e. workers or management) as failing to perform their role obligations.
>
> (Gouldner, 1954, p. 232)

Gouldner explores the many functions of rules in situations of social conflict. He draws our attention, therefore, to the extent to which rules and discretion must be studied in the context of relationships in which the parties on either side seek to influence the freedom of movement of the other.

There is much in common between Gouldner's work and that of Crozier discussed above. It is important to move away from the older emphasis in organisation theory which saw the rules/discretion relationship from the perspective of superiors concerned to limit discretion, as far as acceptable, in the interests of rational management. Instead, attention should be directed towards the extent to which both rules and discretion are manipulated and bargained over within hierarchies. Fox (1974), coming to the examination of this issue from a concern with industrial relations, interestingly relates rule imposition to low-trust relationships. He picks up the top-down concern with detailed prescription and shows how this creates or reinforces low-trust relations:

> The role occupant perceives superordinates as behaving as if they believe he cannot be trusted, of his own volition, to deliver a work performance which fully accords with the goals they wish to see pursued or the values they wish to see observed.
>
> (Fox, 1974, p. 26)

A vicious circle (or 'cercles vicieux bureaucratiques' in Crozier's language) may be expected to ensue. The subordinate who perceives that he or she is not trusted feels little commitment to the effective performance of work. This particularly affects the way the remaining discretionary parts of the work are carried out. The superior's response is to try to tighten control and further reduce the discretionary elements. The irreducible minimum of discretion that is left leaves the subordinate with some weapons against the superior: the prescribed task is performed in a rigid, ritualised, unimaginative and slow way.

This means that some rather similar phenomena may emerge by different routes. One may be defined as discretion, the other as rule breaking. The former emerges from recognition of the power and status of implementers (this word is used deliberately instead of subordinates). This is the high-trust situation described by Fox, and applies to much professional discretion within public administration. The latter is seized by low-level staff regarded as subordinates rather than implementers who, in practice, superiors fail to control. One is legitimised, the other is regarded – by the dominant elements in the hierarchy – as illegitimate. To the member of the public on the receiving end they may be indistinguishable.

Much of the organisation theory explored here indicates that discretion and rule breaking cannot be simply contrasted. Actors may be faced with situations in which rules conflict, in which rules are ambiguous, or in which so many rules are imposed that effective action becomes impossible. In these situations choices are made between rules, or about how they are to be respected. Hence occasions arise in which subordinates can paralyse the organisation by working to rule, by obsessively following rules which under normal operating conditions everyone would tacitly recognise as only to be applied in unusual situations.

One of the authors has discussed elsewhere (Hill, 1969) the way in which social security officials may operate when they suspect fraud. They are able to operate rules and procedures in a heavy-handed way to ensure that claims are fully investigated and claimants are made fully aware of the consequences of detection. If, however, they operate like this in more normal situations they will severely slow down the processing of claims and deter genuine applicants.

Alternatively, Blau (1955) shows how front-line bureaucrats disregard rules to enable them to relate more effectively to their peers and to the members of the public with whom they deal. In this sense rule bending or breaking operates as a substitute for discretion to generate a responsive organisation. However, there are issues here about the legitimacy of such adaptation, and the extent to which it may be used to favour some clients but not others. The discussion of Merton's (1957) portrayal in the next chapter of 'over-conforming' bureaucrats who create problems because they apply the letter and not the spirit of the law, and of Lipsky's (1980) work on 'street-level bureaucracy' (see Chapter 13), returns to this theme.

This excursion into the treatment of discretion in organisation theory suggests, therefore, that there are a number of reasons why discretion is likely to be an important phenomenon in bureaucracies. At times, confusion arises between notions of organisation flexibility in which discretion, particularly professional discretion, is accepted as an inherent feature and notions of conflict between formal requirements and informal behaviour (or more explicitly between rule making or enforcement and rule breaking). Hupe argues (2013, p. 435) that all researchers on this topic:

> share a focus on *discretion-as-used*. They also acknowledge, to a larger or smaller degree, the influence of the discretion granted in a specific policy statute, as a relative one. Hence the usage of the same term for both phenomena hides in fact a rather fundamental difference in meaning. On the one hand the term discretion refers to a determinant of output and thus regards an independent variable, on the other to empirical variation in behaviour which needs to be explained. Then discretion is a dependent variable.

This confusion may be a reflection of the fact that in reality these phenomena cannot be easily separated. Organisations are not simply fixed entities within which informal behaviour may develop. They are in a permanent state of change with both new rules and new forms of rule breaking occurring as conflicting interests interact. Streeck and Thelen (2005), whose perspective on the need to appreciate the complexity of institutional arrangements was discussed earlier (see Chapter 5), stress:

- 'the meaning of a rule is never self-evident and always subject to and in need of interpretation' (2005, p. 14);
- rule makers have cognitive limits;
- 'rule takers do not just implement the rules . . . but also try to revise them in the process of implementation, making use of their inherent openness and under-definition' (ibid., p. 15);
- 'there are limits to the extent to which socially authorized agencies . . . can prevent unintentional or subversive deviation from . . . rules' (ibid.).

The granting of discretion may be a conscious ingredient of the formal design at one extreme, or a reluctant concession to organisational realities at the other. Conversely, new limitations upon discretion may stem from attempts by superiors to assert their hierarchical rights, or from aspirations of subordinates to introduce greater certainty for their activities. In this last sense, therefore, there is no simple equation between rule making and hierarchical control or between the preservation of discretion and subordinate freedom.

This final point needs emphasising further. Baumgartner (1992) criticises the legal concern that discretionary behaviour is unpredictable and argues that 'social laws' make it predictable. Her essay analyses the impact of a variety of sociological features of official encounters upon their outcomes reminding us that 'rules' in a sociological sense may be as readily 'made' in the course of official behaviour as promulgated by policy makers and managers. These 'rules', moreover, may have characteristics which give them a power that is difficult to resist. Feldman, in an essay in the same volume as Baumgartner's, offers a clever analogy:

> The difference between the formal limits and the social context limits to discretion can be likened to the difference between a wall and a rushing stream of water. The wall is firm, clearly delineated, and it hurts when you run into it. The rushing stream . . . moves; its speed varies; it is more powerful in the middle than on the edges. It does not always hurt to go into the stream; indeed it may at times be pleasurable. The wall, however, can be assaulted and broken down while the stream rushes on creating a path for itself against the mightiest resistance.
>
> (Feldman, 1992, p. 183)

Summing up on rules and discretion

In examining rules and discretion, several issues need to be given attention. First, the complex interaction of the two concepts must be emphasised. Issues about rigid rule frameworks are implicitly issues about the absence of discretion. Concerns about excessive discretion are concerns about the limitations of the rule systems within which it is embedded. Hardly ever is there either absolute rule dominance or unstructured discretion.

Second, therefore, as stressed throughout this book, policy (in which rules and discretion are mixed together) must be seen in a wider social and political context, which is likely to affect the way discretion manifests itself and the attempts that are made to control it. Discretion may arise from ambiguity, sometimes deliberate, in public policy.

Third, while acknowledging political reasons why discretionary power may be conferred, the discussion has not disregarded the extent to which this phenomenon arises as a consequence of inherent limits to control. As Prottas (1979) argues:

> A general rule in the analysis of power is that an actor with low 'compliance observability' is relatively autonomous. If it is difficult or costly to determine how an actor behaves and the actor knows this, then he is under less compulsion to comply.
>
> (Ibid., p. 298)

Fourth, as this last observation reminds us, there is a need to analyse discretion as a facet of organisational life in a complex relationship to rule breaking. It is important to relate discretion to issues about organisational complexity, reward systems, motivation and morale.

Fifth, we should not disregard the extent to which the concern about discretion is a normative one. Under what circumstances may discretion be said to be a problem, and for whom? To what extent does the balance established between discretion and rules distribute differential advantages and disadvantages to the parties involved, and particularly to the members of the public affected by the policy?

Finally, in noting that discretion has been regarded as a problem, we should recognise that a variety of strategies of organisational control have developed to try to deal with it. The traditional approach has been to try to control it through tighter rules and procedures. More recently, identification of the ubiquitous nature of the phenomenon has led rather to attempts to structure through the use of performance indicators and the benchmarking of best practice (a topic explored further in Chapter 15).

Bureaucratic Organisations in Comparative Perspective

Taking its starting point from Max Weber's classic delineation of bureaucracy as an ideal-type this chapter has explored the way in which sociological studies of organisations took Weber as their starting point and at the same time argued that his approach leads to too strong an emphasis (even indeed an advocacy of) the importance of formal characteristics. Then, another discourse about aspects of formality has been identified, led in this case by lawyers emphasising the importance of rules in public policy. Critiques of both discourses direct our attention to forms of organisation which, though adopting some formal arrangements and using rules, diverge from the ideal-type of bureaucracy or other organisational models embodied in the founding theories.

In the comparative study of public administration, scholars have suggested that there are important variations in the organisational models used for government in which the general ideas emanating both from Weber and from the administrative lawyers take different institutional forms from country to country. Necessarily for the purpose of comparison they have developed typologies or 'family groups', and as is the case with scholarly innovations of this kind they offer a temptation to play the endless 'game' of adjusting and re-shaping typologies. Here we are faced with the dilemma of wanting to offer the flavour of this activity, inasmuch as it is relevant for our discussion, without being drawn into the 'game'. What we will do here is give a very brief account of some useful exercises in typologisation and then highlight some of the issues that are brought out by them. Whilst in some respect this typologisation sits rather independently of the approaches to the comparison of policy-making processes discussed in Chapter 6, it can be seen as a variant of the 'National Pattern Approach'. But if it is seen in that way questions may be raised about the extent to which its origins need to be explained as well.

Painter and Peters (2010, p. 19) identify nine 'families or groups of countries, each sharing some common administrative inheritance':

1. Anglo-American (e.g. USA, UK, Ireland, Canada, New Zealand)

2. Napoleonic (e.g. France, Spain and other Southern European countries)

3. Germanic (e.g. Germany, Austria, Switzerland, Netherlands)

4. Scandinavian (e.g. Denmark, Sweden, Norway, Finland)

5. Latin American

6. Postcolonial South Asian and African

7. East Asian

8. Soviet

9. Islamic

Not surprisingly such a long list poses questions about comparison that have been little addressed. It is differences between the first four families in their list that have been given most attention. Kuhlmann and Wollman's (2014) venture into administrative comparison confines its attention to Europe and identifies the same first four families in the list and then adds a fifth European variant 'Central Eastern and South Eastern' obviously influenced by the Soviet tradition.

Pollitt and Bouckeart (2000) approach the task of classification by way of the identification of 'structural, cultural and functional elements' (p. 40) going on to choose:

1. State structure – that is whether federal or unitary, and the extent of co-ordination.

2. Nature of executive government at the central level – majoritarian, consensual or somewhere between.

3. The nature of 'minister'/ 'mandarin' relations.

4. Administrative culture: a complex categorisation in which the notion of the 'Rechtsstaat' is used. This involves the perspective that the administrative machine is in the service of the 'state' rather than simply the 'government'.

5. Diversity of sources of political advice.

They then go on to compare nations along these dimensions, resisting further typologisation.

There are several points pertinent to the concerns of this chapter that emerge from a look at comparative administration. Most important here is identification that Weber's bureaucratic model was formulated in the context of the idea of the *Rechtsstaat*. Pollitt and Bouckaert say of this perspective:

> The state is a central integrating force within society, and its focal concerns are with the preparation, promulgation and enforcement of laws. It follows from this that most civil servants will be trained in the law. . . . In such a culture the instinctive bureaucratic stance will be one of rule following and precedent.
>
> (2000, p. 53)

The key contrast here is then with what Pollitt and Bouckaert call the 'public interest model' where the state is less dominant and government is 'regarded as something of a necessary evil' (p. 53). We see in this later categorisation what is often seen as the 'Anglo-Saxon' model 'based on liberal and utilitarian philosophies of the state . . . characterised by an instrumental concept of statehood' (Kuhlmann and Wollmann, 2014, p. 18).

We see thus in this contrast reasons why Weberian notions vary in their importance in administrative systems and why some countries may be more ready that others to adopt delegated, competitive or even privatised policy delivery systems. But why, if the main comparative distinction is this one, are these comparative authors at pains to identify a distinction between Napoleonic and Germanic systems and to recognise a distinctive Scandinavian system in Western Europe? For Kuhlmann and Wollmann an important difference between the Napoleonic and Germanic systems is 'the important role of the subnational-decentralised level and the principle of subsidiarity' (ibid., p. 17). While for Germany and Austria this is perhaps a particular feature of the imposed post-1945 settlement, for Switzerland it is a fundamental characteristic (Giauque, 2013).

The Scandinavian system can, according to Kuhlmann and Wollmann, be differentiated from the other *Rechtsstaat* systems in terms of 'the openness of the recruiting and career system and the explicit accessibility of the administrative system by the citizens' (2014, p. 18). This raises points both about the extent of to which the Weberian bureaucratic model is less dominant, but also about the extent to which issues about implementation involve negotiative perspectives and the acceptance of official discretion. It is notable that significant challenges to top-down perspectives on implementation have come from Scandinavians. We could perhaps add the Netherlands to this category, but we have promised not to play the game of critiquing typologies.

Indeed, rather than follow down the road of further discussion of the typologies, it is perhaps important here to say that – just as was exemplified by the shift in thinking within private enterprise between the Taylorist model and more flexible forms – so government has seen innovations which limit the extent to which it is appropriate to over-stress differences between administrative types.

CONCLUSIONS

This chapter started by examining the way in which Max Weber's theory of bureaucracy has been seen as defining a model for organisational control that has been widely adopted. We are again, as in so much of any discussion of the policy process, in a literature where issues about what does happen and issues about what should happen are often confused. The Weberian ideal-type is seen both as an analytical way of conveying the essential character of hierarchical administration and as an ideal model widely espoused by the architects of administrative systems. Organisational sociologists came along somewhat later to suggest that the reality of organisational life may be more complex. It was also the case that many of them indicated that they thought it should be rather different.

Nevertheless, the Weberian model was attractive to those who wanted to stress that public servants should administer impartially policies devised by politicians and treat equally citizens when delivering policy outputs. In taking that view they were supported by a legal view of the desirability of rule following and a hostility to administrative discretion. The discussion of this then indicates a fascinating parallel literature to both the implementation debate and evaluation of the bureaucratic model, seeing the issues about the relationship between rules and discretion to be very complex and some forms of discretion as inevitable. The chapter ends, however, by showing how a comparative perspective may be developed on these issues, recognising important institutional and cultural differences between countries.

13 The policy process at the street level

SYNOPSIS

Earlier chapters have paid relatively little attention to the roles of middle- and lower-level employees of public administrations. They have presented them as working within complex, partially controlled organisations, granted various degrees of discretion and required to collaborate with other actors of the policy subsystem, but there has been no examination of the implications of their own dispositions and motivational structures for these situations. This chapter explores this issue. In that sense this chapter may be seen as shifting attention from the examination of bureaucracy in Chapter 12 to the examination of bureaucrats here. First, it examines some rather old but still relevant theory, developed by sociologists influenced by the work of Max Weber, which stresses the way in which work in bureaucratic organisations may involve the selection (or the creation) of personalities who will be rigid rule followers and tend to give more attention to the means by which policy is enacted than to its ends. This will then be contrasted with the 'street-level bureaucracy' perspective of Michael Lipsky, with its particular implications for those working with relatively unroutinised service and professional roles, which stresses the many ways in which officials may actually strongly shape or even create policy. This leads on to an examination of the issues about the roles of professionals in public sector bureaucracies. The chapter finishes with a discussion of Mashaw's analysis of issues about professional autonomy, a topic which leads towards issues about accountability (which will be examined in Chapter 15).

Bureaucratic behaviour and the bureaucratic personality

It was suggested in Chapter 12 that the administrative organisation has typically a complex structure of a kind which many writers have described as bureaucratic. For a number of commentators, however, bureaucracy implies something more than a complex organisation. For them, bureaucracies are characterised as rigid and slow, with effective action hampered by red tape, which is defined as the 'rules, regulations, and procedures that remain in force and entail a compliance burden, but do not advance the legitimate purposes the rules were intended to serve' (Bozeman, 2000, p. 12). Although the main arguments on this topic are concerned with the inherent limitations of elaborate formal procedures, several writers have sought to show that bureaucratic rigidity is in some respects a consequence either of the impact of working in a rule-bound context upon the personalities of individuals, or of a tendency for bureaucracies to recruit people with inflexible personalities.

In the study of public bureaucracy, this organisation personality theory links up with a theme that has had a place in popular mythology for many centuries, a theme which several European novelists have developed most effectively: the portrayal of the clerk in public service as an individual whose life becomes dominated by the complex rules that have to be followed in dealings with the public. The novels of Charles Dickens, particularly *Little Dorrit* and *Bleak House*, portray individuals trying to find their way through complex bureaucratic and legalistic systems. Other novels that particularly echo Weber's analysis of bureaucracy are based on experience of bureaucracy in the decaying Austro-Hungarian Empire. This is particularly true of the two novels *The Castle* and *The Trial* written by Franz Kafka, a lawyer who worked in an insurance company, to the extent that he has stimulated comparisons between his viewpoint (of the individual lost in the system) with that of Weber (of the system) (Derlein, 1991; Warner, 2007; Jørgensen, 2012).

A pioneering essay on organisational sociology by Merton (1957) takes up this theme and attempts to explain the conditions under which bureaucratic personalities are likely to be found. Merton argues as follows:

1. An effective bureaucracy demands reliability of response and strict devotion to regulations.
2. Such devotion to the rules leads to their transformation into absolutes; they are no longer conceived as relative to a set of purposes.
3. This interferes with ready adaptation under special conditions not clearly envisaged by those who drew up the general rules.
4. Thus, the very elements which conduce towards efficiency in general produce inefficiency in specific instances. (Merton, 1957, p. 200)

Merton goes on to suggest that the position of those in authority is markedly simplified if subordinates are submissive individuals conditioned to follow their superiors uncritically. Moreover, the implication of much managerial training is that the successful operation of a system of authority will depend upon creating bureaucratic personalities.

In his essay, Merton argues that in Weber's analysis of bureaucracy 'the positive attainments and functions of bureaucratic organisation are emphasised and the internal stresses and strains of such structures are almost wholly neglected' (1957, p. 197). He contrasts this with the popular emphasis upon the imperfections of bureaucracy. Merton argues that bureaucrats are likely to show particular attachment to rules that protect the internal system of social relationships, enhance their status by enabling them to take on the status of the organisation and protect them from conflict with clients by emphasising impersonality. Because of their function in providing security, rules of this kind are particularly likely to be transformed into absolutes. Policy goals are then distorted as means are treated as ends.

Merton's essay is applied to bureaucratic organisations in general, but there are reasons why it may be particularly applicable to public administration. First, public officials are placed in a particularly difficult position vis-à-vis their clients. They may be putting into practice political decisions with which they disagree; they are facing a public who cannot normally go elsewhere if their demands are unsatisfied, as they often can with private enterprise; and the justice of their acts is open to public scrutiny, by politicians and sometimes by courts of law. They are thus under particular pressure to ensure that their acts are in conformity with rules. Rules are bound to play a major part in their working lives.

Second, the careers of public officials are normally organised very much along the lines of Weber's bureaucratic model. Indeed, in this respect at least, state bureaucracies often come very close to Weber's ideal type. The demand for fairness in selection and promotion leads to the development of highly regularised career structures. It tends to be very difficult to justify dramatic or unconventional promotions, and therefore public service careers are likely to be oriented towards what F. Morstein Marx (1957) called 'the economics of small chances'. Marx explains this expression in the following way:

> In the first place, the ideology of service itself minimises the unabashed display of consuming ambition. In some respects, indeed, service is its own reward. Moreover, the mass conditions to which personnel policy and procedure must be addressed in large-scale organisations cry out for recognition of the normal rather than the exceptional. Meteoric rise of the outstandingly able individual is therefore discouraged quite in the same way as favouritism and disregard of rules are discouraged. Advancement, if it is not to attract suspicious or unfriendly eyes, must generally stay in line with the 'normal'. Exceptions call for too much explaining. All this tends to make reward for accomplishment something that comes in small packages at fairly long intervals.
>
> (Marx, 1957, p. 97)

Such a career structure obviously puts an onus upon conformity, and will tend to create a situation in which if a public official becomes conspicuous for disregarding rules it will be more likely to hamper than enhance his or her career.

Marx characterises the public service as 'the settled life' in which security is valued above high rewards (ibid., p. 102). He says: 'the merit bureaucracy is not the place for those who want to make money, to rise fast, to venture far, or to stand on their own'. Marx concedes that senior public officials are usually required to be of a reasonably high calibre, but suggests that those who compete for entry will be mostly the 'solid – as contrasted with the brilliant but restive, for instance' (ibid.).

Marx goes on to suggest that the career structure he describes reinforces the pressure for uniformity within a government bureaucracy which arises from the political need for equity and consistency. Thus he claims: 'When the common rule and the common mind combine, the natural consequence is a narrowness of perspective – a weakness more aggravating than mediocrity in administrative performance' (ibid., p. 103). Marx's essay may be regarded as rather dated. It has been perhaps displaced by the theory discussed in Chapter 3 which focuses upon the potential for 'rent seeking' in public bureaucracies removed from pressure of competition. Yet Marx is theorising about roles rather than simply embarking on taken for granted assumptions about self-interest.

Marx suggests, then, that the bureaucratic personality will be both a product of the fact that only certain types of people choose to join the public service, or indeed the fact that selection procedures may pick out certain types of people, and a product of the bureaucratic environment. The concept of 'Public Service Motivation', which was presented in Chapter 3, also assumes that public employees are committed to particular 'public service values' and are thus predisposed to respond to motives grounded uniquely in public administrations (see Perry and Wise, 1990, p. 368). From a (human resources) management perspective, such values are a key asset for the organisation and, consequently, are highly valued during the initial selection of civil servants and their on-going socialisation on the workplace. In sum, the two influences upon personality operate to reinforce each other. Merton (1957) also recognises this interaction as a key problem for research. He asks:

> To what extent are particular personality types selected and modified by the various bureaucracies (private enterprise, public service, the quasi-legal political machine, religious orders)? Inasmuch as ascendancy and submission are held to be traits of personality, despite their variability in different stimulus situations, do bureaucracies select personalities of particularly submissive or ascendant tendencies? And since various studies have shown that these traits can be modified, does participation in bureaucratic office tend to increase ascendant tendencies? Do various systems of recruitment (e.g. patronage, open competition involving specialised knowledge or general mental capacity, practical experience) select different personality types?
>
> (Ibid., p. 205)

There are, therefore, a number of related issues to consider here: (1) to what extent certain types of people choose to embark on bureaucratic careers; (2) the impact of selection processes in selecting certain types from amongst those who seek to enter bureaucratic careers; (3) the extent to which personalities who do not fit the organisational environment are not motivated at work, do not perform well and, eventually, drop out in the course of their careers; and (4) the extent to which success or failure in climbing a career ladder is associated with personality characteristics. Reporting a more recent empirical study, Oberfield (2009) found support both for the view that rule-following would be explicable in terms of 'consistent' personality and for postulating 'that organizations would pattern rule-following identities' (ibid., p. 753).

However, the relationships between personality traits, job characteristics (including the level of rule formalisation, or red tape), motivation and work outcomes (e.g. organisational commitment, individual performance, work satisfaction, intention to quit, etc.) remain often very complex. According to the Public Service Motivation approach, most bureaucrats enter the public sector because they have aspirations for pursuing the common good, including perhaps a desire to help others and compassion for the end beneficiaries of public policies. They embark on a bureaucratic career with the aim of fulfilling their personal needs. So doing, they expect to encounter favourable organisational realities and to reach a high level of congruence between their individual values and skills, on one hand, and the goals and resources of the bureaucratic organisation they work for, on the other hand. If they feel a high level of 'person-organization fit' (Kristof, 1996), then they will be more satisfied, committed and willing to remain in place. On the contrary, if they experience a big gap between their individual preferences and their organisational environment, then they will probably have a lower job satisfaction and a higher intention to leave, or they will adopt a resigned attitude. Empirical studies have shown, in particular, that a high level of red tape or procedural constraints, within a bureaucracy, clearly increases the level of resignation among bureaucrats, who are highly motivated by public service values but who face too many formal rules to achieve their objectives (Giauque et al., 2012).

Merton and Marx are, of course, attempting to analyse systematically the widely accepted stereotype of the bureaucratic official. But because it deals with a stereotype the bureaucratic personality theory runs into difficulties. On the most superficial level, the public official's role is difficult to distinguish from the role played by a very high proportion of employed persons in a modern complex society – in which case there is nothing very special about the role of the public official. On the other hand, if an attempt is made to analyse roles more deeply it will be found that distinctions can be made both between the many different roles in a public bureaucracy, and also between alternative adjustments to formally similar roles. It is in this sense that Giauque et al. (2013) explore the social psychology of organisational behaviour, postulating the need also to recognise circumstances in which 'unbureaucratic personalities' willing to bend rules may be salient in public organisations. Another variation on this, particularly pertinent to some of the issues raised in the next section, concerns attitudinal variations attributable to differences in 'belief in a just world' (Lerner, 1980; see also Wilkins and Wenger, 2015).

The bureaucratic personality theory is both too specific, in trying to single out certain kinds of organisational roles in a context in which most people are organisational employees, and too general, in implying the existence of uniformity of roles in organisations where such uniformity does not exist.

An important contribution to organisation theory that modern management training has taken seriously recognises that there are problems about creating over-submissive subordinates, and that there are advantages to be gained from having bureaucrats who are unwilling to be excessively bound by formal rules (Argyris, 1964; McGregor, 1960). Moreover, subordinates will resist over-formalisation, and so it may be said that they will try to avoid becoming bureaucratic personalities.

There is a secondary criticism of the theory that there is a tendency to assume the existence of a bureaucratic personality when in practice such behaviour may be a means of protecting the individual from total involvement in the work situation. On this theme a more recent vein of writing is more relevant. It focuses on the pressures upon bureaucrats, and helps to explore, more effectively than the bureaucratic personality theory, how policies become reshaped as public officials seek to bring some order into their own lives. This is the work on street-level bureaucracy by Michael Lipsky (1980) and his associates. For these writers the issue is not the apparent total rule conformity suggested by Merton but rather the way in which officials make choices to enforce some rules, particularly those which protect themselves, while disregarding others.

Street-level bureaucracy

The theory of street-level bureaucracy is set out in Lipsky's book of that title, published in 1980 and re-issued in an amended version in 2010. It is further developed in work by two of his former research students, Weatherley (1979) and Prottas (1979). It has prompted a wide range of work on the behaviour of public officials (see Hupe et al., 2015, for a review of this work and some examples of modern applications of Lipsky's ideas).

Lipsky says of his own book: 'I argue that the decisions of street-level bureaucrats, the routines they establish, and the devices they invent to cope with uncertainties and work pressures, effectively become the public policies they carry out' (Lipsky, 1980, p. xii). He suggests that very often this process of street-level policy making does not involve, as might be hoped, the advancement of the ideals many bring to personal service work but rather the development of practices that enable officials to cope with the pressures they face. He says:

> people often enter public employment with at least some commitment to service. Yet the very nature of this work prevents them from coming close to the ideal conception of their jobs. Large classes or huge caseloads and inadequate resources combine with the uncertainties of method and the unpredictability of clients to defeat their aspirations as service workers.
>
> (Ibid.)

Lipsky argues that street-level bureaucrats develop methods of processing people in a relatively routine and stereotyped way. They adjust their work habits to reflect lower expectations of themselves and their clients. They:

> . . . often spend their work lives in a corrupted world of service. They believe themselves to be doing the best they can under adverse circumstances and they develop techniques to salvage service and decision-making values within the limits imposed upon them by the structure of work. They develop conceptions of their work and of their clients that narrow the gap between their personal and work limitations and the service ideal.
>
> (Ibid., p. xii)

Thus Lipsky handles one of the paradoxes of street-level work. Such workers see themselves as cogs in a system, as oppressed by the bureaucracy within which they work. Yet they often seem to the researcher, and perhaps to their clients, to have a great deal of discretionary freedom and autonomy. This is particularly true of the many publicly employed semi-professionals – people like teachers and social workers who secure a degree of that autonomy allowed to professional workers. These are the people whose roles Lipsky and his colleagues are particularly interested in.

Lipsky analyses the paradox suggested above in the following way. He outlines the many ways in which street-level bureaucrats (SLBs) are able to manipulate their clients. He stresses the non-voluntary status of clients, suggesting that they only have limited resources inasmuch as the street-level bureaucrat needs their compliance for effective action (ibid., p. 57). This is a view supported by two other American writers, Hasenfeld and Steinmetz (1981), who argue that it is appropriate to see bureaucrat–client relationships as exchanges, but that in social services agencies serving low-status clients the latter have little to offer except deference. They point out, as does Lipsky, that 'clients have a very high need for services while the availability of alternatives is exceedingly limited' (Hasenfeld and Steinmetz, 1981, pp. 84–5). Accordingly, 'the power advantage social services agencies have enables them to exercise considerable control over the lives of the recipients of their services' (ibid., p. 85). Clients have to wait for help, experience 'status degradation', have problems in securing access to information, and are taught ways to behave (ibid., pp. 89–92). They possess a generally weaker range of tactics with which to respond.

It needs to be noted that these applications of Lipsky's theory highlight situations in which 'clients' are weaker than the street-level bureaucrats. But the theory goes wider to encompass all kinds of official-citizen interactions. If, as Nielsen (2015, p. 119) argues 'we focus on public regulation and regulatory inspectors instead of, say, social services, we focus on a group of SLBs that often interact with a highly heterogeneous and quite powerful group of "clients". She goes on to argue:

> Contrary to many studies of SLBs, which focus on the interaction with the unemployed, social clients, criminals, the early retired and so on,

regulatory inspectors interact with a group of clients where – at least a good part of them – may be comparatively resourceful regarding knowledge and economic and political power.

(Ibid., p. 119)

The implication in such cases is that the manipulation highlighted above may not apply, on the contrary it may be the 'clients' who are the manipulators. Indeed 'client' may not be an appropriate word to use in this context.

Lipsky, picking up the issues about discretion (discussed in the previous chapter), also stresses that the street-level bureaucrat cannot readily be brought under the control of a superior. He argues:

> The essence of street-level bureaucracies is that they require people to make decisions about other people. Street-level bureaucrats have discretion because the nature of service provision calls for human judgement that cannot be programmed and for which machines cannot substitute.

(Ibid., p. 161)

In this sense Lipsky portrays the street-level bureaucrat as making policy, carrying out a political role that determines 'the allocation of particular goods and services in the society' (ibid., p. 84). Weatherley summarises this view as follows:

> A view of policy as determining frontline behaviour is insufficient for explaining what workers actually do and why, and how their activities affect clients. Of course, teachers do teach, caseworkers dispense public assistance, public defenders defend indigent clients, and doctors treat patients, and their work activities are certainly responsive to public policy. But their activities are also responsive to a number of other influences over which the policy-maker and administrator may only have limited or no control. The pyramid-shaped organisation chart depicting at the bottom the front-line worker as passively receiving and carrying out policies and procedures dispensed from above is a gross oversimplification. A more realistic model would place the front-line worker in the center of an irregularly shaped sphere with vectors of differing size directed inward.

(Weatherley, 1980, p. 9)

Lipsky is widely misrepresented simply as the writer who demonstrates how difficult it is to control the activities of street-level bureaucrats. If that was actually what he had to say, he could merely be seen as someone reinforcing the top-down control-oriented perspective. In those terms he is co-opted in support of the political Right's argument for market solutions to distribution problems, to circumvent the capacity of suppliers to control public monopoly services. In fact, however, what Lipsky says is rather different, indeed much more subtle. He speaks of the street-level bureaucrat's role as an 'alienated' one (Lipsky, 1980, p. 76), stressing such classic features of alienation as that work is only on 'segments of the product', that there is no control over outcomes or over 'raw materials' (clients' circumstances), and that there is no control over the pace of work. Lipsky also emphasises the 'problem of resources': street-level bureaucrats face uncertainty about just what personal resources are necessary for their jobs, they find that work situations and outcomes are unpredictable, and they face great pressures of inadequate time in relation to limitless needs. He stresses patterns of practice as 'survival mechanisms', a perspective that is echoed in Satyamurti's (1981) study of English urban social work teams. There she speaks of the use of 'strategies of survival' by social workers under pressure which nearly always led people with the 'best of intentions' to do 'less for clients than they might have' and often behave in 'ways that were positively damaging' (Satyamurti, 1981, p. 82). The conclusion this literature comes to is that difficult work environments lead to the abandonment of ideals and to the adoption of techniques that enable clients to be 'managed'.

It is appropriate to emphasise again here the inclusion within this discussion of activities that are regulatory rather than service of benefit providing. Alienation may be particularly influenced by powerlessness deriving from the power of those whose activities street-level bureaucrats aim to control and the complexity of the issues at stake. Loyens addresses this issue in a study of two kinds of law enforcement officers – police officers and labour inspectors facing difficult problems dealing with illegal employment and economic exploitation in Belgium. She identifies five coping styles to deal with alienation:

> [T]wo of these coping styles can be considered positive feedback mechanisms that reinforce feelings of fatalism: acquiescence and emotional habituation. However, the street-level bureaucrats in this study also tried to reduce feelings of policy alienation by applying the coping styles 'just do your job from a sense of duty', 'get your share' and 'bond with the victim', which are conceptualised as negative feedback mechanisms.
>
> (2015, p. 113)

Street-level bureaucracy, power and interests

Loyens' analysis of forms of coping as a response to alienation highlights the way in which street-level bureaucrats are seen as both powerless and powerful. Is there an element of inconsistency? In a way what is being provided is a new variant on the Marxist dictum, 'Man makes his own history, even though he does not do so under conditions of his own choosing'. This is certainly partly the case. Street-level bureaucrats make choices about the use of scarce resources under pressure; contemporary fiscal pressure upon human services makes it much easier for officials to emphasise control than to try to put into practice service ideals. Lipsky does not really try to link his analysis to a macro-sociological perspective which would enable him to claim that the illusory freedom of street-level bureaucrats only operates as an instrument of class oppression and manipulation, and not in any other direction. Maynard-Moody and Musheno (2004, p. 156) come closer to that perspective, arguing that street-level bureaucrats 'cannot reject the state-agent role and the demands and tensions it brings to their work. [They] cannot shed the responsibility that comes with the state-assigned power over others'.

Lipsky's analysis rather tends to show that the street-level bureaucrat's *freedom* to make *policy* is largely used to provide a more manageable task and environment. He talks of 'defenses against discretion', emphasising, as Smith (1981) and Zimmerman (1971) have, the extent to which street-level bureaucrats develop rigid practices which may be described by the observer as involving rule conformity even though the rules are imposed upon themselves. This emphasis tends to support interpretations of street-level bureaucracy theory which stress the power of bureaucrats in terms of their capacity to look after their own interests.

Lipsky argues that there is a problem about matching limited resources to apparently much greater needs that is recognised by all sensitive members of social services agencies. Accordingly, therefore, considerable efforts are made to prioritise need and to develop rational ways to allocate resources. The problem is that 'theoretically there is no limit to the demand for free public goods' (Lipsky, 1980, p. 81). Therefore it is important to accept that welfare agencies will always feel under pressure. Lipsky says that the resource problem for street-level bureaucrats is often irresolvable 'either because the number of people treated . . . is only a fraction of the number that could be treated, or because their theoretical obligations call for higher quality treatment than it is possible to provide to individual clients' (ibid., p. 37). Adjustments to caseloads further the quality of work but leave the worry about quantity, and vice versa. It is always possible to make out a case for new resources. Marginal changes in those resources will not necessarily result in visible changes in stress for individual workers.

This equally seems to provide support for the cynical cutting of caseloads. Certainly Lipsky suggests that this is how it is sometimes seen. An agency that has great difficulty in measuring success or providing data on quantity of 'output' is inevitably vulnerable to cutting. Lipsky cogently shows how this response heightens the feeling of stress for individual workers and thus intensifies recourse to the manipulation of clients. Retrenchment and redundancy are particularly threatening to the remaining vestiges of altruism in the human services. In this sense it may be suggested that incremental growth does little to relieve stress, but incremental decline intensifies it considerably. This tends to portray street-level bureaucrats as the realistic – or is it fatalistic – instruments of the 'status quo'.

But then a substantial section of Lipsky's analysis is concerned with the way in which street-level bureaucrats categorise their clients and respond in stereotyped ways to their needs. Lipsky speaks of these as 'psychological coping mechanisms' and elaborates the importance of simplified views of the client of his or her situation and of responsibility for his or her plight to facilitate this (Lipsky, 1980, chapter 10). Many studies of the police have shown how distinctions are made there between different kinds of citizens which enable officers to develop responses in uncertain situations. In addition, stereotyping offers short-cuts to decision making on how to approach people, how to determine whether to act on suspicion and so on (for reviews of the literature on policy discretion see Grimshaw and Jefferson, 1987; Holdaway, 1983; Reiner, 1992). Lipsky argues that such is the need for street-level bureaucrats to differentiate clients 'that it seems as useful to assume bias (however modest) and ask why it sometimes does not occur, than to assume equality of treatment and ask why it is regularly abridged' (Lipsky, 1980, p. 111).

An issue that is related to simplifying assumptions in categorising different kinds of clients is the adoption of stereotyped responses to clients in general. In Chapter 10 Schneider and Ingram's constructivist approach to policy formulation was noted, here we have a reflection of their observations impacting upon implementation. The need to stereotype in order to cope may enhance tendencies towards racist and other prejudiced behaviour. This 'management' of complex decision situations can, depending of course on your point of view, have both benign and malign effects. Box 13.1 highlights some examples.

Box 13.1	Policy evolution in the hands of street-level bureaucrats

A Californian study (Meyers et al., 1998) shows that policy reforms requiring 'welfare' recipients to increase their labour market participation were largely ignored by workers who were primarily concerned with carrying out normal eligibility interviews. We see here a point emphasised by Meyers et al. (1998) that the implementation of a new policy often needs to be seen as a demand which people may have difficulty in accommodating with their existing view about how their work should be done.

Another example of street-level bureaucrat modification of policies they find difficult to put into practice comes from two studies of the ineffectiveness of a new provision in the US AFDC ('welfare') law that expected beneficiaries to be penalised if their children did not attend school regularly. Ethridge and Percy (1993) show that the policy was premised upon a 'rational actor' theory in which quite complex linkages were expected. They set this out in terms of steps in a logical chain: parents want to maximise AFDC payments, parents are able to monitor the school attendance behaviour of their children and interpret messages about this, parents are able to control the behaviour of their children, and the threat of sanctions will lead parents to take action. They go on to show how difficult it was for staff to operationalise these in practice. Stoker and Wilson (1998) focus more precisely upon flaws in the verification process for this policy. They explore how staff encountered weaknesses with the two alternatives, one at least of which was essential for verification: the transfer of administrative information from other agencies or the production of evidence from clients that they had complied with the requirements of the legislation. Clearly, whilst from one point of view these phenomena may be seen as 'disobedience' at the street level, from another they can be regarded as the improvement of a flawed policy.

These questions about choices open to street-level bureaucrats are taken up in a different way in contemporary literature that re-visits the 'representative bureaucracy theme' (see Chapter 10, Box 10.4). Where the earlier literature had raised questions closely linked to democratic theory, postulating that inasmuch as civil services have power they should be socially representative, this literature explores the predispositions of street-level staff in terms of the extent to which the way they exercise their discretion carries advantages (or disadvantages) for their clientele. These studies explore the impact of the ethnicity, gender or social class of implementers upon their decisions. A study of equal educational opportunities argued:

> Political forces (. . .) were able to influence policy outputs to benefit minority students. This political influence is indirect. Black school board members influence the selection of black administrators who in turn influence the hiring of black teachers. Black teachers then mitigate the impact of bureaucratic decision rules and provide black students with better access to educational opportunities.
>
> (Meier et al., 1991, pp. 173–4; see also Pitts, 2005)

Similarly a study of loan allocations for rural housing shows the impact of variations in the number of staff from minority groups, between different offices, upon loans to people from that group (Selden, 1997). A study by Chaney and Saltzstein (1998) shows that female representation in police forces is positively correlated with active responses to domestic violence. Riccucci and Meyers, in a review of this subject (2004), make an important distinction between 'active' and 'passive' representation. Where the former implies explicit recognition of a representative role, passive representation is concerned with less explicit effects that follow from the social or demographic characteristics of bureaucracies. Hence the crucial question is, 'Are passive and active representation linked? That is to say, do ascribed characteristics of an individual . . . relate to or predict policy preferences, as well as actions to achieve certain policy *outcomes*?' (ibid., p. 585).

These issues about the alternative influences on street-level behaviour highlight the 'agency' aspect that is sometimes disregarded in interpretations of the theory that simply stress disobedience and/or self-interest. Choices may be made in which explicit commitments and values may be advanced. As Meyers and Vorsanger put it:

In some studies these workers are portrayed as occupying a powerless position downstream of political and bureaucratic decisions; in others they emerge as loyal public servants who pursue the public good even when it means bending agency regulations; in still others they are described as self-interested bureaucrats whose coping mechanisms frustrate the will of elected officials.

(2003, p. 245)

We see, therefore, in the work on 'representative bureaucracy' a recognition that street-level bureaucrats may be seen as using their discretion in favour of specific interests. This goes beyond the notions of officials seeking a 'quiet life'. It raises then questions about the extent there may be manipulation of the implementation system in response to interests. In the representative bureaucracy work the analysis looks back to an argument that democracy may be enhanced by attention to the origins of public officials. In some of these American studies the underlying implication is that the interests of people disadvantaged in the political system as a whole (notably ethnic minorities) can be furthered in this way. But of course this argument may be turned on its head inasmuch as personnel selection decisions could be manipulated in contrary directions.

This leads us on to wider questions about how street-level work is managed. Brodkin's study reported in Box 13.2 shows how forms of street-level behaviour that are very negative for the individual needs of clients may be driven by managerial pressures. Certainly, as Lipsky suggests, rationing processes are involved in the exercise of discretion by street-level bureaucrats. But, as suggested by Schneider and Ingram (see Chapter 10) it should not be presumed that the parameters of that rationing are determined by the street-level bureaucrats themselves.

Box 13.2	Brodkin's exploration of the impact of management on street-level bureaucracy in the US welfare system

Brodkin argues that her article 'challenges the premise that how policy work is done does not matter so long as performance benchmarks are met' (2011, p. 253), suggesting that this view disregards how street-level discretion interacts with performance incentives.

Her ethnographic study looks at the implementation in Chicago of what is often called 'welfare reform' in the United States, the Temporary Assistance to Needy Families, noting:

'successful' performance in caseload reduction achieved by informally increasing the cost to individuals of getting and keeping benefits does not represent the same outcome as caseload reduction achieved by advancing opportunities for individuals to make it in the labor market. Governance arrangements that measure performance in terms of caseload reduction and work participation rates cannot distinguish between these fundamentally different types of practices.

(ibid., p. 259)

She illustrates her argument with reference to a person she calls 'Mr Frank', typical of those workers rewarded as high performers. She shows how he achieves 'efficiency' by such devices as:

- Scheduling a group of clients to come all at the same time (so they waste their time not his).
- Removing from his caseload those who resisted that requirement.
- Requiring them to use a pay phone to contact him even when they were in the waiting room.
- Not bothering to match clients to specific job opportunities but simply acting on the assumption that this particular sorting would occur when placements clearly did not work.
- Sending troublesome clients to the worst placements.
- Continuing using agencies that he knew provided unsatisfactory services.

She concludes:

> . . . Mr Frank not only demonstrated – but articulated – a logic of street-level work under new managerial arrangements, a logic largely unbalanced by countervailing incentives regarding access, responsiveness, and appropriateness of caseworker judgments about services and needs. More broadly, it indicates how adaptive practices can be simultaneously functional for the agency and the state, but dysfunctional for welfare recipients seeking to make it in the labor market or simply trying to maintain access to income support provided by law.

(Ibid., p. 267)

The question to raise about Brodkin's account is whether it is really the case that 'management' does not recognise the realities of street-level adaption to performance requirement, or whether it does not care.

Public administration is changing with the development of new technology. Tasks are structured and regulated by the use of information and communication technologies. Since the actual functions of these technologies in terms of standardisation is contested, the actual consequences for discretion and autonomy will depend on the type of street-level bureaucracy – and the category of functionaries working in them. Essentially office technology shifts discretion around rather than eliminates it. This issue has been explored by Bovens and Zouridis (2002) who suggest that issues about discretion may be transformed, as

Public servants can no longer freely take to the streets, but are always connected with the organization via the computer. Client data must be filled in, with the help of fixed templates, in electronic forms. Knowledge management systems and digital decision trees have strongly reduced the scope of administrative discretion.

(p. 177)

Their analysis suggests that there may be a complex shift going on here, first to what they call the 'screen level' and subsequently to the 'system level'. Box 13.3 describes their illustration of this process using the example of student grants in the Netherlands. At 'screen level' there are issues about how data is interpreted and how special cases and complaints are handled. At 'system level' discretionary power is located in system design.

Box 13.3	From street-level discretion, through screen level to system level: administration of the system of student grants and loans in the Netherlands (Bovens and Zouridis, 2002)

In the Netherlands a system of scholarships was established early in the twentieth century to assist 'gifted young people lacking financial means'. That system was very personalised, with officials interviewing applicants and following their progress through higher education. Decisions could depend upon comparatively arbitrary views of deservingness.

In the 1960s the system was 'mechanised' and gradually computers were more and more used for processing applications. 'By the early 1980s, the leeway available to the allocating officer had largely been reduced to accepting or rejecting the decisions proposed by the computer.' Later in that decade, 'form processors replaced allocating officers'. Discretionary elements only remained when there were appeals or complaints.

In the later 1990s the system changed again, to involve a wholly automated process of form completion and decision making. This is described as the shift to 'system level'. Bovens and Zouridis note, however, that what is disputable at this stage of policy evolution is the algorithms used for this process, which brings onto the agenda issues about public access to these and the right to contest them.

This is clearly an important development. While (as was argued in the last chapter) it may be questioned whether discretion can be entirely eliminated, these developments may be making the analyses of Merton and Marx more relevant for our understanding of the work of bored officials sitting behind computer screens or in call centres. At the same time, rather more attention needs to be given to a group of bureaucrats whose work has been comparatively neglected: the junior management staff who supervise street-level work, since much of the responsibility for decisions about how detailed data collection should occur lies with them. It should also be noted that system design is often in the hands of private companies working under contract to public authorities (for example, in the UK in respect of local administration of housing benefit).

This identification of key decisions that are neither embedded in policy nor made right at street level is an example of the way in which policy is likely to be elaborated in various, often interactive ways, between the 'stages' of the process, and suggests that the links between street-level bureaucrats and those above them in any hierarchy must be given attention. In some respects, in particular, the roles of the direct line managers of those in the front line tend to have been neglected. The public management literature is trying to rectify this neglect, with however a distinctly prescriptive perspective on the capacity of managers to enforce hierarchically determined goals (see, for instance, Riccucci, 2005).

Other work on street-level bureaucracy, however, draws attention to the extent to which there may be a need to see managers as street-level bureaucrats too. Evans argues:

> In emphasising both the similarity of all front-line workers and their fundamental difference from their supervisors and managers, Lipsky ignores the ways in which, for professional staff particularly, this distinction is blurred and highly permeable. *Street-level bureaucracy* also brackets off the discretion of managers – the new organisational professionals *par excellence* – and characterises their use of discretion as simply motivated to implement the policy that they have been given as best they can.
>
> (2015, p. 288; see also Evans, 2010)

Murray's study of child protection in Scotland offers evidence in support of this observation. Street-level behaviour, that might be deemed to involve disregard of policy, is shown to derive from assumptions of social workers about appropriate action which are shared by their immediate managers who tacitly condone this action (Murray, 2006). But Murray also suggests that the perspectives of clients – even as in the case of her study 'involuntary clients' – also shape policy outputs (Murray, 2006, pp. 221–4). There are some important issues here about team working in which street-level behaviour is shaped by immediate managers or by peers (or of course by both in combination) (see Foldy and Buckley, 2009). We return to the latter point in a discussion of 'coproduction' in the next section.

Finally, that example from childcare social work reminds us that it is important not to lose sight of the fact that some policies are more readily routinised than others, and there are policies where there may be strong value systems or interests that resist routinisation. In his last chapter Lipsky connects his analysis of street-level bureaucracy with some of the discussion of professionalism in bureaucracy. Are professionals different, and can the enhancement of professionalism provide a corrective to the forms of bureaucratic behaviour outlined in Lipsky's analysis? The next section will suggest that the presence of professionals in bureaucracy can make some difference to the ways in which policy is implemented, but this does not imply that the answer to the normative question posed by Lipsky is a clear 'yes'. Professional power is a sub-category of bureaucratic power in this context, with some distinctive characteristics of its own which raise equally important questions.

Professionalism in the bureaucracy

Some discussions of flexibility within organisations seem to offer solutions to the problems about bureaucracy outlined by Merton, Marx and Lipsky. They suggest that organisational employees should be expected to have and use expertise, and be trusted by their managers to use discretion to tackle their work tasks in an adaptive way (van der Aa and Van Berkel, 2015). In short, they should be 'professionals'. The paradox about this solution is that it conflicts both with that other modern theme, rooted in public choice theory, which sees public employees as untrustworthy and professionals as the most likely of all to distort the organisation in their own interests, and with a wider body of literature (from the Left as well as the Right) which has warned against professional power. Before we look at some more specific aspects of this issue, we need to look at the standard analysis of professionalism.

Sociologists have made many attempts to define professions. An influential essay by Greenwood (1957) suggests that 'all professions seem to possess: (1) systematic theory, (2) authority, (3) community sanction, (4) ethical codes, and (5) a culture' (p. 45). However, this list of the attributes of a profession mixes occupational characteristics with societal treatment of that occupation. One can only analyse theory, codes and culture in their social context. An analysis of professions needs at the very least to separate the occupational characteristics that give some groups high prestige (and corresponding power if they possess scarce and needed skills) from the way in which the state and society treat them. In practice there is a very complex interaction between these two groups of factors. It is more fruitful, therefore, to see a profession as an occupation whose members have had some success in defining 'the conditions and methods of their work . . .' and in establishing 'a cognitive base and legitimation for their occupational autonomy' (DiMaggio and Powell, 1983, p. 152).

With these considerations in mind, consider the case of medicine. Of course it is true that doctors possess expertise, and that the public, in its quest for good health, values that expertise. But much medical knowledge is accessible to all. What is therefore also important about the position of the medical profession today is that the state has given that profession a monopoly over many forms of care, allowed it to control its own education and socialisation process, and in many countries created a health service or health insurance system in which its decision-making prerogatives are protected (Harrison et al., 1990; Moran and Wood, 1993; see also Chapter 6 for empirical examples of the key role played by the medical profession in the regulation of biomedicine).

There is a vein of writing on professions within organisations which sees professional power and autonomy as threatened by bureaucratic employment (see Wilensky, 1964). This is misleading, since professionals may secure dominant roles within organisations. Professionalism is often a source of power *within* organisations. The core of that argument is contained in the example of the doctors quoted above. They have often succeeded in persuading politicians and administrators that the public will receive the best service if their discretionary freedom is maximised, and if they are given powerful positions in the organisations that run the health services.

The arguments about expertise, linked with both the emotive nature of our concerns about health and the social status that the medical profession acquired before medical services were provided on any large scale by the state, have reinforced that professional claim to dominance. Other, later established, professions with a weaker base in either expertise or social status have tried to claim similar privileges – teachers and social workers, for example.

Ironically, the argument about the role professions may play in bureaucracy has been fuelled by the contrast popularly drawn between the concepts of bureaucracy and professionalism. As Friedson (1970) has argued:

> In contrast to the negative word 'bureaucracy' we have the word 'profession'. This word is almost always positive in its connotation, and is frequently used to represent a superior alternative to bureaucracy. Unlike 'bureaucracy' which is disclaimed by every organisation concerned with its public relations, 'profession' is claimed by virtually every occupation seeking to improve its public image. When the two terms are brought together, the discussion is almost always at the expense of bureaucracy and to the advantage of profession.
>
> (Friedson, 1970, pp. 129–30)

Hence, professionals stress their altruism, arguing that they are motivated by an ethic of service which would be undermined if their activities were rigidly controlled. In some respects this is a question-begging argument. If public servants are given a high degree of autonomy their actions need to be motivated by ideals of service. The maintenance of ethical standards is important if a group of people have extensive influence on the welfare of individuals. However, the ethical codes of the major professions are often more concerned with protecting members of the group from unfair competition from their colleagues, or from 'unlicensed outsiders', than with service to the public. Moreover, even the public concept of 'good health' is to a considerable extent defined for us by the medical profession: in particular, the measures necessary to sustain it, or restore it when it is absent, are largely set out in terms of the activities of the medical profession when in practice many other aspects of our lifestyles and forms of social organisation are also important (Illich, 1977; Kennedy, 1981).

We trust and respect doctors, and ask them to take responsibilities far beyond those justifiable in terms of expertise. They are allowed to take decisions on when life-support systems may be withdrawn, to ration kidney machines and abortions, to devise and test new biomedical technologies, to advise on where the limits of criminal responsibility may lie and so on. Such powers have emerged gradually as a complex relationship has developed between the state, society and the profession. That relationship has been legitimated partly as a result of the evolution of the medical profession's ethics and culture and partly because those with power in our society have been willing to devolve authority to it (see Johnson, 1972). The two phenomena, moreover, are closely interrelated – internal professional control has made feasible the delegation of responsibility, but equally the latter has made the former more necessary to protect professional autonomy.

Montpetit et al. (2005) have investigated such a phenomenon by comparing the policies implemented in six Western countries to regulated assisted reproductive technology (e.g. *in vitro* fertilisation, genetic selection of embryos, stem cell research and cloning). Germany has probably the most restrictive policy worldwide, which prohibits the resort by medical physicians and researchers to several reproductive techniques. By contrast, doctors in Belgium have a great autonomy and are almost free to apply any available technique. They can self-regulate their own laboratory and clinical practices. The comparative study applies the 'social construction' framework (Schneider and Ingram, 1997; see Chapter 10) to assess if restrictive versus permissive policies can be attributed to the social constructions of the policy target groups? Empirical evidence shows that trust in medical professionals varies across countries, even if medical physicians belong in all countries to powerful groups. Opinion surveys on citizen's perception of doctors and researchers reveal that these target groups are rather constructed as 'contenders' (high power, but negative image) in Germany, whereas they are constructed as 'advantaged groups' (high power and positive image) in Belgium. Consequently, and as expected theoretically by Schneider and Ingram (1997), the Belgian policy design delegates regulatory power to the physicians, who can perfectly protect their professional autonomy. Their German counterparts do not benefit from such a delegation of power, as the state directly forbids many researches and therapeutic applications (see also Chapter 6).

In discussions of professionalism an elitist or structuralist perspective may be seen (see Chapter 2) in which a professional group is part of a ruling consensus, able to secure, or alternatively granted, privileges that ensure its dominance in a specific policy area (see Harrison and McDonald, 2008, chapter 2, for a discussion of the applicability of this idea to medicine). Occupations like medicine are not simply accorded the status of profession by virtue of their own characteristics. Professional status cannot simply be won, as some of the aspirant occupations seem to assume, by becoming more expert and devising an ethical code. It depends upon the delegation of power, and on the legitimisation process in society. In the case of doctors that legitimisation process may well owe a great deal to our fears concerning ill health and to their special expertise; nevertheless, some theorists have argued that it must also be explained in class terms. Harrison and McDonald (2008) have analysed the way in which medical power was established during the nineteenth century through a developing relationship with other powerful groups in society. It is clearly relevant, therefore, to ask questions about the comparable autonomy enjoyed by other established professions whose expertise is much more accessible (lawyers, for example).

The argument in defence of professional autonomy, that professionals possess inaccessible expertise, is not sufficient on its own. We need to look at the situations in which that expertise is used. There are two key issues here.

The first of these is *indeterminacy*, the extent to which it is impossible to predetermine the situations in which expertise will be needed. The complexity of the situations that doctors have to face, and the solutions to medical problems, are not always of a kind that can be programmed automatically. If they were we would merely have to enter our symptoms into a computer and it could offer solutions. Of course, in very many situations this is possible. The difficulty is that judgements may be needed where the solution is not obvious or there are reasons to distrust the obvious. Paradoxically, of course, indeterminacy is most evident when expertise does not offer ready solutions as in many issues about mental health.

The second issue is *invisibility*, the extent to which detailed surveillance of work is impossible. Under an anaesthetic we have to trust the surgeon to react quickly to the unexpected. We cannot debate the implications of what has been found. It is equally inappropriate to have a manager looking over the surgeon's shoulder asking for an account of what is happening, or a medical committee waiting to be convened to debate the next step.

These two issues of indeterminacy and invisibility are not peculiar to the classic cases of professional decision making, as in medicine. They apply also to the police officer alone on the beat who comes upon the unexpected around a corner (though note the point about cameras discussed below). Whilst the police are not seen as 'expert' in the medical sense, there is a similar issue here about ensuring that they are as well trained as possible, to enable them to deal with the unexpected.

With respect to these issues the notion of 'trust' is crucial – it was explored (in Chapter 12) in relation to Fox's (1974) analysis of discretion in organisations. The argument against Fordism within organisations rests fundamentally upon the idea that desired creative responses to exceptional situations occur when individuals have been trusted to exercise discretion. Where it is hoped that public officials will play an active role in developing new approaches to their tasks and more sophisticated service to the public, there may be a strong case for granting them a high degree of autonomy. In individual services there is a need to make a choice between the case for a reliable service which can only be changed by initiative from the top and a less predictable service which may nevertheless be flexible in practice. The organisation that makes extensive use of professionals is one in which there is high expertise in the lower ranks, a complex task to perform, difficulties in developing effective patterns of supervision and a need for flexibility and openness to change. A strong group of arguments for autonomy come together. In this sense professionals are street-level bureaucrats who have been able to develop special claims to autonomy. But, as suggested above, they claim to differ from other public officials in that their relationships with their clients are governed by ethical codes and by altruistic values which others lack.

 ## Analysing autonomy: Mashaw's approach

These questions about autonomy are important for accountability (which will be examined in Chapter 15). These themes are linked together by Mashaw's work, in which he advances the notion of three 'models' of justice (1983, chapter 2):

- the *bureaucratic rationality model*, which demands that decisions should accurately reflect the original policy makers' objectives;
- the *professional treatment model*, which calls for the application of specialist skills in complex situations and where intuitive judgements are likely to be needed;
- the *moral judgement model*, where fairness and independence matter.

The features of these three models are set out in Table 13.1.

Both the 'professional treatment' model and the 'moral judgement' model are offered as justifications for high discretion; in so doing they raise issues about alternative modes of accountability to that posed by 'bureaucratic rationality', where a combination of political and legal accountability can be deemed broadly applicable. This approach is obviously rooted in the notion that different kinds of policy imply a need for different forms of governance (see the discussion about authority, transaction and persuasion as three kinds of governance, which were presented in Table 10.1 in Chapter 10). While Mashaw's first model involves the exercise of top-down authority, his second and third involve variations of the persuasion mode of governance. What will therefore be discussed here are the separate characteristics of his second and third models.

Table 13.1 Task diversity and models of discretionary justice

Model	Primary goal	Organisation	Example
Bureaucratic rationality	Programme implementation	Hierarchical	Income maintenance
Professional treatment	Client satisfaction	Interpersonal	Medicine
Moral judgement	Conflict resolution	Independent	Pollution control

Source: Adapted from Mashaw, 1983, p. 31.

The case for regarding professional treatment – particularly medical treatment – as a special kind of public policy process has been set out above in terms of the issues of expertise, indeterminacy, invisibility and trust. The case against this is that these issues are used to obscure professional power, and used to deliver a protected work environment, occupational control and high rewards. This is a long-running argument. To what extent is its configuration changing in favour of those who seek to exercise control over professionalism? Harrison (2015) argues that 'developments in "evidence-based medicine" and health quasi-markets have undermined the assumed indeterminacy of medicine upon which clinical autonomy is largely based' and goes on therefore to argue that 'the potential for bureaucratisation of clinical practice, though not unlimited, is somewhat greater than long-established theories about the esoteric and tacit nature of medical practice would suggest' (2015, p. 123).

It has been noted that it is possible to show that a high percentage of professional work situations do not involve indeterminacy and do not have to be invisible. The rare and unexpected diagnostic situations, the medical or surgical emergencies where it is not possible to stop to debate or to consult a protocol, form but a small percentage of many doctors' work. Television hospital dramas give us a distorted view of a profession that is much more routine much of the time. Protocols are increasingly being developed to govern medical decision making, offering rules for many situations and yardsticks against which actions can subsequently be judged. Computerised decision models are being developed for many conditions.

The consequence is that, as has already been stressed in the discussion of discretion (see Chapter 12), professional treatment involves discretion within some sort of framework of what may loosely be called 'guidance'. It is important to see guidance as a continuum, with rules at the strong end and advice at the weak end. Concepts like 'codes' and 'directives' can be found towards the strong end and ones like 'pathways' and 'protocols' towards the weak end. There are issues, then, about determinacy or indeterminacy in relation to any activity which guidance seeks to structure. Thus, in medicine there are distinctions to be drawn between the relatively strong guidelines in relation to the administering of anaesthetics or the performance of some orthopaedic operations on the one hand, and the much weaker ones in relation to much psychiatric medicine on the other.

An important aspect to consider when looking at the impact of guidance is where the guidance comes from. The top-down model of public policy sees such guidance as structured through a sequence of measures with a legislative enactment at its apex. But guidance may be simply ministerial advice about 'best practice'. Then within the professional treatment model the interesting thing about notions of best practice is that the source of guidance will often be from within the profession. Guidance may thus come from either the current professional consensus on practice or from research evidence. However, since the governance arrangements for public service professionals involve professional practitioners as staff within, or advisers to, government departments, a distinction cannot necessarily be easily drawn between guidance from government and guidance from the profession. In the British National Health Service various advisory bodies have been developed by the government incorporating representatives of the professions to deal with these issues.

On looking at how guidelines affect occupational practice, there is also a need to give attention to the sanctions that follow from disregarding them. We have to recognise that there is a variety of possibilities about how adherence to guidelines may be enforced:

- requirements for immediate reporting back to a superior;
- regular collection of monitoring data;
- intermittent inspections;
- attention to whether practice followed guidelines when something has gone wrong or complaints arise.

That is surely not an exhaustive list. Enforcement of guidelines may involve all of these phenomena, or just some of them, or of course none at all. To make sense of the impact of a guidance these issues need attention alongside issues about what the guidance is trying to regulate. It is also pertinent here to point out that the increasing use of surveillance cameras extends the capacity of superiors to check that guidelines are being followed in some contexts, at least retrospectively or when complaints are made.

There are also issues about who enforces guidance. The argument about *self-regulation* by professions concerns the extent to which enforcement of good practice can be delegated to the profession. However, alongside this there are issues (particularly evident in relation to the last of the items in the list above) about either the extent to which enforcement comes through a legal process and/or about the extent to which the public customers/consumers/beneficiaries of the service may have a role in the enforcement process.

Turning now to Mashaw's third model, while there may be doubts about his label for this model, the 'moral judgement model', it draws attention to many situations where the key official role involves regulation – a form of law enforcement where the state has prescribed or is seeking to control certain activities. Much that has been said about the professional treatment model also applies to this one. These activities may in general terms be described as 'professional' but they also have much in common with criminal law enforcement. Law enforcement is particularly difficult where there is an absence of unambiguous support for the enforcing agency. Studies of the police have drawn attention to particular difficulties where there is an absence of people who regard themselves as victims (drug and alcohol offences, prostitution and traffic offences where no one is injured) or where there are groups in the community that will try to protect the criminal. Public health inspectors, pollution control officials and factory inspectors, as law enforcement agents, have to operate in a similar way to the police. The difficulties that beset the police are even more likely to apply in relation to the wide range of civil law regulatory tasks that concern officials like this – where the 'offenders' see themselves as engaged in carrying out their legitimate business, not as polluters or producers of impure food, etc.

This model particularly highlights two other conditions which often apply to these regulatory situations. First, what is being enforced by the regulator is a standard – about unreasonably high levels of pollution, etc. – that is likely to be disputed. Second, there are likely to be conflicts of interest between those who are the source of the alleged problem and those who are affected by it. On top of all this, the second alleged 'interest' is often a latent one, because:

- either the 'victims' the regulators have a duty to protect do not know they have a problem (when, for example, pollution cannot be detected by the sense of smell, etc.);
- or they regard the problem as the lesser of two evils (when they perceive it as a choice between a polluted environment and employment – see Blowers, 1984; Crenson, 1971);
- or they are quite satisfied with a situation that others consider unsatisfactory (residents suffering from dementia in a poor-quality care home, for example).

In some cases the conflict is between a quite specific individual interest and a very general public interest. In all these situations enforcement is likely to be controversial and the enforcers may lack clear-cut forms of public support. In many systems professionals with regulatory responsibilities therefore work not with absolute rules but with principles about best practice established by expert officials and operationalised using discretionary powers (see Hill in Downing and Hanf, 1983). The relationship between rules and discretion in these situations may involve 'framework laws', with officials and regulatees negotiating to fill in the details so that gradually the law becomes more codified.

What is often involved in these cases, given that officials need to work very closely with the objects of their regulatory activities, is a process of bargaining between regulator and regulatee (Hawkins, 1984; Peacock, 1984). Such bargaining will not merely deal with costs and consequences, but will also be likely to take into account past behaviour (has the compliance record of the regulatee been satisfactory?) and the likely impact of any outcome on the behaviour of others. Hanf has described this process as one of 'coproduction' in which the determinants of regulatory behaviour need to be seen as 'embedded in the social worlds within and outside the regulatory agency' (Hanf in Hill, 1993, p. 109; Hanf in Moran and Prosser, 1994). Whilst the field of pollution control provides particularly good examples of this 'coproduction', it is also evident in other cases where complex activities are being regulated – the running of a private residential care home or nursing home, for example.

In both the professional treatment and the moral judgement cases there are reasons why systems are likely to have sought to find some sort of balance between rules and discretion in which both are significant. In this discussion key issues have been stressed which tip the balance in the discretion direction: indeterminacy, standards, trust and enforcement difficulties. It was noted at the beginning of this section that Mashaw's models particularly concern the link between different administrative tasks and forms of accountability. But in that case do they cover all the possibilities? Adler has argued that they do not do this. He points out that they 'have been challenged by a *managerialist model* associated with the rise of new public management, a *consumerist model* which focuses on the increased participation of consumers in decision-making, and a *market model* which emphasizes consumer choice' (2006, p. 622). These may be seen as accountability issues: simple arguments about levels of discretion make little sense in the absence of consideration of the structures in which it is used. We return to this in Chapter 15.

CONCLUSIONS

Since the purpose of this book is to explore how public policy is made rather than to advance propositions about alternative ways of making or controlling it, to go beyond noting the phenomenon of professional power to the exploration of the extent to which it should be seen as a 'problem' would be beyond its brief. However, later (in Chapter 15) issues about ways in which attempts are made to secure accountability in public policy are explored, and there it will be necessary to return to these particular issues about professional power.

In this chapter street-level officials (of all kinds) have been identified as key influences upon policy outputs. The main reasons why this is the case were, of course, explored earlier in the examination of rules and discretion (Chapter 12). But it has also been shown that these need to be analysed within their institutional contexts. This chapter has highlighted two rather different analyses of the phenomena, one which emphasises the passivity of officials and one which emphasises their active roles. There is no necessary contradiction here. Individuals are both constrained by the structures in which they work and shape their work roles in various ways in conformity with their needs and (public service) values. An examination of the roles of street-level bureaucrats can be seen as involving an exploration of the strengths and weaknesses of institutional theory. Action at the street level makes manifest institutional constraints whilst also demonstrating ways in which actors who seem to be in weak roles as organisational change agents can (and sometimes have to) nevertheless operate creatively.

14 The policy process in the age of governance

SYNOPSIS

Whilst throughout the book attention has been given to arguments that the policy process in the modern world needs to be seen as having a complexity to which the label 'governance' rather than 'government' should be attached, this has not been examined in any detail. This chapter starts by exploring that argument a little more and then proceeds to look at the two main manifestations of the alleged change: inter-organisational complexity within the nation state and changing relationships between states which impact upon domestic policy processes. The former phenomenon involves both complex vertical and horizontal relationships between public institutions, and the formation of networks composed by state and private actors (none of these by any means new phenomena, but probably now more important). The latter ranges across various issues: the impact of global institutions, the development of groupings of nations like the European Union and the sharing of common problems across institutional boundaries.

Much of the literature on governance goes on from the examination of these developments to the exploration of the changing relationship between state and society and the issues that this poses for representative democracy. A final section in the chapter identifies some of these points and indicates their importance for the discussion of accountability and democratic legitimacy in the next chapter.

Introduction

When a new term is brought into use to replace a long familiar one it is always desirable to be sceptical about whether it is really necessary. This is certainly the case in respect of the development of the use of the term 'governance' to encompass the policy-making process instead of government. It is not helpful that those who write about governance either supply multiple alternative usages (see for example Kooiman, 1999, who identifies 10 different meanings of the term) or suggest, when engaged in such a labelling exercise, 'it has too many meanings to be useful' (Rhodes, 1997).

Central to the analyses of those who argue for attention to be given to governance is evidence of complexity, making political problem solving through forms of representative government in a unitary nation state difficult if not impossible (see Box 14.1 below). It is hoped that it is not necessary to emphasise that complexity at this stage in a book in which there has been a stress on understanding the importance of power in society, the simplistic use of the stages model of the policy process has been challenged and a variety of ideas have been advanced to help to unpack agenda setting, policy formulation and implementation.

Box 14.1	Major traits of governance

Benz and Papadopoulos (2006, pp. 2–3) identify the following major traits of governance as a new mode of policy making:

1. *Plurality of actors*: participation of elected officials and state administration, but also inclusion of experts, interest groups, NGOs and private firms;
2. *Polycentric networks*: absence of a clear hierarchy between various decision centres;
3. *Functional boundaries*: structures of decisions are defined according to the frontiers of the problem to be solved, instead of the existing territorial or institutional boundaries;
4. *Negotiation as mode of coordination*: mutual adjustment and accommodation of interests is more frequent than unilateral decision.

The non-hierarchical, boundary-spanning and flexible character of governance does not imply that government is totally irrelevant, as governance relies on the interplay of both formal and informal institutions. However, the governance dynamics raises important questions for the democratic accountability of (state) actors involved in fragmented policy networks (see Chapter 15).

This chapter will not engage in any precise way with the rather diffuse debate about what governance actually means but rather focus on the characteristics of the policy process in the modern world which are seen as requiring governance, and making older ways of exploring government inapplicable. Dryzek and Dunleavy put the issue like this: 'Does governance involve dissolution of the state itself? Certainly it entails the further blurring of the boundaries between state, economy and civil society (though those boundaries have never been completely clear cut)' (Dryzek and Dunleavy,

2009, p. 149). A central issue here is thus about whether there is a need to recognise problems about those explanations of the policy process which work with simple, government oriented, hierarchical models of the policy process. Most discussions of governance indicate that the change away from this should not be exaggerated. Pierre and Peters, for example, argue:

> We believe that the role of the state is not decreasing . . . but rather that its role is transforming, from a role based in constitutional powers towards a role based in coordination and fusion of public and private resources . . . Furthermore, the ongoing globalisation challenges the traditional model of the state but is not necessarily a threat to the state as such.
>
> (Pierre and Peters, 2000, p. 25)

Hence three questions may be identified. The first is whether there are transformations occurring in the overall relationship between state and society. The second is about the extent to which the policy process within the modern state involves complex interactions between many organisations – state and non-state – making the policy process very much an inter-organisational process. The third is about processes occurring in the relationship between the nation state and other states or indeed the rest of the world (where the shorthand term 'globalisation' is often used), which add to and perhaps make more complex the internal government process. The discussion in this chapter will be primarily about the issues raised in the second and third points here. At the end, it will come back to the very general first point, one that was also addressed in Chapter 4 on corporatism and networks.

Inter-organisational processes within the nation state

One of the main contributions from Pressman and Wildavsky's influential analysis of implementation was shown to be the argument that the number of links in an implementation chain can be shown, logically, to have an impact on the effectiveness of a policy transmission process (see Chapter 11). The starting point for this argument is a version of the old children's game in which a message is whispered from one end of a line to the other. Inaccuracies arise in transmission and new constructions are fabricated to try to retain the sense of the message. But of course, in the implementation process (as was noted in Chapter 11) this is not just a matter of communication. The chain or transmission line image is very often too great a simplification of the inter-organisational arrangements. Some of the links in the chain may be more complex. Imagine a complication to the children's game in which at various points in the chain two or more children had to listen to the message and then decide what its content was before passing it on. But then again, recognise that we are talking about more than mere communication when we explore inter-organisational communication in the real world; hence making sense will be influenced by roles and interests. This implies (sticking with the children's game analogy) negotiation about what they would like the message to be! There are differences of roles and interests along the 'line' and negotiations between parties. At the same time there are institutional links which may contribute to minimising dissent (e.g. majority vote of Parliament in a centralised system; judicial review by the Supreme Court), or indeed in some circumstances to increasing it (e.g. disjointed decisions by various levels of power in a federalist system). In short, a pervasive feature of modern governance is that implementation, and indeed all aspects of the policy process, very often involves interaction within inter-organisational systems where there are multiple actors, multiple interests and multiple institutional venues.

Some efforts to solve inter-organisational collaboration problems involve integration, so that the coordination issues are contained within single organisations. Since this often involves the creation of organisations that are large and complex, it may be argued that internalising the issues makes little difference at the end: inter-organisational problems (e.g. coordination between two ministries) are merely turned into intra-organisational ones (e.g. coordination between two departments within the same ministry). Furthermore, since collaboration issues are ubiquitous, any specific integrated arrangements may leave some coordination problems unresolved.

Many writers have sought to offer advice to governments on the best ways to achieve service delivery integration. Alongside the questions about where the organisational boundaries should be drawn, there are many prescriptions for inter-organisational collaboration. O'Toole summed up the problems about making policy recommendations on these issues in an article published in 1986, but the situation has not changed since then. He noted that 'the field is complex, without much cumulation or convergence. Few well-developed recommendations have been put forward by researchers, and a number of proposals are contradictory. Almost no evidence or analysis of utilization in this field has been produced' (O'Toole, 1986, p. 181). O'Toole goes on to attribute the lack of progress to (a) 'normative disagreement' and (b) 'the state of the field's empirical theory'.

It is appropriate to talk about inter-organisational links that are both horizontal and vertical. This is the obvious way to talk about this subject, as shown in Figure 14.1. This figure assumes a national organisation passing policy recommendations through two regional ones to local ones. The chart shows hierarchical links. However, the development of policy may require horizontal links. For example, even if the organisations at each level are all-embracing, multi-purpose ones, there may be activities for which collaboration is essential. A simple example of this would be the management of a river which passes through both regions and all four local areas.

Water basin management in Belgium is an emblematic example to illustrate how vertical and horizontal coordination issues frequently interact in policy processes (Aubin and Varone, 2004). The two main Belgian rivers, the Meuse and the Scheldt, have their source in France, cross Flanders and

Figure 14.1   A simple organisation chart.

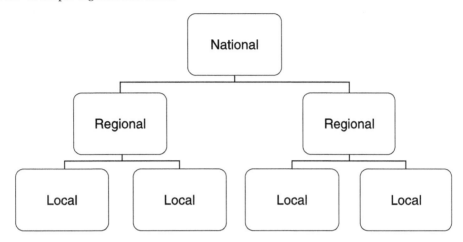

Wallonia, and then flow into the sea in the Netherlands. This hydrological context implies that downstream water users (i.e. drinking water for house-holds) depend functionally upon the activities of upstream water users (i.e. water withdrawals for irrigation and water pollution through manure disposal or industry emissions). To achieve a sustainable river management, all competing water users should thus take part in policy formulation and implementation. This requires both vertical coordination between munici-palities, regions and states; and horizontal coordination between all sector-specific policies that have an impact on water quantity and quality (e.g. agriculture, industry, tourism, hydropower, navigation). Two international commissions for the Meuse and the Scheldt have been put in place to foster such an integrated water management. These commissions aim eventually to become real 'water basin authorities' with extensive regulatory powers to collect taxes, forbid some water uses and sanction users' misconduct. However, this institutional solution remains fragile and the expected outcomes appear to be highly uncertain as soon as we seriously consider the recurrent political conflicts between Wallonia and Flanders.

In the real world of public policy the range of possible permutations on the simple design presented in Figure 14.1 and the case of integrated water basin management is considerable. There may be any one of the following, singly or in combination:

■ many more organisations from different branches of government (i.e. executive, legislative and judicial);

■ organisations with overlapping jurisdictions;

■ organisations that are involved in different policy domains (health/social care/education, etc.);

■ organisations with cross-cutting authority relationships (local organisa-tions required to cooperate at the local level but accountable to different national organisations).

In an earlier edition of this book these complexities were illustrated by a diagram of the English education and training system (from Ainley, 2001, p. 220). The trouble was that the picture provided was out of date before it was published, such has been the continuing evolution of efforts to shape institutional arrangements in that policy area. Furthermore it needs to be borne in mind that no diagram can do justice to the fact that the links in such a chart vary in strength and importance. Indeed it is probable that a chart of that kind published by an official body will be influenced by a view of what should or should not be emphasised.

A chart like Figure 14.1, derived as it is from a computer package designed to help people draw organisational charts, embodies assumptions about hierarchy. Power equalities are normally implied along the horizontal dimension but not along the vertical one. The vertical dimension is normally used to convey the notion of hierarchy. In the complex world of modern governance there is a danger of falling too easily into assumptions about the existence of hierarchy. There may be various respects in which the bodies at either regional or local level in that diagram claim autonomy from central control. These issues become prominent when there are disputes about devolution as in Spain and the United Kingdom. Box 14.2 highlights aspects of the way in which devolution in the UK is raising a succession of questions about control over the policy process. At the same time, even without disputes about local autonomy, where bodies at the same level may be notional 'equals' there may be power inequalities. Hence even in the simple example given above of control over a river, one local authority may be a large and rich one that is reluctant to modify its policies to satisfy the demands of smaller and poorer ones.

Box 14.2   The devolution debate within the United Kingdom

The Scottish independence referendum in 2014, in which the people of Scotland came very close to voting to leave the United Kingdom, may be seen as a stage in a process in which since 1998 Scotland has increasingly gained control over policy making, particularly in relation to social policy. The 2014 vote accelerated that process because, in its efforts to persuade the Scottish people to support the Union, the UK government promised further devolution. These promises took the constitutional debate into some of the most complex aspects of devolution, concerning financial arrangements and voting rights. The debate goes on, and it may be predicted that it will only be a matter of time before new pressures towards independence will emerge. These may also be affected by UK withdrawal from the EU.

There is more limited devolution to Wales, but this too has increased since 1998. Despite the small size of their country some of the people of

Wales (where nationalist politics has a long history) argue that where Scotland goes they can follow.

But it is also important not to forget the fact that there has been controversy about devolution in Northern Ireland ever since 1922, when the south of Ireland (Eire) secured independence from Britain. The 1922 settlement gave extensive powers to the Northern Ireland government. But in that part of the UK the constitutional settlement became unstable in the 1960s as the Irish 'nationalist' minority challenged 'unionist' political dominance (we could have used the words 'Catholic' and 'Protestant' there, but hesitate – in this secular age – to label this as simply a religious division). Direct rule by the UK government was imposed in 1974 and devolution was not restored until after the Good Friday agreement of 1998. That agreement provided for constitutional arrangements that gave a permanent share of power to the nationalist minority. It also set up consultative arrangements between Northern Ireland and Eire. The situation remains unstable.

A forthcoming book by Derek Birrell and Ann-Marie Gray *Delivering Social Welfare: Governance and Service Provision in the UK* tackles the difficult task of explaining the increasingly complex arrangements for delivering social policy across the separate constituent countries of the UK.

The vertical dimension

Clearly, analysis of the vertical dimension owes a great deal to the contribution of Pressman and Wildavsky, noted above, with their subtitle highlighting the 'distance' between Washington and Oakland and emphasising the links in the implementation chain (see Chapter 11). This is a theme that has been taken up in several important American contributions to the study of implementation, and by European scholars as well (see for instance Mayntz, 1980). In their joint book *Implementation Theory and Practice: Toward a Third Generation* (1990), Goggin, Bowman, Lester and O'Toole set out what they call a 'communications model' for the analysis of implementation which has a very strong emphasis upon what affects the acceptance or rejection of messages between layers of government. They set out a large number of hypotheses in which 'inducements and constraints' between federal and state level and between the latter and the local level figure prominently.

Stoker (1991) identifies as a crucial flaw in the American top-down literature, the extent to which it is concerned with failures to exert federal authority in a system of government that was designed to limit that authority (see also Ferman, 1990, on this theme). Stoker therefore contrasts two alternative approaches to the solution of implementation problems, and, taking his lead from Lindblom (1977), he labels these approaches 'authority' and 'exchange'. The authority approach involves suggesting ways to simplify or circumvent the barriers to compliance. The exchange approach requires the achievement of cooperation. There are problems with the exchange approach, however, since this takes us back into questions about how to distinguish policy formulation and implementation in situations in which both (or all) of the partners in the exchange relationship have the right or power to create policy. This leads him to formulate a third alternative in which there is a 'governance' role to 'manipulate the conditions of the implementation process to encourage co-operative responses to conflicts of interest' (Stoker, 1991, p. 50). This is an activity in which 'reluctant partners' are induced to collaborate. In this sense Stoker takes up an argument from Stone (1989) that it is important to give attention to 'power to' accomplish collective goals as opposed to 'power over' recalcitrant others. This leads him on to an exploration of the extent to which different 'implementation regimes' can arise, or be created. Here Stoker uses game theory, drawing particularly upon scholars who have developed this to explore relationships between nations (Axelrod, 1984; Axelrod and Keohane, 1985; Oye, 1985). What is important for Stoker is the extent to which games are repeated, and occur in contexts in which there is a 'history of interaction between participants' and 'the expectation of future interaction' (Stoker, 1991, p. 74).

Cline (2000) contrasts the theoretical contribution from Goggin and his associates with that from Stoker. Exaggerating their emphases a little, he characterises the former as seeing action as involving solving communication problems between agencies, while the latter is seen as about collaboration problems. In the first case the issue is about how to get the 'messages' right, in the second it is about the management of a bargaining process. It is clearly both.

The literature from the United States varies in the extent to which the federal nature of that state is emphasised. Later this chapter will return to issues like these which arise in respect of supra-national systems (exploring amongst other things the arguments about the extent to which the European Union may be seen to be an embryonic federal system). Lane and Ersson (2000), when trying to identify a classification of states in terms of whether they are federal or not, note that while power sharing between layers of government is seen to be a key identifying characteristic of a federation, it also occurs outside federations. Hence 'one cannot simply equate federalism with a decentralized state structure, because unitary states could also harbour considerable decentralization' (p. 87). Geographical decentralisation may be seen as a continuum running from strong federalism through weak federalism, to countries where local governments have clearly entrenched autonomy, to those where it is very much weaker. In applying this to the UK today (see Box 14.2) it is pertinent to suggest that devolution of power to Scotland, Wales and Northern Ireland involves a partial federalism (or, taking a predictive stance inasmuch as the first steps soon led to further ones, it may be more appropriate to speak of embryonic federalism?).

This institutional dimension has been discussed extensively in the typology of Western democracies developed by Lijphart (see the section on National Patterns in Chapter 6) and other scholars of comparative politics.

For example, Vatter (2009) proposes a more fine-grained measurement of the levels of power (i.e. the federal-unitary dimension in Lijphart's work). He combines two sub-dimensions, namely a federalism scale that represents the constitutional provisions for the 'right to decide', and a decentralisation scale that indicates the 'right to act' which non-central actors have de facto (see also Keman, 2000, p. 199 and p. 222). The international comparison of countries along the federal-unitary dimension shows that, among advanced OECD democracies, only New Zealand seems to be more unitary than the UK, but the devolutionary process noted above seems to be moving the UK away from being the epitomal example of the unitary state.

It is also relevant to raise questions about the extent to which, even in apparently unitary systems, local governments are to some degree autonomous originators of policy. Some efforts have been made to distinguish local government systems in different countries, exploring issues about levels of autonomy (see, for example, John, 2001; Page and Goldsmith, 1987).

But the issues here are very complex, and are becoming more so as new forms of governance are developed which blur hierarchical lines and bring new actors from 'civil society' into the policy process.

Many observers of British central/local government relations have observed reductions in local autonomy, charting the increasing distrust of local government by the centre across the period of Conservative rule between 1979 and 1997 (see, for example, Lansley et al., 1989). The election of a Labour government might have been expected to make a difference, yet in many respects controls over local government still tended to increase after that. Newman explores this theme, drawing attention to the conflicts in policy between strong central commitments and a belief in the case for decentralisation. But this is made more complicated by a desire to bring new participants and new forms of participation into the policy process. Hence she notes that 'many of the policy changes being introduced speak "over the heads" of local governments direct to neighbourhoods and communities' (Newman, 2001, p. 78). Box 14.3 provides an illustration of this point.

The example of the school system given in Box 14.3 highlights a further complication. When looking at potential autonomies in the policy process there are other organisational layers that need to be taken into account below local governments. There may be delegation of autonomies to schools. And 'below' that we are perforce into some of the questions about discretionary powers amongst street-level staff.

As an approach to this problem which does not altogether solve it, but which may help with its analysis, Peter Hupe and Michael Hill have drawn a distinction between 'layers' in the administrative system and 'levels' within policy-making activities. They refer to layers as 'separate co-governments exercising authority, with a certain territorial competence and a relative autonomy' (Hill and Hupe, 2003, p. 479). But then there are levels in the policy-making systems. These were discussed in Chapter 8 with reference to the work of Kiser and Ostrom as 'constitutional', 'collective choice' and 'operational' levels. The notion here is that policy processes involve nesting decisions which set quasi-institutional contexts for each other. The confusion that we want to avoid by highlighting the *layers/levels* distinction is that these should not be expected to be the same. Hence whilst in some situations it will be true that responsibility for policy structuration is delegated through a sequence of layers – nation state governments setting the main policy parameters, regional governments designing organisational arrangements and local governments dealing with policy delivery – it is fallacious to expect this neat equation to apply as a matter of course. Rather, the dynamic of relations between layers in many systems involves a succession of struggles for control over action running up and down Kiser and Ostrom's levels.

Box 14.3	Developments in the governance of education in England

Bache (2003) shows how since 1997 UK central government has enhanced its control over education, suggesting that the shift from government to governance in this case involves strengthening schools and bringing new actors (including private companies) into education policy in such a way that local authorities have been weakened. Of importance here are three things:

■ first, central government have modified the complex formulae governing the funding of education in ways which force increasing proportions of the money going to local government to be passed on in predetermined ways to schools;

■ second, new types of publicly funded schools have been developed with higher levels of autonomy;

■ third, there is scrutiny of the performance of local authorities as managers of the school system, which includes powers – which have been used – to take functions away from them.

Some of the most interesting research on the issues about relationships between layers in the policy process has been done by Peter May on environment policy, in which the nature of the 'mandates' between layers of government are explored. May carried out a range of work comparing local government responses in the United States (1993), but then he extended his work to Australia and New Zealand (1995). May and Burby (1996) compared inter-governmental policy mandates designed to prevent environmental hazards in Florida (USA) and New South Wales (Australia). The Florida mandate involved detailed prescriptions for local planning and regulation and imposed severe sanctions on governments that disregarded the law. The New South Wales mandate used what May and Burby describe as a cooperative approach, requiring local governments to engage in a planning process and offering inducements, including promises of future funding, to encourage them to do so.

May and Burby found that the approach adopted in Florida had several advantages, it:

> proved to be much more successful in securing the compliance of local governments with procedural requirements . . . [and] it seems to have an edge – at least in the short run – in building commitment of elected officials to state policy objectives.
>
> (May and Burby, 1996, p. 193)

But they go on to argue that:

> The scorecard . . . is not uniformly in favor of coercive intergovernmental mandates. The cooperative policy as implemented in New South Wales had the advantage of securing strong substantive compliance once different risk levels and other factors were taken into account. Stated differently, amongst the more committed and higher risk jurisdictions, the cooperative policy is at least as effective in motivating local actions in support of state policy goals. Moreover, among those complying with the prescribed processes, the quality of substantive compliance appears to be higher under cooperative policies.
>
> (May and Burby, 1996, pp. 193–4)

This sort of approach starts to tease out some of the complexities in the processes under which authorities relate to each other in a loose superordinate system. There are some intriguing unanswered questions with this research, about the extent to which there are in play here also unmeasured institutional or cultural differences between the countries. In another article produced at around the same time May reflected on the translatability of Australian and New Zealand systems of intergovernmental cooperation to the United States:

> These settings share many commonalities with the United States in terms of government roles, assignment of property rights, and other factors governing land use and environmental management. However, the American system is exceptional for its procedural and legal complexity with respect to intergovernmental regulatory programs. Breaking through these complexities and associated adversarial climate would seem to be additional challenges for success.
>
> (May, 1995, p. 113)

This exploration of the cooperation/coercion dimension is interesting since questions about the nature of central/local government relationships have been widely explored in these terms.

The policy networks and communities literature (see Chapter 4) is also relevant here, in analysing if not in explaining some of these relationships. Clearly, when disparate actors are linked together on some relatively continuous basis this may affect the likelihood of cooperation. As far as central local relationships are concerned, where there are organisations to represent local governments in their negotiations with central government they may contribute to policy coordination (Blom-Hansen, 1999; Rhodes, 1981). This point is clearly also pertinent to the issues about horizontal collaboration discussed in the next section.

Adding the horizontal dimension

Recognising the importance of collaboration between organisations, governments have been prone to argue the case for greater cooperation and tried to set up devices to facilitate joint planning and working. Theorists have sought to assist this task, in the process generating some very complex attempts to model the factors that affect inter-organisational collaboration. This discussion will identify some of the key themes in this literature.

It is important to recognise that collaborative relationships run along a continuum from very detached interactions to arrangements that come close to integration. As noted above, collaboration issues occur within organisations as well as between them. Choices about organisational arrangements for policy processes need to consider what 'boundaries' there are, and what effects they have. There are, then, issues about what collaboration may entail. Perri 6 (2004, Table 3, p. 109) distinguishes collaboration over policy formulation, programme coordination, integration of service relationships and integration of services to individual clients. These distinctions remind us of two key points: (1) the danger of letting stagist thinking get in the way of understanding the complexities of intra-organisational relationships, and (2) the extent to which this subject is complicated (as analysed in relation to vertical collaboration in the last section) by issues about autonomies.

Organisation theories which focus upon the internal concerns of organisations naturally suggest that these will inhibit collaboration with others. The focus is then upon situations in which 'exchanges' are likely to be in the interest of organisations (Levine and White, 1961; for a wider discussion see Hudson, 1987). It is possible to postulate a variety of situations in which exchanges will be seen to be of mutual benefit to separate organisations. For example, an interest group may deliver relevant information (e.g. statistics about the problem to be solved) to a public administration in exchange for a privileged access to the policy-making process (e.g. official seat in an expert committee developing the policy proposal). Conversely, situations can be identified in which suggested exchanges will be rejected as offering no mutual benefit or as benefiting one party and not the other.

Very many organisational activities intrinsically involve relationships with others, including other organisations. Often even key public organisations are weak and need to engage with others to perform tasks. For example, they organise consultations with target groups to assess the practical feasibility and political acceptability of a policy proposal, or they delegate implementation tasks to professional groups in order to reduce costs and resistance by target groups. While the UK has remarkably large local authorities, in countries such as the Netherlands and France there are many small authorities (particularly outside the main towns) that need to work with other local governments or with private organisations to secure quite basic services. Without exchanges many such organisations will fail. In this sense narrow internal concerns are likely to be self-defeating.

Theory on this topic tends to have been developed in relation to manufacturing firms, which need exchange relationships to provide inputs of raw materials, etc. and to secure the successful sale of outputs, or produced goods. One of the problems faced by capitalist enterprises is control over these input and output relationships. Notwithstanding liberal economic theory's hostility to monopoly or oligopoly, seeking this control is portrayed as 'rational' behaviour from an organisational point of view. When separate organisations trade with each other the process of finding the best bargain is not cost free. These costs have been described as 'transaction costs' (Coase, 1937; Williamson, 1975; 1985). Furthermore, when that trading needs to be on a regular basis there is likely to be a need for a 'contract' that sets out obligations on either side, lasts for a period of time and is ultimately renegotiable. Making, monitoring and revising contracts entails costs. Both sides are likely to seek long-run stability. One way of doing this is through amalgamation.

Williamson has gone on to analyse these issues in terms of a contrast between 'markets' and 'hierarchies' (1975). His supposition is that whilst in general market relationships are superior because of their flexibility and because of the role competition can play in keeping down costs, this may not apply if 'transaction costs' are high. When these are high the incorporation of suppliers, distributors, etc. into hierarchies may become a desirable strategy.

The literature on 'markets and hierarchies' has made a contribution to the institutional theory discussed in Chapter 5. It suggests answers to questions about the design of systems of interacting *public* policy organisations. The reasons for exploring it here are thus two developments that have been seen as examples of the shift from government to governance:

1. that there are significant attempts by governments to take note of the public choice criticism of bureaucracy and to try to transform some hierarchies into markets (see for instance the New Public Management reform that was launched three decades ago; Hood and Dixon 2015); contracts between public organisations or between public and private organisations are becoming an increasing feature of the public policy process;
2. that even without contracts the issues about transaction costs are relevant to the exchange relations between public organisations, and there are issues about the consequences of choices between forms of organisation which incorporate many functions under one department and forms which leave them in separate bodies (see Flynn, 1993; Walsh, 1995).

However, Thelen and Steinmo, amongst others, argue that seeing 'institutions as efficient solutions to collective action problems, reducing transaction costs . . . in order to enhance efficiency' begs 'the important questions about how political power figures into the creation and maintenance of these institutions . . .' (Thelen and Steinmo, 1992, p. 10).

A general problem with the use of the concept of 'exchange' is that it tends to direct attention to comparatively equal transactions. The history of capitalist growth contains many stories of company expansion in order to control transactions with other organisations. There is therefore a need to explore the inequalities and 'power dependencies' in organisational interactions (Kochan, 1975; Aldrich, 1976).

Analysis of exchanges between organisations needs to be sited within an overall analysis of social power. One writer who has done this, Benson (1975), has criticised writers who concentrate on the problems of securing the coordination of public services and neglect the broader influences that affect coordination. Benson maintains that inter-organisational analysis is at one level concerned with examining the dependency of organisations on each other for resources such as money and authority, but that at another level it must focus on the interests built into the structure of a particular policy sector. We have explored aspects of these in Chapters 4 and 8. Benson goes on to give these observations a structuralist formulation, writing of 'the rules of structure formation'. Summing up these aspects of Benson's work, Ranade and Hudson say that '[the] implications of his analysis are that organisational life is marked by a constant struggle for survival and domain control, and collaboration will only be entered into where there is some mutual benefit to be derived from doing so' (Ranade and Hudson, 2003, p. 39).

Benson's theory clearly takes us back to some of the ideas about structural determinism explored in Chapter 2, particularly those ideas that derive from Marxist theory. A somewhat similar position is reached, in a way which is less determinist and draws less upon the concept of 'interests', by the institutionalist theorists (discussed in Chapter 5). Thus March and Olsen argue:

> Institutional theories supplement exchange theories of political action in two primary ways: first, they emphasise the role of institutions in defining the terms of rational exchange . . . Second, without denying the reality of calculations and anticipations of consequences, institutional conceptions see such . . . as occurring within a broader framework of rules, roles and identities.
>
> (March and Olsen, 1996, p. 250)

Institutional theory is relevant for the exploration of the barriers to change that are erected when efforts are made to get separate organisations to work together in new ways. If traditional bureaucratic organisations have well-established, complex institutional arrangements that include standard operating procedures, organisational cultures and value systems, then there will be resistance to ways of working with others that threaten these. There have been many efforts since 1997 to get British government departments to work together better on cross-cutting issues and problems (Flynn, 1993; Kavanagh and Richards, 2001). It has become commonplace to emphasise the 'silo' approach to government which makes inter-departmental collaboration difficult. Indeed, the strength of organisational boundaries and 'departmentalism' are classical themes of public administration research. Gulick (1937) argued that resources, civil servants and policy tasks should be grouped on the basis of their homogeneity. Different principles can be applied to foster such organisational homogeneity. For instance, departments can be defined by the functional purpose of the organisation (e.g. controlling water pollution), the target groups to be dealt with (e.g. industries, farmers or households), the process used (e.g. chemical analysis) or the geographical perimeter where the policy is delivered (e.g. a river basin). Furthermore, homogeneous departments develop their own organisational culture and face specific resources allocation (e.g. yearly budget) and accountability structures (e.g. supervision by one minister). They have thus very few incentives to collaborate with other departments, if this collaboration is detrimental to the achievement of their own objectives. Even where departments make efforts to form partnerships with other departments, 'delivering on the core business will obviously take precedence' (Ranade and Hudson, 2003, p. 41; see also Exworthy and Powell, 2004; James and Nakamura 2015; see also Chapter 15). Questions then arise, from the efforts of the institutional theorists to explain change (discussed in Chapter 5), about how 'access points' or 'critical junctions' may occur, which are seized upon by those who want to create more 'joined-up government' or 'holistic government'. Inasmuch as these changes to the arrangements for 'governance' occur against a background of externally generated change or the evolution of international organisations, for example, these critical change opportunities may be occurring. Equally, success in generating change, may create a platform for further change.

DiMaggio and Powell (1983) explore – in a way which rejects 'functionalist or Marxist' explanations of organisational change (p. 156) – what they call 'isomorphic processes' which tend to make organisations similar to one another. They offer a series of hypotheses on this topic – including factors like internal organisational uncertainties and external resource dependencies to explain this convergence.

Another way into this issue without using structuralist theory is to recognise that individual members of organisations also have other affiliations. They belong to families, voluntary organisations, political parties, churches, etc. This may mean that they have commitments to other organisations which interact with the organisation that employs them. That may seem a rather trivial point, but there are circumstances in which it is definitely not. The most significant of these for public policy is where individuals are members of professional groups that extend across a number of organisations. The impact of this is then further enhanced by intra-organisational divisions, with different professional groups in separate sections or hierarchical systems. To describe this phenomenon Ouchi (1980) has added 'clans' as a third element to be looked at within organisational relationships alongside markets and bureaucracies. Degeling (1993), analysing hospitals as organisations, writes of them as often locales in which members of distinct authority structures are loosely linked in the provisions of services. The separateness of medicine, nursing, allied health and hotel services, recognised in the formal structure of most hospitals, attests to the past capacity of these occupational groups to stake out and preserve their control over particular aspects of treatment provision.

(Degeling, 1993, p. 33)

Laffin (1986) identifies how these professional communities may have an influence upon relations between organisations, and DiMaggio and Powell (1983) argue that professional communities are important in generating convergence in organisational structures. A related issue is the need to recognise that individual participants in organisations have careers which may spread across more than one organisation. Significant personnel changes occur in some of the organisations particularly affected by the establishment of a quasi-market system in Britain, which may involve fairly rapid moves between purchasers and providers or between local government and the health service. Where individuals come from and where they hope to go to must surely influence their willingness to engage with others.

Those who have explored ways to enhance inter-organisational cooperation have explicitly suggested a need for the fostering of roles which help individuals to look outwards from their own organisation (Hudson, 1987; Huxham and Macdonald, 1992). Such individuals have been described as 'reticulists' (Friend et al., 1974), 'boundary spanners' (Ranade, 1998; van Meerkerk and Edelenbos, 2014), 'institutional entrepreneurs' (Eisenstadt, 1980; Oliver, 1991) or the 'entrepreneurs frontières' in French (Bergeron, 2013). Questions then arise about the extent to which, given the dominant impact of intra-organisational concerns for individual careers, such roles may be created or encouraged. A variety of devices may be adopted to this end: the setting up of special joint units, the designation of collaboration as a key ingredient of a work task, joint training, the temporary secondment of staff and so on. The success of these ventures depends upon some of the considerations already discussed – the feasibility of meaningful exchanges, the overall power context, the extent to which there are shared values. But inasmuch as they must be seen in terms of individual motivation as well as organisational motivation there are key considerations to take into account about the extent to which they yield rewards – explicit or implicit, financial or psychic – for the persons involved or for the organisations from which they originate. A concern of a number of writers on this subject has been the conflict between hierarchical intra-organisational pressures and the search for inter-organisational linkages. Pollitt thus argues:

It would not be difficult to slide into the worst of both worlds – a combination of traditional 'vertical' organizations, still carrying the principal legal responsibilities and means of delivery, and an overlay of fashionable new units or teams, which cream off the most talented staff but lack either clear lines of accountability or the implementation capacity to get things done.

(Pollitt, 2003, p. 72; see also Powell et al., 2001)

This tricky issue is not only relevant at the micro-level of an individual organisation, but also for a coalition of organisations. Beyers and Braun (2013) have addressed the internal versus external pressures at the meso-level of interest groups' coalitions. Their contribution is explored further in Box 14.4.

Box 14.4	Beyers and Braun's analysis of internal and external pressures on coalitions

The challenge is to coordinate policy making between groups' coalitions which, at the same time, want to maintain their internal cohesion. Beyers and Braun have investigated the Dutch trade policy, and conducted interviews with representatives of groups and members of the Parliament or government agencies. They measured the 'strong ties' between groups belonging to the same advocacy coalition and 'weak ties' bridging more distant groups that are members of alternative coalitions. The empirical findings showed that if a group occupies a central node in a coalition (i.e. bonding position), then it can represent the coalition's homogeneous policy preferences and gain access to elected officials. By contrast, a group linking different coalitions (i.e. bridging position) is able to stimulate information exchanges between heterogeneous policy positions and, so doing, produce new ideas about problem solving that are primarily attractive to bureaucrats. This study confirms the hypothesis of the 'strength of weak ties' that was initially formulated by Granovetter (1973).

Networks revisited

It has already been acknowledged that in many cases both vertical and horizontal interactions between organisations are involved. In this context it is perhaps more appropriate to speak of networks, the 'net' notion here implying both directions. The contemporary importance of network theory was explored in Chapter 4. Rhodes describes governance as 'governing with and through networks, or, to employ shorthand, it refers to steering networks' (Rhodes, 2003, p. 67). There is an interesting bringing together of potentially conflicting ideas here. Earlier, we saw network theory used to characterise the whole policy process. But to talk of 'steering' networks suggests a coordinating role for someone or something that steers. Bevir (2013) uses the term of 'metagovernance' to grasp the state's capacity to steer a policy network and to insure its long-term legitimacy. In relation to policy implementation, clearly the notion is that there is an element of hierarchical steering *from the government*.

Hence we have alternatives here. One is to talk of networks as informally coordinated systems, in which case the general organisational theory issues discussed in the last section are sufficient for our analysis. Alternatively, there are questions to be considered about the relationship between any efforts to pull the network from 'above': about the management of networks.

These issues are explored in research by Exworthy et al. (2002) (see Box 14.5). They show how action depends upon horizontal linkages at national level (between government departments) and vertical linkages between those departments and local agencies and then also horizontal linkages at the local level. Adapting Kingdon's analysis of policy agenda setting (discussed in Chapter 9), they suggest that in examining policy implementation in multi-organisational contexts there is a need to recognise the relationship between 'big windows' at national level and 'little windows' at local level. Decisions rest upon the successful integration of three streams (another concept from Kingdon):

- a policy stream concerned with goals and objectives;
- a process stream dealing with 'causal, technical and political feasibility' (Exworthy et al., 2002, p. 266);
- a resource stream, using that concept to embrace, of course, finance but also other resources.

While we do not want here to go back into a repetition of the discussion of network theory in Chapter 4, it is important to recognise how this theory is pertinent whenever action is likely to involve multi-organisational collaboration. The question is: to what extent is this a universal characteristic of public policy. Fritz Scharpf takes an extreme view:

> It is unlikely, if not impossible, that public policy of any significance could result from the choice process of any single unified actor. Policy formulation and policy implementation are inevitably the result of interactions among a plurality of separate actors with separate interests, goals and strategies.
>
> (Scharpf, 1999, p. 347)

Box 14.5	Exworthy, Berney and Powell (2002) on network linkages in British health inequalities policy

Health inequalities policy is the kind of policy that can easily become merely symbolic if it is not firmly endorsed by key actors at all levels. It can easily be seen as an optional extra when there are mainstream policy delivery goals. The fact that action to eliminate health inequalities competes with other policy goals is significant here both in inhibiting horizontal collaboration and in blunting policy transmission between levels. It is argued that:

> many local practitioners have been disappointed that, although the government had emphasised health inequalities, they had not put in place the range of initiatives that (they thought) would be necessary to effect demonstrable change ... [t]hey claimed that joined-up government centrally (and partnerships locally) had not been translated into better policy-making processes. The rhetoric of tackling health inequalities had not yet matched the reality for these individuals. It is not just national expectations that have foundered locally but also local expectations that have foundered centrally.
>
> (Exworthy et al., 2002, p. 92)

More cautiously Koppenjan and Klijn speak of 'complex problems' as 'increasingly resolved in a setting of mutual dependencies' (2004, p. 5). The expression 'wicked problem' is used in this context with Koppenjan and Klijn arguing:

> Complex and highly undetermined types of interactions characterize wicked problems. This strategic uncertainty is not easy to reduce and can never be completely eliminated. In a complex society characterized by network formations and horizontalization, actors have discretion to make their own choices. Unexpected strategic turns are an intrinsic characteristic of interaction processes surrounding wicked problems.
>
> (Ibid., p. 7; see also Ferlie et al., 2011, for an alternative analysis of this issue)

So is complexity an inherent feature of modern societies? Or is this particularly the case in respect of '(super-)wicked problems' (Rittel and Webber, 1973; Levin et al., 2012) or 'messy problems' (Jochim and May, 2010), implying that there may be simpler problems where this is not the case? Many of the examples in Koppenjan and Klijn's book concern major environmental problems (flood control, pollution reduction, etc.) where a very elaborate policy process is likely to be necessary, and their reflection can be easily applied to other contemporary wicked problems such as climate change, terrorism, migration flux or the regulation of international finance.

But is the emphasis then on the inevitability of networks, or on the need for a network approach for the management of some (argued to be frequently evident) kinds of policies? There is an ambiguity in writing about 'wicked problems' as to whether this 'wickedness' is intrinsic in the nature of the problems or whether it derives from the fact that effective solutions require multi-actor collaboration, probably through networks. In other words there may be integrated hierarchical solutions possible, which have been ruled out for some reason. Which came first – wicked problem – or complex organisational arrangements that make those problems 'wicked'? But that is to dichotomise too simply; rather, as in Matland's analysis of the relationship between policy complexity and power conflict, a problem may be rendered wicked by difficulties in getting agreement. Then also it is quite possible that complex organisational arrangements contribute to that. In sum, policy scholars face the challenge of identifying which factors trigger the social construction of wicked problems and their access to the political agenda (as already discussed in Chapter 9).

In these cases the analysis of policy problem solving is largely about stages 'upstream' from implementation – such as widening the circle of those who are involved in problem solving (in other words a combination of policy formulation and decision making; or even agenda setting). Then these complex inter-organisational structures needed for problem solution imply another departure from the staged model of the policy process. One cannot speak simply of implementation if organisations (with different control structures) need to work together to solve problems like flood control. Very high levels of discretion are needed if inter-organisational negotiation is to work properly. This leads Koppenjan and Klijn on to a concern with the management of networks. While their work is largely prescriptive in this respect, what they have done is to highlight another issue about the complexity of modern governance.

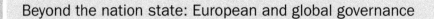

Beyond the nation state: European and global governance

There are observations (in Chapters 8 and 10) about how scholars have tended to handle issues about international relations in a literature that is often unrelated to the policy process literature. Even if this is justifiable the recognition that internal policy decision processes may be influenced by relationships with other nations now requires attention to links beyond the individual nation state. Propositions about such links range from developments from globalisation theory through a burgeoning European literature on the impact of the European Union to observations about issues that emerge from problems shared by nations (particularly adjacent nations). On top of this there are issues about the extent to which non-governmental participants in the policy process and beyond nation states may themselves be international in nature. This discussion will explore these issues in that order.

Constraints upon national policy choices arising from global international organisations are most evident in respect of the regulation of economies and the terms of trade between nations. In respect of the former two organisations stand out – the International Monetary Fund and the World Bank – both established after the Second World War to try to diminish the problems arising when nations regulate their economies in efforts to secure competitive advantages over others. Crucial here too has been the extent to which trading relationships require currency stability, and arguably the existence of an international reserve currency. Alongside these has been the World Trade Organization embodying the commitment to maximising free trade. In practice the issues about constraints on nation states are likely to be most evident for countries that are relatively weak because of their small size or poor economic base. In that sense the power of the United States needs to be recognised, and to some extent the international organisations identified above have been seen as indirect instruments of American domination. What is also important is the way in which the international organisations come into play when a nation's economy is in difficulties. This has been particularly salient for many of the world's poorest countries inasmuch as help with economic difficulties comes with prescriptions about how to deal with them, which explicitly or implicitly limit policy options. A similar situation also occurred in Europe after the 2008 economic crisis in the Eurozone. Several member states of the Eurozone (mainly Greece, Portugal, Ireland, Spain and Cyprus) needed the urgent assistance of the so-called 'Troika' (i.e. European Commission, European Central Bank and International Monetary Fund) to refinance their public debt. These countries had to implement a series of austerity measures (wages cut in public sector, privatisation, policy retrenchments, etc.) and a fundamental restructuration of debt to get bail-out loans from the Troika. These structural adjustments generated massive social protests.

However, given that the policy prescriptions are contestable it is important to recognise that there is competition between international organisations. However one does the arithmetic – counting states or counting people – a countervailing force exists within globalisation from the fact that the weak nations outnumber the strong. Deacon (1997; 2007) has done an extensive amount of work on this theme. He argues:

> The ideas about desirable national social policy carried and argued for by the international organisations . . . reveals something approaching a 'war of position' between those agencies arguing for a more selective, residual role for the state together with a larger role for private actors in health, social protection and education provision and those who take the opposite view.
>
> (Deacon, 2007, p. 171)

That proposition is about social policy – where views about economic development have particularly involved constraints of government action – but Deacon's position applies across the board.

A comparatively recent arrival on the global agenda is global warming. Mitigation of its impact (particularly reducing the burning of fossil fuels) depends upon international action. Even adaptation to its impact should be seen as having knock-on effects for other nations (for example, if the Dutch strengthen their sea walls this will affect adjacent nations). So we have here an issue where international collective action is essential. Since the end of the 1980s there have been increasing efforts to reach international agreements on policies to deal with climate change (see Box 14.6). Not much has been achieved yet on this issue; conflict between the rich historic high polluters (particularly the United States) and the emerging new economic powers (particularly China) threatens progress. But the point is that when any nation state now looks at its environmental policy this issue is on the agenda and other nations are concerned about what it does or does not do.

In respect of global warming, policy making is evident at two or more levels. The international process does no more than establish an overall objective and norms and targets for nation states. There then needs to be a process in which those are translated into national policies taking into account situations and resources. A satisfactory process requires interaction between these levels, inasmuch as the overall goals need to be realistic. Then within nation states the collaboration of multiple actors from different policy sectors – energy producers, transportation firms, industrial manufacturers but also individual households and consumers – needs to be secured.

Box 14.6	International efforts to deal with the issue of global warming

Early achievements to bring nations together to deal with the issue of global warming did no more than put it on the agenda. This was important for the development of a worldwide scientific activity. Extensive international collaborative action pulled together the facts about the situation and facilitated the development of estimates about effects. The crucial step forward was the Kyoto Protocol of 1997, imposing specific emission targets for each industrial country over a future five-year commitment period. A later Copenhagen Accord of 2009 tried to build on this; it had some success but there was also some weakening of the overall aspiration. Finally, the 2015 United Nations Climate Change Conference (so-called COP 21) negotiated in December 2015 a new global agreement that sets a goal of limiting global warming to less than 2 degrees Celsius compared to pre-industrial levels. This Paris agreement will become legally binding (in 2017) if joined by at least 55 countries which together represent at least 55 percent of global greenhouse emissions.

Other international agreements between nations do in some respects make the securing of agreements easier. A key example here is the European Union where shared concerns, and a complex economic settlement, has facilitated joint action in the prescription of targets and policies to apply across the member states. Beyond Europe the presence of international trading agreements has also played a role in bringing nations together around shared goals.

One other issue worth a brief mention before leaving the global agenda is that there is a large scale international activity collecting information on policy performance by nation states. Some of the United Nations agencies are important in this respect, particularly the World Health Organization. For the richer nations the Organization for Economic Co-operation and Development is a key body; it has invested a great deal of effort into the production of comparative data. Alongside macro-statistics about the functioning of the economy and the role of the state, and a sequence of reports on the performance of individual members, are survey activities. An interesting example here is the Program for International Student Assessment (PISA) exercise which compares educational achievements, and then gets used in national debates about the needs for more attention to, for example, numeracy and literacy levels. We have here an example of a 'discourse' with, notwithstanding the contestable nature of some of the statistics used, an influence on national policies (Desrosières, 2002).

Coming now down from the global level, bodies that coordinate the activities of groups of nations are important for national policy process. Within Europe it is of course the European Union that is the most significant body. This is a union of countries described on its own web site as 'progressively building a single Europe-wide market in which people, goods, services, and capital move among Member States as freely as within one country'. Self-evidently that implies collective policy-making processes but of course also 'EU decisions pervade the policy-making activities of individual European countries, both the member states and their neighbours' (Wallace et al., 2010, p. 4). The presence of long-term treaty obligations reinforced over time in a context in which withdrawal would be a very complicated process creates institutional constraints that are very important for national policy-making processes. It is clearly important that in this context institutionalisation involves an elaborate set of organisational arrangements with EU-wide bodies set up with their own staff.

It is important to bear in mind that while the 'free movement' goal set out above, in respect of the EU, embraces the notion of a single market it also implies a range of less expected ways in which national policies may be seen to need to be coordinated. Some of the more contested EU decisions have concerned these, and in some respect EU politics involves a sequence of disputes between those who take a broad view of what the EU might do and those who take a narrower view. For some the broad view extends to an aspiration to create a federal state. At the time of writing one aspect of that broad view is particularly in focus: the coordination of economic activities through monetary union (the Euro as a single currency). Some member states use the Euro (e.g. Germany and France), others do not. The economic difficulties of some Euro members require attention from that sub-group as a whole, yet the EU lacks the powers to directly manage (through taxation and expenditure control) the Euro member states in the way a fully-fledged federal state (like the United States) does. Hence federalism is just an aspiration, probably one very hard to realise.

Within the ranks of EU scholars there have been arguments then about the extent the policy process may be viewed as akin to that of a federation, with consequences for the component states that can be analysed in rather the same way that Pressman and Wildavsky wrote about implementation in the United States or whether analysis requires an inter-governmental perspective derived from international relations theory (Jordan, 1997, 2001; for an overview of these arguments see chapter 2 in Wallace et al., 2010).

This issue has been discussed in Chapter 10 and mentioned in Chapter 11. In the former it is suggested that the most appropriate way to approach this issue is in terms of the notion of 'policy interdependence', taking various forms within the EU. That formulation reflects the contribution to this subject of Holzinger and Knill (see Table 10.3).

Going beyond the often contested issues about the capacity of the EU to impose policies it is important to recognise that there are issues – particularly evident in the crowded European space – where even in the absence of institutions designed to try to secure policy coordination there would be likely to be influences upon policy making within nation states. Below the macro level of global warming there are pollution issues which cross boundaries because of air and water flows. It is not surprising to find that in the EU the combination of concerns about these with the 'common market' considerations has led to particularly strong efforts to influence national policies. Fisheries policy provides another example – indeed one where the issues spread beyond the EU borders – where the concern is about the sharing and conservation of a shared resource (see the discussion of the 'tragedy of the commons' in Chapter 3). Another rather more fraught issue – on which there are divisions within the EU – concerns control over migration from outside. Parallel examples to all these can be found around the world.

We encounter thus much looser influences on national policies, inasmuch as there are problems that are best solved in collaboration with neighbouring states or even just pressures to be 'good neighbours'. At this stage issues about international collaboration and issues about policy interdependence rather converge.

Finally this section needs to go back to one of the wider issues within the governance literature about the shift away from the emphasis on the state as policy maker, since this has a supra-national dimension too. In its simplest form this implies just a proposition that given the significance of the efforts of interest groups to influence government we will find situations in which those groups are supra-national and organise to influence policy makers at whatever level they operate. Callanan (2011), looking at how local governments may both lobby their own central governments and lobby in Brussels, writes of 'venue' shopping affected by the issues and by the institutional arrangements within nation states (see also Dür and Mateo, 2012). Hence national governments will be subject to pressure from such groups. Moreover, as is very clear from studies of the EU, if policies are being made for groups of nations it is not at all surprising that national interest groups will seek to work together with those from other nations. This is particularly evident in respect of the major organisations of employers and employees and of the large business organisations, and gets explicit recognition within the EU policy-making system:

> The founding treaties established the Economic and Social Committee . . . as a point of access to the policy process for socio-economic groups. Its creation borrowed from the corporatist traditions in some of the member

countries. It has not, however, become an influential body in the policy process. Instead socio-economic groups have found their own more direct points of access since the 1960s.

(Wallace et al., 2010, p. 86)

But this is also a theme within the literature on globalism. Strong statements of this perspective emphasise the extent to which economic activities are organised globally; there are global companies that exceed many nation states in wealth and some activities (notably finance) are quite explicitly organised on a global scale (see Chapter 2 on the structural power of business). So we find statements from globalism theorists like: 'traditional nation-states have become unnatural, even impossible business units' (Ohmae, 1996, p. 5) and 'the magnitude of capital flows is exceeding the capacities of even the most powerful government to manage the pressures they generate' (Peterson, 1996, p. 268).

It is undisputable that many nation states are not able to steer multinational corporations. However, Steurer (2013) and Risse (2006) makes the point that these private transnational actors are submitted to new external accountability mechanisms: 'Many new global governance arrangements and trisectoral public policy networks have sprung to increase social corporate responsibility including, for example, the UN's Global Compact (Ruggie, 2002), the Global Reporting Initiative, the Dow Jones Sustainability Index, and others' (Risse, 2006, p. 199). Of course, the policy effects of these not state-centric and not hierarchical governance schemes remain to be seen in practice. In any case, if policy scholars want to grasp the emergence and the effectiveness of these new modes of global governance, they probably have to think outside the analytical box of domestic policy processes and to adopt a new epistemological position beyond 'methodological nationalism' (Coleman, 2012, p. 684).

So far, we have discussed how the governance of policy processes faces three major challenges: the vertical coordination between layers of government, the horizontal coordination between policy sectors and the coordination at the international or global level. The next analytical step would be to consider the interdependences between these three challenges. Varone et al. (2013) have developed the concept of 'functional regulatory space' in order to investigate new forms of public action, which address wicked problems spanning several policy sectors, institutional territories and levels of government. This concept integrates previous policy approaches that focused either on boundary-spanning regime (Jochim and May, 2010), territorial institutionalism (Carter and Smith, 2008) or multi-level governance (Hooghe and Marks, 2003). It puts the emphasis on the political 'rescaling process' (Brenner, 2004), which simultaneously implies new inter-policies dynamics, the redefinition of regulatory territorial perimeters and multi-level re-arrangements. In other words, the emergence of a functional regulatory space corresponds not only to the sum of these three different processes, but is a result of the interdependencies between the concomitant transformations of various policy scales. For instance, changes in policy hierarchy (e.g. structural measures implemented to reduce public debts in southern European countries) often depends on the redefinition of territorial (e.g. frontiers of the Eurozone) and institutional scales (i.e. shifts of political power from the national State to the European level). Box 14.7 illustrates it for the new European way of managing airspace.

Box 14.7	Combining sectors, territories and levels: political rescaling process towards Functional Airspace Blocks

The regulation of the European sky through so-called 'Functional Airspace Blocks' is an empirical example of such an emerging Functional Regulatory Space. The continuous growth of aviation traffic has prompted an increase in the rivalries surrounding the use of airspace and ground infrastructure, resulting also in safety concerns (e.g. increasing cases of near-collision). In this context, the EU adopted the Single European Sky legislative package in March 2004 with the aim of decreasing delays and congestion. This new strategy notably reorganises air traffic management irrespective of national borders. The newly created functional airspace blocks are designed according to the traffic needs and main commercial routes. This means that military forces are invited to integrate the blocks and renounce the exclusive use of portions of the airspace.

The functional airspace blocks are (1) *cross-sectors* arrangements as they link together three formerly autonomous policy subsystems, namely national defence, air transport and environmental protection. (2) They have *cross-border perimeters* that encompass several portions of countries. For instance the Functional Airspace Block Europe Central (FABEC) manages the airspace of six countries. (3) Finally a *multi-level* governance characterises FABEC as it is run by a Council comprised of civil and military representatives from the six countries. The national governments are put in the difficult position of remaining liable for their national airspace while transferring its management to the supra-national agency. It seems obvious that a single European agency could control air traffic, at least for the upper airspace. However, the decision is highly sensitive, and the national governments prefer a gradual integration of air traffic controllers in order to avoid protest by unions.

Of course, additional examples need to be analysed in depth if we want to identify the key factors underlying the emergence of a functional regulatory space. Good candidates for such an empirical analysis are the creation of basin authorities for the sustainable management of watersheds; the development of the Eurozone to regulate monetary, financial and macroeconomic issues; the 'Schengen Area' arrangement for border control, security and immigration policies; or terrorism and homeland security strategy in European countries (see Christensen et al., 2015 for Norway) or in the United States (see Jochim and May, 2010).

Transformations in the overall relationship between state and society

In the discussion above concentration has been upon the specific phenomena that affect the policy process, shifting it away from the simple hierarchical model alleged to be at the heart of traditional analyses of 'government'. But it was noted at the beginning of the chapter that the governance literature postulates a rather more fundamental shift in the relationship between state and society. There are questions here about how much this shift comes about because of changes in society: lower acceptance of traditional authorities, rising materialism and hedonism, more mobility, the development of electronic means of communication and social networks, distrust of politics, to name a few of the developments. Alternatively this is interpreted more in terms of changes to the state:

> Liberal democratic theory emphasises a sharp distinction between state and society. With the emergent collaborative strategies in policy implementation and public service delivery that distinction becomes difficult to uphold, something that, in turn, has triggered a series of issues related to accountability and the exercise of political power.
>
> (Pierre, 2009, p. 592)

There is no need to get hung up on exact explanations, there are interacting influences here. Where, however, is this taking the policy process? An extreme view of what is happening is provided by Hajer in an article whose title summarises his position precisely 'Policy without polity? Policy analysis and the institutional void' (2003). He argues:

> The weakening of the state goes hand in hand with the international growth of civil society, the emergence of citizen-actors and new forms of mobilization . . . *there are no clear rules and norms according to which politics is to be conducted and policy measures are to be agreed upon.*
>
> (Ibid., p. 175, his italics)

Hajer goes on to itemise five elements in this:

- A 'dispersed' decision making order, a point referring specifically to limitations on the capacity of a single (probably nation state) actor to deal with a specific problem.

- A 'new speciality of policy making and politics' following on that first point with emphasis on the geographical location of issues.
- A need to rethink 'participation and democratic governance'.
- The undermining of 'classical' (scientific) expertise.
- The 'expansive' context of policy making, meaning the way issues interconnect with each other.

Hajer's argument – rather like some of the other broad arguments about governance and globalism – emphasises complexity, and highlights what is most difficult about contemporary decision making. It is his second point that has received the most attention in the literature on governance, leading to exploration of the extent to which there may be said to be a 'democratic deficit' and accordingly a need for new perspectives on how people participate in politics. At the time this book is being completed the issues about the management of the Eurozone or of the movement of migrants into Europe are highlighting problems in respect of Kingdon's trilogy of problems, policies and politics: where the problems are supra-national, and so are many of the policies, but there are then problems about the extent to which the critical politics (how to impose constraints on citizens) is within individual nation states. The issues about the democratic deficit at the European level take us in a direction that is not the main concern of this book, but for which an understanding of the policy process is important. The next chapter offers a further exploration of some aspects of this topic.

CONCLUSIONS

Perri 6 comments that 'coordination is an eternal and ubiquitous problem in public administration' (2004, p. 131). However, whilst not dissenting from that generalisation, it is important to recognise the extent to which it is a characteristic of modern governance that inter-organisational collaboration issues are very salient. Writers vary in the way they stress the elements in the definition of governance, but in the context of this chapter the gloss John puts on the terms is particularly relevant:

> Governance is a flexible pattern of public decision-making based on loose networks of individuals. The concept conveys the idea that public decisions rest less within hierarchically organised bureaucracies, but take place more in long-term relationships between key individuals located in a diverse set of organisations located at various territorial levels.
>
> (John, 2001, p. 9)

Clearly, inasmuch as that is true then – unless we are to engage in a reductionist approach of simply focusing on those 'key individuals' – the exploration

(*continued*)

of inter-organisational relationships is important for an understanding of the policy process.

A recognition of the importance of inter-organisational relationships can be seen not just as arising from the pragmatic concerns of practitioners but also from the recognition in policy process theory of the importance of networks and policy communities, and of the way in which institutional configurations influence action. It may even, as Benson argues, extend to issues about the wider structural context.

But while much of the literature on governance stresses these issues in terms of relationships within nation states it has been shown here that there may be aspects of the relationships between states and even the relationships between states and non-state 'global' actors which are also important for the understanding of the policy process.

The chapter ends by highlighting how these new complexities are changing relationships between state and society, with implications for democracy. The big questions about this go beyond the main concern of this book but there is a need to consider how issues about public policy accountability are changing in this context. The next chapter explores this further.

Conclusion: evaluation and accountability

SYNOPSIS

This book is about the description of the policy process and not a prescriptive text. In this concluding chapter two concepts are addressed that belong to a large extent to the prescriptive branches of policy analysis: evaluation and accountability. In examining how these issues are addressed in the modern world there is a need to take into account the complexity of the policy process explored throughout the book and highlighted at the end of the discussion of governance in the last chapter. If there is a 'democratic deficit' arising from the complexity of governance, can new forms of evaluation and new approaches to accountability reduce that deficit?

Evaluation appears as a final step in stages models of the policy process. Yet, whilst for any policy process with a concrete output the other stages will have occurred in some form (however coalesced or convoluted), it will very often be the case that there is no evaluation process. And, even when evaluation does occur the literature on that subject suggests that it is often seen as an unsatisfactory and problematical process with little in the way of substantive implications for subsequent policy activities. On the one hand it is seen as something important for many versions of the 'rational model' of the policy process: a process of identifying whether something that was supposed to happen actually did happen. Traditionally the evaluation literature puts the case for rational evaluation against the rough and tumble of the political context in which it occurred. The idea that a policy process should involve the explicit identification of objectives, translated as effectively as possible into action and thus susceptible to evaluation afterwards, dies hard. On the other hand, in the real world of policy that ideal is rarely attained. What will be provided in this chapter are observations on the efforts to solve the problems in relation to this presentation of the issues about the process.

The wish to evaluate and accountability are logically linked. Inasmuch as there is a view that someone should be in control of a policy process it is pertinent – even perhaps necessary – to examine whether that control was successfully exercised. This is most evident in that model of democratic politics that sees the policy process as the translation into action of the will of the people, but it is by no means absent from models that adopt a more complex view of what accountability implies. Here the examination of issues about accountability, which will follow the section on evaluation, will look at what is involved in processes of holding public officials to account and the ways in which this is an area of dispute. It will be shown that there are many forms of accountability, including ones that supplement or challenge traditional top-down approaches. Then issues about the way professionalism poses problems for these models are explored, picking up on themes developed in Chapter 13. This takes the discussion first to the extent to which new modes of account-ability are embodied in the 'New Public Management' (NPM) movement and second to some important ideas about direct accountability to the public.

A final section explores issues about both evaluation and accountability in the context of modern governance, recognising the way in which mixed modes of accountability often co-exist and pose questions of choice for policy makers. In this way it will sum up the stress in this book on the diversity of policy issues and of policy process contexts, which leave issues about evaluation and accountability very much areas of dispute.

Evaluation

It is understandable that questions will be asked about what specific policies have achieved. Once a policy has been programmed and implemented, ex post evaluations aim at measuring the effects generated by this policy. To do so, the evaluator has to reconstruct, both conceptually and empirically, the complex causal chain from policy's inception through to implementation activities of public administration (outputs) and then on to behavioural changes of target groups and, eventually, the desired effects of the policy on society (outcomes). Furthermore, evaluation criteria relate the identified policy effects to other policy elements to enable a value judgement to be made on the policy effects. For instance, the effectiveness criteria relates the policy outcomes to the formulated policy objectives (doing the right thing?). The efficiency criteria compares the policy outcomes to the resources invested in the policy implementation (doing the thing right?). Such a policy evalu-ation is a useful tool to deliver empirical evidence on policy effects, to show whether policy measures and policy instruments work and, consequently, to modify the policy design and its implementation arrangement. There are obvious links between the desire to ensure that policy is 'evidence based' (a fundamental feature of the 'rational model' of policy formulation as set out by Simon, see Chapter 10) and then the need to see what it has achieved, with a natural feedback cycle to subsequent policy improvement. There is no wish here to argue against that ideal; rather, the question is: why does this occur so rarely in practice, as suggested by studies on evidence-based policy making (e.g. Sanderson, 2004; Solesbury, 2001)? Discussions of evaluation offer many answers to this question.

An important group of those answers concern themselves with social science methodology. For them the problems are rooted in issues about the difficulties of formulating a positive social science and using methods that facilitate the testing of policy impact. For those wedded to positivist social science an important problem is the difficulty in developing, in the real world, a pure experimental situation to isolate the net effects of a policy. The model here is the controlled trial method used in medicine with matched groups, one of which gets the new treatment to be tested (i.e. experimental group) while the other does not (i.e. control group). In practice it is rare for there to be situations in which entirely arbitrary distinctions (based on controlled random selection) between who gets and who does not get the benefit of a new policy can be made. Logically some policies could not be evaluated in that way (excluding some people from general benefits, like the reduction of pollution or a low inflation rate), but it is also the case that ethical objections may be raised even when such approaches are possible and politicians will be unhappy about what are seen to be arbitrary exclusions from benefits (excluding some people from crime prevention, education or welfare services). There is then a search for alternatives that come close to that: broadly matched areas (see Walker and Duncan's discussion of the use of this in the UK, 2007, p. 176) or designs that compare matched groups of people who could but in fact did not secure access to the benefits of the new policy (i.e. quasi-experimental evaluation designs).

Alternatives to rigorous experimental designs have however been criticised for the difficulties they have in controlling key variables (see Spicker, 2006, pp. 173–4). Policy objectives are often expressed in terms of desired end states: reduction in poverty, air pollution, crime or unemployment, etc. Throughout this book arguments have been advanced about the complexity of policy, and about the need to be sceptical about proclaimed policy goals. In any case the relationship between even the most explicit and controlled policy process and its achievements may be affected by events and changes in the real world on which the policy is expected to have an impact. In theory quasi-experimental designs may try to avoid these problems – choosing very specific policy changes and adopting statistical techniques designed to isolate external influences – but they run into severe difficulties (Pawson and Tilley, 1997).

Krane sums up a discussion of methodological conflicts in this field with the observation: 'To learn that all methods are fallible and limited is not surprising news; what remains, albeit tragic, is the continuing methodological polarisation preached by some evaluators' (Krane, 2001, p. 107). In the context of this book it would be digressing too far from the main concerns to discuss the extent to which it is possible to develop social science methodologies that overcome the problems identified above. Moreover such a discussion would take us into the bigger issue of the feasibility of positivist methodologies. This is of course one of the themes that has hovered in the background in many places in the book, it was explicitly addressed in

Chapters 1 and 6. It is only appropriate to address it further here inasmuch as a further problem about evaluation studies is that there are difficulties in establishing agreed outcome variables. In policy interventions desired outcomes may be disputed. The customers of services may have expectations of services that are not shared by those who deliver them. Exceptionally services may be designed to control behaviour rather than to deliver what people want. The choice of an outcome variable may require the researcher to recognise competing policy goals, and indeed perhaps even make a choice: answering the question 'whose side am I on'?

Fischer adopts an interestingly mixed approach to this problem in his ('empowering') evaluation approach. He explores the evaluation of a classic American policy intervention, the Head Start programme, to enhance the educational achievements of disadvantaged children, showing how different conclusions may be drawn about its results in terms of four considerations (Fischer, 2006):

- 'verification': a typical positivist evaluation measuring the achievement of stated objectives (did the test scores of children in the experiment increase more than those not in it?);

- 'validation': raising issues about the relevance of the programme in terms of definitions of the problem it claims to address (recognising that Head Start might be about more than education performance, for example about reducing cultural exclusion);

- 'vindication': asking whether the programme contributes value for society as a whole (raising questions about whether Head Start was an appropriate response to the issues about social exclusion);

- 'social choice': raising wider ideological questions about what the programme is trying to do (suggesting that there are wider questions about social exclusion in society and about the role education plays in relation to it).

The objective here is not to explore further the methodological challenge presented by Fischer's book but rather to note that his analysis highlights the fact that evaluation is in a broad sense a 'political' activity. After reviewing evaluations of the Australian policy related to the mandatory detention of asylum seekers, Slattery (2010) similarly insists on the political inherency of any evaluation process. He concludes that either the evaluators are able to manage the political forces shaping the evaluation scope, or the evaluation findings bear the risk of being instrumentalised to reinforce existing power relations. It is here then that we see the key to the issue raised in the introduction that there is rarely a systematic connection between evaluation and policy improvement. It is interesting to note how Walker and Duncan, in an essay that may broadly be seen as making a case for evaluation, observe that:

A moment's thought reveals that policy evaluation is not a necessary concomitant of a democratic system, especially an adversarial one such as exists in Britain. Politics is a battle for minds that is won by ideas and driven by ideology and the ballot box. Hence policies have not only to 'work', but also to be seen to work; public opinion is a key ingredient in the policy process. If politicians are ideologically committed to a policy, they may be less amenable to the 'wait and see' logic inherent in prospective evaluation.

(Walker and Duncan, 2007, pp. 169–70)

This leads Walker and Duncan down the practical road of seeing evaluation as a limited activity, part of the policy development process. This is described as 'formative evaluation', defined by Spicker as

Undertaken at intermediate stages in the policy cycle. Formative evaluations can take place to see whether guidelines have been followed, whether an agency is ready to start work, to see whether an agency is being properly managed, or to see whether contract terms have been complied with.

(Spicker, 2006, p. 168)

This approach offers, of course, another challenge to the stages emphasis in much earlier writing about policy, and challenges the view of evaluation as a distinctive end process.

In fact, of course, inasmuch as the policy process involves (as has been argued in many places in this book) continual processes of adjustment anything other than formative evaluation may be very difficult. In respect of some policies – notably macro-economic policy and activities involving decisions about going to war – evaluation seems to be likely to involve a speculative activity like that undertaken by some historians exploring how history might have been different had some fateful decision not been taken. Evaluators frequently apply a counterfactual reasoning. They conduct thought experiments about what would have happened if (a specific component of) a policy had not been implemented. Of course, the precise identification of causal chains is very complex and remains speculative, and evaluators always face the 'Cleopatra's nose' problem as described by James Fearon (1991):

According to Pascal, if Cleopatra's nose had been shorter, Anthony might not have been so infatuated, and the course of Western history might have been different. Does this imply that the gene controlling the length of Cleopatra's nose was a cause of WWI?

(Fearon, 1991, p. 190)

Much more pragmatically Marsh and McConnell's (2010) contribution to this topic tackles the issues about complexity through a taxonomy of dimensions of policy success applicable to, at least, less fundamental policy issues. They provide an elaborate table of 'indicators' and 'evidence' of 'policy success', from which only the former are reproduced in Table 15.1.

Marsh and McConnell are of course aware that 'whatever dimensions of policy are being considered, there are significant complexities involved in assessing success' (see also McConnell, 2010). What constitutes success can differ according to the perspective and/or interests of the participant in, or observer of, the policy process' (ibid., p. 581).

Table 15.1   Marsh and McConnell's indicators of dimensions of policy success

Process
Legitimacy in the formation of choices: that is, produced through due processes of constitutional and quasi-constitutional procedures and values of democracy, deliberation and accountability
Passage of legislation: was the legislation passed with no, or few, amendments?
Political sustainability: did the policy have the support of a sufficient coalition?
Programmatic
Operational: was it implemented as per objectives?
Outcome: did it achieve the intended outcomes?
Resource: was it an efficient use of resources? Internal efficiency evaluations, external audit reports/assessments, absence of critical media reports
Actor/interest: did the policy/implementation benefit a particular class, interest group, alliance, political party, gender, race, religion, territorial community, institution, ideology, etc.?
Political
Government popularity: is the policy politically popular? Did it help government's re-election chances? Did it help secure or boost its credibility?

Source: Abridged version of Marsh and McConnell, 2010, Table 1, p. 571.

This leads on to the question: in a policy process in which there are contending 'actors', what may those various actors gain from an evaluation process? For Knoepfel et al. (2007, pp. 243–9) policy evaluations represent a particular form of policy advice. Such evaluations may be made both by governments and by their opponents. There may then be variations in the extent to which they remain in an exclusive and narrow advisory context, providing information and recommendations for action solely at the disposal of the actors who commissioned them, or they may make their evidence more widely available. There may then be variations in the ways that evaluations are used strategically to support the status quo, to attack policy developments or to support the case for further change. Later in the chapter we will see how the collection of performance indicators (very much linked to the 'New Public Management' reforms), which can loosely be seen as a form of evaluation, looms large in modern public management. The word 'loosely' is used there since these may be seen often as rather more measures of policy outputs than of outcomes, and are thus – along the lines outlined by Fischer – very narrow and contestable evaluation indices.

In this way we are reminded that evaluation is also a political process. This leads radical analyses of evaluation to stress the case for adding other actors to those 'top' ones that are typically seen as in charge of policy evaluation, to seek ways of securing participation in the evaluation process (Taylor and Balloch, 2005). This recognition of alternative 'stakeholders', however, may need a view of the place of evaluation in a democracy in which power holders may to some extent be prepared to pay for uncomfortable assessments of their activities. To argue for a wider approach to evaluation may be seen as an aspect of the challenge to the top-down perspective embodied in representative democracy. In this respect Krane contrasts 'the perspective of overhead democracy' in which evaluators 'are funded by and report their findings to their political superiors' with the possibility of 'operating out of a model of discursive democracy, where local communities are permitted substantial autonomy and self-rule' (Krane, 2001, p. 118). Hoppe (1999) goes beyond that simple contrast. His notion of policy analysis as 'puzzling' and 'powering' brings together the rational aspiration to 'speak truth to power' with a recognition that it is 'utopian to think of a power free politics' (Hoppe, 2010, p. 259). He recommends

> a governance of problems . . . that adopts responsible hope as its basic attitude. Power and coercion, rejection of mutual learning between rulers and ruled through deliberation and argumentation, sophisticated answers to wrong-problem problems – they are certainly here to stay. A responsible governance of problems therefore allows and furthers policy analysis in the face of power. A hopeful governance of problems assumes and actively pursues that dedicated analysis and clever citizens always, sooner or later, find ways to inject solid puzzling in biased powering.
>
> (Hoppe, 2010, p. 262)

Hoppe's argument takes us beyond the concerns of this book with analysis 'of' policy into an important argument about how people should think of analysis 'for' policy. However, it is important to keep in mind that, from a normative perspective, evaluation should contribute to the *secondary*, outcome-based legitimation of public policies, by showing how policy effects contribute to solving collective problems (i.e. democracy as 'government *for* the people'). Evaluations feedbacks are thus complementary to the *primary*, input- and throughput-based legitimation of State action, which rely on open and democratic decision-making processes (i.e. democracy as 'government *by* the people'). This conception of evaluation as a necessary legitimacy exercise (Scharpf, 1999; Knoepfel et al., 2007) leads us on to the topic of legal and democratic accountability, since how this relationship works out in practice depends much upon how that operates.

Accountability: introduction

Accountability has been described as 'probably one of the most basic yet most intractable of political concepts' (Uhr, 1993, p. 13). Thomas, in a review of its use, argues for its restriction to describe situations 'where an authoritative relationship exists in a formal sense' (Thomas, 2003, p. 555). Yet he recognises that there is a much wider usage:

> The meaning of accountability has consistently widened over the years. The term is now frequently used to describe situations where the core features of an authoritative relationship and a formal process of enforcement are not necessarily present. Certainly, the public no longer sees

accountability in strictly legal and organizational terms. For them, accountability is a broader professional, ethical and moral construct that is achieved only when public officials, both elected and appointed, serve with a commitment to do the right things.

(Thomas, 2003, p. 550)

This widening involves two things. One of these is recognition of the complexity of the accountability relationship in the context of modern governance, with the range of intra- and inter-organisational complexities that have been explored in earlier chapters. This is therefore something that cannot be disregarded in this discussion. The other is a confusion of 'accountability' and 'responsibility'. Criticising this confusion, Gregory says: 'accountability is a matter of political and organizational housekeeping, whereas responsibility is often about moral conflict and issues of life and death' (2003, p. 558). While Gregory goes on to suggest that there are problems with accountability systems that disregard these wider issues, it is appropriate to adopt the perspective embodied in that quotation for this chapter since the concern here is with ways in which actors in the policy process are held to account, not with those wider ethical issues.

If one's starting point is a narrow rather than a wide definition of accountability, it must be recognised that 'accountability is an unapologetic bureaucratic concept' (Kearns, 2003, p. 583) which is particularly enshrined in traditional notions of representative government. In the study of public administration the accountability theme emerged early on in the efforts to separate politics and administration, rooted in the idea that in a democratic state politics should set the goals for administration to put into practice. That idea lives on, despite all the evidence that this distinction is difficult to make in practice. Hence, there is one approach to accountability, which we may still call the dominant one, which places politics, in the form of top-down representative government, in the driving seat.

That approach to accountability is accompanied by a legalistic view of what gives policy action legitimacy, namely that it should be within the framework of the 'rule of law'. This can involve, in some of the more philosophical approaches to this topic, notions like principles of 'natural' or 'common' law which derive from universal principles independent of the actions of governments (a view that features significantly in discussions of human rights and international legal principles). But in many cases, legitimacy is seen as lying in the extent to which action is authorised by either constitutional rules or specific legislation. The legal approach may offer a challenge to the political approach, when judges question political decisions, for instance through the constitutional review of laws. But both are in the last resort top-down mandates, the product of what are seen as legitimate political processes.

Therefore, the dominant approach to accountability can be seen as a top-down one, normally buttressed by some notion of representative democracy. However, if representative democracy is to be really meaningful it needs to be recognised that the ultimate accountability of governments is to the people. In the face of deficiencies in the doctrines of representative government there are claims that people should have direct control over policy processes in ways other than, or additional to, representative democracy. Embodied in those propositions is a great deal of complexity, which could take us into issues in political philosophy well beyond the brief of this book. What is clear is that as far as policy processes are concerned, claims that functionaries should be accountable to the government are still very much in evidence.

Alongside the democratic challenge to top-down accountability will be found two other forms of accountability: bureaucratic and professional. Pollitt defines the former as 'accountability to the codes and norms within the bureaucratic context' and the latter as 'accountability to the standards laid down by one's professional body' (Pollitt, 2003, p. 93). Both of these have come under attack as involving a rejection of the democratic forms of accountability. The defence to this charge involves arguing that they embody apolitical notions of direct duty of service to the public. In that sense doctors, for example, may argue that they are accountable to their patients for the service they provide and to their peers who monitor those standards of service. But that brings us close to the widening of the concept of accountability to embrace responsibility as well, a moral responsibility that overrides ordinary accountability.

It is not proposed to evaluate here the justifications on offer for the various forms of accountability – the point here is to acknowledge that accountability is a complex and contested concept. Box 15.1 summarises the various forms of accountability.

Box 15.1	Forms of accountability

Political – direct accountability to elected representatives (recognising that these arrangements may be complex since often there are alternatives – presidents and parliaments, central and local governments, etc.).

Hierarchical – accountability to the 'head' of an organisation, a version of accountability that is often embodied in the political concept of accountability; but since the one does not logically embrace the other this should not be taken for granted.

Direct democratic – direct accountability to the public (complicated by issues about who the public are in particular cases: patients, parents, pupils, tenants, etc. or everyone, and by the fact that these will be in specifically defined geographical areas).

Legal – forms of accountability that may be secured through the courts. This may be a reinforcement to political accountability but there will be situations in which legal legitimacy overrides political legitimacy.

Professional – governed by profession-related principles which, like some legal ones, may be considered to override political accountability.

Bureaucratic – normally a derivative from political, hierarchical or legal accountability but may be seen in some cases to involve overriding 'responsibilities' similar to those embodied in some versions of professional accountability.

Developed from Pollitt's typology (2003, Table 4.1, p. 93).

All of the forms of accountability, including the direct democratic one, are often expressed in relatively simplistic top-down forms. What is meant by that is that executive bodies – prime ministers and cabinets, elected representatives of parents, supreme courts, professional governing bodies, bureau chiefs, etc. – demand that others are accountable to them. The very complexity of the policy process and of modern governance makes the achievement of any simple form of accountability difficult.

Accountability to the top: the political model

Kaare Strom (2000) has conceptualised parliamentary democracies as a top-down chain of delegation and accountability. He relies on the principal-agent theory that we briefly introduced in Chapter 3 to describe how citizens may indirectly hold elected officials and civil servants accountable for their policy decisions. In its ideal-typical form, a parliamentary democracy is characterised by four successive delegation steps: (1) from voters to elected representatives; (2) from elected representatives to the cabinet and prime minister; (3) from the cabinet to the head of the executive department and, eventually, (4) from the department head to their respective civil servants. At each stage, a principal (the citizen) delegates policy-making competencies to a principal (e.g. MPs); vice versa, this agent is accountable to the principal and might be sanctioned (e.g. through the next parliamentary elections) if the expected policies are not delivered. For instance, a top civil servant is accountable to a minister. The minister is supervised by the prime minister. And the cabinet is under the tight control of the legislature. This approach insists on the fact that delegation is inherently risky and that various accountability mechanisms need to be put in place. These accountability tools include ex ante screenings and selection procedures (e.g. before hiring a civil servant) and ex post reporting requirements and institutional checks (e.g. minister testifying during a committee hearing) (Strom et al., 2006, pp. 37–9).

This general approach fits very well the Westminster model of democracy, and Brown sets out the importance of the top-down perspective for public administration, whilst amplifying it to take into account local democracy, in the UK in the following way:

The formal characteristic of any public service is that in the last resort a lay politician carries responsibility for it to an elected assembly. There is a chain of command leading from the bedside and the local insurance office to the front bench in the House of Commons. In the personal social services the chain leads first to the committee room in county hall and then, because of his overall duty to guide the development of the service, to the secretary of state.

These lines of accountability give the public, through its elected representatives, the opportunity to question and influence the operation of public services. They provide constitutional channels through which grievances can be ventilated. In the very last resort they provide a means through which the electorate can withdraw support from an administration whose policies it dislikes, and substitute one more to its liking. This is the ultimate sanction in public administration.

(Brown, 1975, p. 247)

Brown is right to emphasise how this is the starting point for most discussions of accountability. He then, of course, goes on to recognise the limitations to this approach, saying: 'A moment's reflection, however, suggests that this needs to be supplemented in some directions and perhaps qualified in others if services are to be efficiently administered in the public interest' (ibid.). Day and Klein similarly, in an exploration of the 'career' of the concept of accountability, chart a progression from 'simple to complex models' (1987, chapter 1).

A recognition of these complexities has characterised the analysis of public administration at least since Woodrow Wilson's classical essay (1887) on the distinction between politics and administration. While that has been seen as supporting the view that administration must be subordinate to politics, it in fact sought to prescribe a way of separating the two in the context of the realities of American politics. Wilson sought thus to combine democratic accountability with efficient administration. Wilson was both identifying an important problem about administrative accountability and recognising that the United States faced great difficulties in coming to terms with a set of institutional arrangements that made political problem solving very difficult.

The alternative view on Wilson's politics/administration dichotomy is that this is a distinction that bears little relation to the reality of political and administrative behaviour. Evidence for this has been explored in various places in this book. But what is important about Woodrow Wilson's perspective is the way his ideal division influenced thinking about the management of government and public policies. It finds resonances not just in discussion of representative democracy but also in arguments about the 'rule of law', the concern of the next section.

The legal model of accountability and the problem of discretion

Two key ingredients in the 'rule of law' according to Wade (1982, p. 22) are:

1. 'that everything must be done according to the law', which when applied to the powers of government means that 'every act which affects the legal rights, duties or liberties of any person must be shown

to have a strictly legal pedigree. The affected person may always resort to the courts of law, and if the legal pedigree is not found to be perfectly in order the court will invalidate the act, which he can then safely disregard';

2. 'that government should be conducted within a framework of recognized rules and principles which restrict discretionary power'.

The particular way those principles are enunciated by Wade may have characteristics that are peculiar to Anglo-Saxon countries, but the general thrust of the principles is accepted wherever it is claimed that governments operate within the 'rule of law'. In administrative law systems, the criterion of legality is also a basic principle: all policy interventions should be rooted in a legal basis. Note that this principle applies not only to domestic law, but also to the compatibility between national and European law. In case of discrepancy, a member state of the European Union can be brought before the European Court of Justice.

The importance of the 'rule of law' and legality as a basis for legitimate rule is explored in Weber's third type of authority: 'rational–legal'. This was examined in Chapter 12. Weber argues (in a text originally put together in the early years of the twentieth century):

> Today the most usual basis of legitimacy is the belief in legality, the readiness to conform with rules which are formally correct and have been imposed by accepted procedure.
>
> (Weber, 1947, p. 131)

Weber goes on to distinguish a social order derived from voluntary agreement from one that is imposed – but he calls this distinction 'only relative'. The first of the ideas which he sees as central to the 'effectiveness' of legal authority is:

> That any given legal norm may be established by agreement or by imposition, on grounds of expediency or rational values or both, with a claim to obedience at least on the part of the members of the corporate group. This is, however, usually extended to include all persons within the sphere of authority or of power in question – which in the case of territorial bodies is the territorial area – who stand in certain social relationships or carry out forms of social action which in the order governing the corporate group have been declared to be relevant.
>
> (Ibid., p. 329)

In that rather convoluted argument, of course, lies the concept of the state. The second idea is that 'every body of law consists essentially in a consistent system of abstract rules which have been intentionally established' (ibid., p. 330).

Thus issues about the legitimacy of official rules, and the related discretions they may explicitly or implicitly convey, may be disputed with reference to their specific source, to their constitutional context or to wider principles. However, this is not a simple matter.

In the United Kingdom the absence of a written constitution gives debate about public law a peculiar shape which derives from the fact that the primary source of law is Parliament. The central concern is with whether the rules applied by public officials have the formal sanction of Parliament and whether departures from those rules (discretion) are formally authorised (or not formally proscribed) by statute. A secondary concern is with the capacity of the court system – as supplemented in the modern world by simpler grievance procedures such as tribunals and ombudsmen – to respond in situations in which citizens (singly or in organised groups) regard official behaviour as falling outside those statutorily determined boundaries.

The peculiarities of the UK system (shared of course by some Commonwealth countries) contrast with those of countries with written constitutions and a supreme adjudicative body entrusted with the protection and interpretation of that constitution. In such countries, an additional test of the legitimacy of any policy process-related action will be its compatibility with the constitution. In France, for example, the Constitutional Council assesses the compatibility of legislative and regulative texts with the constitution. In addition, the Council of State examines if the regulatory decisions proposed by the executive are compatible with previous legislative provisions. However the contrast between the UK system and other political systems is not as stark as it may seem. The absence of a written constitution should not be understood to imply the absence of a constitution (see King, 2007). While historically judges in the UK have taken a very cautious view of their responsibilities in this respect, in the last quarter of the twentieth century they began to take a more active view. This was then reinforced by the extent to which membership of the European Union required the UK to give attention to European law, and even more significantly by an Act of Parliament, the Human Rights Act (1998) which incorporated the European Convention on Human Rights into UK law, with the implication that the judges could scrutinise the compatibility of new laws with the provisions of that Act. This opens up a potential for conflict between accountability to the law and accountability to government.

But much of the detailed role of the law in dealing with accountability concerns questions about the extent to which powers exercised by administrators have been formally authorised by government. It thus particularly deals with administrative discretion. Hence what the law textbooks provide is a portrait of the law as trying to keep administrative discretion under control. In so doing the law is presented as the defender of the citizen against the arbitrary exercise of power. Wade (1982) perceives administrative law as an attempt to ensure that the 'whole new empires of executive power' conform to the principles of liberty and fair dealing. This perspective leads Wade to argue that the key issue is ensuring that the law can control 'the exercise of the innumerable discretionary powers which Parliament has conferred on the various authorities' (p. 4). His emphasis is on ensuring that such authorities do not act *ultra vires* by exceeding their statutory power or following the wrong procedures. Authorities cannot escape such control by being offered statutes that give them unlimited power, since 'in practice all statutory powers have statutory limits, and where the expressed limits are indefinite, the courts are all the more inclined to find that limits are implied. The notion of unlimited power has no place in the system' (ibid., p. 50). While it is clearly possible to see in this view of the rule of law a control over arbitrary government, it is largely transformed into a notion of control over arbitrary administration.

Two things further complicate this boldly stated application of the model of the 'rule of law'. One is the difficulties citizens experience in using the law to protect themselves from the executive. The other, very much within our terms of reference, is that these so-called statutory powers are very complicated. One view, abandoned by any realistic critic of the United Kingdom legislative system at least 50 years ago, was that all rules should be embodied in formal Acts of Parliament. The reality is that there is a great deal of subordinate rule making, not only in 'regulations' which are hypothetically open to parliamentary scrutiny, but also in a variety of departmental guidance circulars, codes and working instructions to officials. These were a key concern of the discussion of policy formulation in Chapter 10.

The very institutional complexity of the policy system means that there is a wide range of bodies which have responsibilities to interpret and perhaps amplify their statutory mandates. Hence, it is not possible to draw a simple distinction between statutory rules deriving from the legislature and the discretion of officials. The intermediary departments, executive agencies, local governments and so on, which, from the old-fashioned perspective, can be seen as discretionary actors themselves, engaged in subordinate rule-making processes. A considerable body of case law governs these processes.

Traditionally, UK administrative law textbooks give attention to administrative discretion as a 'taken for granted' phenomenon within the political system. They point out that the concern of the courts has been with (a) whether or not the discretionary powers that are exercised have been clearly delegated by statute; (b) whether the exercise of those powers is within the boundaries of natural justice (are they exercised reasonably and with regard to due process?); and (c) the principle that if a statute grants discretionary powers then the officials using them should not devise rules which in practice fetter that discretion.

These questions are highly relevant for the so-called 'independent regulatory agencies' that were recently institutionalised in liberalised network industries such as telecommunications, electricity, airlines or postal services (Thatcher, 2005). As a matter of fact, these agencies are granted a formal independence from elected officials and, at the same time, large regulatory powers. Their accountability to politicians, citizens and regulated industry is thus a key issue. Some authors argue that the rapid development of independent regulatory agencies, in various policy sectors and countries, leads gradually to the emergence of an 'indirect representative democracy' (Levi-Faur, 2005). We should no longer speak of a delegation of authority and policy-making tasks to elected representatives (as suggested by Kaare

Strom) as we observe a second-level of indirect delegation: citizens still elect representatives, but these representatives delegate their policy-making power to experts who are seating in independent regulatory agencies and who administer policies quasi-autonomously. This is a major transformation in the delegation and accountability chain from citizens to policy makers.

The 'rule of law' approach to the issue of accountability primarily reinforces the top-down model of accountability, embodied in the notion of the primacy of politics in a context of representative democracy, but it may suggest that there should be wider principles to which citizens can appeal. It sets up a tension between accountability to a legislature and accountability to the courts, which takes its most clear form in the way in which the American constitution gives the Supreme Court a super-ordinate role. It has led to recognition that the Supreme Court can be in some circumstances a 'policy maker'. A corresponding interesting feature in Europe is the role of the European Court, which is reinforced by an international search for ways of specifying and enforcing universal human rights (Stone Sweet, 2004; Kelemen, 2011).

This excursion into issues about legal control over policy introduces something else: concerns about the extent to which law may be comparatively impotent in the face of the complex issues of administrative discretion. A recognition of the limits to legal control over administration or independent regulatory agencies as well as the limits to top-down political control stimulates a search for other models of accountability. The debate about that has particularly centred on issues about professionalism.

Accountability, discretion and professionalism

Chapter 13 explored the arguments about professional discretion, showing how a case for professional autonomy has been made. That case tends to be most strongly made in relation to the role of medical doctors. Medical autonomy is traditionally defended in terms of the sanctity of the doctor/patient relationship and the needs of good medical practice. In this argument the most important form of accountability is seen as being to the patient, but it takes the paternalistic form of suggesting that the doctor's expertise enables him or her to determine what is in the patient's best interests. That is reinforced by arguments about indeterminacy in many situations and about the need for a relationship of 'trust'. A wider protection is then alleged to be offered by the fact that the doctor's behaviour is subject to scrutiny by his or her professional 'peers', who were given responsibility (by the state) for training and accreditation, and have the power to take disciplinary action against malpractice.

However, individual clinical decisions are not merely the concern of the practitioner, the profession and the patient, at least as far as publicly financed medicine is concerned. In a situation of resource constraints (which must be regarded as a normal situation for a publicly financed health service) a response to the needs of any patient involves claims on scarce resources. It must thus – taking an overall view – be to some extent at the expense of a response to others. That issue comes to the fore most poignantly where there is manifestly a lack of resources relative to an identified need – as is the case with very expensive but comparatively unused medicines, various forms of treatment for kidney disease, organ transplants or in a hard-pressed emergency unit. It is also present inasmuch as there are cost differences between professionals who carry out ostensibly the same practices, increasingly given attention in the management of public services. Concerns about these issues are then heightened by the fact that there are often waiting lists for treatments and operations. Overall, it may be contended that there is a ubiquitous requirement for all clinical work to be planned and organised against a backcloth of resource issues, which are surely public concerns.

If the need for wider public control is conceded, the question then becomes: who is to do the controlling? Here we find, alongside straightforward top-down arguments for political and legal control, some alternatives (or some combination of them): lay managers, professionally qualified managers, other professional colleagues and patients. There are problems with accountability in respect to each of these.

Clearly, the standard control model for the policy process involves appointed managers working within a remit supplied by politicians. The intense need for cost control over services like health has increased the propensity to see lay managers as having a key role to play. That view has been reinforced by the availability of new technologies (computerised medical records, systems to identify the costs of 'normal' medical procedures like those offered by the identification of 'diagnosis related groups', etc.) and the introduction of performance indicators as one key element of 'New Public Management' (see below).

This approach to the management of professional activity is opposed by two alternatives. One is control by managers who are drawn from the ranks of the service professionals themselves. There has been a long-standing argument about this approach to the management of professionals: do these managers retain their old professional loyalties or become co-opted to the ranks of the lay managers? There seems good reason to believe, confirmed by research led by Degeling (Degeling et al., 1998; 2003), that the truth lies somewhere between these two positions. These 'managers' obviously offer scope for the development of a more sophisticated, shared accountability, but they do not, of course, open up the system to public accountability in the widest sense.

The other alternatives are variations of this. These are either the creation of a cadre of people who are involved in management but still practising their profession, or collective self-management through collegial shared participation. This is a managerial model widely favoured by professionals. However, there are well-founded suspicions that – particularly when review processes are not shared outside the professional group (medical audit, for example; Harrison and Pollitt, 1994) – this approach to management preserves traditional professional domination. There are also questions about whether this is an efficient use of members of an expert workforce.

This discussion has deliberately explored the doctor/patient relationship, but the arguments explored are also applicable to other, similar relationships, such as those between teacher and pupil. A view that the case of professional autonomy is weaker outside the medical profession has been embodied in arguments that in many cases it is more appropriate to speak of semi-professions rather than professions (Etzioni, 1969).

All the managerial approaches to increasing the accountability of professional service groups involve the development of performance indicators, and often then related cost measures. The use of these can be seen as a particular feature of modern approaches to accountability, embodied in concepts of New Public Management. These will be explored next (we return to issues of direct accountability to patients after that).

The impact of 'New Public Management'

It has been difficult to decide where to include a discussion of 'New Public Management' (NPM) in this book. Inasmuch as the NPM movement has been motivated by concerns about accountability, this is the appropriate place. However, whilst issues like control over professional autonomy have been one of the movement's preoccupations, this has been accompanied by a concern that the obvious alternative to this autonomy, top-down control of a bureaucratic kind, is also inadequate. In this respect, this discussion might have been included in Chapter 12, where the sociological work on the deficiencies of the top-down model was outlined, or in Chapter 13 where issues about street-level autonomy were examined. NPM is a response to dilemmas about public bureaucracy that go back at least as far as Max Weber's time, and it draws upon the sociological analysis of organisations stimulated by Weber's work and by the arguments about Taylorism or Fordism as well as the rational choice critique of organisational behaviour. In discussing it here, then, it is important to recognise the potential contradiction within NPM between a strong stress on accountability and a rejection of traditional forms of top-down control.

Hood (1991) identifies seven 'doctrines' to which 'over the last decade, a "typical" public sector policy delivery unit in the UK, Australia, New Zealand and many other OECD [Organization for Economic Co-operation and Development] countries would be likely to have had some exposure' (p. 4). These ideas have travelled quickly from country to country, promoted by fashionable 'gurus'. Hood does not mention the United States, but perhaps the most influential of all the NPM tracts, a book by Osborne and Gaebler (1992), comes from that country. The seven doctrines Hood identifies are set out in Box 15.2.

Box 15.2	Hood's summary of NPM 'doctrines'

1. 'Hands-on professional management in the public sector'
2. 'Explicit standards and measures of performance'
3. 'Greater emphasis on output controls'
4. '. . . disaggregation of units in the public sector'
5. '. . . greater competition in the public sector' (to this may be added actual privatisation)
6. '. . . private sector styles of management'
7. '. . . greater discipline and parsimony in resource use'.

Source: Adapted from Table 1 in Hood, 1995, pp. 4–5.

In some respects the expression NPM is simply useful shorthand for a variety of innovations, widespread across the world, which are 'dominating the bureaucratic reform agenda' (Hood, 1991, p. 3). There is a danger that the use of this shorthand expression may convey the sense of a unified and compatible set of initiatives. In a later essay (1995), despite having established himself as the leading analyst of the phenomenon, Hood attacks the view that NPM is a 'new global paradigm' and highlights some of the inconsistencies within the work of its leading exponents.

Hood indicates that NPM has been attacked for its concern to place issues about efficiency before equity (Pollitt, 1990), but he argues that NPM advocates would assert that efficiency 'can be conceived in ways which do not fundamentally conflict with equity' (Hood, 1999, p. 10, citing Wilenski, 1986).

That takes us into issues about the relationship between efficiency and accountability. Some of the NPM movement's concerns come directly from the rational choice attack (see Chapter 3) upon traditional public bureaucracy which links the two. But others – notably (1) and (4) in Hood's list (see Box 15.2) – have their roots in Peters and Waterman's (1982) concerns about human relations in the organisation and the desire to create organisations where 'excellence' can be achieved by a committed workforce left to perform delegated tasks without undue surveillance. This seems to conflict with the rational choice view that public sector managers cannot be trusted to operate autonomously (see Kettl, 1997; Terry, 1998). A particular feature of NPM in practice has been an attack upon the traditional autonomy claims of the established professions – medicine, teaching, etc. Paradoxically, the new 'hands-on professional' managers are seen as a countervailing force to traditional professionals (Hoggett, 1996).

If the ideas are taken together as a package, these conflicts may be resolved to the satisfaction of the New Right perspective by stressing that market discipline imposes its own accountability. Managerial autonomy does not enable managers to 'buck the market'. Others, like the 'aristocratic' old professions, it is argued, must also learn to come to terms with market discipline. But that presumes that real market discipline can be established in a public service.

Hence for others not wedded to the New Right perspective or unconvinced about the feasibility of creating a market, this mixture of measures seems to preserve the autonomy of those 'hands-on' managers at the top whilst ensuring the efficiency of response by lower-level workers to their demands through the increased insecurity entailed in the combination of strict standards and competition from alternative providers (Hoggett, 1996). Relevant here is Pollitt's summary of the impact of NPM (2003, chapter 2), in which what is particularly stressed is its emphasis upon the use of performance targets to impose accountability. In that sense NPM can be seen as an effort to secure tight controls over public organisations without recourse to traditional bureaucracy.

A characteristic of NPM in the United Kingdom (and probably in Australia and New Zealand too) is that it has been very much a 'top-down' movement. Reform of central administration has not involved decentralisation. The 'disaggregated units' Hood refers to have been subject to tight controls. There are grounds for arguing – with respect to the development of quasi-autonomous agencies – that the operational freedom of these consists merely of a freedom to take the blame. At the lower levels British local government has experienced steadily tightening financial control, strong steering to ensure that its interpretation of NPM is compatible with that of the government and requirements to accept and stimulate competition that has weakened its capacity to respond to local political forces (Butcher, 2002; Deakin and Walsh, 1996; Hoggett, 1996; Walsh, 1995).

The 'search for excellence', or 'reinvented government', has involved an attempt to put a 'post-Fordist' form of administrative organisation into place to combat the bureaucratic 'diseases' associated with traditional hierarchies. Yet there is a conflict between this remedy for inefficient government and 'rational choice' theory, which sees bureaucratic autonomy as a key cause of the uncontrollable growth of government. It is also necessary to note the conflict between the case for the flexible organisation in which staff have high discretion and the use of rules to secure accountability.

The solution to this dilemma has been seen to involve two ideas. One of these is that control should deal with broad general parameters, leaving much detail to be settled at the 'street level'. This is the idea of the loose/tight organisation of 'steering' not 'rowing' (Osborne and Gaebler, 1992). Steering is seen as involving the setting of the financial framework and the specification of a range of incentives (Kickert, 1995, pp. 149–50). It must be questioned how much this is really new, and how much it is merely another approach to analysing the hierarchical structure of discretion, explored in relation to the points quoted from Simon and from Dunsire in Chapter 12 (see also Hoggett's criticism of Kickert: Hoggett, 1996). Nevertheless it does suggest the need for the co-existence of two forms of accountability.

The other approach to control involves emphasis upon retrospective controls requiring the collection of information on performance, hence bringing the discussion here back to issues about evaluation. Rewards or sanctions are applied on the basis of such data. The crucial sanction may be the termination of a contract if a quasi-market system is operating. Some commentators on

British public policy in the 1990s have seen developments of this kind as a retreat from accountable public administration (Baldwin, 1995). Others have seen it as a rather bogus loosening of control – taking out some actors who might have played a role in accountability such as local government (see Glennerster et al., 1991) – whilst financial constraints and fear of sanctions reinforce strong central control (Deakin and Walsh, 1996). Some forms of managerial control have been enhanced at the expense of professional autonomy, particularly where those managers hold values compatible with the pro-market 'Right' (Hoggett, 1996). Clarke and Newman (1997) have seen 'new managerial regimes as producing a field of tensions', an 'unstable settlement between bureau-professional power and the new managerialism' (Newman, 2001, p. 31).

At the same time it is still necessary to draw another lesson about the use of rational devices in the control of administrative behaviour, for example management by objectives and quantitative staff assessment, from Blau's old study (1955). He demonstrates how performance indicators used in the evaluation of work may distort bureaucratic behaviour. Individuals not only set out to 'cook' their own performance statistics but choose to emphasise those activities that will maximise the score achieved by themselves and their agency (see Box 13.2 reporting Brodkin's account of what may happen in this case). The proverb 'what gets measured gets done' is frequently verified in organisations managed through performance indicators: civil servants game the system (Hood and Bevan, 2006), react strategically to performance incentives, and tend to focus only on the delivery of services that are measured through performance indicators and can (potentially) increase 'their' organisational budget or their individual salary (if a performance-related pay had been introduced). By contrast, they deliberately neglect administrative tasks (e.g. horizontal coordination with other administrations) and policy outputs that are not monitored with performance indicators, even if these outputs are essential for policy quality and effectiveness (Varone and Giauque, 2001). Organisational egoism and individual selfishness are potentially reinforced by performance indicators, at the expense of inter-organisational coordination and team work.

In addition, it is through the use of output measures (about administrative activities and costs) rather than outcome measures (about policy effects on society), whose collection and analysis is facilitated by computer technologies, that much retrospective control over discretion is sought. This is one of the ingredients in the curious mix of apparent neo-Fordism with a reversion to Fordism in the public sector (Hoggett, 1996; Pollitt, 1990). This shortsighted view of outputs is problematic as it allows only to assess the efficiency of an administrative organisation, and not policy effectiveness. To be clear, we do not argue that cost efficiency is not an important evaluation criteria, but we claim that policy effectiveness should come first. From a policy-making perspective, it make sense to evaluate if a policy is able to solve a collective problem (doing the right thing?) before assessing if the allocation of administrative resources is optimal (doing the thing right?) (Knoepfel et al., 2007, p. 244).

Furthermore, some implementation activities and policy effects are much more easily measured than others, hence performance indicators that offer a distorting impression of a public service activity as a whole may come to have an excessive influence. Allied to this issue is the fact that some of those measurements most likely to impress are those that embody data on costs or can be translated into money terms. Therefore issues about effectiveness in education have often been translated quite spuriously into indicators of 'value added' for individuals and/or the national economy (Wolf, 2002).

Measurement activities may empower another group of people: experts in measurement and other forms of auditing. Such people may be every bit as difficult to bring under accountability systems as the people whose activities they measure. Hence Power has exposed some of the problems with auditing, raising questions about how auditors are audited (or more often, how they are not audited) (Power, 1997). Overall, what may be occurring is the enhancement, at the expense of professional service staff, of the power of those who monitor and measure their work, creating new kinds of 'professional dominance' among accountants, lawyers and managers (see Alford, 1975, and Ham, 1992, on 'corporate rationalisers', and developments of this theme in Harrison et al., 1990).

The NPM movement claims to have ways to deal with these issues, but the discussion of their complexity suggests reasons to be sceptical about those claims. This is supported by Hood's analysis of the extent to which management changes under the influence of NPM produce 'side-effects and even reverse effects'. He borrows Sieber's (1981) notion of 'fatal remedies' – 'producing the opposite of the intended effect' – to analyse these (Hood, 1995, pp. 112–16). Among them the erosion of trust and the adverse effects of elaborate rule structures and reporting requirements loom large (see also Power's (1997) attack on 'the audit explosion').

Research evaluations of the key NPM developments have been slow to emerge. There are grounds for believing that realistic competitive 'markets' are hard to create and, thus, that the achievements of NPM will be limited. Christopher Hood and Ruth Dixon (2015) have made a major contribution to the evaluation of NPM in the United Kingdom by examining systematically the main NPM hypothesis that government would 'work better and cost less' after the NPM reforms. To make their case Hood and Dixon present impressive time series on service performance, robust statistics and graphs, to satisfy the 'evidence hunger' and appetite for numbers of NPM proponents. They conclude that the UK government works slightly worse and costs a bit more after NPM. They claim that after 30 years of administrative reform:

> NPM and associated digital developments over much of UK central government's operations seem to have had little dramatic long-term effects in the area for which the strongest claims were made by both advocates and critics about its likely impacts (i.e. cutting running costs) even if the country often claimed to be the originator of NPM and undoubtedly one of its most enthusiastic cheerleaders.
>
> (Hood and Dixon, 2015, p. 192)

Hood and Dixon argue that NPM does not lead to a complete collapse of trust in public administration and service delivery.

Inter-organisational complexity (see Chapter 14 on horizontal, vertical and global coordination issues) is one key challenge in policy-making processes. The question arises whether NPM reform in general, and performance indicators in particular, tend to reduce or increase coordination difficulties. We have suggested above that performance indicators focusing on the outputs delivered by one single administrative unit might lead to organisational egoism. However, there may also be 'shared performance indicators' that target many departments. The UK Public Service Agreement adopted in 2008 developed such shared performance indicators for both outputs and outcomes. The aim was to foster horizontal coordination of departments through shared objective setting, shared monitoring of progress and shared feedbacks and incentives to improve policy performance. Despite this policy coordination tool, the organisational logic was still dominant:

> The potential for blame diffusion between departments was more significant in cross-departmental targets than single-departmental targets. Departments tended to focus on planning the delivery of single-departmental targets because it was clearer who was to be blamed if policy delivery failed for those targets.
>
> (James and Nakamura, 2015, p. 404)

In sum, the Public Service Agreement system was too weak to incentivise horizontal coordination and was eventually abolished in 2010 by the incoming Conservative–Liberal government. As indicated the combination of a mixture of themes and aspirations with the continuing imperatives of a top-down oriented approach to governance limits the applicability of NPM as something radically different.

Alternative ways of conceptualising NPM have been put forward which recognise the force of the Peters and Waterman (1982) critique of bureaucracy and accept the importance of performance measures as indices to be shared with the public but reject the market orientation of much of the rest of the thinking. This approach tackles the issue of accountability not by the adoption of market devices but by trying to put bottom-up notions of accountability in place of the traditional top-down ones (Hoggett, 1991; Stewart and Clarke, 1987). This is explored in the next section.

Consumer control as an alternative

A good approach to exploring the issue of consumer control is offered by Hirschman's (1970) analysis of the options available to consumers (in both public and private systems) as being 'exit, voice or loyalty'. This approach, which can be seen as related to ideas about the use of 'rational choices' by people, suggests that the exit option is the simplest. But is it easy to use and does it effectively secure accountability to consumers?

A feature of NPM that has been noted is the development of competition within public services, either through competitive arrangements within these or by allowing private providers to offer public services. It is important to note that the exit option depends not just upon the availability of alternatives but also on information about what these alternatives actually offer. Constraints are also imposed by the fact that exit carries 'transaction' costs for consumers (getting appropriate information, negotiating changes and adapting to new arrangements). Market systems are more likely to provide realistic choices at the point at which people start consuming a service – choose a doctor, a hospital or a school, for example – rather than when they are already consuming it. In that sense it is not so much 'exit' options that people have in systems of public choice as 'entry' options. These points are particularly pertinent as far as health and social care services are concerned.

'Voice', the alternative to exit, involves seeking ways to increase 'grassroots' public accountability through forms of participation (e.g. consumers' charters, satisfaction surveys). Perhaps the chief characteristic of this approach has been to seek to establish ways of decentralising decision making to the local government level or below it (particularly where, as in the UK, local authorities are large).

This leads us to an approach to professional accountability that has been widely canvassed, one which offers a combination of political accountability and accountability to consumers by stressing localised 'political' control mechanisms. Thus Lipsky argues for a new approach to professional accountability in which there is more emphasis upon client-based evaluation of their work (Lipsky, 1980, final chapter). Similarly, Wilding (1982) writes of the need to realise 'a new relationship between professions, clients and society' (p. 149), precisely because others have so little control over them. Stewart and Clarke (1987) offer a related approach in terms of the idea of a 'public service' orientation committed to accountability to local citizens' groups.

The main, perhaps rather dismissive, point to make here is that it represents more an aspiration than a properly tried form of accountability. It comes into direct conflict with concerns about territorial justice, which emphasise the need for uniformity of services. It can also be seen as difficult to integrate with concerns about interactions between services – the demand for 'joined-up government' (see Newman, 2001, for an analysis of these tensions in the UK). However, as indicated at the beginning of this chapter, if accountability ultimately means accountability to citizens, then the issues about how to do this other than through representative government are bound to be on the agenda.

Accountability and governance

While academics may dismiss the political preoccupation with top-down accountability, the issue remains very much alive. It has, however, to confront the reality that new approaches to public administration make the issues about control over the policy process much more complicated. Central to this development was, first, the exploration of public policy delivery through private organisations using market mechanisms and public–private partnerships, followed by recognition of the importance of inter-organisational coordination and networks for policy delivery. This is summed up by Pollitt as follows:

> there are two sets of reasons why a simple, single accountor and single accountee model of accountability is an inadequate description of reality. First, many public managers find themselves working in partnerships or contractual relationships, where different parties are accountable for different aspects of a joint activity (multiple accountors). Second, even where a public manager is working within a single institution they will often have several lines of accountability – political, legal, professional, bureaucratic (multiple accountees).
>
> (Pollitt, 2003, p. 94)

These are the more concrete issues within the shift from government to governance explored in Chapter 14 and expressed in wider terms by Hajer and Pierre as leading to a potential for democratic deficit, and requiring therefore the emergence of new modes of participation.

A 'realistic' approach to evaluation and accountability

The title Hogwood and Gunn used for their book on policy analysis, *Policy Analysis for the Real World*, implied a realism absent in some other work. In their concluding section, indeed, they indicate that they are 'interested in the role of policy analysis in the policy process rather than simply the academic study of the policy process' (1984, p. 268). In the first chapter of this book the latter approach was justified in terms of the argument that effective engineering needs to be grounded in a good understanding of physics rather than by drawing a distinction between an academic analysis and an analysis for the real world. In that sense the claim of realism in the heading of this section rests upon the view that those two notions, inevitably particularly important for prescriptive policy analysis – evaluation, concerned with asking what actually happened, and accountability, concerned about who is in control – need to be put in the context of the exploration of the characteristics of the policy process explored in the previous chapters of this book.

The approach adopted in books like Hogwood and Gunn's, defended as equally oriented to assisting those in favour of or against specific policy initiatives (ibid., p. 269), is open nevertheless to the accusation that the key concepts come from ideologically or politically dominant perspectives. Throughout this book the problems in respect of one particular dominant perspective – the stages model or policy cycle – have been emphasised. However, there are alternative problems that have to be faced by any attempt to offer a detached and value-neutral account of the policy process. The physics/engineering distinction does not actually work well for the social sciences, where there is no broadly accepted framework of theory in which law-like propositions and hypotheses can be located. Instead there are contending schools of thought, and there are good reasons for suggesting that social scientists cannot be detached observers of social reality. Moreover the closer one gets to matters of fundamental ideological and political differences the more likely this will be true.

A particularly problematical area for any discussion of the policy process is the fact that some of the most challenging propositions in the field are theories deduced from general assumptions about political activity which have been subjected to little empirical testing, in a discipline in which testing is in any case a difficult activity. This issue was particularly highlighted in the discussion of rational choice theory in Chapter 3. However, whilst that theory is particularly open to challenge inasmuch as it sweeps up a range of difficult explanatory problems using one over-riding assumption – that behaviour is self-interested – there are other theoretical propositions in the book that raise comparable if more limited difficulties (some of the ideas embedded in institutional theory for example).

There are also difficulties arising from the fact that where evidence is available to enable generalisations about the policy process to be advanced this tends to come from studies in a single country, with its own distinctive culture and institutional system. It is then a risky undertaking to offer those generalisations outside the context in which they were developed. For example, it was noted that Kingdon's account of agenda setting which is advanced as generally useful is nevertheless based solely on careful observation in the United States. Similarly it was shown that concerns about the working of federalism in that same country have had a major influence on the development of implementation theory. However, as is indicated in Chapter 6, comparative studies are beginning to address these issues.

Finally, while the objective of emphasising description and explanation rather than prescription was emphasised in Chapter 1 and has been re-emphasised elsewhere, it has been necessary to draw upon policy analysis writings which mix these two, drawing prescriptions from observations or assumptions about the 'real world' as they see it. That brings us back to the subject matter of this chapter, concerned as it is with two questions that are of fundamental importance for prescriptive policy analysis: what happened, and how was control over the policy process exercised? Those then have to be the starting points for the prescriptive questions. All participants are concerned about the issues about 'what happened'. Evaluation questions, in principle, concern us all. The interest in notions like consumer participation in evaluation and the sharing of learning from evaluation (see Taylor and Balloch, 2005) show an aspiration to embrace this perspective. On the other hand much actual evaluation work is embedded in a traditional top-down concern that those with power to influence policy get what they want. A wide rather than a narrow view of policy accountability can operate as a counterweight to that. But the concern here has been to emphasise the way in which accountability is contested. The great virtue of the work of the early top-down theorists, eager to make prescriptions for rational policy making, was that they emphasised issues about purposive action and control over policy processes. Those issues remain important regardless of the stance one takes on who should be in control.

CONCLUSIONS

Evaluation and accountability are inevitably subjects that attract considerable controversy in discussions of public policy. In conformity with this book's concern with examining the policy process, this chapter has tried to avoid taking a stance in the debate about who should be in control and how they should do it. It has noted that the view that, in a system of representative government, the administration of public policy should be hierarchically controlled by elected representatives has dominated the literature. When a traditional top-down view of the system has been challenged, that challenge has involved either the assertion that the complexity of modern governance requires that it should be supplemented by other forms of accountability or efforts to establish alternative 'democratic' legitimacy from a bottom-up perspective.

However, identification of the complexity of accountability has long involved a recognition of forms of legal accountability (normally reinforcing hierarchical political accountability but occasionally challenging it). More complexity has then been added by a recognition of ways in which the elaborate nature of many public activities involves extensive discretionary decision making. Consideration therefore needs to be given to the roles of professional groups and to the way in which forms of co-production occur. An alternative approach to these issues, coming particularly from the 'rational choice' school of thought, suggests that in various respects consumer participation can be enhanced to deal with these issues through market and quasi-market mechanisms providing 'exit' (or as noted above, more realistically 'entry') options. An alternative is to try to strengthen 'voice' at the 'street level'.

All of this adds up to recognising that accountability in modern governance is bound to be complex. It will often be mixed, involving multiple forms of accountability to multiple groups. This has then, as noted, consequent implications for how it is evaluated. In examining these issues, attention needs to be given to the very different ways in which different public policies are made manifest, a theme that has recurred throughout this book.

Many of the key themes in the book as a whole have surfaced again in this chapter. The traditional approach to evaluation and accountability has been seen as part of that consensus about representative government within which

(continued)

the rational model of decision making and the top-down model of implementation also belong. This has been challenged both by an ideological pluralism which sees the need for multiple 'accountabilities' and by those who see networks and complex institutional arrangements as making any simple form of accountability difficult. In the background, and not analysed much in this chapter but emphasised in the early chapters of the book, lies another view – one which sees the structure of power as imposing severe limits on any form of popular accountability.

Throughout the book it has been stressed that there is a need to think about the policy process as a whole, even when analysis requires parts of the process to be separated out. It has also been stressed that it is important to see that the policy process is embedded in the structure of power in society. At the same time there is a need to recognise that it is not easy to generalise about the policy process, inasmuch as different policy issues emerge in different ways in different institutional contexts. The art of policy process analysis needs to involve a capacity to see connections, and to compare and contrast, whilst being sceptical about all-encompassing generalisations.

References

6, P. (2004) 'Joined-up government in the Western world in comparative perspective: A preliminary literature review and exploration', *Journal of Public Administration Research and Theory*, 14(1), pp. 103–38.

Aberbach, J.D., Putman, R.D. and Rockman, B.A. (1981) *Bureaucrats and Politicians in Western Democracies*. Cambridge, MA: Harvard University Press.

Adler, M. (2006) 'Fairness in Context', *Journal of Law and Society*, 33(4), pp. 615–38.

Ainley, P. (2001) 'From a national system locally administered to a national system nationally administered: The new Leviathan in education and training in England', *Journal of Social Policy*, 30(3), pp. 457–76.

Albrow, M. (1970) *Bureaucracy*. London: Pall Mall.

Alden, C. and Aran, A. (2012) *Foreign Policy Analysis*, Abingdon: Routledge.

Aldrich, H.E. (1976) 'Resource dependence and inter-organizational relations: Local employment service offices and social services sector organizations', *Administration and Society*, 7(4), pp. 419–54.

Alford, R. (1975) *Health Care Politics*. Chicago: University of Chicago Press.

Allison, G.T. (1971) *Essence of Decision*. Boston, MA: Little Brown.

Anderfuhren-Biget, S. Varone, F. and Giauque, D. (2014) 'Policy Environment and Public Service Motivation', *Public Administration,* 92(4), pp. 807–25.

Anderweg, R.B. and Irwin, G.A. (2002) *Governance and Politics in the Netherlands*, 2nd edn. Basingstoke: Palgrave Macmillan.

Argyris, C. (1964) *Integrating the Individual and the Organisation*. New York: Wiley.

Armingeon, K. (2011) 'A prematurely announced death?', in Mach, A. and Trampusch, C. (eds) *Switzerland in Europe. Continuity and Change in the Swiss Political Economy*, pp. 165–85. London: Routledge.

Arts, W. and Gelisen, J. (2002) 'Three worlds of welfare capitalism or more?' *Journal of European Social Policy*, 12(2), pp. 137–58.

Ashford, D.E. (1986) *The Emergence of the Welfare States*. Oxford: Blackwell.

Atkinson, A. (2015) *Inequality: What Can Be Done?* Cambridge, MA: Harvard University Press.

Aubin, D. and Varone, F. (2004) 'The evolution of the water regimes in Belgium' in Kissling-Näf, I. and Kuks, S. (eds) *The Evolution of National Water Regimes in Europe. Transition in Water Rights and Water Policies*, pp. 143–85. Dordrecht/Boston/London: Kluwer Academic Publishers.

Auster, R.D. and Silver, M. (1979) *The State as a Firm: Economic Forces in Political Development*. The Hague: Martinus Nijhoff.

Axelrod, R. (1981) 'The Evolution of Cooperation', *Science*, 221(4489), pp. 1390–6.

Axelrod, R. (1984) *The Evolution of Cooperation*. New York: Basic Books.

Axelrod, R. and Keohane, R. (1985) 'Achieving cooperation under anarchy: Strategies and institutions', *World Politics*, 39(1), pp. 226–54.

Bache, I. (2003) 'Governing through governance: Education policy control under New Labour', *Political Studies*, 51(2), pp. 300–14.

Bachrach, P. (1969) *The Theory of Democratic Elitism*. London: University of London Press.

Bachrach, P. and Baratz, M.S. (1962) 'Two faces of power', *American Political Science Review*, 56, pp. 641–51.

Bachrach, P. and Baratz, M.S. (1963) 'Decisions and nondecisions: An analytical framework', *American Political Science Review*, 57, pp. 947–52.

Bachrach, P. and Baratz, M.S. (1970) *Power and Poverty*. New York: Oxford University Press.

Baldwin, P. (1990) *The Politics of Social Solidarity*. Cambridge: Cambridge University Press.

Baldwin, R. (1995) *Rules and Government*. Oxford: Oxford University Press.

Bardach, E. (1977) *The Implementation Game. What Happens after a Bill Becomes a Law*, Cambridge, MA: MIT Press.

Barnard, C. (1938) *The Functions of the Executive*. Cambridge, MA: Harvard University Press.

Barr, J. (2011) *A Line in the Sand: Britain, France and the Struggle for the Mastery of the Middle East*. London: Simon and Schuster.

Barrett, M. (1980) *Women's Oppression Today*. London: Verso.

Barrett, S. and Fudge, C. (eds) (1981) *Policy and Action*. London: Methuen.

Barrett, S. and Hill, M.J. (1981) 'Report to the SSRC Central London: Methuen. Local Government Relations Panel on the "core" or theoretical component of the research on implementation' (unpublished).

Bauer, M.W. and Gaskell, G. (eds) (2002) *Biotechnology: The Making of a Global Controversy*. Cambridge: Cambridge University Press.

Baumgartner, F. and Jones, B. (1993) *Agendas and Instability in American Politics*. Chicago: University of Chicago Press.

Baumgartner, F., Breunig, C., Green-Pedersen, C., Jones, B.D., Mortensen, P.D., Nuytemans, M. and Walgrave, S. (2009) 'Punctuated Equilibrium in Comparative Perspective', *American Journal of Political Science* 53(3), pp. 603–20.

Baumgartner, F., De Boef, S. and Boydstun, A. (2008) *The Decline of the Death Penalty and the Discovery of Innocence*. Cambridge: Cambridge University Press.

Baumgartner, M.P. (1992) 'The myth of discretion', in Hawkins, K. (ed.) *The Uses of Discretion*. Oxford: Clarendon Press.

Beer, S.H. (1965) *Modern British Politics*. London: Faber & Faber.

Beetham, D. (1987) *Bureaucracy*. Milton Keynes: Open University Press.

Béland, D. (2001) 'Does labor matter? Institutions, labor unions and pension reform in France and the United States', *Journal of Public Policy*, 21(2), pp. 153–72.

Béland, D. (2005) 'Ideas and social policy: An institutionalist perspective', *Social Policy and Administration*, 39(1), pp. 1–18.

Béland, D. (2007) 'The social exclusion discourse: ideas and policy change', *Policy and Politics*, 35(1), pp. 123–40.

Bell, D. (1960) *The End of Ideology*. New York: Free Press.

Bemelmans-Videc, M.L., Rist, R. and Vedung, E. (eds) (2003) *Carrots, Sticks, and Sermons. Policy Instruments and their Evaluation*. Herdon, VA: Transaction Publishers.

Benson, J.K. (1975) 'The inter-organizational network as political economy', *Administrative Science Quarterly*, 20(June), pp. 229–49.

Bentley, A.F. (1967) *The Process of Government*. Cambridge, MA: Belknap Press.

Benz, A. and Papadopoulos, Y. (2006) 'Introduction. Governance and democracy: concepts and key issues', in Benz, A. and Papadopoulos, Y. (eds) *Governance and Democracy. Comparing National, European and International Experiences*, pp. 1–26. London: Routledge.

Berger, P.L. and Luckman, T. (1975) *The Social Construction of Reality*. Harmondsworth: Penguin Books.

Bergeron, H. (2013) 'Elements pour une sociologie de l'entrepreneur-frontière', *Revue française de sociologie*, 54(2), pp. 263–302.

Bernauer, T. and Meins, E. (2003) 'Technological revolution meets policy and the market: Explaining cross-national differences in agricultural biotechnology regulation', *European Journal of Political Research*, 42, pp. 643–83.

Bevir, M. (2013) *A Theory of Governance*. Berkeley: University of California Press.

Beyers, J. and Braun, C. (2013) 'Ties that count. Explaining interest group access to policymakers', *Journal of Public Policy*, 34(1), pp. 93–121.

Birkland, T.A. (1998) 'Focusing events, mobilization, and agenda setting', *Journal of Public Policy*, 18(1), pp. 53–74.

Birrell, D. and Gray, A-M. (forthcoming) *Delivering Social Welfare: Governance and Service Provision in the UK*. Bristol: Policy Press.

Blau, P.M. (1955) *The Dynamics of Bureaucracy*. Chicago: University of Chicago Press.

Blom-Hansen, J. (1999) 'Policy-making in central–local government relations: Balancing local autonomy, macroecnomic control and sectoral policy goals', *Journal of Public Policy*, 19(3), pp. 237–64.

Blowers, A. (1984) *Something in the Air: Corporate Power and the Environment*. London: Harper and Row.

Blyth, M. (2002) *Great Transformations: Economic Ideas and Institutional Change in the Twentieth Century*. Cambridge: Cambridge University Press.

Bonoli, G. and Shinkawa, T. (eds) (2005) *Ageing and Pension Reform Around the World*. Cheltenham: Elgar.

Bonvin, J-M. and Moachon, E. (2007) 'The impact of contractualism in social policies: The case of active labour market policies in Switzerland', *International Journal of Sociology and Social Policy*, 27(9–10), pp. 401–12.

Bonvin, J-M. and Moachon, E. (2013) 'The local dimension in labour market policies: Promoting autonomy or enforcing compliance?' in Otto, H.-U and Ziegler, H. (eds) *Enhancing Capabilities: The Role of Social Institutions*, pp. 55–70. Opladen and Farmington Hills: Barbara Budrich.

Booth, T. (1988) *Developing Policy Research*. Aldershot: Avebury.

Bottomore, T.B. (1966) *Elites and Society*. Harmondsworth: Penguin.

Bovens, M. and 't Hart, P. (1996) *Understanding Policy Fiascos*. Brunswick, NJ: Transaction Publishers.

Bovens, M. and Zouridis, S. (2002) 'From street-level to system-level bureaucracies: How information and communication technology is transforming administrative discretion and constitutional control', *Public Administration Review*, 62(2), pp. 174–84.

Bovens, M., 't Hart, P. and Peters, B.G. (eds) (2001) *Success and Failure in Public Governance*. Cheltenham: Edward Elgar.

Bowen, E.R. (1982) 'The Pressman–Wildavsky paradox', *Journal of Public Policy*, 2(1), pp. 1–21.

Bozeman, B. (2000) *Bureaucracy and Red Tape*. Upper Saddle River, NJ: Prentice Hall.

Bradach, J.L. and Eccles, R.G. (1991) 'Price, authority and trust: From ideal types to plural forms', in Thompson, G., Frances, J., Levacic, R. and Mitchell, J. (eds) *Markets, Hierarchies and Networks: The Coordination of Social Life*, pp. 277–92. London: SAGE.

Braverman, H. (1974) *Labor and Monopoly Capital*. New York: Monthly Review Press.

Braybrooke, D. and Lindblom, C.E. (1963) *A Strategy of Decision*. New York: The Free Press.

Brenner, N. (2004) *New State Spaces: Urban Governance and the Rescaling of Statehood*, Oxford: Oxford University Press.

Brittan, S. (1977) *The Economic Consequences of Democracy*. London: Temple Smith.

Brodkin, E.Z. (2011) 'Policy Work: Street-Level Organizations Under New Managerialism', *Journal of Public Administration Research and Theory*, 21(2), pp. 253–77.

Brown, R. (1975) *The Management of Welfare*. Glasgow: Fontana/Collins.

Browne, A. and Wildavsky, A. (1984) 'Should evaluation become implementation', in Pressman, J. and Wildavsky, A., *Implementation*, 3rd edn, pp. 206–31. Berkeley: University of California Press.

Buchanan, J.M. and Tullock, G. (1962) *The Calculus of Consent*. Ann Arbor, MI: University of Michigan Press.

Bull, D. (1980) 'The anti-discretion movement in Britain: Fact or phantom?' *Journal of Social Welfare Law*, pp. 65–83.

Bulmer, M. (ed.) (1987) *Social Science Research and Government*. Cambridge: Cambridge University Press.

Bulmer, S. and Padgett, S. (2004) 'Policy transfer in the European Union: An Institutionalist Perspective', *British Journal of Political Science*, 35, pp. 103–26.

Bulpitt, J. (1983) *Territory and Power in the United Kingdom*. Manchester: Manchester University Press.

Burns, T. and Stalker, G.M. (1961) *The Management of Innovation*. London: Tavistock.

Butcher, T. (2002) *Delivering Welfare*, 2nd edn. Buckingham: Open University Press.

Cairney, P. and Jones, M.D. (2016) 'Kingdon's multiple streams approach: What is the empirical impact of this universal theory', *Policy Studies Journal*, 44(1), pp. 37–58.

Callanan, M. (2011) 'EU decision-making: reinforcing interest group relationships with national governments', *Journal of European Public Policy*, 18(1), pp. 17–34.

Campbell, C. and Wilson, G.K. (1995) *The End of Whitehall: Death of a Paradigm?* Oxford: Blackwell.

Caramani, D. (ed.) (2014) *Comparative Politics* (Third edition). Oxford: Oxford University Press.

Carter, C. and Smith, A. (2008) 'Revitalizing public policy approaches to the EU: 'territorial institutionalism', fisheries and wine' *Journal of European Public Policy*, 15(2), pp. 263–81.

Castles, F.G. (1998) *Comparative Public Policy: Patterns of Post-war Transformation*. Cheltenham: Edward Elgar.

Chadwick, A. (2000) 'Studying political ideas: A public political discourse approach', *Political Studies*, 48, pp. 283–301.

Chaney, C.K. and Saltzstein, G.H. (1998) 'Democratic control and bureaucratic responsiveness: The police and domestic violence', *American Journal of Political Science*, 42(3), pp. 745–68.

Chapman, R.A. (1970) *The Higher Civil Service in Britain*. London: Constable.

Child, J. (1972) 'Organization structure, environment and performance: The role of strategic choice', *Sociology*, 6, pp. 1–22.

Christensen, T., Lagreid, P. and Rykkja, L.H. (2015) 'The challenges of coordination in national security management – the case of the terrorist attack in Norway', *International Review of Administrative Sciences,* 81(2), pp. 352–72.

Christiansen, P.M., Nørgaard, A.S., Rommetvedt, H., Svensson, T., Thesen, G. and Öberg P-O. (2010). 'Varieties of democracy: Interest groups and corporatist committees in Scandinavian policy making', *Voluntas*, 21(1), pp. 22–40.

Clarke, J. and Newman, J. (1997) *The Managerial State: Power, Politics and Ideology in the Remaking of Social Welfare*. London: SAGE.

Clegg, S. (1990) *Modern Organizations*. London: SAGE.

Clegg, S., Courpasson, D. and Phillips, N. (2006) *Power and Organizations*, London: SAGE.

Cline, K.D. (2000) 'Defining the implementation problem: Organizational management versus cooperation', *Journal of Public Administration Research and Theory*, 10(3), pp. 551–71.

Coase, R.H. (1937) 'The nature of the firm', *Economica*, 4, pp. 386–405.

Cobb, R.W. and Elder, C.D. (1983) *Participation in American Politics: The Dynamics of Agenda-Building*. Baltimore: Johns Hopkins University Press.

Cobb, R.W., Ross, J.K. and Ross, M.H. (1976) 'Agenda building as a comparative political process', *American Political Science Review*, 70(1), pp. 126–38.

Cohen, J. and Rogers, J. (1995) *Associations and Democracy*. London: Verso.

Cohen, M.D., March, J.G. and Olsen, J.P. (1972) 'A garbage can model of organizational choice', *Administrative Science Quarterly*, 17, pp. 1–25.

Cohen, R. (1987) *The New Helots: Migrants in the International Division of Labour*. Aldershot: Avebury.

Colebatch, H. and Larmour, P. (1993) *Market, Bureaucracy and Community*. London: Pluto.

Colebatch, H., Hoppe, R. and Noordegraaf, M. (2010) 'The lessons for policy work', in Colebatch, H., Hoppe, R. and Noordegraaf, M. (eds) *Working for Policy*, pp. 227–45. Amsterdam: Amsterdam University Press.

Coleman, A., Checkland, K. and Harrison, S. (2014) 'Local histories and local sensemaking: a case of policy implementation in the English National Heath Service', in Hill, M. (ed.) *Studying Public Policy*, pp. 209–20. Bristol: Policy Press.

Coleman, W.D. (2012) 'Governance and global public policy', in Levi-Faur, D. (ed.) *The Oxford Handbook of Governance*, pp. 673–85. Oxford: Oxford University Press.

Collier, R.B. and Collier, D. (1991) *Shaping the Political Arena: Critical Junctures, the Labour Movement and Regime Dynamics in Latin America*. Princeton, NJ: Princeton University Press.

Cox, R. (1987) *Production, Power and World Order*. New York: Columbia University Press.

Crenson, M.A. (1971) *The Unpolitics of Air Pollution*. Baltimore, MD: Johns Hopkins University Press.

Crosland, C.A.R. (1956) *The Future of Socialism*. London: Cape.

Crossman, R.H.S. (1975, 1976 and 1977) *Diaries of a Cabinet Minister*, (3 volumes). London: Hamish Hamilton and Jonathan Cape.

Crouch, C. (2011) *The Strange Non-Death of Neoliberalism*. Cambridge: Polity.

Crozier, M. (1964) *The bureaucratic phenomenon*. Chicago: Chicago University Press.

Culpepper, P.D. and Reinke, R. (2014) 'Structural power and bank bailouts in the United Kingdom and the United States', *Politics and Society,* 42(4), pp. 427–54.

Cunningham, G. (1963) 'Policy and practice', *Public Administration*, 41, pp. 229–38.

Dahl, R.A. (1957) 'The concept of power', *Behavioural Science*, 2, pp. 201–15.

Dahl, R.A. (1958) 'A critique of the ruling-elite model', *American Political Science Review*, 52, pp. 463–9.

Dahl, R.A. (1961) *Who Governs?* New Haven, CT: Yale University Press.

Dahl, R.A. and Lindblom, C.E. (1953) *Politics, Economics and Welfare*. Chicago: Chicago University Press.

Dallek, R. (2003) *John F. Kennedy: An Unfinished Life*. London: Allen Lane.

Daugbjerg, C. (1998) *Policy networks under pressure: Pollution control, policy reform, and the power of farmers*. Aldershot: Ashgate.

Daugbjerg, C. and Fawcett, P. (2015) 'Metagovernance, network structure, and legitimacy developing a heuristic for comparative governance analysis', *Administration & Society*, DOI: 0095399715581031.

Davies, H.T.O., Nutley, S.M. and Smith, P.C. (eds) (2000) *What Works?* Bristol: Policy Press.

Davis, K.C. (1969) *Discretionary Justice*. Baton Rouge: Louisiana State University Press.

Dawkins, R. (1976) *The Selfish Gene*. Oxford: Oxford University Press.

Day, P. and Klein, R. (1987) *Accountabilities*. London: Tavistock.

De Winter, L., Della Porta, D. and Deschouwer, K. (1996) 'Comparing similar countries: Italy and Belgium', *Res Publica*, 38(2), pp. 215–35.

Deacon, B. (2007) *Global Social Policy and Governance*. London: SAGE

Deacon, B. with Hulse, M. and Stubbs, P. (1997) *Global Social Policy*. London: SAGE.

Deakin, N. and Walsh, K. (1996) 'The enabling state: The role of markets and contracts', *Public Administration*, 74, pp. 33–48.

Dean, M. (2011) *Democracy under Attack: How the Media Distort Policy and Politics*, Bristol: Policy Press.

Dearlove, J. and Saunders, P. (1991) *Introduction to British Politics*. Cambridge: Polity Press.

Degeling, P. (1993) 'Policy as the accomplishment of an implementation structure: Hospital restructuring in Australia', in Hill, M. (ed.) *New Agendas in the Study of the Policy Process*, pp. 25–56. Hemel Hempstead: Harvester Wheatsheaf.

Degeling, P. and Colebatch, H.K. (1984) 'Structure and action as constructs in the practice of public administration', *Australian Journal of Public Administration*, 43(4), pp. 320–31.

Degeling, P., Kennedy, J., Hill, M., Carnegie, M. and Holt, J. (1998) *Professional Sub-Cultures and Hospital Reform*. Centre for Hospital Management and Information Systems Research, University of New South Wales.

Degeling, P., Maxwell, S., Kennedy, J. and Coyle, B. (2003) 'Medicine, management and modernisation: A "danse macabre"?' *British Medical Journal*, 326, pp. 649–52.

Delley, J-D., Derivaz, R., Mader, L., Morand, C-A. and Schneider, D. (1982) *Le droit en action: étude de mise en oeuvre de la loi Furgler*, Saint-Saphorin: Georgi.

Delphy, C. (1984) *Close to Home: A Materialist Analysis of Women's Oppression*. London: Hutchinson.

Derlein, H-U., (1991) 'Bureaucracy in Art and Analysis: Kafka and Weber', *Journal of Kafka Society of America*, 1–2, pp. 4–20.

Dery, D. (1984) *Problem definition in policy analysis*. Lawrence: University Press of Kansas.

Dery, D. (1999) 'Policy by the way: When policy is incidental to making other policies', *Journal of Public Policy*, 18(2), pp. 163–76.

Desrosières, A. (2002) *The Politics of Large Numbers, a History of Statistical Reasoning*, Cambridge, MA: Harvard University Press.

DiMaggio, P.J. and Powell, W. (1983) 'The iron cage revisited: Institutional isomorphism and collective rationality in organizational fields', *American Sociological Review*, 48, pp. 147–60.

DiMaggio, P.J. and Powell, W. (1991). 'Introduction', in Powell, W. and DiMaggio, P.J. (eds) *The New Institutionalism in Organizational Analysis*, pp. 1–38. Chicago: University of Chicago Press.

Doern, G.B. and Phidd, R.W. (1983) *Canadian Public Policy*. Agincourt, Ontario: Methuen.

Dolowitz, D. and Marsh, D. (1996) 'Who learns what from whom: A review of the policy transfer literature', *Political Studies*, 44, pp. 343–57.

Dolowitz, D. and Marsh, D. (2000) 'Learning from abroad: The role of policy transfer in contemporary policy making', *Governance*, 13(1), pp. 5–24.

Dolowitz, D.P., Hulme, R., Nellis, M. and O'Neill, F. (2000) *Policy Transfer and British Social Policy: Learning from the USA?* Buckingham: Open University Press.

Domhoff, G.W. (1978) *The Powers That Be: Processes of Ruling Class Domination in America*. New York: Random House.

Donnison, D.V. (1977) 'Against discretion', *New Society*, 15 September, pp. 534–6.

Dowding, K. (1995) 'Model or metaphor? A critical review of the policy network approach', *Political Studies*, 43, pp. 136–58.

Downing, P.B. and Hanf, K. (eds) (1983) *International Comparisons in Implementing Pollution Laws*. Boston, MA: Kluwer Nijhoff.

Downs, A. (1957) *An Economic Theory of Democracy*. New York: Harper and Row.

Downs, A. (1967) *Inside Bureaucracy*. Boston, MA: Little Brown.

Downs, A. (1972) 'Up and down with ecology – the "issue-attention cycle"', *The Public Interest*, 28, pp. 38–50.

Dryzek, J.S. (1990) *Discursive Democracy*. Cambridge: Cambridge University Press.

Dryzek, J.S. and Dunleavy, P. (2009) *Theories of the Democratic State*. Basingstoke: Palgrave Macmillan.

Dudley, G. and Richardson, J. (1999) 'Competing advocacy coalitions and the process of "frame reflection": a longitudinal study of EU steel policy', *Journal of European Public Policy*, 6(2), pp. 225–48.

Dunleavy, P. (1981) 'Professions and policy change: Notes towards a model of ideological corporatism', *Public Administration Bulletin*, 36, pp. 3–16.

Dunleavy, P. (1985) 'Bureaucrats, budgets and the growth of the state: Reconstructing an instrumental model', *British Journal of Political Science*, 15, pp. 299–328.

Dunleavy, P. (1986) 'Explaining the privatization boom: Public choice versus radical approaches', *Public Administration*, 64(1), pp. 13–34.

Dunleavy, P. (1991) *Democracy, Bureaucracy and Public Choice*. Hemel Hempstead: Harvester Wheatsheaf.

Dunleavy, P. and O'Leary, B. (1987) *Theories of the State*. London: Macmillan.

Dunsire, A. (1978a) *Implementation in a Bureaucracy*. Oxford: Martin Robertson.

Dunsire, A. (1978b) *Control in a Bureaucracy*. Oxford: Martin Robertson.

Dür, A. and Mateo, G. (2012) 'Who lobbies the European Union? National interest groups in a multilevel polity', *Journal of European Public Policy*, 19(7), pp. 969–87.

Durant, J., Bauer, M.W. and Gaskell, G. (eds) (1998) *Biotechnology in the Public Sphere*. London: Science Museum.

Durkheim, E. (ed. Lukes, S.) (1982) *The Rules of Sociological Method and Selected Texts on Sociology and Its Method*. London: Macmillan.

Dworkin, R. (1977) *Taking Rights Seriously*. London: Duckworth.

Dwyer, P. (2010) *Understanding Social Citizenship: Themes and Perspectives for Policy and Practice*. Bristol: Policy Press.

Dyson, K. (1980) *The State Tradition in Western Europe*. Oxford: Martin Robertson.

Eardley, T., Bradshaw, J., Ditch, J., Gough, I. and Whiteford, P. (1996) *Social Assistance in OECD Countries: Synthesis Report*. London: HMSO.

Easton, D. (1953) *The Political System*. New York: Knopf.

Easton, D. (1965a) *A Systems Analysis of Political Life*. New York: Wiley.

Easton, D. (1965b) *A Framework for Political Analysis*. Englewood Cliffs, NJ: Prentice Hall.

Ebbinghaus, B. (ed.) (2011) *The Varieties of Pension Governance: Pension Privatisation in Europe*. Oxford: Oxford University Press.

Edelman, M. (1971) *Politics as Symbolic Action*. Chicago: Markham.

Edelman, M. (1977) *Political Language: Words that Succeed and Policies that Fail*. New York: Institute for the Study of Poverty.

Edelman, M. (1984) *The Symbolic Uses of Politics*. Urbana: University of Illinois Press.

Edelman, M. (1988) *Constructing the Political Spectacle*. Chicago: University of Chicago Press.

Eisenstadt S.N. (1980) 'Cultural orientations, institutional entrepreneurs, and social change: Comparative analysis of traditional civilizations', *American Journal of Sociology*, 85(4), pp. 840–69.

Ellul, J. (1964) *The Technological Society*. New York: Vintage Books.

Elmore, R. (1980) 'Backward mapping: Implementation research and policy decisions', *Political Science Quarterly*, 94, pp. 601–16.

Elster, J. (1983) *Sour Grapes: Studies in the Subversion of Rationality*. Cambridge: Cambridge University Press.

Engeli, I. and Rothmayr Allison, C. (eds) (2014) *Comparative Policy Studies: Conceptual and Methodological Challenges*. Basingstoke: Palgrave Macmillan

Engeli, I. and Varone, F. (2011) 'Governing morality issues through procedural policies', *Swiss Political Science Review*, 17(3), pp. 239–58.

Engeli, I., Green-Pedersen, C. and Larsen, L.T. (eds) (2012) *Morality Politics in Western Europe: Parties, Agenda and Policy Choices*. Basingstoke: Palgrave Macmillan.

Enthoven, A.C. (1985) *Reflections on the Management of the NHS*. London: Nuffield Provincial Hospitals Trust.

Esping-Andersen, G. (1990) *Three Worlds of Welfare Capitalism*. Cambridge: Polity Press.

Ethridge, M.E. and Percy, S.L. (1993) 'A new kind of public policy encounters disappointing results: Implementing learnfare in Wisconsin', *Public Administration Review*, 53(4), pp. 340–7.

Etzioni, A. (1961) *A Comparative Analysis of Complex Organizations*. New York: Free Press.

Etzioni, A. (1969) *The Semi Professions and Their Organization*. New York: Free Press.

Evans, P.B., Rueschemeyer, D. and Skocpol, T. (eds) (1985) *Bringing the State Back in*. Cambridge: Cambridge University Press.

Evans, R.J. (2000) *In Defence of History*. London: Granta.

Evans, T. (2010) *Professional Discretion in Welfare Services*. Aldershot: Ashgate.

Evans, T. (2015) 'Professionals and discretion in street-level bureaucracy' in Hupe, P.L, Hill, M. and Buffat, A. (eds) (2015) *Understanding Street-Level Bureaucracy*, pp. 279–93. Bristol: Policy Press.

Exley, S. (2014) 'Think tanks and policy networks in English education' in Hill, M. (ed.) *Studying Public Policy*, pp. 179–89. Bristol: Policy Press.

Exworthy, M. and Powell, M. (2004) 'Big windows and little windows: implementation in the "congested state"', *Public Administration*, 82(2), pp. 263–81.

Exworthy, M., Berney, L. and Powell, M. (2002) '"How great expectations in Westminster may be dashed locally": The implementation of national policy on health inequalities', *Policy and Politics*, 30(1), pp. 79–96.

Farmer, D.J. (1995) *The Language of Public Administration: Bureaucracy, Modernity and Post-modernity*. Tuscaloosa, AL: University of Alabama Press.

Farnsworth, K. (2007) 'Business, power, policy and politics', in Hodgson, S.M. and Irving, Z. *Policy Reconsidered: Meaning, Politics and Practices*, pp. 1–17. Bristol: Policy Press.

Farr, J., Hacker, J.S. and Kazee, N. (2006) 'The Policy scientist of democracy: the discipline of Harold D. Lasswell', *American Political Science Review*, 100(4), pp. 379–87.

Fayol, H. (1949) *General and Industrial Management*. London: Pitman.

Fearon, J.D. (1991) 'Counterfactuals and hypothesis testing in political science', *World Politics*, 43(2), pp.169–95.

Feeley, M. and Rubin, E.L. (1998) *Judicial Policy Making and the Modern State: How the Courts Reformed America's Prisons*. Cambridge: Cambridge University Press.

Fehr, E. and Gintis, H. (2007) 'Human motivation and social cooperation: Experimental and analytical foundations', *Annual Review of Sociology*, 33, pp. 43–64.

Feldman, M. (1992) 'Social limits to discretion: An organizational perspective', in Hawkins, K. (ed.) *The Uses of Discretion*, pp. 163–83. Oxford: Clarendon Press.

Ferlie, E., Fitzgerald, L., McGivern, G., Dopson, S. and Bennett, C. (2011) 'Public policy networks and wicked problems: a nascent solution', *Public Administration*, 89(2), pp. 307–24.

Ferman, B. (1990) 'When failure is success: Implementation and Madisonian government', in Palumbo, D.J. and Calista, D.J. (eds) *Implementation and the Policy Process: Opening Up the Black Box*, pp. 39–50. New York: Greenwood Press.

Fernándes, J-L., Kendall, J., Davey, V. and Knapp, M. (2007) 'Direct payments in England: Factors linked to variations in local provision', *Journal of Social Policy*, 36(1), pp. 97–122.

Ferragina, E. and Seeleib-Kaiser, M. (2011) 'Welfare regime debate: Past, present and futures?', *Policy and Politics*, 39(4), 583–612.

Fischer, F. (2003) *Reframing Public Policy*. Oxford: Oxford University Press.

Fischer, F. (2006) *Evaluating Public Policy*. Mason, OH: Thomson Wadsworth.

Fischer, M. and Sciarini, P. (2013) 'Europeanization and the inclusive strategies of executive actors' *Journal of European Public Policy*, 20(10), pp. 1482–98.

Flynn, R. (1993) 'Coping with cutbacks and managing retrenchment in health', *Journal of Social Policy*, 20(2), pp. 215–36.

Foldy, E.G. and Buckley, T.R. (2009) 'Re-creating street-level practice: The role of routines, work groups and team learning', *Journal of Public Administration Research and Theory*, 20, pp. 23–52.

Foucault, M. (1980) *Power/Knowledge: Selected Interviews and Other Writings, 1972–77*. Brighton: Harvester.

Fox, A. (1974) *Beyond Contract: Work, Power and Trust Relations*. London: Faber.

Fox, C.J. and Miller, H.T. (1995) *Postmodern Public Administration: Toward Discourse*. Thousand Oaks, CA: SAGE.

François, P. and Vlassopoulos, M. (2008) 'Pro-social motivation and the delivery of social services', *Economic Studies*, 54(1), pp. 22–54.

Frederickson, H.G. and Smith, K.B. (2003) *The Public Adminstration Theory Primer*. Boulder, CO: Westview Press.

Freeman, G.P. (1985). 'National policy styles and policy sectors: Explaining structured variations', *Journal of Public Policy*, 5(4), pp. 467–96.

Friedman, T.L. (1999) *The Lexus and the Olive Tree: Understanding Globalisation*. New York: Farrar, Straus and Giroux.

Friedrich, C.J. (1940) 'The nature of administrative responsibility', *Public Policy*, 1, pp. 3–24.

Friedson, E. (1970) *Professional Dominance*. New York: Atherton.

Friend, J.K., Power, J.M. and Yewlett, C.J.L. (1974) *Public Planning: The Inter-Corporate Dimension*. London: Tavistock.

Fukuyama, F. (1992) *The End of History and the Last Man*. New York: Free Press.

Fukuyama, F. (2011) *The Origins of Political Order: From Prehuman Times to the French Revolution*. New York: Farrar, Straus and Giroux.

Fukuyama, F. (2014) *Political Order and Political Decay: From the Industrial Revolution to the Globalization of Democracy*. New York: Farrar, Straus and Giroux

Gains, F. and Stoker, G. (2011) 'Special advisers and the transmission of ideas from the policy primeval soup', *Policy and Politics*, 39(4), pp. 485–98.

Galbraith, J. K. (1963) *American Capitalism*, Penguin Edition. Harmondsworth: Penguin Books.

Galligan, D.J. (1986) *Discretionary Powers*. Oxford: Clarendon Press.

Gamble, A. (1994) *The Free Economy and the Strong State*, 2nd edn. Basingstoke: Macmillan.

Gamble, A. (2009) *The Spectre at the Feast*. Basingstoke: Palgrave Macmillan.

Gaskell, G. and Bauer, M.W. (eds) (2001) *Biotechnology 1996–2000: The Years of Controversy*. London: NMSI Trading Ltd.

Gava, R. (2014) *Trusting Bankers: Continuity and Change in Swiss Banking Policy*, PhD Thesis, University of Geneva (SES 832).

Gaventa, J. (1980) *Power and Powerlessness: Quiescence and Rebellion in an Appalachian Valley*. Oxford: Clarendon Press.

George, V. and Wilding, P. (2002) *Globalisation and Human Welfare*. Basingstoke: Palgrave.

Giauque, D. (2013) 'L'administration publique fédérale Suisse en comparaison internationale: à la recherche d'une tradition administrative', in Ladner, A., Chappelet, J-L., Emery, Y., Knoepfel, P., Mader, L., Soguel, N. and Varone, F. (eds) *Manuel d'administration publique suisse*, pp. 31–45. Lausanne: Presses polytechniques et universitaires romandes.

Giauque, D., Ritz, A., Varone, F. and Anderfuhren-Biget, S. (2012) 'Resigned but satisfied: the negative impact of public service motivation and red tape on work satisfaction', *Public Administration*, 90(1), pp. 175–93.

Giddens, A. (1976) *New Rules of Sociological Method*. London: Hutchinson.

Giddens, A. (1984) *The Constitution of Society*. Cambridge: Polity Press.

Gilardi, F. (2008) *Delegation in the Regulatory State: Independent Regulatory Agencies in Western Europe*. Cheltenham: Edward Elgar.

Gilardi, F. (2014) 'Methods for the analysis of policy interdependence', in Engeli, I. and Rothmayr Allison, C. (eds) *Comparative Policy Studies: Conceptual and Methodological Challenges*, pp. 185–204. Basingstoke: Palgrave Macmillan.

Gilbert, B.B. (1966) *The Evolution of National Insurance in Great Britain*. London: Michael Joseph.

Glennerster, H., Power, A. and Travers, T. (1991) 'A new era for social policy: A new Enlightenment or a new Leviathan?' *Journal of Social Policy*, 20(3), pp. 389–414.

Goggin, M.L., Bowman, A.O'M., Lester, J.P. and O'Toole, L.J., Jr. (1990) *Implementation Theory and Practice: Toward a Third Generation*. Glenview: Scott Foresman/Little, Brown.

Goodin, R.E. (1996) *The Theory of Institutional Design*. Cambridge: Cambridge University Press.

Gordon, I., Lewis, J. and Young, K. (1977) 'Perspectives on policy analysis', *Public Administration Bulletin*, 25, pp. 26–30.

Gough, I. (1979) *The Political Economy of the Welfare State*. London: Macmillan.

Gouldner, A.W. (1954) *Patterns of Industrial Bureaucracy*. Glencoe, IL: Free Press.

Gouldner, A.W. (1957–58) 'Cosmopolitans and locals: Towards an analysis of latent social roles', *Administrative Science Quarterly*, 2, pp. 281–306 and 444–80.

Granovetter, M.S. (1973) 'The strength of weak ties', *American Journal of Sociology*, 78(6), pp. 1360–80.

Grant, A. (2008) 'Does intrinsic motivation fuel the prosocial fire? Motivational synergy in predicting persistence, performance, and productivity', *Journal of Applied Psychology*, 93(1), p. 48.

Grant, W.P. (1989) *Pressure Groups, Politics and Democracy in Britain*. London: Phillip Allan.

Gray, P.D. and 't Hart, P. (eds) (1998) *Public Policy Disasters in Europe*. London: Routledge.

Green, D.P. and Shapiro, I. (1994) *Pathologies of Rational Choice Theory*. New Haven, CT: Yale University Press.

Green-Pedersen, C. and Walgrave, S. (eds) (2014) *Agenda Setting, Policies, and Political Systems: A Comparative Approach*. Chicago: University of Chicago Press.

Greenwood, E. (1957) 'Attributes of a profession', *Social Work*, 2, pp. 45–55.

Greenwood, R., Hinings, C.R. and Ranson, S. (1975) 'Contingency theory and the organisation of local authorities: Part one. Differentiation and integration', *Public Administration*, 53, pp. 1–24.

Gregory, R. (2003) 'Accountability in modern government', in Peters, B.G. and Pierre, J. (eds) *Handbook of Public Administration*, pp. 557–68. London: SAGE.

Grimshaw, R. and Jefferson, T. (1987) *Interpreting Policework: Policy and Practice in Forms of Beat Policing*. London: Allen & Unwin.

Gulick, L. (1937) 'Notes on the theory of organization, with special reference to government', in Gulick, L. and Urwick, L. (eds) *Papers on the Science of the Organization*, pp. 1–46. New York: Columbia University Press.

Gunn, L. (1978) 'Why is implementation so difficult?' *Management Services in Government*, 33, pp. 169–76.

Gusfield, J.R. (1981). *The Culture of Public Problems: Drinking-Driving and the Symbolic Order*. Chicago: University of Chicago Press.

Haas, P. (2004) 'When does power listen to truth? A constructivist approach to the policy process', *Journal of European Public Policy*, 11(4), pp. 569–92.

Habermas, J. (1987) *The Theory of Communicative Action*. Cambridge: Polity Press.

Hacker, J.S. and Pierson, P. (2002) 'Business power and social policy: Employers and the formation of the American welfare state', *Politics and Society*, 30(2), pp. 277–325.

Hacker, J.S. and Pierson, P. (2010) *Winner-Take-All Politics*. New York: Simon and Schuster.

Haider-Markel, D.P. and Meier, K.J. (1996) 'The politics of gay and lesbian rights: Expanding the scope of conflict', *The Journal of Politics*, 58(2), pp. 332–49.

Hajer, M. (2003) 'Policy without polity? Policy Analysis and the institutional void', *Policy Sciences*, 36, pp. 175–95.

Hall, P.A. (1986) *Governing the Economy: The Politics of State Intervention in Britain and France*. Cambridge: Polity Press.

Hall, P.A. (ed.) (1989) *The Political Power of Economic Ideas: Keynesianism across Nations*. Princeton: Princeton University Press.

Hall, P.A. (1993) 'Policy paradigms, social learning and the state: The case of economic policy making in Britain', *Comparative Politics*, 25, pp. 275–96.

Hall, P.A. and Soskice, D. (2001) *Varieties of Capitalism: The Institutional Foundations of Comparative Advantage*. Oxford: Oxford University Press.

Hall, P.A. and Taylor, R.C.R. (1996) 'Political science and the three new institutionalisms', *Political Studies*, 44(5), pp. 936–57.

Hallin, D.C. and Mancini, P. (2004) *Comparing Media Systems: Three Models of Media and Politics*. Cambridge: Cambridge University Press.

Ham, C. (1992) *Health Policy in Britain*, 3rd ed. London: Macmillan.

Ham, C. and Hill, M.J. (1984) *The Policy Process in the Modern Capitalist State*. Hemel Hempstead: Harvester Wheatsheaf.

Hanf, K. (1993) 'Enforcing environmental laws: The social regulation of co-production', in Hill, M. (ed.) *New Agendas in the Study of the Policy Process*, pp. 88–109. Hemel Hempstead: Harvester Wheatsheaf.

Hanneman, R. and Riddle, M. (2005) *Introduction to Social Network Methods*. Riverside, CA: University of California, Riverside (published in digital form at http://faculty.ucr.edu/~hanneman/).

Hardin, G. (1968) 'The tragedy of the commons', *Science*, 162, pp. 1243–8.

Hargrove, E.C. (1975) *The Missing Link*. Washington, DC: The Urban Institute.

Harrison, S. (2015) 'Street-level bureuacracy and professionalsim in health services' in Hupe, P.L, Hill, M. and Buffat, A. (eds) (2015) *Understanding Street-Level Bureaucracy*, pp. 61–78. Bristol: Policy Press.

Harrison, S. and McDonald, R. (2008) *The Politics of Health Care in Britain*. London: SAGE.

Harrison, S. and Pollitt, C. (1994) *Controlling Health Professionals*. Buckingham: Open University Press.

Harrison, S., Hunter, D.J. and Pollitt, C. (1990) *The Dynamics of British Health Policy*. London: Unwin Hyman.

Hasenfeld, Y. and Steinmetz, D. (1981) 'Client–official encounters in social service agencies', in Goodsell, C.T. (ed.) *The Public Encounter*, pp. 83–101. Bloomington: Indiana University Press.

Hawkins, K. (1984) *Environment and Enforcement*. Oxford: Clarendon Press.

Hay, C. (2002) *Political Analysis: A Critical Introduction*. Basingstoke: Palgrave.

Hay, C. (2004) 'Theory, stylized heuristic or fulfilling prophecy? The status of rational choice theory in public adminstration', *Public Administration*, 82(1), pp. 39–61.

Hayek, F.A. (1944) *The Road to Serfdom*. London: Routledge and Kegan Paul.

Hayek, F.A. (1960) *The Constitution of Liberty*. London: Routledge and Kegan Paul.

Haynes, P. (2003) *Managing Complexity in the Public Services*. Maidenhead: Open University Press.

Hayward, J. and Menon, A. (eds) (2003) *Governing Europe*. Oxford: Oxford University Press.

Head, B.J. and Alford, J. (2008) 'Wicked problems: Implications for policy and management', paper delivered to the Australasian Political Studies Association Conference.

Heclo, H. (1972) 'Review article: Policy analysis', *British Journal of Political Science*, 2, pp. 83–108.

Heclo, H. (1974) *Modern Social Politics in Britain and Sweden*. New Haven, CT: Yale University Press.

Heclo, H. and Wildavsky, A. (1981) *The Private Government of Public Money*. London: Macmillan.

Heidenheimer, A.J., Heclo, H. and Adams, C.T. (1990) *Comparative Public Policy*. New York: St. Martin's Press.

Herzberg, F. (1966) *Work and the Nature of Man*. New York: Staples Press.

Hilgartner, S. and Bosk, C.L. (1988) 'The rise and fall of social problems: A public arenas model', *American Journal of Sociology*, 94(1), pp. 53–78.

Hill, M. (1969) 'The exercise of discretion in the National Assistance Board', *Public Administration*, 47, pp. 75–90.

Hill, M. (1972) *The Sociology of Public Administration*. London: Weidenfeld & Nicolson.

Hill, M. (ed.) (1993) *New Agendas in the Study of the Policy Process*. Hemel Hempstead: Harvester Wheatsheaf.

Hill, M. (2006) *Social Policy in the Modern World*. Oxford: Blackwell.

Hill, M. (2007) *Pensions*. Bristol: Policy Press.

Hill, M. and Hupe, P. (2003) 'The multi-layer problem in implementation research', *Public Management Review*, 5(4), pp. 471–90.

Hill, M. and Hupe, P. (2006) 'Analysing policy processes as multiple governance: Accountability in social policy', *Policy and Politics*, 34(3), pp. 557–73.

Hill, M. and Hupe, P. (2014) *Implementing Public Policy*. Third Edition. London: SAGE.

Hill, M., Aaronovitch, S. and Baldock, D. (1989) 'Non-decision making in pollution control in Britain: Nitrate pollution, the EEC Drinking Water Directive and agriculture', *Policy and Politics*, 17(3), pp. 227–40.

Hills, J. and Stewart, K. (2005) *A More Equal Society?* Bristol: Policy Press.

Hindmoor, A. (2006) *Rational Choice*. Basingstoke: Palgrave Macmillan.

Hirschman, A.O. (1970) *Exit, Voice and Loyalty*. Cambridge, MA: Harvard University Press.

Hirst, P. and Thompson, G. (1992) 'The problem of "globalisation": International economic relations, national economic management and the formation of trading blocs', *Economy and Society*, 21(4), pp. 355–96.

Hjern, B. and Hull, C. (1982) 'implementation research as empirical constitutionalism', in Hjern, B. and Hull, C. (eds) *Implementation Beyond Hierarchy*. Special issue of *European Journal of Political Research*, pp. 105–15.

Hjern, B. and Porter, D.O. (1981) 'Implementation structures: A new unit of administrative analysis'. *Organisational Studies*, 2, pp. 211–27.

Hobsbaum, E.J. (1997) *On History*. London: Weidenfeld and Nicolson.

Hodgson, S.M. and Irving, Z. (2007) *Policy Reconsidered: Meaning, Politics and Practices*. Bristol: Policy Press.

Hofferbert, R. (1974) *The Study of Public Policy*. Indianapolis: Bobbs Merrill.

Hofferbert, R.I. and Budge, I. (1992) 'The party mandate and the Westminster model: Election programmes and government spending in Britain, 1948–1985', *Political Studies,* 53, pp. 379–402.

Hoggett, P. (1991) 'A new management for the public sector?' *Policy and Politics*, 19, pp. 143–56.

Hoggett, P. (1996) 'New modes of control in the public service', *Public Administration*, 74(1), pp. 9–32.

Hogwood, B. (1987) *From Crisis to Complacency? Shaping Public Policy in Britain*. London: Oxford University Press.

Hogwood, B.W. and Gunn, L. (1981) *The Policy Orientation*. University of Strathclyde: Centre for the Study of Public Policy.

Hogwood, B.W. and Gunn, L. (1984) *Policy Analysis for the Real World*. London: Oxford University Press.

Hogwood, B.W. and Peters, B.G. (1983) *Policy Dynamics*. Brighton: Harvester.

Holdaway, S. (1983) *Inside the British Police: A Force at Work*. Oxford: Blackwell.

Holzinger, K. and Knill, C. (2005) 'Causes and conditions of cross-national policy convergence', *Journal of European Public Policy*, 12(5), pp. 775–96.

Hood, C. (1976) *The Limits of Administration*. Chichester: Wiley.

Hood, C. (1986) *The Tools of Government*. Chatham, NJ: Chatham House.

Hood, C. (1991) 'A public management for all seasons'. *Public Adminstration,* 69(1), pp. 3–19.

Hood, C. (1995) 'Contemporary public management: A new global paradigm?' *Public Policy and Administration*, 10(2), pp. 104–17.

Hood, C. (1999) *The Art of the State*. Oxford: Clarendon Press.

Hood, C. (2007) 'Intellectual obsolescence and intellectual makeovers: Reflections on the tools of government after two decades', *Governance,* 20(1) pp. 127–44.

Hood, C. and Bevan, G. (2006) 'What's measured is what matters: Targets and gaming in the English public health care system', *Public Administration,* 84(3), pp. 517–38.

Hood, C. and Dixon, R. (2015) *A Government that Worked Better and Cost Less?* Oxford: Oxford University Press.

Hooghe, L. and Marks, G. (2003) 'Unraveling the central state, but how? Types of multi-level governance', *American Political Science Review,* 97(2), pp. 233–43.

Hoppe, R. (1999) 'Policy analysis, science and politics: from "speaking truth to power" to "making sense together"', *Science and Public Policy*, 26(3) pp 201–10

Hoppe, R. (2010) *The Governance of Problems*. Bristol: Policy Press.

Horn, M. (1995) *The Political Economy of Public Administration*. Cambridge: Cambridge University Press.

Horowitz, D. (1977) *The Courts and Social Policy*. Washington: The Brookings Institution.

Howlett, M. (1991) 'Policy instruments, policy styles and policy implementation: National approaches to theories of instrument choice', *Policy Studies Journal*, 19(2), pp. 1–21.

Howlett, M. (2009) 'Process sequencing policy dynamics', *Journal of Public Policy*, 29(3), pp. 241–62.

Howlett, M. and Cashore, B. (2014) 'Conceptualizing public policy' in Engeli, E. and Rothmayr Allison, C. (eds) *Comparative Policy Studies: Conceptual and Methodological Challenges*, pp. 17–33. Basingstoke: Palgrave Macmillan.

Howlett, M. and Migone, A. (2011) 'Charles Lindblom is alive and well and living in punctuated equilibrium land', *Policy and Society*, 30, pp. 53–62.

Howlett, M. and Ramesh, M. (2002) 'The policy effects of internationalization: A subsystem adjustment analysis of policy change', *Journal of Comparative Public Policy: Research and Practice*, 4(1), pp. 31–50.

Howlett, M. and Ramesh, M. (2003) *Studying Public Policy*, 2nd edn. Don Mills, Ontario: Oxford University Press.

Huber, J.D. and Shipan, C.R. (2002) *Deliberate Discretion? The Institutional Foundations of Bureaucratic Autonomy*. Cambridge: Cambridge University Press.

Hudson, B. (1987) 'Collaboration in social welfare: A framework for analysis', *Policy and Politics*, 15(3), pp. 175–82.

Hudson, J. and Lowe, S. (2004) *Understanding the Policy Process*. Bristol: Policy Press.

Hudson, J., Lowe, S., Oscroft, N. and Snell, C. (2007) 'Activating policy networks: A case study of local environmental policy-making in the United Kingdom', *Policy Studies*, 28(1), pp. 55–70.

Hunter, F. (1953) *Community Power Structure*. Chapel Hill, NC: University of North Carolina Press.

Hupe, P.L. (2013) 'Dimensions of discretion: Specifying the object of street-level bureaucracy research.' *DMS – Der Moderne Staat: Zeitschrift für Public Policy, Recht und Management*, 6(2), pp. 425–40.

Hupe, P.L. (2014) 'What happens on the ground: Persistent issues in implementation research', *Public Policy and Administration*, 29(2), pp. 164–82.

Hupe, P.L, Hill, M. and Buffat, A. (eds) (2015) *Understanding Street-Level Bureaucracy*. Bristol: Policy Press.

Huxham, C. and Macdonald, D. (1992) 'Introducing collaborative advantage', *Management Decision*, 30(3), pp. 50–6.

Illich, I. (1977) *Limits to Medicine*. Harmondsworth: Penguin.

Immergut, E.M. (1992) 'The rules of the game: The logic of health policy-making in France, Switzerland and Sweden', in Steinmo, S., Thelen, K. and Longstreth, F. (eds) *Structuring Politics: Historical Institutionalism in Comparative Analysis*, pp. 57–89. Cambridge: Cambridge University Press.

Immergut, E.M. (1993) *Health Policy, Interests and Institutions in Western Europe*. Cambridge: Cambridge University Press.

Ingold, K. and Varone, F. (2012) 'Treating policy brokers seriously: Evidence from the climate policy', *Journal of Public Administration Research and Theory*, 22(2), pp. 319–42.

Ingram, H., deLeon, P. and Schneider, A. (2016) 'Public policy theory and democracy: The elephant in the corner', in Peters, G.B. and Zittoun P. (eds) *Contemporary Approaches to Public Policy*, pp. 175–200. Basingstoke: Palgrave.

Jacques, E. (1967) *Equitable Payment*. Harmondsworth: Penguin.

James, O. and Lodge, M. (2003) 'The limitations of "policy transfer" and "lesson drawing" for public policy research', *Political Studies Review*, 1(2), pp. 179–93.

James, O. and Nakamura, A. (2015) 'Shared performance targets for the horizontal coordination of public organizations: Control theory and departmentalism in the United Kingdom's Public Service Agreement system', *International Review of Administrative Sciences*, 81(2), pp. 392–411.

Jenkins, R. (2007) 'The meaning of policy/policy as meaning', in Hodgson, S.M. and Irving, Z. *Policy Reconsidered: Meaning, Politics and Practices*, pp. 21–36. Bristol: Policy Press.

Jenkins, W.I. (1978) *Policy Analysis*. London: Martin Robertson.

Jensen, M. and Meckling, W. (1976) 'Theory of the firm: Managerial behavior, agency costs and ownership structure', *Journal of Financial Economics*, 3(4), pp. 305–60.

Jewell, C.J. (2007) *Agents of the Welfare State*. New York and Basingstoke: Palgrave Macmillan.

Jochim, A.E. and May, P.J. (2010) 'Beyond subsystems: Policy regimes and governance', *Policy Studies Journal*, 38(2), pp. 303–27.

Johansen, L.N. and Kristensen O.P. (1982) 'Corporatist traits in Denmark 1946–76' in Lehmbruch, G. and Schmitter, P. (eds) *Consequences of Corporatist Policy-Making*, pp. 189–218. London: SAGE.

John, P. (1998) *Analysing Public Policy*. London: Pinter.

John, P. (2001) *Local Government in Western Europe*. London: SAGE.

John, P., Bertelli, A. and Jennings, W. (2013) *Policy Agendas in British Politics*, Houndmills: Palgrave Macmillan.

Johnson, T.J. (1972) *Professions and Power*. London: Macmillan.

Jones, B.D. (2015) 'Agenda setting, punctuated equilibrium, and issue-attention: The evolution of the study of pre-decisional processes', Paper presented at the *Roundtable Panel Public Policy Studies: Origin and Evolution of the Field*, The International Conference on Public Policy, Milan, July 3, 2015.

Jones, B.D. and Baumgartner, F.R. (2005) *The Politics of Attention*. Chicago: University of Chicago Press.

Jones, B.D., Baumgartner, F.R., Breunig, C., Wlezien, C., Soroka, S., Foucault, M., François, A., Green-Pedersen, C., Koski, C., John, P., Mortensen, P.B., Varone, F. and Walgrave, S. (2009) 'A general empirical law of public budgets: A comparative analysis', *American Journal of Political Science*, 53(4), pp. 855–73.

Jones, M.D. (2014) 'Communicating climate change: Are stories better than "just the facts"?', *Policy Studies Journal*, 42(4), pp. 644–73.

Jones, M.D., McBeth, M.K. and Shanahan, E.A. (2014) 'Introducing the narrative policy framework', in Jones, M.D., Shanahan, E.A. and McBeth, M.K. (eds) *The Science of Stories: Applications of the Narrative Policy Framework in Public Policy Analysis*, pp. 1–25. New York: Palgrave Macmillan.

Jones, O. (2014) *The Establishment*. London: Allen Lane.

Jones, P. and Cullis, J. (2003) 'Key parameters in policy design: The case of intrinsic motivation', *Journal of Social Policy*, 32(4), pp. 527–48.

Jordan, A. (1997) 'Overcoming the divide between comparative politics and international relations approaches to the EC: What role for "post-decisional politics"?' *West European Politics*, 20(4), pp. 43–70.

Jordan, A. (2001) 'The European Union: An evolving system of multi-level governance . . . or government?' *Policy and Politics*, 29(2), pp. 193–208.

Jordan, A.G. (1986) 'Iron triangles, woolly corporatism and elastic nets: Images of the policy process', *Journal of Public Policy*, 1, pp. 95–123.

Jordan, A.G. and Richardson, J.J. (1987) *British Politics and the Policy Process*. London: Unwin Hyman.

Jordana, J., Levi-Faur, D. and Fernandez i Marin, X. (2011) 'The global diffusion of regulatory agencies: Channels of transfer and stages of diffusion', *Comparative Political Studies*, 44(10), pp. 1343–969.

Jørgensen, T.B. (2012) 'Weber and Kafka: The rational and the enigmatic bureaucracy', *Public Administration*, 90(1), pp. 194–210.

Jowell, J. (1973) 'The legal control of administrative discretion', *Public Law*, pp. 178–220.

Katzenstein, P.J. (1985) *Small States in World Markets*. Ithaca: Cornell University Press.

Katzenstein, P.J. (2003) 'Small states in world markets revisited', *New Political Economy*, 8(1), pp. 9–30.

Katznelson, I. (2013) *Fear Itself: The New Deal and the Origins of Our Time*. New York: Liveright.

Kavanagh, G. and Richards, D. (2001) 'Departmentalism and joined-up government: Back to the future', *Parliamentary Affairs*, 64(1), pp. 1–18.

Kay, A. (2011) 'UK monetary policy change during the financial crisis: Paradigms, spillovers and goal co-ordination', *Journal of Public Policy*, 31(2), pp. 143–61.

Kearns, K.P. (2003) 'Accountability in a seamless economy', in Peters, B.G. and Pierre, J. (eds) *Handbook of Public Administration*, pp. 581–9. London: SAGE.

Kelemen, R.D. (2011) *Eurolegalism. The Transformation of Law and regulation in the European Union*. Cambridge, MA: Harvard University Press.

Kelsey, J. (1995) *The New Zealand Experiment*. Auckland: Auckland University Press.

Keman, H. (2000) 'Federalism and policy performance' in Wachendorfer-Schmidt, U. (ed.) *Federalism and Political Performance*, pp. 196–227. London: Routledge.

Kennedy, I. (1981) *The Unmasking of Medicine*. London: Allen & Unwin.

Kerr, C. (1973) *Industrialism and Industrial Man*. Harmondsworth: Penguin Books.

Kettl, D.F. (1997) 'The global revolution in public management: Driving themes, missing links', *Journal of Policy Analysis and Management,* 16(3), pp. 446–62.

Kickert, W.J.M. (1995) 'Steering at a distance: A new paradigm of public governance in Dutch higher education', *Governance*, 8(1), pp. 135–57.

Kickert, W.J.M. and van Vucht, F.A. (eds) (1995) *Public Policy and Administration Sciences in the Netherlands*. Hemel Hempstead: Harvester Wheatsheaf.

Kickert, W.J.M., Klijn, E.H. and Koppenjan, J.F.M. (eds) (1997) *Managing Complex Networks: Strategies for the Public Sector*. London: SAGE.

King, A. (2007) *The British Constitution*. Oxford: Oxford University Press.

King, A. and Crewe, I. (2013) *The Blunders of Our Governments*. London: One World.

Kingdon, J.W. (1995) *Agendas, Alternatives and Public Policies*. New York: Addison, Wesley, Longman.

Kingsley, J.D. (1944) *Representative Bureaucracy*. Yellow Springs, OH: Antioch Press.

Kisby, B. (2007) 'Analysing policy networks: Towards an ideational approach', *Policy Studies*, 28(1), pp. 71–90. Taylor & Francis Ltd, www.tandfonline.com. Reprinted by permission of the publisher.

Kiser, L.L. and Ostrom, E. (1982) 'The three worlds of action: A metatheoretical synthesis of institutional approaches', in Ostrom, E. (ed.) *Strategies of Political Inquiry*, pp. 179–222. Beverly Hills, CA: SAGE.

Klijn, E-H. and Skelcher, C. (2007) 'Democracy and governance networks. Compatible or not?', *Public Administration*, 85, pp. 587–608.

Klijn, E-H., Steijn, B. and Edelenbos, J. (2010) 'The impact of network management on outcomes of governance networks', *Public Administration*, 88, pp. 1063–82.

Klingemann, H., Hofferbert, R. and Budge, I. (1994) *Parties, Policies and Democracy*. Oxford: Westview Press.

Knapp, A. and Wright, M. (2001) *The Government and Politics of France*, 4th edn. London: Routledge.

Knill, C. and Lenschow, A. (1998) 'Coping with Europe: The impact of British and German administrations on the implementation of EU environmental policy', *Journal of European Public Policy*, 5(4), pp. 595–614.

Knoepfel, P. and Weidner, H. (1982) 'Formulation and implementation of air quality control programmes: Patterns of interest consideration', *Policy and Politics*, 10(1), pp. 85–109.

Knoepfel, P., Larrue, C. and Varone, F. (2006) *Analyse et pilotage des politiques publiques*. Chur: Verlag Ruegger.

Knoepfel, P., Larrue, C., Varone, F. and Hill, M. (2007) *Public Policy Analysis*. Bristol: Policy Press.

Knoke, D. (1990) *Policy Networks: The Structural Perspective*. Cambridge: Cambridge University Press.

Kochan, T.A. (1975) 'Determinants of power boundary units in an interorganizational bargaining relation', *Administrative Science Quarterly*, 20, pp. 435–52.

Kodate, N. (2014) 'Focusing events, priority problems and governance arrangements: regulatory reforms in the health and eldercare sector in Sweden and Japan', in Hill, M. (ed.) *Studying Public Policy*, pp. 101–14. Bristol: Policy Press.

Koelble, T.A. (1995) 'The new institutionalism in political science and sociology', *Comparative Politics*, 27(2), pp. 231–43.

Kooiman, J. (1999) 'Social-political governance: Overview, reflections and design', *Public Management*, 1(1), pp. 67–92.

Koppenjan, J. and Klijn, E-H. (2004) *Managing Uncertainties in Networks*. London: Routledge.

Koppenjan, J., Kars, M., and van der Voort, H. (2009) 'Vertical politics in horizontal policy networks: Framework setting as coupling arrangement', *Policy Studies Journal*, 37(4), pp. 769–92.

Krane, D. (2001) 'Disorderly progress on the frontiers of policy evaluation', *International Journal of Public Administration*, 24(1), pp. 95–123.

Krasner, S. (1984) 'Approaches to the state: Alternative conceptions and historical dynamics', *Comparative Politics*, 16, pp. 223–46.

Kriesi, H. (1980) *Entscheidungsstrukturen und Entscheidungsprozesse in der Schweizer Politik*. Frankfurt: Campus Verlag.

Kristof, A.L. (1996) 'Person-organization fit: An integrative review of its conceptualizations, measurement, and implications', *Personel Psychology*, 49(1), pp. 1–49.

Kübler, D. (2001) 'Understanding policy change with the advocacy coalition framework: An application to Swiss drug policy', *Journal of European Public Policy*, 8(4), pp. 623–41.

Kuhlmann, S. and Wollmann, H. (2014) *Introduction to Comparative Public Administration*. Cheltenham: Edward Elgar.

Kuhn, R. (2007) 'Media management', in Seldon, A. (ed.) *Blair's Britain*, pp. 123–42. Cambridge: Cambridge University Press.

Laffin, M. (1986) 'Professional communities and policy communities in central–local relations', in Goldsmith, M. (ed.) *New Research in Central–Local Relations*, pp. 108–21. Aldershot: Gower.

Lampinen, R. and Uusikylä, P. (1998) 'Implementation deficit – Why member states do not comply with EU directives', *Scandinavian Political Studies*, 21(3), pp. 231–51.

Landerer, N. (2014) *The Mediatization of Political Decision-Making Processes*, PhD Thesis, University of Geneva.

Landry, R. and Varone, F. (2005) 'Choice of policy instruments: Confronting the deductive and the interaction approaches', in Eliadis, P., Hill, M.M. and Howlett, M. (eds) *Designing Government. From Instruments to Governance*, pp. 106–31. Montreal and Kingston: McGill-Queen's University Press.

Lane, J-E. (1987) 'Implementation, accountability and trust', *European Journal of Political Research*, 15(5), pp. 527–46.

Lane, J-E. and Ersson, S.O. (2000) *The New Institutional Politics: Performance and Outcomes*. London: Routledge.

Lansley, S., Goss, S. and Wolmar, C. (1989) *Councils in Conflict: The Rise and Fall of the Municipal Left*. London: Macmillan.

Lascoumes, P. and Le Galès, P. (2007) 'Innovation and Innovators Inside Government: From Institutions to Networks', *Governance* 20(1), pp. 1–21.

Lascoumes, P. and Le Galès, P. (2007) *Sociologie de l'action publique*. Paris: Armand Colin.

Laski, H.J. (1925) *A Grammar of Politics*. London: Allen & Unwin.

Lasswell, H.D. (1936) *Politics: Who Gets What, When, How*. Cleveland, OH: Meridian Books.

Lasswell, H.D. (1951) 'The policy orientation', in Lerner, D. and Lasswell, H.D. (eds) *The Policy Sciences*. Stanford, CA: Stanford University Press, pp. 3–15.

Lasswell, H.D. (1968) 'The policy sciences', in *Encyclopedia of the Social Sciences*, vol. 12. New York: Macmillan.

Lasswell, H.D. (1970) 'The emerging conception of the policy sciences', *Policy Sciences*, 1, pp. 3–14.

Latham, E. (1952) *The Group Basis of Politics*. Ithaca, NY: Cornell University Press.

Laumann, E.O. and Knoke, D. (1987) *The Organizational State: Social Choice in National Policy Domains*. Madison: University of Wisconsin Press.

Le Grand, J. (1997) 'Knights, knaves and pawns? Human behaviour and social policy', *Journal of Social Policy*, 26(2), pp. 149–70.

Le Grand, J. (2003) *Motivation, Agency and Public Policy*. Oxford: Oxford University Press.

Leece, J. and Bornat, J. (eds) (2006) *Developments in Direct Payments*. Bristol: The Policy Press.

Lenin, V.I. (1917) *State and Revolution*. Moscow: Foreign Languages Publishing House.

Lerner, M. (1980) *The Belief in a Just World: A Fundamental Delusion*. New York: Plenum Press.

Levi-Faur, D. (2004) 'Comparative research designs in the study of regulation: How to increase the numbers of cases without compromising the strengths of case-oriented analysis' in Jordana, J. and Levi-Faur, D. (eds) *The Politics of Regulation: Institutions and Regulatory Reforms for the Age of Governance*, pp. 177–99. Cheltenham: Edward Elgar.

Levi-Faur, D. (2005) 'The global diffusion of regulatory capitalism', *The Annals of the American Academy of Political and Social Science*, 598, pp. 12–32.

Levi-Faur, D. (2006a) 'Varieties of regulatory capitalism: Getting the most out of the comparative method', *Governance*, 19(3), pp. 367–82.

Levi-Faur, D. (2006b) 'A question of size? A heuristics for stepwise comparative research design', in Rihoux, B. and Grimm, H. (eds) *Innovative Comparative Methods for Policy Analysis*, pp. 43–66. New York: Springer.

Levin, K., Cashore, B., Bernstein, S. and Auld, G. (2012) 'Overcoming the tragedy of super wicked problems: constraining our future selves to ameliorate global climate change', *Policy Sciences*, 45, pp. 123–52.

Levine, S. and White, P. (1961) 'Exchange as a conceptual framework for the study of interorganisational relationships', *Administrative Science Quarterly*, 5, pp. 583–601.

Lewin, L., Lewin, B., Bäck, H. and Westin, L. (2008) 'A kindler, gentler democracy? The consensus model and Swedish disability politics', *Scandinavian Political Studies,* 31(3), pp. 291–310.

Lieberman, R.C. (2002) 'Ideas, institutions and political order: Explaining political change', *American Political Science Review*, 96(4), pp. 697–712.

Lijphart, A. (1971) 'Comparative politics and the comparative method', *American Political Science Review*, 65(3), pp. 682–93.

Lijphart, A. (1975) *The Politics of Accommodation: Pluralism and Democracy in the Netherlands*, 2nd edn. Berkeley, CA: University of California Press.

Lijphart, A. (1984) *Democracies: Patterns of Majoritarian and Consensus Government in Twenty-One Countries*. New Haven, CT: Yale University Press.

Lijphart, A. (1999) *Patterns of Democracy*. New Haven, CT: Yale University Press.

Lindblom, C.E. (1959) 'The science of "muddling through"', *Public Administration Review*, 19, pp. 78–88.

Lindblom, C.E. (1965) *The Intelligence of Democracy*. New York: The Free Press.

Lindblom, C.E. (1977) *Politics and Markets*. New York: Basic Books.

Lindblom, C.E. (1979) 'Still muddling, not yet through', *Public Administration Review*, 39, pp. 517–25.

Linder, S.H. and Peters, B.G. (1991) 'The logic of public policy design: Linking policy actors and plausible instruments', *Knowledge in Society*, 4, pp. 15–51.

Lipsky, M. (1980) *Street-Level Bureaucracy*. New York: Russell Sage.

Littler, C.R. (1978) 'Understanding Taylorism', *British Journal of Sociology*, 29(2), pp. 185–202.

Local Government Association (2013) *Changing Behaviours In Public Health: To Nudge or to Shove*. London: Local Government Association.

Lowe, P. (1986) *Countryside Conflicts*. Aldershot: Gower.

Lowi, T.A. (1972) 'Four systems of policy, politics and choice', *Public Administration Review*, 32, pp. 298–310.

Lowndes, V. (1996) 'Varieties of new institutionalism: A critical appraisal', *Public Administration,* 74, pp. 181–97.

Lowndes, V. and Skelcher, C. (1998) 'The dynamics of multi-organizational partnerships: An analysis of changing modes of governance', *Public Administration*, 76, Summer, pp. 313–33.

Loyens, K. (2015) 'Law enforcement and policy alienation: Coping by labour inspectors and federal police officers', in Hupe, P.L, Hill, M. and Buffat, A. (eds) *Understanding Street-Level Bureaucracy*, pp. 99–114. Bristol: Policy Press.

Lukes, S. (1974) *Power: A Radical View*. London: Macmillan.

Lukes, S. (2005) *Power: A Radical View* [Second Edition]. London: Macmillan.

Mach, A. (2007) 'Interest Groups', in Klöti, U., Knoepfel, P., Kriesi, H., Linder, W., Papadopoulos, Y. and Sciarini, P. (eds) *Handbook of Swiss Politics*, pp. 359–80. Zürich: NZZ.

MacMillan, M. (2001) *Peacemakers: Six Months that Changed the World*. London: John Murray.

MacMillan, M. (2009) *The Uses and Abuses of History*. London: Profile Books.

MacRae, C.D. (1977) 'A political model of the business cycle', *Journal of Political Economy*, 85, pp. 239–64.

Majone, G. (1994) 'The rise of the regulatory state in Europe', *West European Politics,* 17(3), pp. 77–101.

Majone, G. and Wildavsky, A. (1978) 'Implementation as evolution', in Freeman, H. (ed.) *Policy Studies Review Annual*. Beverley Hills, CA: SAGE.

March, J.G. and Olsen, J.P. (1984) 'The new institutionalism: Organisational factors in political life', *American Political Science Review*, 78, pp. 734–49.

March, J.G. and Olsen, J.P. (1989) *Rediscovering Institutions*. New York: Free Press.

March, J.G. and Olsen, J.P. (1996) 'Institutional perspectives on political institutions', *Governance*, 9(3), pp. 248–64.

Marchildon, G.P. (2014) 'Agenda setting in a parliamentary federation: Universal Medicare in Canada', in Hill, M. (ed.) *Studying Public Policy*, pp. 75–87. Bristol: Policy Press.

Marris, P. and Rein, M. (1967) *Dilemmas of Social Reform*. London: Routledge & Kegan Paul.

Marsh, D. and McConnell, A. (2010) 'Towards a framework for establishing policy success', *Public Administration*, 88(2), pp. 564–83.

Marsh, D. and Rhodes, R.A.W. (eds) (1992) *Implementing Thatcherite Policies: Audit of an Era*. Buckingham: Open University Press.

Marsh, D. and Rhodes, R.A.W. (1992) *Policy Networks in British Government*. Oxford: Oxford University Press.

Marsh, D. and Smith, M. (2000) 'Understanding policy networks: Towards a dialectical approach', *Political Studies*, 48(1), pp. 4–21.

Marx, F.M. (1957) *The Administrative State*. Chicago: University of Chicago Press.

Marx, K. (1845) 'Theses on Feuerbach', reprinted in *Marx and Engels: Selected Works*, vol. 2 (1958), pp. 13–15. Moscow: Foreign Languages Publishing House.

Mashaw, J.L. (1983) *Bureaucratic Justice*. New Haven, CT: Yale University Press.

Massey, P. (1995) *New Zealand: Market Liberalization in a Developed Economy*. New York: St. Martin's Press.

Matland, R.E. (1995) 'Synthesizing the implementation literature: The ambiguity-conflict model of policy implementation', *Journal of Public Administration Research and Theory*, 5(2), pp. 145–74.

May, P.J. (1993) 'Mandate design and implementation: Enhancing implementation efforts and shaping regulatory styles', *Journal of Policy Analysis and Management*, 12(4), pp. 634–63.

May, P.J. (1995) 'Can cooperation be mandated? Implementing intergovernmental environmental management in New South Wales and New Zealand', *Publius*, 25(1), pp. 89–113.

May, P.J. (2015) 'Implementation failures revisited: Policy regime perspectives', *Public Policy and Administration*, 30(3–4), pp. 277–99.

May, P.J. and Burby, R.J. (1996) 'Coercive versus cooperative policies: Comparing intergovernmental mandate performance', *Journal of Policy Analysis and Management*, 15(2), pp. 171–201.

May, P.J. and Jochim, A.E. (2013) 'Policy regime perspectives: Policies, politics and governing', *Policy Studies Journal*, 41(3), pp. 426–52.

Maynard-Moody, S. and Musheno, M. (2004) *Cops, Teachers, Counsellors*. Ann Arbor: University of Michigan Press.

Mayntz, R. (ed.) (1980) *Implementation politischer Programme. Empirische Forschungsberichte*. Königstein: Verlag Anton Hain Meisenheim.

Mazur, A.G. and Hoard, S. (2014) 'Gendering comparative policy studies: Towards better science', in Engeli, I. and Rothmayr Allison, C. (eds) *Comparative Policy Studies. Conceptual and Methodological Challenges*, pp. 205–35. Basingstoke: Palgrave Macmillan.

Mazzoleni, G. and Schulz, W. (1999) 'Mediatization of politics: A challenge for democracy?', *Political Communication*, 16(3), pp. 247–62.

McBeth, M.K., Jones, M.D. and Shanahan, E.A. (2014) 'The narrative policy framework' in Sabatier, P.A. and Weible, C.M. (eds) *Theories of the Policy Process*, pp. 225–66. Boulder, CO: Westview.

McCann, M. (1998) 'Law and political struggle for social change: Puzzles, paradoxes, and promises in future research', in Schultz, D. (ed.) *Leveraging the Law. Using the Courts to Achieve Social Change*, pp. 219–349. New York: Peter Lang.

McCombs, M. and Shaw, D.L. (1972) 'The agenda-setting function of mass media', *Public Opinion Quarterly*, 36, pp. 176–87.

McConnell, A. (2010) *Understanding Policy Success*. Basingstoke: Palgrave Macmillan.

McDonald, M. and Budge, I. (2005) *Elections, Parties, Democracy: Conferring the Median Mandate*. Oxford: Oxford University Press.

McGregor, D. (1960) *The Human Side of Enterprise*. New York: McGraw Hill.

McLellan, D. (1971) *The Thought of Karl Marx*. London: Macmillan.

Meier, K.J. (1994) *The Politics of Sin: Drugs, Alcohol and Public Policy*. Armonk: Shape.

Meier, K.J., Stewart, J. Jr and England, R.E. (1991) 'The politics of bureaucratic discretion: Educational access as an urban service', *American Journal of Political Science*, 35(1), pp. 155–77.

Meny, Y. and J-C. Thoenig (1989) *Politiques publiques*. Paris: Presses universitaires de France.

Merelman, R.M. (1968) 'On the neo-elitist critique of community power', *American Political Science Review*, 62, pp. 451–60.

Merton, R.K. (1957) *Social Theory and Social Structure*. Glencoe, IL: Free Press.

Meyer, J.W. and Rowan, B. (1977) 'Institutionalized organizations: Formal structure as myth and ceremony', *American Journal of Sociology*, 83(1), pp. 340–63.

Meyer, T. (2002) *Media Democracy: How the Media Colonize Politics*. Cambridge: Polity.

Meyer, T., Bridgen, P. and Reidmüller, B. (eds) (2007) *Private Pensions versus Social Inclusion: Non-State Provision for Citizens at Risk in Europe*. Cheltenham: Edward Elgar.

Meyers, M.K. and Vorsanger, S. (2003) 'Street Level Bureaucrats and the Implementation of Public Policy' in B.G. Peters and J. Pierre (eds) *Handbook of Public Administration*, pp. 245–54. London: SAGE.

Meyers, M.K., Glaser, B. and MacDonald, K. (1998) 'On the front lines of welfare delivery: Are workers implementing policy reforms?', *Journal of Policy Analysis and Management*, 17(1), pp. 1–22.

Meynaud, J. (1965) *Technocracy*. London: Faber.

Middlemas, K. (1979) *Politics in Industrial Society*. London: Andre Deutsch.

Middlemas, K. (1986) *Power, Competition and the State*. Oxford: Blackwell.

Miliband, R. (1969) *The State in Capitalist Society*. London: Quartet.

Millet, K. (1970) *Sexual Politics*. New York: Avon Books.

Mills, C.W. (1956) *The Power Elite*. New York: Oxford University Press.

Milward, H.B. and Francisco, R.A. (1983) 'Subsystem politics and corporatism in the United States', *Policy and Politics*, 11(3), pp. 273–93.

Milward, H.B., Provan, G. and Else, B.A. (1993) 'What does the "hollow state" look like?', in Bozeman, B. (ed.) *Public Management: The State of the Art*, pp. 309–22. San Francisco: Jossey-Bass.

Moe, T.M. (1980) *The Organisation of Interests*. Chicago: University of Chicago Press.

Moe, T.M. (2015) 'Vested interests and political institutions', *Political Science Quarterly*, 130(2), pp. 277–318.

Montpetit, E., Rothmayr Allison C. and Varone, F. (2005) 'Institutional vulnerability to social constructions: Federalism, target populations, and policy designs for assisted reproductive technology in six democracies', *Comparative Political Studies*, 38(2), pp. 119–42.

Montpetit, E., Varone, F. and Rothmayr Allison, C. (2007). 'Regulating ART and GMOs in Europe and North America: A qualitative comparative analysis', in Montpetit, E., Rothmayr Allison, C. and Varone, F. (eds) *The Politics of Biotechnology in North America and Europe: Policy Networks, Institutions and Internationalization*, pp. 263–86. Lanham: Lexington Books.

Mooney, C.Z. (1999) 'The politics of morality policy', *Policy Studies Journal*, 27(4), pp. 675–80.

Mooney, C.Z. (ed.) (2001) *The Public Clash of Private Values*. New York: Chatham House.

Moran, M. and Prosser, T. (1994) *Privatisation and Regulatory Change in Europe*. Buckingham: Open University Press.

Moran, M. and Wood, B. (1993) *States, Regulation and the Medical Profession*. Buckingham: Open University Press.

Moravcsik, A. (1994) *Why the European Union Community Strengthens the State: Domestic Politics and International Cooperation*. Harvard: Center for European Studies (Working Paper 52).

Mosca, C. (1939) *The Ruling Class*, trans. H.D. Kahn. London: McGraw Hill.

Mosley, P. (1984) *The Making of Economic Policy*. Brighton: Wheatsheaf.

Moynihan, D.P. (1969) *Maximum Feasible Misunderstanding*. New York: Free Press.

Muller, P. (2003) *Les politiques publiques*. Paris: Presses universitaires de France.

Murray, C. (2006) 'State intervention and vulnerable children: Implementation revisited', *Journal of Social Policy*, 35(2), pp. 211–28.

Musgrave, R.A. (1959) *The Theory of Public Finance*. New York: McGraw Hill.

Neilsen, V.L. (2015) 'Law enforcement behaviour of regulatory inspectors', in Hupe, P.L, Hill, M. and Buffat, A. (eds) (2015) *Understanding Street-Level Bureaucracy*, pp. 115–31. Bristol: Policy Press.

Newman, J. (2001) *Modernising Governance*. London: SAGE.

Niskanen, W.A. (1971) *Bureaucracy and Representative Government*. New York: Aldine-Atherton.

Niskanen, W. (1991) 'A reflection on bureaucracy and representative government' in Blais, A. and Dion, S. (eds) *The Budget Maximising Bureaucrat: Appraisals and Evidence*, pp. 13–32. Pittsburg: University of Pittsburg Press.

Nohrstedt, D. (2009) 'Do advocacy coalitions matter? Crisis and change in Swedish nuclear energy policy', *Journal of Public Administration Research and Theory*, 20(2), pp. 309–33.

Nohrstedt, D. (2014) 'Understanding the political context of nuclear energy policy change in Sweden', in Hill, M. (ed.) *Studying Public Policy*, pp. 55–67. Bristol: Policy Press.

Nordhaus, W. (1975) 'The political business cycle', *Review of Economic Studies*, 42, pp. 169–90.

Nordlinger, E.A. (1981) *On the Autonomy of the Democratic State*. Cambridge, MA: Harvard University Press.

Norgaard, A.S. (1996) 'Rediscovering reasonable rationality in institutional analysis', *European Journal of Political Research*, 29, pp. 31–57.

Nuffield Council on Bioethics (2007) *Public Health: Ethical Issues*, http://nuffield-bioethics.org/project/public health.

O'Connor, J. (1973) *The Fiscal Crisis of the State*. New York: St. Martin's Press.

O'Toole, L.J. Jr (1986) 'Policy recommendations for multi-actor implementation: An assessment of the field', *Journal of Public Policy*, 6(2), pp. 181–210.

Obama, Barack (2015) 'Executive Order – Using Behavioral Science Insights to Better Serve the American People', 2015, September 15.

Oberfield, Z.W. (2009) 'Rule following and discretion at government's frontlines: Continuity and change during organization socialization', *Journal of Public Administration Research and Theory*, 20, pp. 735–55.

Öberg, P-O., Svensson, T., Christiansen, P.M., Nørgaard, A.S., Rommetvedt, H. and Thesen, G. (2011) 'Disrupted exchange and declining corporatism: Government authority and interest group capability in Scandinavia', *Government and Opposition*, 46(3), pp. 365–91.

Ohmae, K. (1996) *The End of the Nation State*. New York: Free Press.

Oliver, A. (2013) 'From nudging to budging: Using behavioural economics to inform public sector policy', *Journal of Social Policy*, 42(4) pp. 685–700.

Oliver, C. (1991) 'Strategic responses to institutional processes', *Academy of Management Review* 16(1), pp. 145–79.

Olson, M. (1965) *The Logic of Collective Action*. Cambridge, MA: Harvard University Press.

Olson, M. (1982) *The Rise and Decline of Nations*. New Haven, CT: Yale University Press.

Osborne, D. and Gaebler, T. (1992) *Reinventing Government*. Reading, MA: Addison Wesley.

Ostrom, E. (1998) 'A behavioural approach to the rational choice theory of collective action', *American Political Science Review*, 92(1) pp. 1–22.

Ouchi, W.G. (1980) 'Markets, bureaucracies and clans', *Administrative Science Quarterly*, 25, pp. 129–41.

Oye, K. (1985) 'Explaining cooperation under anarchy: Hypotheses and strategies', *World Politics*, 39(1), pp. 1–24.

Page, E.C. (2003) 'The civil servant as legislator: Law making in British administration'. *Public Administration*, 81(4), pp. 651–79.

Page, E.C. and Goldsmith, M. (1987) *Central and Local Government Relations*. Beverley Hills, CA: SAGE.

Page, E.C. and Jenkins, B. (2005) *Policy Bureaucracy*. Oxford: Oxford University Press.

Painter, M. and Peters, B.G. (eds) (2010) *Tradition and Public Administration*. Basingstoke: Palgrave.

Pampel, F.C. and Williamson, J.B. (1989) *Age, Class, Politics and the Welfare State*. Cambridge: Cambridge University Press.

Panitch, L. (1980) 'Recent theorisations of corporatism: Reflections on a growth industry', *British Journal of Sociology*, 31(2), pp. 159–87.

Panitch, L. (1994) 'Globalisation and the state', in Miliband, R. and Panitch, L. (eds) *The Socialist Register, 1994*. London: Merlin.

Pappi, F. and Henning, C. (1998) 'Policy networks: More than a metaphor?', *Journal of Theoretical Politics,* 10(4), pp. 553–75.

Pareto, V. (1966) *Sociological Writings* (ed. S.E. Finer). London: Pall Mall.

Parsons, W. (1995) *Public Policy.* Aldershot: Edward Elgar.

Pawson, R. and Tilley, N. (1997) *Realistic Evaluation.* London: SAGE.

Peacock, A. (ed.) (1984) *The Regulation Game.* Oxford: Blackwell.

Perri 6: *see* 6, P.

Perrow, C. (1972) *Complex Organizations: A Critical Essay.* Cleanview, IL: Scott Foresman.

Perry, J.L. (1996) 'Measuring public service motivation: An assessment of construct reliability and validity', *Journal of Public Administration Research and Theory,* 6(1), pp. 5–22.

Perry, J.L. and Wise, L.R. (1990) 'The motivational bases of public service', *Public Administration Review,* 50, pp. 367–73.

Peters, B.G. and Pierre, J. (eds) (2003) *Handbook of Public Administration,* London: SAGE.

Peters, B.G. and Pierre, J. (eds) (2006) *Handbook of Public Policy,* London: SAGE.

Peters, B.G., Pierre, J. and King, D.S. (2005) 'The politics of path dependency: Political conflict in historical institutionalism', *Journal of Politics,* 67(4), pp. 1275–1300.

Peters, T. and Waterman, R. (1982) *In Search of Excellence.* New York: Harper Collins.

Peterson, E.R. (1996) 'Surrendering to markets' in Roberts, B. (ed.) *New Forces in the World Economy,* pp. 265–78. Cambridge, MA: MIT Press.

Pierce, J., Siddiki, S., Jones, M.D., Schumacher, K., Pattison, A. and Peterson, H. (2014) 'Social construction and policy design: A review of past applications', *Policy Studies Journal,* 42(1), pp. 1–29.

Pierre, J. (ed.) (2000) *Debating Governance.* Oxford: Oxford University Press.

Pierre, J. (2009) 'Reinventing governance, reinventing democracy?', *Policy and Politics,* 37(4), pp. 591–609.

Pierre, J. and Peters, B.G. (2000) *Governance, Politics and the State.* Basingstoke: Macmillan.

Pierson, P. (1993) 'When effect becomes cause: Policy feedback and political change', *World Politics,* 45(4), pp. 595–628.

Pierson, P. (1994) *Dismantling the Welfare State?* Cambridge: Cambridge University Press.

Pierson, P. (2000) 'Increasing returns, path dependence and the study of politics', *American Political Science Review,* 92(4), pp. 251–67.

Pierson, P. (ed.) (2001) *The New Politics of the Welfare State.* Oxford: Oxford University Press.

Piketty, T. (2014) *Capital in the Twenty-First Century.* Cambridge, MA: Bellknap.

Piliavin, J.A. and Grube, J.A. (2002) 'Role as resource for action in public service', *Journal of Social Issues,* 58(3), pp. 469–85.

Pitts, D. (2005) 'Diversity, representation and performance: Evidence about race and ethnicity in public organizations', *Journal of Public Administration Research and Theory*, 15(4), pp. 615–31.

Platt, L., Sunkin, M. and Calvo, K. (2010) 'Judicial review litigation as an incentive to change in local authority public services in England and Wales', *Journal of Public Administration Research and Theory*, 20, pp. 243–60.

Polanyi, K. (1944) *The Great Transformation*. Boston, MA: Rinehart.

Pollitt, C. (1990) *Managerialism and the Public Services*. Oxford: Blackwell.

Pollitt, C. (2003) *The Essential Public Manager*. Maidenhead: Open University Press.

Pollitt, C. and Bouckaert, G. (2000) *Public Management Reform: A Comparative Analysis*. Oxford: Oxford University Press.

Pollitt, C. and Bouckaert, G. (2009) *Continuity and Change in Public Policy and Management*. Cheltenham: Edward Elgar.

Polsby, N.W. (1963) *Community Power and Political Theory*. New Haven, CT: Yale University Press.

Powell, G.B., Dalton, R.H. and Strom, K. (eds) (2012) *Comparative Politics Today* (Tenth edition). Boston, MA: Longman.

Powell, M., Exworthy, M. and Berney, L. (2001) 'Playing the game of partnership', in Sykes, R., Bochel, C. and Ellison, N. (eds) *Social Policy Review*, pp. 39–62. Bristol: Policy Press.

Power, M. (1997) *The Audit Explosion*. London: Demos.

Pralle, S.B. (2009) 'Agenda-setting and climate change', *Environmental Politics*, 18(5), pp. 781–99.

Pressman, J. and Wildavsky, A. (1973 [1st edn], 1979 [2nd edn], 1984 [3rd edn]) *Implementation*. Berkeley: University of California Press.

Prindle, D. (2012) 'Importing concepts from biology into political science: The case of punctuated equilibrium', *Policy Studies Journal*, 40(1), pp. 21–44.

Prottas, J.M. (1979) *People Processing: The Street-Level Bureaucrat in Public Service Bureaucracies*. Lexington, MA: D.C. Heath.

Przeworski, A. and Wallerstein, M. (1988) 'Structural dependence of the state on capital', *American Political Science Review*, 82(1), pp. 11–29.

Pusey, M. (1991) *Economic Rationalism in Canberra*. Cambridge: Cambridge University Press.

Putnam, R. (1988) 'Diplomacy and domestic politics: The logic of two-level games', *International Organization*, 42(3), pp. 427–60.

Radaelli, C.M., Dunlop, C.A. and Fritsch, O. (2013) 'Narrating impact assessment in the European Union', *European Political Science*, 12(4), pp. 500–21.

Ragin, C.C. (1987) *The Comparative Method: Moving Beyond Qualitative and Quantitative Strategies*. Los Angeles: University of California Press.

Ranade, W. (1998) *Making Sense of Multi-Agency Groups*. Newcastle: Sustainable Cities Research Institute.

Ranade, W. and Hudson, B. (2003) 'Conceptual issues in inter-agency collaboration', *Local Government Studies*, 29(3), pp. 32–50.

Raynsford, N. (2007) 'Policy development in a 24/7 media environment', *Policy and Politics*, 35(3), pp. 557–65.

Reiner, R. (1992) *The Politics of the Police*. 2nd Edition. New York: Harvester Wheatsheaf.

Reissman, L. (1949) 'The study of role conceptions in bureaucracy', *Social Forces*, 27, pp. 305–10.

Rex, J. (1986) *Race and Ethnicity*. Milton Keynes: Open University Press.

Rhodes, R.A.W. (1981) *Control and Power in Central–Local Government Relations*. Farnborough: Saxon House.

Rhodes, R.A.W. (1988) *Beyond Westminster and Whitehall*. London: Unwin Hyman.

Rhodes, R.A.W. (1995) 'From prime ministerial power to core executive', in Rhodes, R.A.W. and Dunleavy, P. (eds) *Prime Minister, Cabinet and Core Executive*. Basingstoke: Macmillan, pp. 11–37.

Rhodes, R.A.W. (1997) *Understanding Governance: Policy Networks, Governance, Reflexivity and Accountability*. Buckingham: Open University Press.

Rhodes, R.A.W. (2003) 'What is new about governance and why does it matter?', in Hayward, J. and Menon, A. (eds) *Governing Europe*, pp. 61–73. Oxford: Oxford University Press.

Rhodes, R.A.W. (2007) 'The everyday life of a minister: A confessional and impressionist tale', in Rhodes, R.A.W., t' Hart, P. and Noordegraaf, M. (eds) *Observing Government Elites*, pp. 21–50. Basingstoke: Palgrave Macmillan.

Rhodes, R.A.W. (2011) *Everyday Life in British Government*. Oxford: Oxford University Press.

Riccucci, N.M. (2005) *How Management Matters: Street-Level Bureaucrats and Welfare Reform*. Washington, DC: Georgetown University Press.

Riccucci, N.M. and Meyers, M.K. (2004) 'Linking passive and active representation: The case of frontline workers in welfare agencies', *Journal of Public Administration, Research and Theory*, 14(4), pp. 585–97.

Richards, D. and Smith, M.J. (2002) *Governance and Public Policy in the UK*. Oxford: Oxford University Press.

Richardson, J. (ed.) (1982) *Policy Styles in Western Europe*. London: Allen & Unwin.

Richardson, J.J. and Jordan, A.G. (1979) *Governing under Pressure*. Oxford: Martin Robertson.

Ripley, R.B. and Franklin, G.A. (1982) *Bureaucracy and Policy Implementation*. Homewood: Dorsey Press.

Risse, T. (2006). 'Transnational governance and legitimacy', in Benz, A. and Papadopoulos, Y. (eds) *Governance and Democracy. Comparing National, European and International Experiences*, pp. 179–99. London: Routledge.

Rittel, H.W.J. and Webber, M.M. (1973) 'Dilemmas in a general theory of planning', *Policy Sciences*, 4, pp. 155–69.

Robinson, S.E. (2006) 'A decade of treating networks seriously', *Policy Studies Journal*, 34(4), pp. 589–98.

Roethlisberger, F.J. and Dickson, W.J. (1939) *Management and the Worker*. Cambridge, MA: Harvard University Press.

Rose, R. (1991) 'What is lesson drawing?' *Journal of Public Policy*, 11(1), pp. 3–30.

Rose, R. (1993) *Lesson Drawing in Public Policy*. Chatham, NJ: Chatham House.

Rosenberg, G. (1991) *The Hollow Hope: Can Courts Bring about Social Change?* Chicago: University of Chicago Press.

Rothmayr Allison, C. and Saint-Martin, D. (2011) 'Half a century of "muddling": Are we there yet?' *Policy and Society*, 30, pp. 1–8.

Rothstein, B. (1992) 'Labor-market institutions and working-class strength', in Steinmo, S., Thelen, K. and Longstreth, F. (eds) *Structuring Politics: Historical Institutionalism in Comparative Analysis*, pp. 33–56. Cambridge: Cambridge University Press.

Rothstein, B. (1998) *Just Institutions Matter: The Moral and Political Logic of the Universal Welfare State*. Cambridge: Cambridge University Press.

Ruggie, J.G. (2002) 'The theory and practice of learning networks: Corporate social responsibility and the global compact', *Journal of Corporate Citizenship*, 5, pp. 27–36.

Sabatier, P.A. (1986) 'Top-down and bottom-up approaches to implementation research: A critical analysis and suggested synthesis', *Journal of Public Policy*, 6(1), pp. 21–48.

Sabatier, P.A. (1988) 'An advocacy coalition framework of policy change and the role of policy-oriented learning therein', *Policy Sciences,* 21, pp. 129–68.

Sabatier, P.A. (1999) 'The need for better theories', in Sabatier, P.A. (ed.) *Theories of the Policy Process*, pp. 3–17. Boulder, CO: Westview Press.

Sabatier, P.A. (ed.) (1999) *Theories of the Policy Process*. Boulder, CO: Westview Press.

Sabatier, P.A. (ed.) (2007) *Theories of the Policy Process*, Second Edition. Boulder, CO: Westview Press.

Sabatier, P.A. and Jenkins-Smith, H. (eds) (1993) *Policy Change and Learning: An Advocacy Coalition Approach*. Boulder, CO: Westview Press.

Sabatier, P.A. and Jenkins-Smith, H. (1999) 'The advocacy coalition framework: An assessment', in Sabatier, P.A. (ed.) *Theories of the Policy Process*, pp. 117–66. Boulder, CO: Westview Press.

Sabatier, P.A. and Weible, C.M. (2007) 'The advocacy coalition framework: Innovations and clarifications', in Sabatier, P.A. (ed.) *Theories of the Policy Process*, pp. 189–222. Boulder, CO: Westview Press.

Sabatier, P.A. and Weible, C.M. (eds) (2014) *Theories of the Policy Process*, 3rd edn. Boulder, CO: Westview Press.

Sabel, C.F. (1982) *Work and Politics*. Cambridge: Cambridge University Press.

Sætren, H. (2014) 'Implementing the third generation research paradigm in policy implementation research: An empirical assessment', *Public Policy and Administration*, 29(2), pp. 84–105.

Salaman, G. (1979) *Work Organisations*. London: Longman.

Salisbury, R.H. (1979) 'Why no corporatism in the United States?', in Schmitter, P.C. and Lembruch, G. (eds) *Trends Towards Corporatist Intermediation*, pp. 213–25. London: SAGE.

Sanderson, I. (2004) 'Getting evidence into practice: Perspectives on rationality', *Evaluation* 10(3), pp. 366–79.

Satyamurti, C. (1981) *Occupational Survival*. Oxford: Blackwell.

Scharpf, F.W. (1997) *Games Real Actors Play: Actor-Centered Institutionalism in Policy Research*. Boulder, CO: Westview Press.

Scharpf, F.W. (1999) *Governing in Europe: Effective and Democratic?* Oxford: Oxford University Press.

Schattschneider, E.E. (1960) *The Semi-Sovereign People*. New York: Holt, Rinehart and Winston.

Schiffino, N., Ramjoué, C. and Varone, F. (2009) 'Biomedical policies in Belgium and Italy: From regulatory reluctance to policy changes', *West European Politics*, 32(3), pp. 559–85.

Schmidt, V.A. (2002) *The Futures of European Capitalism*. Oxford: Oxford University Press.

Schmitter, P. (1974) 'Still the century of corporatism?' *Review of Politics*, 36, pp. 85–131.

Schneider, A.L. and Ingram, H. (1997) *Policy Design for Democracy*. Lawrence: University Press of Kansas.

Schumpeter, J. (1947) *Capitalism, Socialism and Democracy*, 2nd rev. edn. London: Allen & Unwin.

Schwarzmantel, J. (1994) *The State in Contemporary Society*. Hemel Hempstead: Harvester Wheatsheaf.

Sciarini, P. (2015) 'From corporatism to bureaucratic and partisan politics: Changes in decision-making processes over time', in Sciarini, P. and M. Fischer, D. Traber (eds) *Political Decision-Making in Switzerland. The Consensus Model under Pressure*, pp. 24–50. Houndmills: Palgrave Macmillan.

Scott, W.R. (1995) *Institutions and Organizations*. Thousand Oaks, CA: SAGE.

Selden, S.C. (1997) 'Representative bureaucracy: Examining the linkage between passive and active representation in the farmers' home administration', *American Review of Public Administration*, 27(1), pp. 22–42.

Seldon, A. (ed.) (2001) *The Blair Effect*. London: Little Brown.

Seldon, A. (ed.) (2007) *Blair's Britain*. Cambridge: Cambridge University Press.

Self, P. (1985) *Political Theories of Modern Government*. London: Allen & Unwin.

Self, P. (1993) *Government by the Market?* Basingstoke: Macmillan.

Selznick, P. (1949) *TVA and the Grass Roots*. Berkeley: University of California Press.

Selznick, P. (1957) *Leadership in Administration*. New York: Harper & Row.

Selznick, P. (1996) 'Institutionalism "old" and "new"', *Administrative Science Quarterly*, 41, pp. 270–7.

Shambaugh, D. (1995) *Deng Xiaoping*. Oxford: Clarendon Press.

Shapiro, M. (1996) 'The globalization of judicial review', in Friedman, L. and Scheiber, H. (eds) *Legal Culture and the Legal Profession*, pp. 119–35. Boulder, CO: Westview Press.

Shaxson, N. (2011) *Treasure Islands: Tax Havens and the Men who Stole the World*. London: The Bodley Head.

Shinkawa, T. (2005) 'The politics of pension reform in Japan: Institutional legacies, credit claiming and blame avoidance', in Bonoli, G. and Shinkawa, T. (eds) *Ageing and Pension Reform Around the World*. Cheltenham: Elgar.

Sibony, A-L. and Alemanno, A. (2015) 'The emergence of behavioural policy-making: A European perspective', in Alemanno, A. and Sibony, A-L. (eds) *Nudge and the Law. A European Perspective*, pp. 1–25. Oxford: Hart Publishing.

Sieber, S. (1981) *Fatal Remedies: The Ironies of Social Intervention*. New York: Plenum.

Simon, H.A. (1945) *Administrative Behaviour*. New York: The Free Press.

Simon, H.A. (1957) *Administrative Behaviour*, 2nd edn. New York: Macmillan.

Skocpol, T. (1994) *Social Policy in the United States*. Princeton, NJ: Princeton University Press.

Skocpol, T. and Finegold, K. (1982) 'State capacity and economic intervention in the early New Deal', *Political Science Quarterly*, 97, pp. 255–78.

Slattery, D. (2010) 'The political inherency of evaluation: The impact of politics on the outcome of 10 years of evaluative scrutiny of Australia's mandatory detention policy', *Evaluation Journal of Australasia*, 10(1), pp. 17–27.

Smith, B.C. (1976) *Policy Making in British Government*. London: Martin Robertson.

Smith, B.C. (1988) *Bureaucracy and Political Power*. Brighton: Harvester.

Smith, G. (1981) 'Discretionary decision-making in social work', in Adler, M. and Asquith, S. (eds) *Discretion and Welfare*, pp. 47–88. London: Heinemann.

Smith, G., John, P., Stoker, G., Cotterill, S., Richardson, L., Moseley, A. and Wales, C. (2011) *Nudge, Nudge, Think, Think: Experimenting with Ways to Change Civic Behaviour*. London and New York: Bloomsbury Academic.

Smith, K.E. (2007) 'Health inequalities in Scotland and England: The contrasting journey of ideas from research into policy', *Social Science and Medicine*, 64, pp. 1438–49.

Smith, M., Richards, D., Geddes, A. and Mathers, H. (2011) 'Analysing policy delivery in the United Kingdom: The case of street crime and anti-social behaviour', *Public Administration*, 89(3), pp. 975–1000.

Smith, M.J. (1993) *Pressure, Power and Policy*. Hemel Hempstead: Harvester Wheatsheaf.

Smith, M.J. (2011) 'Tsars, leadership and innovations in the public sector' *Policy and Politics*, 39(3), pp. 343–60.

Solesbury, W. (2001) *Evidence Based Policy: Whence it Came and Where it's Going* (Working Paper 1). London: ESRC UK Centre for Evidence Based Policy and Practice.

Solomos, J., Findlay, B., Jones, S. and Gilroy, P. (1982) 'The organic crisis of British capitalism and race: The experience of the seventies', in Centre for Contemporary Cultural Studies, *The Empire Strikes Back*, pp. 9–46. London: Hutchinson.

Spicker, P. (2006) *Policy Analysis for Practice*. Bristol: Policy Press.

Steurer, R. (2013) 'Disentangling governance: A synoptic view of regulation by government, business and civil society', *Policy Sciences*, 46, pp. 387–410.

Stevens, A. (2011) 'Telling policy stories: An ethnographic study of the use of evidence in policy-making in the UK', *Journal of Social Policy*, 40(2), pp. 237–55.

Stewart, J. and Clarke, M. (1987) 'The public services orientation: Issues and dilemmas', *Public Administration*, 65, pp. 161–77.

Stewart, K. (2007) 'Equality and Social Justice' in Seldon. A. (ed.) *Blair's Britain*, pp. 408–35. Cambridge: Cambridge University Press.

Stewart, K. (2011) 'A treble blow? Child poverty in 2010 and beyond' in C. Holden, M. Kilkey and G. Ramia (eds) *Social Policy Review 23*, pp. 165–84. Bristol: Policy Press.

Stigler, G. (1971) 'The theory of economic regulation', *Bell Journal of Economics and Management Science*, 3, pp. 3–18.

Stoker, R.P. (1991) *Reluctant Partners: Implementing Federal Policy*. Pittsburgh, PA: University of Pittsburg Press.

Stoker, R.P. and Wilson L.A. (1998) 'Verifying compliance: Social regulation and welfare reform. *Public Administration Review*, 58(5), pp. 395–405.

Stone, C. (1989) *Regime Politics: Governing Atlanta, 1946–1988*. Lawrence: University Press of Kansas.

Stone, D. (2002) *Policy Paradox: The Art of Political Decision Making*, 2nd edn. New York: W.W. Norton.

Stone Sweet, A. (2004) *The Judicial Construction of Europe*. Oxford: Oxford University Press.

Streeck, W. (2014) *Buying Time: The Delayed Crisis of Democratic Capitalism*. London: Verso.

Streeck, W. and Thelen, K. (eds) (2005) *Beyond Continuity: Institutional Change in Advanced Political Economies*. Oxford: Oxford University Press.

Strom, K. (2000) 'Delegation and accountability in parliamentary democracies', *European Journal of Political Science*, 37, pp. 261–89.

Strom, K., Müller, W.C. and Bergman, T. (2006) 'The (moral) hazards of parliamentary democracy', in Braun, D. and Gilardi, F. (eds) *Delegation in Contemporary Democracies*, pp. 27–51. London: Routledge.

Strömbäck, J. and Esser, F. (2009) 'Shaping politics: Mediatization and media interventionism', in Lundby, K. (ed.) *Mediatization: Concepts, Changes, Consequences*, pp. 205–24. New York: Peter Lang.

Strömbäck, J. and Esser, F. (2014) 'Mediatization of politics: Towards a theoretical framework', in Esser, F. and Strömbäck, J. (eds) *Mediatization of Politics: Understanding the Transformation of Western Democracies*, pp. 3–28. Basingstoke: Palgrave Macmillan.

Surel, Y. (2000) 'The role of cognitive and normative frames in policy-making', *Journal of European Public Policy*, 7(4), pp. 495–512.

Swank, D. (1992) 'Politics and the structural dependence of the state in democratic capitalist nations', *American Political Science Review*, 86(1), pp. 38–54.

Tate, N. (1995) 'Why the expansion of judicial power?' in Tate, N. and Vallinder, T. *The Global Expansion Of Judicial Power*, pp. 27–37. New York: New York University Press.

Taylor, D. and Balloch, S. (eds) (2005) *The Politics of Evaluation*. Bristol: Policy Press.

Taylor, F.W. (1911) *The Principles of Scientific Management*. New York: Harper.

Taylor, I. (2003a) 'Policy on the hoof: The handling of the foot and mouth disease outbreak in the UK, 2001', *Policy and Politics*, 31(4), pp. 535–46.

Taylor, M. (2003b) *Public Policy in the Community*. Basingstoke: Palgrave Macmillan.

Taylor-Gooby, P. (ed.) (2001) *Welfare States under Pressure*. London: SAGE.

Taylor-Gooby, P. (2002) 'The silver age of the welfare state: Perspectives on resilience', *Journal of Social Policy*, 31(4), pp. 597–622.

Taylor-Gooby, P. (2013) *The Double Crisis of the Welfare State and What We Can Do about It*. Basingstoke: Palgrave Macmillan.

Terry, L.D. (1998) 'Administrative leadership, neo-managerialism, and the public management movement', *Public Administration Review*, 58(3), pp. 194–200.

Thaler, R.H. and Sunstein, C.R. (2008) *Nudge: Improving Decisions about Health, Wealth, and Happiness*. New Haven, CT: Yale University Press.

Thatcher, M. (2004) 'Varieties of capitalism in an internationalized world: Domestic institutional change in European telecommunications', *Comparative Political Studies*, 37(7), pp. 751–80.

Thatcher, M. (2005) 'The third force? Independent regulatory agencies and elected politicians in Europe', *Governance*, 18(3), pp. 347–73.

Thatcher, M. (2007) *Internationalisation and Economic Institutions. Comparing European Experiences*. Oxford: Oxford University Press.

Thelen, K. and Steinmo, S. (1992) 'Historical institutionalism in comparative politics', in Steinmo, S., Thelen, K. and Longstreth, F. (eds) *Structuring Politics: Historical Institutionalism in Comparative Analysis*, pp. 1–32. Cambridge: Cambridge University Press.

Theobald, H. and Kern, K. (2011) 'The introduction of long-term care policy schemes: Policy development, policy transfer and policy change', *Policy and Politics*, 39(3), pp. 325–42.

Thomas, P.G. (2003) 'Accountability: Introduction', in Peters, B.G. and Pierre, J. (eds) *Handbook of Public Administration*. London: SAGE.

Thompson, G., Frances, J., Levacic, R. and Mitchell, J. (eds) (1991) *Markets, Hierarchies and Networks: The Coordination of Social Life*. London: SAGE.

Thompson, J.B. (1989) 'The theory of structuration', in Held, D. and Thompson, J.B. (eds) *Social Theory of Modern Societies: Anthony Giddens and His Critics*. Cambridge: Cambridge University Press.

Thurber, J.A. (1991) 'Dynamics of policy subsystems in American politics', in Cigler, A.J. and Loomis, A. (eds) *Interest Group Politics*, 3rd edn. Washington, DC: Congressional Quarterly, pp. 302–48.

Tilly, C. (1991) 'Domination, Resistance, Compliance . . . Discourse', *Sociological Forum*, 6(3), pp. 593–602.

Toke, D. and Marsh, D. (2003) 'Policy networks and the GM crops issue: Assessing the utility of a dialectic model of policy networks', *Public Administration*, 81(2), pp. 229–51.

Tresch, A., Sciarini, P. and Varone, F. (2013) 'The relationship between media and political agendas: Variations across decision-making phases', *West European Politics*, 36(5), pp. 897–918.

Tribe, L.H. (1990) *Abortion: The Clash of Absolutes*. New York: Norton.

Truman, D. (1958) *The Governmental Process*. New York: Alfred Knopf.

Tullock, G. (1967) *The Politics of Bureaucracy*. New York: Public Affairs Press.

Tullock, G. (1976) *The Vote Motive*. London: Institute of Economic Affairs.

Uhr, J. (1993) 'Redesigning accountability: From muddles to maps', *Australian Quarterly*, Winter, pp. 1–16.

van Aelst, P. and Walgrave, S. (2011) 'Minimal or massive? The political agenda-setting power of the mass media according to different methods', *International Journal of Press/Politics*, 16(3), pp. 295–313.

Vandenabeele, W. (2007) 'Toward a public administration theory of public service motivation: An institutional approach', *Public Management Review*, 9, pp. 545–56.

van der Aa, P. and van Berkel, R. (2015) 'Fulfilling the promise of professionalism in street-level practice', in Hupe, P.L., Hill, M. and Buffat, A. (eds) *Understanding Street-Level Bureaucracy*, pp. 263–78. Bristol: Policy Press.

van der Heijen, J. (2014). 'Selecting cases and inferential types in comparative public policy research', in Engeli, I. and Rothmayr Allison, C. (eds) *Comparative Policy Studies: Conceptual and Methodological Challenges*, pp. 35–56. Basingstoke: Palgrave Macmillan.

van Meerkerk, I. and Edelenbos, J. (2014) 'The effect of blundary spanners on trust and performance of urban governance networks: Findings from survey research on urban development projects in the Netherlands', *Policy Sciences*, 47, pp. 3–14.

Van Meter, D. and Van Horn, C.E. (1975) 'The policy implementation process: A conceptual framework', *Administration and Society*, 6(4), pp. 445–88.

Varone, F. (1998) *Le choix des instruments des politiques publiques. Une analyse comparée des politiques d'efficience énergétique du Canada, du Danemark, des Etats-Unis, de la Suède et de la Suisse*. Berne: Paul Haupt Verlag.

Varone, F. and Aebischer, B. (2001) 'Energy efficiency: The challenges of policy design', *Energy Policy*, 29(8), pp. 615–29.

Varone, F. and Giauque, D. (2001) 'Policy management and performance-related pay: Comparative analysis of service contracts in Switzerland', *International Review of Administrative Sciences*, 67(3), pp. 543–65.

Varone, F. and Schiffino, N. (2004) 'Regulating biotechnologies in Belgium: Diverging designs for ART and GMOs', *Archives of Public Health*, 62, pp. 83–106.

Varone, F., Nahrath, S., Aubin, D. and Gerber, J-D. (2013) 'Functional regulatory spaces', *Policy Sciences*, 46(4), pp. 311–33.

Varone, F., Rothmayr Allison, C. and Montpetit, E. (2006) 'Regulating biomedicine in Europe and North America: A qualitative-comparative analysis', *European Journal of Political Research*, 45(2), pp. 317–43.

Varone, F., Rothmayr Allison, C. and Montpetit, E. (2007). 'Comparing biotechnology policy in Europe and North America: A theoretical framework', in Montpetit, E. (eds)

The Politics of Biotechnology in North America and Europe: Policy Networks, Institutions and Internationalization, pp. 1–33. Lanham: Lexington Books.

Vatter, A. (2009) 'Lijphart expanded: three dimensions of democracy in advanced OECD countries', *European Political Science Review,* 1(1), pp. 125–54.

Vick, N., Tobin, R., Swift, P., Spandler, H., Hill, M., Coldham, T., Towers, C. and Waldock, H. (2006) *An Evaluation of the Impact of the Social Care Modernisation Programme on the Implementation of Direct Payments*, unpublished report of the Health and Social Care Advisory Service to the Department of Health.

Virtanen, T. (2014) 'Implementation of the structural development policy of Finnish higher education', in Hill, M. (ed.) *Studying Public Policy*, pp. 221–31. Bristol: Policy Press.

Visser, J. and Hemerijk, A. (1997) *A Dutch Miracle: Job Growth, Welfare Reform and Corporatism in the Netherlands*. Amsterdam: Amsterdam University Press.

Vogel, D. (1995) *Trading Up: Consumer and Environmental Regulation in a Global Economy*. Cambridge, MA: Harvard University Press.

Vogel, D. (1996) *Freer Markets, More Rules: Regulatory Reforms in Advanced Industrial Countries*. London: Cornell University Press.

Vogel, D. (2004) 'The hare and the tortoise revisited: The new politics of risk regulation in Europe and the United States', in Levin, M. and Shapiro, A. (eds) *Transatlantic Policymaking in an Age of Austerity. Diversity and Drift*, pp. 177–202. Washington, DC: Georgetown University Press.

Wade, H.W.R. (1982) *Administration Law*, 5th edn. Oxford: Oxford University Press.

Walgrave, S. and Varone, F. (2008) 'Punctuated equilibrium and agenda-setting: Bringing parties back in. Policy change after the Dutroux Crisis in Belgium', *Governance*, 23(1), pp. 365–95.

Walgrave, S., Varone, F. and Dumont, P. (2006) Policy with or without parties? A comparative analysis of policy priorities and policy change in Belgium, 1991 to 2000', *Journal of European Public Policy*, 13(7), pp. 1021–38.

Walker, A. and Wong, C-K. (2004) 'The ethnocentric construction of the welfare state', in Kennett, P. (ed.) *A Handbook of Comparative Social Welfare*. Cheltenham: Edward Elgar.

Walker, C. (2015) 'Discretionary payments in social assistance', in Hupe, P.L., Hill, M. and Buffat, A. (eds) (2015) *Understanding Street-Level Bureaucracy*, pp. 45–60. Bristol: Policy Press.

Walker, R. and Duncan, S. (2007) 'Knowing what works: Policy evaluation in central government', in H. Bochel and S. Duncan (eds) *Making Policy in Theory and Practice*, pp. 169–90. Bristol: Policy Press.

Wallace, H., Pollack, M. And Young, A.R. (2010) *Policy Making in the European Union*. Oxford: Oxford University Press.

Wallas, G. (1948) *Human Nature in Politics*. London: Constable.

Wallerstein, I. (1979) *The Capitalist World Economy*. Cambridge: Cambridge University Press.

Wallis, J. (1997) 'Conspiracy and the policy process: A case study of the New Zealand experiment', *Journal of Public Policy*, 17(1), pp. 1–29.

Walsh, K. (1995) *Public Services and Market Mechanisms*. Basingstoke: Macmillan.

Ward, M.D., Stovel, K. and Sacks, A. (2011) 'Network analysis and political science', *Annual Review of Political Science*, 14, pp. 45–264.

Warner, M. (2007) 'Kafka, Weber and Organization Theory', *Human Relations*, 60(7), pp. 1019–38.

Weatherley, R. (1979) *Reforming Special Education: Policy Implementation from State Level to Street Level*. Cambridge, MA: MIT Press.

Weatherley, R. (1980) 'Implementing social programs: The view from the front line'. Paper delivered at the annual meeting of the American Political Science Association, Washington, DC.

Weaver, R.K. (1986) 'The politics of blame avoidance', *Journal of Public Policy*, 6, pp. 371–98.

Weber, M. (1947) *The Theory of Social and Economic Organization* (trans. A.M. Henderson and T. Parsons). Glencoe, IL: Free Press.

Weber, M. (1997) *The Methodology of the Social Sciences*. New York: Free Press.

Weible, C.M. (2007) 'An advocacy coalition framework approach to stakeholder analysis: Understanding the political context of California marine protected area policy', *Journal of Public Administration Research and Theory*, 17, pp. 95–117.

Weible, C.M., Sabatier, P.A. and McQueen, K. (2009) 'Themes and variations: Taking stock of the advocacy coalition framework', *Policy Studies Journal*, 37(1), pp. 121–40.

Weir, M., Orloff, S. and Skocpol, T. (eds) (1988) *The Politics of Social Policy in the United States*. Princeton, NJ: Princeton University Press.

Wildavsky, A.B. (1979) *Speaking Truth to Power. The Art and Craft of Policy Analysis*. New Brunswick and London: Transaction Publishers.

Wilding, P. (1982) *Professional Power and Social Welfare*. London: Routledge.

Wilenski, P. (1986) *Public Power and Public Administration*. Sydney: RAIPA.

Wilensky, H.L. (1964) 'The professionalisation of everyone', *American Journal of Sociology*, 70, pp. 137–58.

Wilensky, H.L. (1975) *The Welfare State and Equality*. Berkeley: University of California Press.

Wilkins, V.M. and Wenger, J.B. (2015) 'Street-level bureaucrats and client interaction in a just world', in Hupe, P.L., Hill, M. and Buffat, A. (eds) *Understanding Street-Level Bureaucracy*, pp. 155–67. Bristol: Policy Press.

Wilks, S. and Wright, M. (1987) 'Conclusion: Comparing government–industry relations: States, sectors and networks', in Wilks, S. and Wright, M. (eds) *Comparative Government Industry Relations: Western Europe, the United States and Japan*, pp. 274–313. Oxford: Clarendon Press.

Williamson, O. (1975) *Markets and Hierarchies*. New York: Free Press.

Williamson, O. (1985) *The Economic Institutions of Capitalism*. New York: Free Press.

Wilson, J.Q. (1973) *Political Organizations*. Beverley Hills, CA: SAGE.

Wilson, W. (1887) 'The study of administration', *Political Science Quarterly*, 2, pp. 197–222.

Winkler, J. (1976) 'Corporatism', *Archives Européennes de Sociologie*, 17(1), pp. 100–36.

Winter, S.C. (2003) 'Implementation perspectives: Status and reconsideration', in Peters, B.G. and Pierre, J. (eds) *Handbook of Public Administration*, pp. 212–22. London: SAGE.

Winter, S.C. (2006) 'Implementation', in Peters, B.G. and Pierre, J. (eds) *Handbook of Public Policy*, pp. 151–66. London: SAGE.

Wolf, A. (2002) *Does Education Matter? Myths about Education and Economic Growth*. London: Penguin Books.

Wolfinger, R.E. (1971) 'Nondecisions and the study of local politics', *American Political Science Review*, 65, pp. 1063–80.

Wood, D.B. and Waterman, R. (1994) *Bureaucratic Dynamics*. Boulder, CO: Westview Press.

Woodward, J. (1965) *Industrial Organisation: Theory and Practice*. London: Oxford University Press.

World Bank (1994) *Averting the Old Age Crisis*. Oxford: Oxford University Press.

Yom, S. (2015) 'From methodology to practice: Inductive iteration in comparative research', *Comparative Political Studies,* 48(5), pp. 616–44.

Young. A.R. (2003). 'Political transfer and "trading up"? Transatlantic trade in genetically modified food and U.S. politics', *World Politics*, 55, pp. 457–84.

Young, K. (1977) 'Values in the policy process', *Policy and Politics*, 5(2), pp. 1–22.

Zahariadis, N. (2008) 'Ambiguity and choice in European public policy', *Journal of European Public Policy*, 15(4), pp. 514–30.

Zimmerman, D.H. (1971) 'The practicalities of rule use', in Douglas, J.D. (ed.) *Understanding Everyday Life*, pp. 221–38. London: Routledge and Kegan Paul.

Index